W9-CSW-176

FOURTH EDITION

Asian Philosophies

JOHN M. KOLLER
Rensselaer Polytechnic Institute

Prentice
Hall

Upper Saddle River, New Jersey 07458

Library of Congress Cataloging-in-Publication Data

Koller, John M.
   Asian philosophies / John M. Koller.—4th ed.
     p. cm.
   Includes bibliographical references and index.
   ISBN 0-13-092385-0
   1. Philosophy, Asian. I. Title.

   B121 .K555 2002
   181—dc21
                        2001021684

VP, Editiorial Director: Charlyce Jones Owen
Acquisitions Editor: Ross Miller
Editiorial Assistant: Carla Worner
VP, Director of Production
   and Manufacturing: Barbara Kittle
Senior Managing Editor: Jan Stephan
Production Liasion: Fran Russello
Project Manager: Linda B. Pawelchak
Manufacturing Manager: Nick Sklitsis
Prepress and Manufacturing Buyer:
   Sherry Lewis

Cover Director: Jayne Conte
CoverDesign: Bruce Kenselaar
Cover Image: We Wei, "Scholar Seated Under
   a Tree," China. Ink & traces of colour on
   silk. 14.7 x 8.25. Chinese and Japanese
   Special Fund. © 1996/All Rights Reserved.
   Courtesy of Museum of Fine Arts, Boston.
Marketing Manager: Chris Ruel
Copy Editing: Melissa Martin
Proofreading: Ellen Denning

This book was set in 10/11 Times Ten by DM Cradle Associates
and was printed and bound by The Courier Companies.
The cover was printed by Lehigh Press.

©2002, 1998 by Pearson Education, Inc.
Upper Saddle River, New Jersey 07458

First and second editions titled *Oriental Philosophies*
and copyright ©1985, 1970 by Charles Scribner's Sons

Printed in the United States of America
10 9 8 7 6 5 4 3 2

ISBN 0-13-092385-0

Pearson Education LTD., *London*
Pearson Education Australia PTY. Limited, *Sydney*
Pearson Education Singapore, Pte. Ltd.
Pearson Education North Asia Ltd., *Hong Kong*
Pearson Education Canada, Ltd., *Toronto*
Pearson Educación de Mexico, S.A. de C.V.
Pearson Education—Japan, *Tokyo*
Pearson Education Malaysia, Pte. Ltd.

To My Daughter
Christy Koller

And in Memory of My Son
John Thomas Koller

Contents

Preface xiii

Introduction xv

PART I
INDIAN PHILOSOPHIES

CHAPTER 1
Historical Perspectives 3

Historical Overview 3
Dominant Features 7
Review Questions 11
Further Reading 12

CHAPTER 2
Vedas and Upanishads 14

Indus Culture 14
Vedic Thought 15
The Upanishads 19

Review Questions 26
Further Reading 26

CHAPTER 3
The Jain Vision   **28**

Brief Overview 28
Historical Context 29
Bondage 30
Way of Liberation 34
Faith, Knowledge, and Conduct 36
Impact of Jain Thought 41
Review Questions 42
Further Reading 42

CHAPTER 4
Society and the Individual   **44**

Bhagavad Gita 44
Human Aims 46
Social Classes 49
Life-Stages 51
Review Questions 52
Further Reading 52
Notes 53

CHAPTER 5
Self and the World: Samkhya-*Yoga*   **54**

Samkhya: A Dualistic Theory of Reality 54
Causality 55
Evolution of the World 57
Yoga: The Way of Discipline 60
Review Questions 65
Further Reading 65
Notes 66

CHAPTER 6
Knowledge and Reality: Nyaya-Vaisheshika 67

The Problem of Knowledge 67

The Means of Knowledge 68
The Objects of Knowledge: The Vaisheshika Categories 73
Review Questions 76
Further Reading 77

CHAPTER 7

Self and Reality: Mimamsa and Vedanta   78

Mimamsa 78
Vedanta 81
Shankara's Nondualism 82
The Qualified Nondualism of Ramanuja 88
The Dualistic Vedanta of Madhva 90
Review Questions 92
Further Reading 92
Note 93

CHAPTER 8

Theistic Developments   94

Vishnu 95
Kali 99
Shiva 101
Review Questions 104
Further Reading 104

CHAPTER 9

Islam   106

Basic Teachings of Islam 107
Development of Sufi Thought 109
The Sufi Path 113
Interaction Between Muslims and Hindus 114
Religion and Politics 118
Review Questions 120
Further Reading 121
Notes 122

CHAPTER 10

Continuing Tradition   123

Gandhi 124

Aurobindo 125
Iqbal 127
Radhakrishnan 130
Review Questions 132
Further Reading 132
Notes 133

PART II
BUDDHIST PHILOSOPHIES

CHAPTER 11
Historical Perspectives   137

Central Teaching 137
India at the Time of the Buddha 138
After the Buddha 139
Mahayana and Theravada 139
Philosophical Traditions 142
Buddhism in China 145
Buddhism in Korea and Japan 145
Buddhism in the West 146
Review Questions 146
Further Reading 146

CHAPTER 12
The Life and Teachings of the Buddha   148

The Buddha 148
The Four Signs 149
Quest for Enlightenment 151
The Buddha's Teachings 155
The Noble Eightfold Path 160
Review Questions 164
Further Reading 164
Notes 166

CHAPTER 13
Interdependent Arising   **167**

Principle of Conditioned Existence 167
The Wheel of Becoming 168
Mindfulness 175
Review Questions 180
Further Reading 180
Notes 181

CHAPTER 14
Sarvastivada   **182**

Sarvastivada Teachings 182
Foundations of Abhidharma 183
Arguments Against Substance 186
Review Questions 191
Further Reading 191
Notes 191

CHAPTER 15
Perfection of Wisdom   **193**

Perfection of Wisdom Tradition 193
Diamond Sutra 196
Heart Sutra 198
Review Questions 201
Further Reading 201
Notes 201

CHAPTER 16
Madhyamaka: The Middle Way Tradition   **203**

Overview of Madhyamaka 203
Middle Way Philosophy of Nagarjuna 204
A Dialogue on the Teaching and Practice of Emptiness 211
Review Questions 216

Further Reading 216
Notes 217

CHAPTER 17
Yogacara   **218**

Overview of Yogacara 218
Existence and Consciousness 219
Knowledge of Reality 226
Review Questions 229
Further Reading 229
Notes 230

CHAPTER 18
Buddhism in Japan: Zen   **231**

Overview 231
Indian and Chinese Foundations 233
Taoist Influences 235
Aims of Zen 236
Practice 238
Teachings 243
Ox-Herding: Stages of Practice 244
Review Questions 251
Further Reading 251
Notes 252

PART III
CHINESE PHILOSOPHIES

CHAPTER 19
Historical Perspectives   **257**

Pre-Confucian China 257
Confucianism 258
Taoism 259
Mohism 260
School of Names 260
Yin-Yang 261

Legalism 262
Early Medieval Developments 262
Chinese Buddhism 263
Neo-Confucianism 264
Basic Characteristics of Chinese Philosophy 265
Review Questions 267
Further Reading 268
Notes 269

 CHAPTER 20
Confucianism   **270**

Confucius 270
Humanity (*Jen*) 271
Propriety (*Li*) 273
Filial Piety (*Hsiao*) 274
Righteousness (*Yi*) 275
Rectification of Names *(Cheng-Ming)* 276
Governing by Virtue 276
Mencius 281
Hsun Tzu 283
Review Questions 284
Further Reading 285
Notes 285

 CHAPTER 21
Taoism: The Natural Way of Freedom   **287**

Lao Tzu 287
The *Tao* and Its Manifestations 290
Chuang Tzu 293
Review Questions 301
Further Reading 302
Notes 303

 CHAPTER 22
Neo-Confucianism: The Grand Harmony   **304**

The Buddhist Challenge 304
Neo-Confucian Beginnings 305

Ch'eng Hao and Ch'eng I 309
Chu Hsi 313
Wang Yang-ming 317
Tai Chen 320
Review Questions 321
Further Reading 322
Notes 323

CHAPTER 23
Recent Chinese Philosophical Thought   **324**

K'ang Yu-wei 325
Chang Tung-sun 326
Hsiung Shih-li 328
Fung Yu-lan 331
Mao Tse-tung 334
Post-Mao Thought 337
Review Questions 340
Further Reading 340
Notes 341

Glossary   **343**

Pronunciation Guide   **348**

Index   **355**

Preface

What are the main ideas that have shaped Asian cultures? What are the fundamental values that have guided the lives of Asian peoples over the millennia? How have the great thinkers of Asia thought about these ideas and values? This book is intended to help answer these questions, enabling us to understand the principal philosophies of the great Asian traditions.

Basic human ideas and values derive from answers to fundamental questions about existence and human life. People everywhere, whether Asian or Western, seek to answer the same basic questions: Who am I? What is real? How do we come to know something? What is the right thing to do? What is good? These questions, however, arise in different contexts and assume different forms for people living at different times and in different places, and the answers given vary accordingly. But these questions, arising out of wonder, out of human suffering, or out of the efforts to improve the conditions of human existence, are questions that every reflective person seeks to answer. And the answers to these questions provide the fundamental ideas and values that guide the development of whole cultures as well as the lives of individual persons.

By studying the great philosophical traditions of Asia, it is possible to understand these traditions' carefully considered answers to these questions, answers that are supported by profound insights and good reasons. Because these answers have guided the thought and action of the peoples of Asia over the centuries, they provide the basic clues to the guiding ideas and values of Asian societies today. And in today's world, where the very future of humankind depends upon understanding and cooperation among people with diverse values and ideas, it is imperative that these values and ideas be understood.

As each of us tries to creatively develop our own philosophy to guide and direct our lives, we can benefit enormously from an understanding of the different ways that the basic questions of life have been answered by philosophers in the Asian traditions.

ACKNOWLEDGMENTS

I would like to express appreciation to the many scholars whose translations and interpretive studies I have used. I also wish to thank the people who have contributed to the writing of this book. These include Roger Ames, Frances Anderson, Russell Blackwood, David Burke, Chung-ying Cheng, Eliot Deutsch, Dewitt and Dorothy Ellinwood, Charles Fu, Premchand Gada, Jennifer Galloway, Robert Garvin, Bina Gupta, Louis Hammer, Derek Heyman, Frank Hoffman, Kenneth Inada, David Kalupahana, Chenyang Li, Joel Marks, G. Mishra, Richard Olmsted, K. H. Parekh, Rama Rao Pappu, C. Ramaiah, Henry Rosemont, Bhagwan Singh, John Schumacher, Joel Smith, Kenneth Sterling, Weiming Tu, Madhu Wangu, Theodore Wright; students who have used earlier editions; friends and colleagues at Rensselaer, especially those in the Department of Philosophy, Psychology, and Cognitive Science; as well as the reviewers of this edition: Chenyang Li, Central Washington University; Balaji Hebbar, George Washington University; E. Ruth Klein; Hope Fitz, Eastern Connecticut State University; Clyde Ebenreck; and Gerald Poliks, College of Dupage. Thanks also to my production editor, Linda B. Pawelchak. I also wish to express appreciation for the support provided by Rensselaer Polytechnic Institute and by the Jain Foundation of North America.
I am especially grateful for the love and support of my wife, Mimi Forman, as well for her many helpful suggestions.

John M. Koller
Great Neck, New York

Introduction

PHILOSOPHICAL QUESTIONS

Philosophical questions arise out of reflection on experience. Experiencing sorrow and grief, we ask, What is suffering? Experiencing pleasure and joy, we ask, What is happiness? Reflecting on the difference between waking experience and dreaming experience, we ask, What is real? Reflecting on mistaken claims to know something, we ask, What is knowledge? Reflecting on our experience of hurting others by our actions and on our own suffering caused by the actions of others, we ask, What are the right and wrong ways of action? And reflecting on our own struggles to achieve personal identity and give meaning to our life, we ask, Who am I? These questions, the fundamental questions of philosophy, are important because their answers ultimately determine the value and meaning of life.

But what about religion? Doesn't religion provide the meaning and value of life by providing the ultimate answers to our questions? This is a difficult question, and to answer it we must distinguish between Western and Asian attitudes. In the modern West, we typically think of religion as grounded in faith rather than knowledge and concerned with attaining spiritual life in the next world. To the extent that religion is concerned with the fulfillment of life in this world, it looks to the commandments of God rather than to human reason for guidance. For the religious person, answers to life's questions are provided by divine revelation through scriptures. Philosophy, in contrast, is thought of as arising out of intellectual curiosity (the word *philosophy* means "love of wisdom" in Greek) and proceeds by way of rational inquiry, rather than by way of faith. Philosophy's dictum is that the unexamined life is not worth living, and that philosophical reflection will show how life should be lived. As self-critical rational inquiry, philosophy is never satisfied with dogmas but is always ready to question not only every answer, but even the questions themselves.

In Asia, because philosophy is regarded as arising out of reflection on the ways of overcoming suffering and improving the quality of human life, there are no rigid distinctions between philosophy and religion. Asian philosophical thought, while it is also self-critical, tends to emphasize insight into and understanding of reality and its importance as a guide to life as its chief characteristics. Indeed, the Indian philosophical traditions are called "visions [of reality]" *(darshana)*, and the Chinese philosophical traditions are called "Way [of life]" *(Tao)*. One consequence of this Asian tendency to see philosophy in practical terms, concerned with human transformation, is the widespread recognition of the relevance of philosophy to life. Philosophy in Asia has not been viewed as ivory tower speculation, something separate from the concerns of daily life. Rather, it has been seen as one of life's most basic and most important activities.

INDIAN PHILOSOPHY

India is famous for the high regard it accords the seeker of wisdom and for its reverence and respect for wise persons. Three thousand years ago, the sages of India were pondering the questions, What is the Self? and What is the nature of ultimate reality? Pursuing these two questions, they came to the realization, twenty-five hundred years ago, that the innermost Self is one with the ultimate reality. The immediate practical problem arising from this discovery was how one could come to know and to realize this inner Self and thereby become one with the very essence of the universe. The theoretical problems raised by this discovery centered on the difficulty of relating the multiplicity and diversity of experienced reality with the sages' insight into the unity of all existence and the difficulty in ascertaining how knowledge of such an ultimate reality could be achieved. Reflection on these issues led to questions about the basis of morality, the nature and function of society, the means of valid knowledge, the principles of logic, the nature of the Self, and the means of self-realization.

As Indian thinkers reflected on these fundamental questions, they often disagreed with one another. Their differing insights and understandings led to the establishment of a variety of philosophical traditions, many of which continue to this day. Although the Vedanta tradition is in agreement with the sages who declared the innermost Self and ultimate reality identical, other traditions reject this vision of reality. Some traditions, such as Nyaya and Vaisheshika, are frankly pluralistic, while others, such as Samkhya and Yoga, are dualistic. The Jain and Buddhist traditions, though they disagreed with each other in significant ways, both rejected the authority of the Vedas and the existence of God, while emphasizing the importance of yogic discipline. The Carvakans, sometimes called Lokayatas, were materialists, denying the existence of God, soul, and any kind of life after death.

Despite this diversity of philosophical views, there has been widespread agreement that the self-discipline of *yoga* is needed to achieve the total integration of life and to attain life's highest goals. According to the *Bhagavad Gita,* an extremely influential Hindu text, this discipline is available to all persons when it is channeled through the activities of worship and devotion, the activities of work, and the activities of knowledge and concentration. From a Hindu perspective, these paths of self-discipline are simply the philosophical wisdom of the ages being put into practice by the people.

There has also been widespread agreement concerning the importance of living morally, fulfilling one's moral duties, especially the duty to avoid hurting other living beings. At least part of the reason why living a moral life is so important is the widespread agreement that all human actions are governed by the principle of *karma*, which says, roughly, that because every action inevitably produces its effects, it is our actions that make us the kinds of persons we become. To become good, we must engage in morally good actions. Performing bad actions will make us into bad persons.

BUDDHISM

One of the traditions that originated in India twenty-five hundred years ago was Buddhism, a tradition that soon spread north, south, and east, becoming an important influence throughout almost all of Asia. The basic problem of life, according to Buddhism, is that of overcoming suffering. The essential teachings of the Buddha revolve around the questions, What is suffering? On what conditions does it depend? How can these conditions be eliminated? What path should one follow to eliminate suffering?

These questions, however, cannot be answered without inquiring into the nature of the self that suffers and the nature of the world that constitutes a source of suffering for the self. The question, How is suffering caused? leads to a general theory of causation that shapes the theories of self and reality that constitute Buddhist metaphysics. The problems of justifying the claims made about the nature of the self and the nature of reality led to theories of logic and knowledge. And the problem of how to overcome suffering led to the development of understanding about morality and mental discipline and a new understanding of consciousness. Thus, the eminently practical problem of finding a way to overcome suffering provokes the reflections that constitute the Buddhist philosophical tradition, a tradition that comprises many subtraditions. Many of the Buddhist traditions began in India as a result of differing interpretations of the Buddha's teachings and different emphases within the teachings. But many traditions began in Tibet, China, Korea, and Japan, for example, as a result of interactions between Buddhism and indigenous philosophical traditions.

CHINESE PHILOSOPHY

The three enduring philosophical traditions in China are Confucianism, Taoism, and Buddhism. Confucianism, which began with the teachings of Confucius in the sixth century BCE, incorporated important features of competing traditions, such as Legalism, Mohism, the School of Names, and Yin-Yang thought, as it developed. Taoism, which began at about the same time, provided not only a counterbalance to Confucian thought, but also much of the philosophical framework and vocabulary necessary for Buddhism to take hold in China and become the third great tradition fifteen hundred years ago.

Before the development of Chinese Buddhism, philosophical thought was concerned primarily with the ways of moral, social, and political life or with understanding the ways of nature. The central problems of Chinese philosophy are reflected in the Confucian question, How can I achieve harmony with humanity? and in the Taoist question, How can I achieve harmony with nature? For two thousand years, because the Confucian writings were made the core curriculum of the imperial university system and the basis of the civil service exams, knowing Confucian thought was a requirement for government service, making Confucianism the official ideology of China. That Confucian thought could be taken as the basis for social and political practice is possible because of the Chinese tendency to regard thought and practice as inseparable from each other, as aspects of the same activity.

As philosophy developed in China, there was an increasing tendency to see human nature in terms of natural processes. To the extent that this identification took place, the problem of achieving harmony with nature was the problem of being in harmony with oneself. In turn, being in harmony with oneself was regarded as the necessary basis for achieving a harmony with other persons. Being in harmony with oneself, in harmony with humanity, and in harmony with Heaven and Earth is the highest good in Chinese philosophy. Because human nature is seen as essentially moral, the dominant concern of Confucian and Neo-Confucian philosophy has been morality. The Confucian questions, How can I be good? and What is the basis of goodness? have been basic questions throughout the history of Chinese philosophy, as has been the Taoist question, How can I achieve harmony with the *Tao*?

The development of Chinese Buddhism in the fourth and fifth centuries BCE fostered an interest in metaphysical questions about the nature of the self and reality and in the relationship of knowledge to liberation, causing Confucian and Taoist thought to become involved with these issues. At the same time, Confucian concerns with fostering the way of humanity and social harmony and Taoist concerns with the workings of nature allowed Buddhism to develop in new ways in China.

INTERACTIONS AND SHARED CONCERNS

Although Buddhism was the main vehicle of interaction between Indian thought and the thought of East and Southeast Asia, it turned out that the influence was largely one way, from India to the rest of Asia. The most notable external influences on Indian thought came from the Greeks who came to India with Alexander the Great and from the Muslims who came to India between the eighth and eleventh centuries and who came to rule India from the thirteenth to the nineteenth centuries.

Many differences may be seen among the philosophies of India, China, and Buddhist Asia, but they all share the practical concern of how to live better.

They agree that the development of moral virtue is an important ingredient of a successful way of life, and that the well-being of the individual cannot be separated from the well-being of the family and the larger social community. They also agree that to follow the way to a better life, we must have a deep understanding of ourselves and the world.

Because it is concerned with the fundamental ideas and values of the people, philosophy has been of primary importance in Asian cultures. Therefore, in order to understand the life and the attitudes of the peoples of Asia, it is necessary to understand their philosophies. And in order to understand their philosophies, it is necessary to look at the traditions in which these philosophies developed and through which they continue to nourish the cultures of Asia. That is why this book focuses on the philosophical traditions of India, China, and Buddhist Asia.

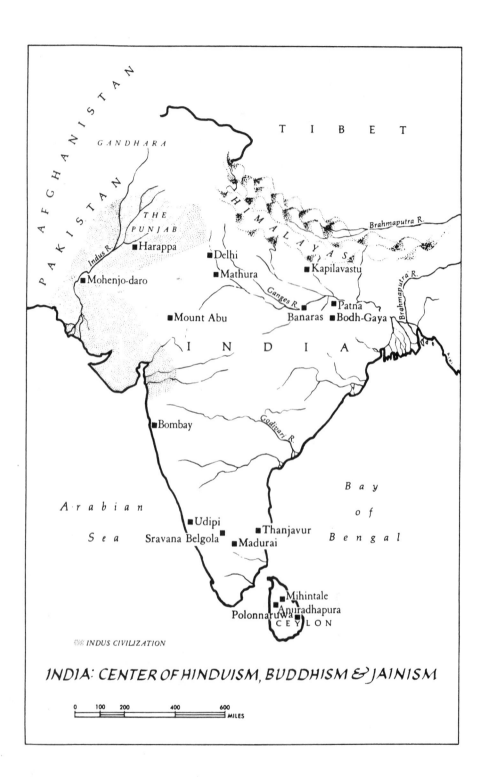

INDUS CIVILIZATION

INDIA: CENTER OF HINDUISM, BUDDHISM & JAINISM

0 100 200   400   600
                        MILES

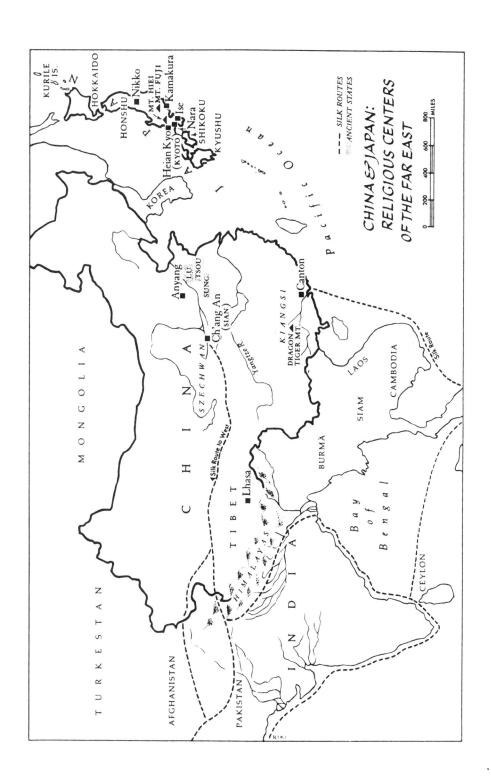

CHINA & JAPAN: RELIGIOUS CENTERS OF THE FAR EAST

PART 1

INDIAN PHILOSOPHIES

Shiva as Lord of the Dance. (Asia Society, New York: Mr. and Mrs. John D. Rockefeller 3rd Collection; photograph by Lynton Gardiner)

Indian Chronology

BCE	Events and Thinkers
2500–1500	Indus civilization
1500–1000	Beginnings of Vedic, Sanskritic India; *Rig Veda, Atharva Veda*
1200–800	*Yajur* and *Sama Vedas*; the *Mahabharata* war
800–400	Early Upanishads (Brihadaranyaka, Chandogya, Taittiriya); the *Mahabharata* epic
600–400	Development of Jainism, (Mahavira); beginning of Buddhism (the Buddha); *Ramayana* (oral form)
500–300	India united under Chandra Gupta and Ashoka; treatises on *dharma, artha, kama*; Patanjali's *Yoga Sutras*; *Vedanta Sutras*; early Samkhya
300 BCE–300 CE	Development of the great systems of philosophy: Samkhya, Yoga, Mimamsa, Vedanta, Nyaya, Vaisheshika, Jainism, Buddhism, and Carvaka
CE	
300–800	Period of the great commentaries on the various philosophical systems; Guadapada (500s); Shankara (700s); beginning of Islam (612)
1000–1500	India comes under Muslim rule; Ibn Sina (981–1037); Al Ghazali (1059–1111); Ibn Arabi (1165–1240); development of theistic philosophies of Vaishnavism and Shaivism; Ramanuja (1100s); Madhva (1200s); Kabir (1440–1518)
1500–1700	Guru Nanak (1449–1538), founder of Sikhism; Akbar (r. 1556–1605); Shaikh Ahmad (1564–1624)
1700–1900	Colonization by Western powers; Ram Mohun Roy (1772–1833), founder of Brahmo Society; Dayananda Saraswati (1824–83), founder of the Arya Society; Ramakrishna (1836–86)
1850–2000	R. Tagore (1861–1941); Gandhi (1869–1948); Aurobindo Ghose (1872–1950); Mohammad Iqbal (1877–1938); Sarvepalli Radhakrishnan (1888–1975); Indian Independence (1947)

CHAPTER 1

Historical Perspectives

When we look at the development of Indian philosophy over the past three thousand years, we can distinguish between different periods of development, each with its own distinct characteristics. We can also see an underlying continuity in which certain basic ideas and attitudes are dominant. This chapter provides an overview of the development of Indian philosophy as a historical context for the more detailed chapters that follow.

HISTORICAL OVERVIEW

Although critical and systematic philosophical thought first emerges in the Upanishads and early philosophical systems in the seventh to the fifth centuries BCE, deeply reflective thought is found already in the *Rig Veda,* which may have been composed as early as 1500 BCE. Since those early beginnings, India has acquired a vast wealth of philosophical vision, speculation, and argument. It is difficult to approach Indian philosophy chronologically, however, for early Indian history is full of uncertainties with respect to names, dates, and places. In India, so much emphasis has been put on the content of the thought and so little emphasis on person, place, and time that in many instances, it is not known who is responsible for the particular philosophy in question. And when the author is unknown, the time and the place can be reckoned only indirectly. Because of this, time is often reckoned in terms of centuries rather than years or decades, and authorship is sometimes attributed to schools rather than to individual persons. Nevertheless, it is possible to

3

see changes in philosophical thinking occurring in a certain historical sequence. That is, it is possible to see the antecedents and successors of various philosophical problems and solutions.

The historical approach is facilitated by adopting a generally agreed upon classification of periods in the development of the philosophical traditions in India. The Vedic period stretches from about 1500 BCE to 700 BCE. The Epic period occurred between 800 BCE and 200 CE. The period of the great systems began in the sixth century BCE and continues, through the commentaries, up to the present time. The Commentary period commenced about 200 CE and continued until about 1700. The Modern period, still in progress, began around 1800, under the influence of Western thought.

The Vedic Period

The Vedic age began when the Sanskrit-speaking peoples began to dominate life and thought in the Indus Valley, around 1500 BCE. Historians used to think that these Sanskrit-speaking peoples who called themselves Aryans came to the Indus Valley in northwest India as conquerors some thirty-five hundred years ago. But recent scholarship has challenged this thesis of conquering Aryans. What we do know is that the earlier Indus culture, which flourished from 2500 to 1500 BCE, and which, judged by its archaeological remains, was quite sophisticated, declined at this time. We also know that the Vedic thought and culture reflected in the *Rig Veda* has a continuous history of dominance in India during the past thirty-five hundred years. It may well be that the cultural traditions of the Vedic peoples mingled with the traditions and customs of the Indus people, and what we now think of as Indian culture began to take shape from about 1500 BCE on.

The earliest Vedic literature was composed between 1500 and 700 BCE. Although concerned primarily with religious practice, occasionally reflective inquiry occurs as Vedic thinkers asked questions about themselves, the world around them, and their place in it. What is thought? What is its source? Why does the wind blow? Who put the Sun—giver of warmth and light—in the sky? How is it that Earth brings forth these myriad life-forms? How do we renew our existence and become whole?

Questions of how, what, and why are the beginning of philosophical reflection. At first, thinkers tried to answer these questions in terms of human agency, attributing events in nature to the gods, who are conceived of as superhuman persons. This tended to encourage religious rather than philosophical thought. Inquiring minds pushed further, however, probing into who the gods are and what lies beyond them. Not satisfied merely to accept the traditional goals of life, these thinkers sought to understand what is truly the highest good and how it can be achieved. They inquired into the nature of knowledge and thought. This kind of thinking in the Vedas marks the beginnings of Indian philosophy.

The main texts of the Vedic period are the *Rig Veda, Sama Veda, Yajur Veda,* and *Atharva Veda.* Each Veda has four parts. The first part, the collection of verses called *samhita,* contains hymns to the gods, questions and reflections, and chants and formulas for success. The second part, called *Brahmana,* consists of arrangements of *samhita* verses for ritual use. The third part, called *Aranyaka,* contains reflections on and interpretations of the rituals. The final part, the Upanishads, contains reflections on the basic questions underlying religious thought and practice.

Philosophically, the Upanishads are the most important Vedic texts, for they contain the most profound inquiries into the meaning of life. Three great visions of life proclaimed by the sages of the Upanishads, for the most part unknown to the earlier Vedic thinkers, have shaped India's self-understanding for the past three thousand years. First, the innermost self, the *Atman,* is one with the ultimate reality, *Brahman.* Second, because life is governed by *karma*, we can become good only by performing good actions. Third, only meditative knowledge can liberate us from the cycle of repeated deaths and suffering.

The Epic Period

The wisdom of the Vedic literature was part of a sacred and carefully guarded tradition, often unavailable to many members of the society or, where available, beyond understanding. To compensate for this, there grew up a folklore recited in stories and poems that managed to transmit many of the ideals of the sacred tradition to the majority of the people. The two most notable collections of materials constituting this literature are India's two great epics, the *Mahabharata* and the *Ramayana.*

The *Mahabharata* is an epic that tells the story of the conquest of the land of India and in so doing provides a guide to life in all its dimensions, from the philosophical and religious to the political. The single most influential part of the *Mahabharata* is the *Bhagavad Gita,* the "Song of the Lord." The *Gita*, in a dialogue between Krishna (God manifested in human form) and Arjuna, explains the nature of humanity and reality, setting out ways of life that enable human beings to achieve spiritual freedom by acting in accord with the deepest nature of the self.

The *Ramayana,* a beautiful poem in four volumes, sets out an ideal order for society as a whole and an ideal way of life for the individual. It presents an ideal for womanhood in the person and life of Sita and an ideal of manhood in the person and life of her husband, Rama, the divine hero of the epic. Through dance, theater, popular stories, and movies, the *Ramayana* is widely known and continues to inspire the people of India even into the twenty-first century.

During the Epic period, important treatises on morality called *Dharma Shastras* were written to explain how the life of the individual and society should be regulated. For example, the *Artha Shastra* of Kautilya explains the need for and the importance of the various means of life, especially political power, and explains how they may be obtained. The *Manu Shastra* explains how justice and order may be secured in society by the king and the institutions of government. The *Shastra* of Yajnavalkya emphasizes the attainment of success and order in the life of the family.

Period of Philosophical Systems

No doubt it was also during this time that the beginnings of the various systems of philosophy were established, for there are references in the *Mahabharata* to certain systems. The beginnings of several systematic philosophical explanations of the world and human nature were already established by 500 BCE, even though their full systemization would be achieved only seven or eight hundred years later. These systems represent the first purely philosophical effort in India, for not only did they attempt to explain the nature of existence, but they did so self-consciously and self-critically, engaging in careful analysis and argumentation to show the correctness of their answers. The summaries of analyses, arguments, and answers were preserved as *sutras,* literally the "threads" on which the whole philosophical system hangs. Extensive commentaries were developed to unpack and explain the summaries contained in the *sutras.*

Buddhism, Jainism, and Carvaka were designated *nastika,* or unorthodox systems, because their authors did not accept the pronouncements of the Vedas as true and final. Neither did the thinkers of these systems endeavor to justify their analyses and solutions by showing them to be in accord with the Vedas. The philosophies of the Nyaya, Vaisheshika, Samkhya, Yoga, Mimamsa, and Vedanta systems, especially in their later development, however, all accepted the authority of the Vedas and were all concerned to show that their analyses and claims were in accord with the central Vedic teachings.

The major division, however, is between Carvaka and the other philosophical systems. Carvaka is the only completely materialistic system; all the others provide for spiritual life. Jainism, for example, attempts to show the way out of karmic bondage. It emphasizes a life of nonhurting that culminates in final release from bondage through meditative self-realization. Buddhism presents an analysis of the nature and causes of human suffering and presents the eightfold path as a cure for suffering.

Turning to the orthodox systems, Nyaya is concerned primarily with a logical analysis of the means of knowing. Vaishesika analyzes the kinds of things that are known, providing a pluralistic metaphysics. Samkhya is a dualistic system that seeks to relate the self to the external world and to explain the world's evolution. Yoga analyzes the nature of the self and explains how the pure Self can be realized. Mimamsa develops a theory of interpretation and knowledge that concentrates on the criteria for the self-validity of knowledge, attempting thereby to establish the truth of the Vedic pronouncements. Vedanta begins with the conclusions of the Upanishads and attempts to show that a rational analysis of knowledge and reality will support those conclusions.

Period of the Great Commentaries

As generations of seers and scholars studied the *sutras* of the various systems, they frequently wrote commentaries on them. In this way, the great commentaries of Gaudapada (sixth century CE), Shankara (eighth century CE), Bhaskara (ninth century CE), Yamuna (tenth century CE), Ramanuja (eleventh century CE), Nimbarka (twelfth century CE), Madhva (thirteenth century CE), and Vallabha (fifteenth century CE) came to be written on the *Vedanta Sutras* of Badarayana. Other systems have a similar history of commentaries.

The Modern Period

As a result of outside influences, especially contact with the West, Indian philosophers began to reexamine their philosophical traditions. Beginning with the studies, translations, and commentaries of Ram Mohun Roy in the nineteenth century, this renewal of ancient traditions has flourished in the past century. Gandhi, Tagore, Ramakrishna, Aurobindo, Vivekananda, and Radhakrishnan are among the more influential of India's modern thinkers. Now, as we enter the twenty-first century, India is enjoying a philosophical renaissance. Rediscovery of ancient traditions, new interpretations of Western thought, creative work in comparative philosophy, and the development of new visions are flourishing side by side, often influencing one another.

DOMINANT FEATURES

From its beginnings in the reflections of the Vedic seers thousands of years ago and continuing to the present, Indian philosophical thought presents an extraordinary richness, subtlety, and variety. This richness and variety make it difficult to summarize Indian philosophy with simple generalizations. Nevertheless, certain dominant features can be identified on the basis of their endurance, their influence on philosophers, or their widespread importance in the lives of a majority of the people.

Practical Character

Next to its richness and comprehensiveness, the most striking feature of Indian philosophical thought is its practical character. From the very beginning, the speculations of India's sages grew out of attempts to improve life. Confronted with physical, mental, and spiritual suffering, they sought to understand the causes, attempting to understand human nature and the universe in order to eliminate these causes.

India's philosophies respond to both practical and speculative motivations. Practical considerations motivated the search for ways to overcome the various forms of suffering. Speculative considerations led to construction of explanatory accounts of the nature of reality and of human existence and to the development of logic and theories of knowledge. But these philosophical efforts were not undertaken separately. The understanding and knowledge derived from speculative curiosity were utilized in the practical attempts to overcome suffering.

Two fundamentally different approaches to the problem of suffering are possible. Both approaches recognize that suffering is the result of a gap between what one is and has, and what one wants to be and wants to have. If there were no difference between what one is and has, and what one wants to be and wants to have, there would be no suffering. But when there is a difference, suffering is inevitable because one's desires are not satisfied. The solution to the problem seems obvious: what is and what is desired must be made identical.

Self-Discipline

But how can this identity be achieved? One approach to the solution is to try to attain what one desires. The person who desires wealth should try to accumulate wealth. The person who wants to be immortal should support medical and technological research that promises to extend life. A second approach consists in adjusting one's desires to what one has. If one is poor and desires wealth, the resulting suffering can be eliminated by removing the desire for wealth. The person who suffers fear of death because of the desire for immortality can eliminate this suffering by accepting death as a part of life.

Basically, it is the second approach that Indian philosophy has emphasized, advocating the control of desires. As a result, the philosophies of India tend to insist on self-discipline and self-control as the way to eliminate suffering.

Self-Knowledge

Because self-discipline and self-control require that one have knowledge of the self, self-knowledge has been a dominant concern of Indian philosophy. Indeed, knowing what the self is and how to realize its perfection through self-discipline has been at the heart of the Indian philosophical enterprise since its beginnings.

Vision

The practical character of Indian philosophy is manifested in a variety of ways. The very word *darshana* that is usually translated as "philosophy" points to this. *Darshana* literally means "vision," that is, what is "seen." In its technical sense, it means what is seen when ultimate reality is investigated. The seers of India, seeking the solution to life's sufferings, investigated the conditions of suffering and examined the nature of human life and the world in order to find the causes of suffering and the means for its elimination. What they found constituted their *darshana,* their philosophy of life.

Truth

Of course, it is possible to be mistaken in one's vision; one may not see things as they really are. Consequently, the philosopher's vision must be verified by providing evidence of its truth. Historically, two methods of verifying philosophical visions are encountered. According to the first method, logical analysis is used to determine whether or not a particular view is false. If the concepts and statements expressing the vision are inconsistent, the vision may be discarded as self-contradictory.

The second method, in recognition of the insufficiency of logic alone, is pragmatic, finding the verification of philosophical views or theories in the quality of resulting practice. Indian philosophers have always insisted that practice is the ultimate test of truth. Philosophical visions must be put into practice and life must be lived according to the ideals of the vision. The quality of the life lived according to those ideals is the ultimate test of any vision. The better life becomes, the closer the vision approaches complete truth.

The criteria for determining the quality of life are, in turn, derived from the basic impetus for philosophy: the drive to eliminate suffering. The vision that makes possible a life without suffering is properly called a true philosophy. Degrees of philosophic truth are determined according to the degree of alleviation of suffering. Put in a positive way, views are true according to the extent that they improve the quality of life.

Placing the positive emphasis for justification of a philosophy on experience rather than logic (though logic is not excluded) requires putting philosophy into practice. The path of practice is part of the vision, and if the path to the realization of the goals of the vision cannot be followed, the vision itself is regarded as inadequate. The saying "Good in theory, but not in practice" makes no sense when applied to Indian philosophies. Good in theory necessarily means good in practice.

Religion and Philosophy

The identification of the way to the good life with the vision of the good life itself is the integrating factor between religion and philosophy in India. Because philosophy is not regarded as being concerned only with theory, its concern with the practical means of attaining the good life allows Indian philosophy to maintain its connection with religion. In the West, philosophy and religion are considered entirely separate because philosophy concerns itself only with the rational and religion is viewed as being concerned not with reason but with faith. According to Indian thought, revelation is a valid way of knowing, along with perception and reasoning, allowing faith and reason to interact to provide a critical view of the good life and the various means thereto. Because in India a philosopher's theory of the good life has to be tested by practice, a philosopher must be concerned with the means for achieving the good life in order to be a philosopher.

Focus on Self

Since Indian philosophy begins with the suffering of human beings, the human subject is of greater importance than the objects that come within the experience of the subject. The self that suffers is always the subject. To treat it otherwise is to regard it as a thing, a mere object. The ultimate self is described in the Upanishads and the Samkhya system as pure subject, the subject that can never become object. The subject is always "the one without a second." For all the systems except Carvaka, it is the qualitative experience of the subject that is of fundamental concern in Indian thought.

Liberation

Above all, Indian philosophy is concerned with finding ways to liberate the self from bondage to fragmented and limited modes of existence, the bondage that causes suffering. According to the Upanishads, the great power *(Brahman)* that energizes the universe and the spiritual energy of the Self *(Atman)* are ultimately the same. This vision of the identity of Self *(Atman)* with ultimate reality *(Brahman)* provides the foundation for the methods of liberation that constitute the practical core of Indian philosophy. It is a vision that sees the various distinct things and processes of the world as manifestations of a deeper reality that is undivided and unconditioned. Within this undivided wholeness are different levels of reality, distinguished by the degree to which they participate in the truth and being of ultimate reality. Because of this unity of existence, the powers needed to achieve liberation are available to every person. But a person must become aware of these powers and the means to harness them for the task of attaining liberation. Hence knowledge, especially self-knowledge, is of major importance.

The emphasis on the ultimate Self in the Upanishads, Vedanta, and Yoga means that relevant philosophical criteria are not primarily quantitative and public. Rather, they belong to self as subject. Therefore it is impossible for one person to subscribe to one "true" philosophy and to regard the others as completely false. Truth in philosophy depends upon the human subject, and another's experience can be known only as an object. There is no knowing—according to ordinary ways of knowing, at least—the other as subject. Consequently, there is no rejecting the other's experience as inadequate or unsatisfactory.

Tolerance

Recognition of the uniqueness of each subject's perspective has led to a tolerant, inclusive attitude that is commonly expressed by saying that while it may be that no vision, by itself, is absolutely true and complete, nevertheless, each vision contains some glimpse of the truth. By respecting the viewpoints and experiences assumed by the various visions, one comes closer to the absolute truth and the complete vision. Philosophical progress is not made by proceeding from falsehood to truth, but by proceeding from partial to more complete truth.

Moral Emphasis

In addition to these features of Indian philosophy that stem from its practical orientation, there is a widespread tendency in Indian thought, going back to the Vedic concept of *rita* (order), to presuppose universal moral justice. The world is seen as a great moral stage directed by justice. Everything good, bad, and indifferent is earned and deserved. The impact of this attitude is to place the responsibility for the human condition squarely upon human beings themselves. We are responsible for what we are and what we become. We ourselves have determined our past and will determine our future, according to Indian thought. It is by our good actions that we become good and by our bad actions that we become bad.

Karma

This principle of self-determination through action is called *karma*. *Karma* literally means "action," but it refers to action in a comprehensive way that includes thoughts, words, and deeds. Furthermore, it includes all the effects of these various kinds of action, both the immediate and visible effects and the long-term and invisible effects. *Karma* is the force that connects all the moments of life to one another and that connects all things to one another. Because of this interconnectedness, each lifetime of a person is but a moment in a continuing cycle in which one may be reborn countless times and in many different forms. But each birth is followed by death, and the cycle rolls on, bringing innumerable deaths and untold suffering. To obtain liberation *(moksha)* from this cycle of suffering is the highest goal of life. Because only discipline and knowledge can exhaust the store of *karma* and liberate a person from the cycle of re-death, they are highly prized in India.

Dharma

Because *karma* connects everything in the universe, every thought, word, or deed affects not only one's own future, but the lives of others as well. Therefore, each person has a responsibility to act so as to maintain the order of the family, society, and the entire cosmos, thereby contributing to the well-being of others. This responsibility is called *dharma,* a word that means to "uphold" or "support" existence. The various duties that make up one's *dharma* provide the moral structure for one's entire social life.

Nonattachment

Rather widespread agreement is found in Indian philosophical thought concerning nonattachment. Suffering results from attaching oneself to what one does not have or even to what one cannot have. These attached objects then become the causes of suffering insofar as they are not attained or are lost. Therefore, if a spirit of nonattachment to the objects of suffering could be cultivated, the suffering itself could be eliminated. Thus, nonattachment is recognized as an essential means to the realization of the good life.

Because of all these features of Indian thought, the people of India have usually accorded the highest respect to philosophers and philosophy. Philosophy shows the way to live, and philosophers are guides along the way.

REVIEW QUESTIONS

1. What are the main periods in the development of Indian philosophy? Briefly characterize the literature of each of these periods, and describe the main differences between periods.
2. What is the basis for the distinction between the "orthodox" and "unorthodox" systems? In what sense is the distinction between Carvaka and all the other systems fundamental?

3. How did confrontation with physical, mental, and spiritual suffering lead to philosophical thought in India?
4. Why is knowledge, especially self-knowledge, regarded as the highest philosophical achievement?
5. Where does Indian thought place responsibility for the human condition?
6. What are the criteria that a successful philosophical theory must satisfy?

FURTHER READING

The Indian Way, by John M. Koller (New York: Macmillan, 1982), is an exploration of the basic features of India's philosophical and religious thought. The seventeen chapters cover major historical developments from the Vedas up to the present time, demonstrating the continuity of basic ideas and values. The aim throughout is to show that these ideas and values are both philosophical and religious.

Sourcebook in Asian Philosophy, by John M. and Patricia Koller (New York: Macmillan, 1991), provides original sources in English translations to accompany *Asian Philosophies.* It contains more than 500 pages of source material selected from the basic texts of the Indian, Chinese, and Buddhist traditions.

Brief Introduction to Hinduism, by A.L. Herman (Boulder, CO: Westview Press, 1991), is a philosophical exploration of Hinduism intended for beginners.

Tradition and Reflection: Explorations in Indian Thought, by Wilhelm Halbfass (Albany: State University of New York Press, 1991), is a collection of essays probing key issues in Indian thought. Issues include the relation between reason and revelation, the basis of social organization, *karma* and rebirth, *dharma,* the nature of knowledge, and justifying human action.

The Indian Mind: Essentials of Indian Philosophy and Culture, edited by Charles A. Moore (Honolulu: University of Hawaii Press, 1967), is a collection of essays by leading Indian philosophers.

Guide to Indian Philosophy, by Karl H. Potter (Boston: G.K. Hall, 1988), is the most recent bibliography of books and articles on various topics in Indian philosophy. Organized according to authors, with a name index and good cross-referencing, this is a useful guide to both secondary and original works.

A Concise Dictionary of Indian Philosophy, rev. ed., by John Grimes (Albany: State University of New York Press, 1996), is a useful dictionary of Sanskrit philosophical terms defined in English.

A History of Indian Philosophy, vols. 1–5, by Surendranath Dasgupta (Cambridge: Cambridge University Press, 1922–1955), is a classic in the field. It is a work of great learning, covering most of India's philosophical thinkers in sufficient depth to give the reader a good sense of major continuities and discontinuities in the history of Indian thought.

Indian Philosophy, vols. 1 and 2, by Sarvepalli Radhakrishnan (London: Allen and Unwin, 1923), has been the most widely used history of Indian philosophy. The sections on the Upanishads and Vedanta are especially good, but all of the major developments through the eleventh century are covered.

The Encyclopedia of Indian Philosophies, edited by Karl Potter (Princeton, NJ, and Delhi: Princeton University Press and Motilal Banarsidass, 1961–2000), provides excellent historical coverage of major schools. The web site (http://faculty.washington.eda/Potter) for the encyclopedia's *Bibliography of Indian Philosophy* is the most complete bibliography available and is updated regularly.

A Survey of Hinduism, 2d ed., by Klaus Klostermaier (Albany: State University of New York Press, 1994), covers both thought and practice and has an excellent, brief chapter on Indian chronology.

CHAPTER 2

Vedas and Upanishads

This chapter explores the visions of self and reality contained in India's earliest literature, the *Rig Veda* and the early Upanishads, texts composed between 1500 and 600 BCE. The ideas expressed in the Vedas and Upanishads are both profound and subtle, the result of centuries of reflective thought about the deepest mysteries of life. They provide insights into the processes of life that constitute a timeless testament of human wisdom, enabling these texts to inspire and nurture Indian culture up to the present time. But at least a thousand years before the *Rig Veda*, the earliest texts of the Sanskrit-speaking Vedic peoples, composed probably around 1500 BCE, the Indus peoples had developed a rich and sophisticated civilization that flourished in the Indus Valley from 2500 to 1500 BCE.

INDUS CULTURE

Indus civilization probably began shortly after 3000 BCE in the lower Indus River valley in what is today Pakistan. By 2000 BCE, it occupied an area approximately one-third the size of present-day India, reaching north to the Himalayas, south almost to Bombay, and from the western coast eastward as far as Delhi. Archaeological studies of one of its largest cities, Mohenjo Daro, reveals something of this civilization's sophistication. Mohenjo Daro had a population of about fifty thousand people in 2000 BCE. Clearly designed with attention to central planning, its paved brick streets were laid out in a rectangular grid pattern. Huge granaries provided ample food storage for the people and livestock. Ceramic tiled underground water and drainage systems represented a mar-

14

velous engineering accomplishment. The degree of standardization achieved indicates the efficiency of their departments of planning and administration, suggesting that the Indus people had a highly efficient centralized social and political organization.

Among the recovered artifacts, fine jewelry reveals the presence of skilled craftsmen, and the great variety of beautiful toys and games (including chess) suggests a culture that valued play and delighted in children. An accurate system of weights and measures, utilizing an efficient binary and decimal system of mathematical computation, reflects both the culture's mathematical accomplishments and its emphasis on trade. Trade was probably extensive, as numerous Indus seals, used to mark ownership, have been found as far away as Mesopotamia.

It is only natural to assume that the sophisticated material culture of Indus civilization was matched by an equally sophisticated system of social and religious thought. This, however, must remain merely an assumption, for no written records are available that would constitute evidence of literary, religious, or philosophical accomplishments. The material clues found in the hundreds of sites that have been identified since Sir John Marshall first discovered the Indus civilization eighty years ago suggest that religion played a major role in this culture. Even the smaller towns and villages have large ceremonial buildings, and numerous masks have been found, suggesting a priesthood. The elaborate bathing facilities indicate a concern for religious purification. Figures in yogic postures on seals suggest that *yoga* may have roots in this early civilization and support the hypothesis that later Indian culture represents a wedding of Indus and Vedic cultures.

From 1500 BCE on, the influence of the Sanskrit-speaking Vedic peoples spread east and south from the Indus Valley, and Indus civilization disappeared, leaving not a single text to reveal its thought. By the fourth century BCE, with the establishment of the Mauryan empire, practically the whole subcontinent was under Vedic political control. The Sanskrit language, of which the Vedas are the oldest surviving expression, became the primary vehicle of Indian thought. Although the Sanskrit tradition reflects borrowing and accommodations from non-Vedic sources, it hides more of these contributions than it reveals. Thus, despite the grandeur of the ancient Indus civilization, it is to the Vedas that we must turn for an understanding of earliest Indian thought.

VEDIC THOUGHT

The Vedas are verses of wisdom that form the core of India's sacred liturgy. Tradition regards Vedic wisdom as timeless and authorless. This wisdom is revealed to great persons whose experience has reached the inner core of existence. It is timeless because it was revealed to the very first human beings even as it is revealed today to all whose experience plumbs the depths of life. It is considered authorless because it is not revealed by persons but by reality itself.

The *Rig Veda*, dating from about 1500 BCE, is the oldest collection of these verses of wisdom. Regarded as the fountainhead of Indian spirituality, it has nourished the culture and inspired India's people for more than three thousand years. Part of the enduring power of the Vedic verses stems from the profound insight into reality they express. But part of their importance stems from the fact that they were the liturgical part of India's great rituals. Vedic India had a powerful ritual orientation. Life was sanctified and given meaning through the ritual recreation of existence, and the liturgy of the cosmos-creating and life-creating rituals consisted primarily of recited, chanted, and sung verses from the Vedas. Thus, through their incorporation into the rituals, these verses were regarded as having the power to join all beings together, renewing life with sacred energy released by the rituals. The Vedas themselves tell us that when these verses are recited, chanted, and sung, they enable all creation to share in the wisdom and energy of the divine reality.

Vedic Deities

Most of the Vedic verses are addressed to gods and goddesses and have a central liturgical function. But this does not mean that they are merely hymns for worship or ritual incantation. Some go much deeper, presenting profound and subtle visions of reality. Indeed, the various deities addressed in these verses are not simply anthropomorphic beings, but symbols of the fundamental powers of existence. Speech, consciousness, life, water, wind, and fire—these are among the auspicious powers symbolized as deities in the Vedas. They represent the powers that create and destroy life, that control the ebb and flow of existence.

Agni. Agni, for example, one of the principal Vedic deities, is the god of fire. The word *agni* means "fire," and Agni is the symbol of fire's awesome power. Out of control, raging flames destroy homes and forests, killing people and animals. But under control, the fire in the hearth transforms raw meat and vegetation into food, providing energy for life. Because of fire's transforming power, both destructive and creative, Agni, lord of the fire, is one of the most important deities of the *Rig Veda*. The Vedic people gained access to Agni through ritual offerings made to the sacrificial fire, thereby obtaining his creative powers and averting his destructive powers. Thus, the offerings to Agni in the rituals that dominated Vedic religious life were, in essence, attempts to control the transformations of existence that affected human life. That is why nearly one-third of the 1,008 hymns are addressed to Agni.

Indra. Indra, perhaps the chief god of an earlier age, is the most human-like of the Vedic deities. As lord of the thunderbolt, Indra vanquishes enemies and protects his people. He defeats the cosmic forces of chaos and darkness, making way for creative forms of existence. But above all, Indra, who is mentioned more often than any other deity in the *Rig Veda,* symbolizes the courage and strength people need to resist their enemies and to protect their families and communities.

Vac. Vac, whose name means "speech," is the goddess of communication. She represents not only words, but the underlying consciousness that makes speech possible. Speech provides a way of controlling things by giving them names. Knowledge, the most powerful means of controlling existence that human beings have, is essentially Vac, consciousness operating through speech.

Other Vedic deities are similar. They symbolize the most fundamental powers that the Vedic people experienced. Although the Vedic deities symbolize the powers of existence, they are usually not thought of as the creators of existence. Indeed, the idea of a creator separate from the universe itself is foreign to the *Rig Veda*. Both the intelligence and the material stuff of the universe are regarded as contained within existence itself and inseparable from each other.

Rita

Because existence was seen as inherently intelligent, the universe was seen as a well-ordered whole. The order present in the cyclical regularities of the seasons and moon phases, and in the stages of growth from embryo to child to adult, originates at the very heart of existence. Known as *rita*, this order, present in the very origin of things, provides the basis for all the norms and rules of life. It is the source of the laws of nature and the principles of society, morality, and justice. *Rita* regulates the functioning of all things, providing the structure and rhythm of existence. Nature, deities, and persons are all subject to the demands of *rita*. What is in accord with *rita* flourishes; what is not, perishes.

Varuna, sometimes called King of the Gods, is the divine custodian of *rita*. He ensures the operation of this cosmic order in all its dimensions and phases, punishing all those who violate this sacred order of the universe. Thus, a song of praise to Varuna includes the following petition: "O Varuna, if we have violated your sacred order through our carelessness, do not harm us, O God, for that transgression" (*Rig Veda* 7.89.5).

Origins of Existence

In the Hymn to the Cosmic Person, the sage reflects on the emergence of sacred order of the cosmos out of the order inherent in the cosmic person. It was assumed that the existence of the universe emerged out of the transformation of prior existence, in this case the prior existence of the cosmic person. But where did this prior existence come from? What existence preceded it? And from what did the very first existence come? When the sages reflected on these questions, they discovered one of the most important insights of the *Rig Veda:* beyond existence and nonexistence there is a wholeness, an undivided reality, that is more fundamental than being or nonbeing.

We can see how the Vedic sages came to this insight and what it meant to them by turning to the famous Hymn of Origins (*Rig Veda* 10.129), perhaps the most profound series of reflections in the entire *Rig Veda*. The first verse announces the intention to inquire into what was prior to existence:

> 1. In the beginning there was neither existence nor non-existence;
>   Neither the world no[r] the sky beyond.
>   What stirred? Where? Who protected it?
>   Was there water, deep and unfathomable?

Here the sage explains that if we are looking for the absolute beginnings of things, before there was anything whatsoever, we can find that source neither in existence nor in nonexistence. If the source is something already existing, then it is not the first source, the absolute beginning. So we cannot say that existence is the source of existence.

If, however, we say that this existence emerged from nonexistence, we contradict experience. Experience reveals only new things emerging out of previous existence through processes of transformation, never something being created out of nothing. But if neither existence nor nonexistence can be the original source of things, what is the alternative? Existence and nonexistence include all possibilities and are the most fundamental categories of thought.

Having arrived at this impasse, the sage asks, How then can we explain where everything came from? We know that things move, that movement or change is the very nature of existence, so there must be some original source of this motion, something that stirred it in the beginning. And just as everything that exists exists in some place, so this original stirring of things into motion must have occurred somewhere. Furthermore, just as all successful activities are protected—by a father, a king, or a god—so this original activity of setting things in motion must have had a protector.

In the last line, the sage refers to an ancient account of the universe emerging out of bottomlessly deep water. Of course, by his own thinking, since the deep water already existed, it could not be the beginningless source of the universe. Perhaps the sage is suggesting that thought cannot go beyond existence and nonexistence. As long as we think of the source of things, we will have to think of some prior existence, even though this means it cannot be the absolute source.

The second verse suggests that prior to existence and nonexistence, before there was night or day, before there was either death or immortality, there was a primordial oneness:

2. Then there was neither death nor immortality,
   Nor any sign of night or day.
   THAT ONE breathed, without breath, by its own impulse;
   Other than that, there was nothing at all.

The sage does not name this primordial oneness; it is called THAT ONE because it is beyond what exists and can be named. What leads the sage to think that there is something beyond existence and nonexistence? Perhaps he thought of them as interrelated opposites, dependent on each other, for we give meaning to nonexistence by relating it to existence (by negating existence), and we give meaning to existence by contrasting it with nonexistence. Existence and nonexistence are like two halves, a negative half and a positive half, of a whole divided into two parts. Unless there were some prior whole to be divided, where would the two halves come from? It is like cutting an apple in half, labeling one half right, the other half left. Right and left are interrelated opposites; their meanings depend on each other. Right and left are different, but without one, the other is impossible. Left half and right half cannot exist unless there is a prior whole that can be divided. In a similar way, the sage may have thought of existence and nonexistence as the results of a division of a prior whole. Language, however, cannot go beyond existence and nonexistence; "is" and "is not" are the fundamental units of language. Consequently, though the sage may intuit the primordial wholeness beyond existence and nonexistence, this wholeness cannot be referred to or described directly.

Recognizing this, the sage turns to the language of paradox to approach the great mystery of the original oneness that is the primordial source of everything. Every attempt to talk about the primordial source reduces it to the limited realms of the existent and nonexistent. But in the language of paradox, each statement negates itself, pointing to something beyond. In paradoxical language, the sage tells us that as the source of life this primordial source breathed, but did not breathe (at least not with the breath of ordinary, existing things); it was motionless, but it moved (though not because of anything outside itself). It was, after all, the original unmoved mover, that which existed prior to creation.

Verse 3 emphasizes that in the beginning, nothing could be seen or differentiated; even the originating source was concealed—as darkness is concealed by darkness. But the third and fourth lines tell us how that darkness was lifted, enabling that original undivided wholeness to manifest itself as creation. Through *tapas*, the powerful transforming energy of ritual, the unmanifest source became manifest as this universe.

> 3. Then there was darkness, concealed in darkness,
>   All this was undifferentiated energy.
>   THAT ONE, which had been concealed by the void,
>   Through the power of heat-energy was manifested.

The last two verses suggest that perhaps the primordial source of the world cannot be known. How can knowledge go beyond existence and nonexistence? Perhaps it must forever remain a mystery.

> 6. Who really knows? Who here can say?
>   When it was born and from whence it came—this creation?
>   The Gods are later than this world's creation;
>   Therefore who knows from whence it came?

> 7. That out of which creation came,
>   Whether it held it together or did not,
>   He who sees it in the highest heaven,
>   Only He knows—or perhaps even He does not know!

THE UPANISHADS

The Upanishads are much more philosophical than the Vedas. Not only do they try to explain the fundamental principles of existence, but they also show a recognition of the need to supply reasons for their claims. They do not, however, present any formal analysis of the criteria of truth and the relation between truth and evidence. For the most part, personal experience of what is claimed is taken as sufficient evidence for the truth of the claim. And while there is general recognition that self-contradictory views cannot be true, it would be going too far to suggest that reason determined the truth or falsity of views, for the principles of logic and reason had not yet been formally worked out.

Consequently, the Upanishads tend to emphasize the content of the vision of the seer more than the means whereby the vision can be justified. The claims in the Upanishads are taken to be the reports of the experience of the seers, not philosophical theories waiting to be justified. It is the experience of the seers that provides the evidence for the truth of the claims being made.

The two key questions of the Upanishads are, What is the true nature of ultimate reality? and Who am I in the deepest level of my existence? These questions presuppose that there is a difference between shallower manifestations and more fundamental essence and between what appears to be real and what is actually real; appearances are understood to depend on a deeper reality.

Quest for Brahman

In seeking the ultimate reality, these seers had no clear concept of what they sought; they simply knew that there must exist that by which all other things existed and which made them great. The name given to this "something" was *Brahman*, which means "that which makes great." It was a nondescriptive name, for it did not name anything definite, either abstract or concrete.

The search for *Brahman* is recorded in the Upanishads as the search for the ultimate external reality. At first, there was an attempt to identify that "something" with religious symbols and rituals, or with natural objects, such as the Sun and the Moon, or with certain psychological functions of human beings. All of these attempts to state what *Brahman* is in terms of something else presuppose limits on that power. But if *Brahman* is ultimate, it is impossible for it to be limited, for there could be nothing beyond it to limit it. As the seers began to realize more clearly that *Brahman* could not adequately be described by appealing to their experience of the world of appearance, they attempted to define this reality in a negative way.

Way of Negation. According to Yajnavalkya in the *Brihadaranyaka Upanishad, Brahman* is not conceivable, not changeable, not injurable, not graspable. According to the *Katha Upanishad, Brahman* is inaudible, invisible, indestructible, cannot be tasted, cannot be smelled, is without beginning or end, and is "greater than the great." *Brahman* is described negatively in the *Mundaka Upanishad* as follows:

> Invisible, incomprehensible, without genealogy, colorless, without eye or ear, without hands or feet, unending, pervading all and omnipresent, that is the unchangeable one whom the wise regard as the source of beings. (I.1.6)

If *Brahman* is that which makes possible time, space, and causality, then it is impossible to regard it as limited by them. Being prior to space, time, and causality means being beyond the characteristics of the empirical universe, and therefore beyond empirical description. Because *Brahman* is beyond thought, it cannot be conceived by thought. Consequently, the nature of *Brahman* remains elusive and mysterious.

Quest for the Ultimate Self *(Atman)*

The sages seeking the ultimate Self asked, What am I, in my deepest existence? This question presupposes that the self is something more than meets the eye, for the bodily organism is not particularly elusive or mysterious. But the question of what the self is that thinks is another matter. How can the "I" that thinks the self to be a bodily organism also be a bodily organism? And is not the "I" that contemplates bodily existence more properly the self than the bodily self?

Undoubtedly, the thinkers of the Upanishads distinguished between what the self appears to be and what it really is. Their search for the innermost essence of human existence is guided by this injunction:

> The Self *(Atman)* which is free from evil, free from old age, free from death, free from grief, free from hunger and thirst, whose desire is the real, whose thoughts are true, he should be sought, him one should desire to understand. He who has found out and who understands that Self, he obtains all worlds and desires. (*Chandogya Upanishad*, VII.7.1)

The question was, What is that wonderful and mysterious Self that lies beyond mere appearances? In trying to answer that question, the seers of the *Taittiriya Upanishad* turned their attention to the various aspects and functions of the individual person as they searched for the ultimate Self. If the Self is thought to be the body, then it is essentially food, they reasoned, for the body is simply digested food. But surely the Self is not to be identified with the body only, for it is something more; it is alive and moving. If the Self is not merely food, they reasoned, perhaps it is the life of food. But they saw that while this would serve to distinguish living from nonliving matter, it does not designate the ultimate Self of the person, for a person is more than simply living food. The person sees, hears, feels, and so forth. Perhaps, the reasoning continues, the Self should be thought of in terms of the mental ability to perceive. But this too seemed inadequate, for thinking and understanding are even more properly Self than perception. Even the thinking and understanding self, however, is rejected as the ultimate Self, for there must be something beyond that gives existence to thinking and understanding. As the *Taittiriya Upanishad* says, "Different from and within that which consists of the understanding is the Self consisting of bliss" (II.5.1).

This search for the ultimate Self was essentially a matter of going deeper and deeper into the foundations of human existence. Matter was regarded as covering for life, which in turn was a covering for the sensing self. And deeper than sensing was intellectual activity. But deeper still was the bliss of total consciousness. Consequently, the Self is not to be identified with any of the lower forms of the person exclusively, but is to be thought of as existing within these various layers of existence, giving them life while remaining distinct from them.

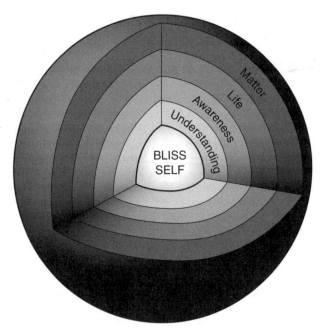

The Layers of Self

In the *Kena Upanishad*, the search for the ultimate Self takes the form of a quest for the ultimate agent or doer of human action. The sage asks, "By whom willed and directed does the mind light on its objects? By whom commanded does life the first, move? At whose will do [people] utter this speech? And what god is it that prompts the eye and the ear?" (I.1)

In the very next paragraph these questions are answered by saying that there is a more basic Self that directs the eye to color, the ear to sound, the understanding to consciousness. And this Self is said to be "other than the known and other than the unknown" (I.4). The question the sage is asking is, What makes possible seeing, hearing, and thinking? But the question is not about physiological or mental processes, it is about the ultimate subject who knows. Who directs the eye to see color or the mind to think thoughts? The sage assumes there must be an inner director, an inner agent, directing the various functions of knowledge.

Distinction Between Subject and Object

What is that inner agent that directs all human activities? The sage says that this ultimate Self cannot be known by any ordinary knowledge: "There the eye goes not, speech goes not, nor the mind; we know not, we understand not how one can teach this" (I.3). The reason this ultimate subject is beyond the eye, beyond the ear, beyond the understanding, is that whatever is seen, heard, and understood is always an object known by the human subject, and not the subject itself.

If we were to say the ultimate Self is known, we would have to ask, Who knows it? Because the Self being sought is the ultimate knowing subject, the "Who" that is known cannot be the ultimate subject because it has become an "it," an object of knowledge. Because any self that is known is an object rather than the knowing subject, it follows that the Self that is the ultimate subject cannot be known as an object.

Nevertheless, because the knowing Self is the ultimate subject, it can be realized directly in total self-awareness, where it is illumined by its own light. Thus, though in one sense, in terms of knowledge of objects, the ultimate Self cannot be known, in another sense, in terms of immediate experience, it can be known intimately and completely in the experience of self-awareness. In self-awareness, the Self is known much more surely and completely than any object of knowledge. Here one finds the certitude of one's own existence, beyond question or doubt, for any attempt to question one's own existence reveals the existence of the questioner.

Prajapati Teaches Indra

In the *Chandogya Upanishad*, the search for the ultimate Self is presented in the form of a story in which Prajapati (representing the creative forces of the universe) instructs Indra (who represents the gods) and Virocana (who represents the demons) about the Self. For thirty-two years they prepare themselves for Prajapati's teaching by practicing self-discipline. At the end of that time Prajapati tells them that the Self is what they see when they look at their reflection in a mirror. What they see is their physical form, clothed and adorned with jewels.

Virocana, delighted with this knowledge, returns to the demon world and teaches that the body is the Self. Such is the teaching of the demons! But Indra reflects on this teaching and sees that if the Self is the same as the body, then when the body perishes so does the Self. This cannot be the immortal Self he is seeking, so he again asks Prajapati about the Self. This time Prajapati tells him that the dream self is the real Self. But still Indra is uneasy. For although the dream self is not absolutely dependent upon the body, nevertheless sometimes it too is subject to pain, suffering, and destruction. So again he asks what the real Self is. And this time he is told that the self that is beyond dreams is the real Self. At first this satisfies Indra, but before he has reached the abode of the gods he realizes that even though the deep-sleeping self is not subject to pain and destruction, nevertheless it cannot be the real Self, because in deep sleep the self is not aware of itself.

By this time Indra has spent a total of 101 years disciplining and preparing himself for that highest knowledge and now is ready to hear the highest teaching. Now Prajapati tells him that the Self being sought transcends all of the selves considered so far. It is true, there is a physical self, which some think to be the only self. And there is the self that is the subject that experiences dreams, a self recognized by some. And there is the self that experiences deep sleep, otherwise deep sleep would be the same as death. But the highest Self goes beyond all of these; it is that which makes possible the self of waking experience, of dreaming experience, and of deep sleep. Those selves are merely instruments of the highest Self, which is the very source of their existence.

The state in which one realizes the ultimate Self that gives existence to the selves of the waking, dreaming, and deep-sleeping person is sometimes called the *turiya*, or the fourth state. Unlike the condition of deep sleep, this state is one of total self-consciousness and illumination. In the *Brihadaranyaka Upanishad*, it is said, "When one goes to sleep, he takes along the material of this all-containing world, himself tears it apart, himself builds it up and dreams by his own brightness, by his own light. Then this person becomes self-illuminated" (IV.3.9).

Although ordinary knowledge, which presupposes the duality of subject and object, of knower and known, is impossible in this fourth state, there is no doubt of the authenticity of its existence. The same Upanishad continues:

> Indeed, while he does not there know, he is indeed knowing, though he does not know [what is usually to be known]; for there is no cessation of the knowing of a knower because of his imperishability [as a knower]. It is not, however, a second thing, other than himself and separate, which he may know. (IV.3.30)

The *Mandukya Upanishad*, which identifies the first state of the self as the waking state, the second as the dreaming state, and the third as the state of deep sleep, describes the fourth state as beyond all dualities, of the essence of the knowledge of the one Self that is *Brahman*.

Thus, in the Upanishads, the question, What am I, in the deepest reaches of my existence? is answered by saying that the very foundation of existence is self-illuminating consciousness. Furthermore, this consciousness can be directly experienced by a person who goes beyond identification with the objectified self. It is significant that the ultimate Self—the *Atman*—can be known directly and immediately through direct experience.

Atman Is Brahman

The discovery of *Atman* is also significant in another way. The seers of the Upanishads who were seeking both the ultimate external reality (*Brahman*) and the ultimate reality of the Self *(Atman)* eventually came to inquire into the relations or connections between these realities. The exciting discovery they now made was that *Atman* was none other than *Brahman*. Only one ultimate reality existed, although it appeared to be two because it could be approached either by looking for the ground of things, or by looking for the ground of the self. Thus, although the search for the ground of external reality, *Brahman*, had appeared to end in frustration because *Brahman* was beyond all possible description, the sages now realized that *Brahman* could be known by the self-certifying experience of complete self-awareness, because *Brahman* was identical with the ultimate subject, *Atman*. Seeking to understand the ultimate nature of the world and self, it had been discovered that the same

Self exists within all beings. Each person shares his or her deepest being (*Atman*) with all other beings. One need only know this Self to know all. And this Self can be known in the surest way possible, for it is self-revealing in consciousness when the objects of consciousness that block out self-illumination are transcended.

The identity of *Atman* and *Brahman* is the greatest discovery made in the Upanishads. This identity is the mystery and sacred teaching (*upanishat*) that is so carefully guarded by the seers of the Upanishads, and that constitutes the fundamental teaching of these treatises.

Tat Tvam Asi

The fundamental teaching of the Upanishads is that by knowing the deepest Self, the *Atman*, all is known. This teaching is presented in the famous passage of the *Chandogya Upanishad* in which Uddalaka teaches his son, Shvetaketu, that in his deepest being he is, indeed, the immortal, unchanging *Atman*.

Shvetaketu had become a pupil at age twelve, and for twelve years, he studied the Vedas. At age twenty-four, thinking himself learned, he was arrogant and conceited. His father then said to him, "Shvetaketu, since you are now so greatly conceited, think yourself well read and arrogant, did you ask for that instruction by which the unhearable becomes the heard, the unperceivable becomes perceived, the unknowable becomes known?" When Shvetaketu asked how such a teaching is even possible, his father responded, "just as, my dear, by one clod of clay all that is made of clay becomes known, the modification being only a name arising from speech while the truth is that it is just clay." The point of this is that the variety and plurality of objects in the world is only a disguise for the unified reality that underlies these objects. And that underlying reality is the reality of the Self.

The instruction then proceeds to the famous teaching:

> That which is the subtle essence, this whole world has for its Self *(Atman)*. That is the true. That is the Atman. That art thou *(tat tvam asi)*, Shvetaketu.

The "subtle essence" referred to is *Brahman*, the source of all existence. Thus, when Shvetaketu learns that he is identical with his deepest self, the *Atman*, and that his *Atman* is identical with *Brahman*, the mystic teaching has been imparted.

Of course, Shvetaketu does not come to know that Self through merely conceptual understanding of this teaching. Conceptual knowledge is always of objects, whereas the Self to be known is pure subject. Yajnavalkya brings this out when he answers Ushasta Cakrayana's request for an explanation of "the *Brahman* that is immediately present and directly perceived, that is the Self in all things," by declaring, "This is your Self that is within all things." When the question is put again, "What is within all things?" Yajnavalkya's reply is, "You cannot see the seer of seeing, you cannot hear the hearer of hearing, you cannot think the thinker of thinking, you cannot understand the understander of understanding. He is your Self which is in all things" (*Brihadaranyaka Upanishad*, III.4.2).

In other words, the *Atman* is the ultimate subject that can never become an object. Consequently, it cannot be known in the way that ordinary objects of consciousness can be known, but must be realized directly in self-illuminating experiences.

The advantages brought to the search for the ultimate reality by the nature of *Atman*-awareness as immediate and direct experience resulted in providing for the establishment of the indubitable existence of *Atman*. But this kind of knowledge also carries with it certain disadvantages. Knowledge of objects is public in a way that direct experience is not. It is open to anyone to examine the evidence for the claims of knowledge about known objects. But one's immediate experience is available only to oneself. Thus, whereas for the one with the experience there is nothing surer than the experience itself, for one lacking the experience there is little or no evidence for the claimed reality. In this respect, the knowledge of *Atman* is similar to the knowledge of love. Only those experiencing love know what it is. Others might make various claims about love, but they obviously lack the appropriate experience. For the person having the experience, nothing could be more sure than its existence, although a person lacking this experience might very well be skeptical of the existence of love. In a similar way, those without faith or experience might be skeptical of the existence of *Atman* and the possibility of *Atman*-realization. But according to the Upanishads, those who have experienced the bliss of *Atman* know the ultimate joy.

REVIEW QUESTIONS

1. What evidence is there that the people of the Indus civilization had reached a relatively high level of culture and thought?
2. What is the significance of the Vedic Hymn of Origins?
3. What are the sages of the Upanishads seeking?
4. How does the *Taittiriya* teaching of sheaths or layers of existence lead to the discovery of *Atman*?
5. What is the meaning of Uddalaka's teaching, "You are That (*Tat tvam asi*)"?

FURTHER READING

Upanishads, translated from the original Sanskrit by Patrick Olivelle (Oxford: Oxford University Press, 1996), is the first accurate translation of all the major Upanishads in contemporary English to appear in the past forty years. Contains a good introductory essay and useful bibliography.

The Roots of Ancient India: The Archaeology of Early Indian Civilization, 2d rev. ed., by Walter A. Fairservis Jr. (Chicago: University of Chicago Press, 1975), is a well-rounded account of the beginnings of Indian civilization.

The Rig Veda: An Anthology, translated and annotated by Wendy Doniger O'Flaherty (New York: Penguin Books, 1981), contains 108 hymns (10 percent of the total) in a modern translation.

The Vedic Experience: Mantramañjari, by Raimundo Panikkar (Los Angeles: University of California Press, 1977), is a collection of teachings from the Vedas, *Brahmanas*, and Upanishads. No other anthology comes close to matching choice of material, quality of translation, and helpfulness of commentaries found in this treasury of Vedic thought.

The Principal Upanishads, edited and translated by Sarvepalli Radhakrishnan (Boston: Unwin Hyman, 1989), contains the Sanskrit text and excellent readable translations of all the early Upanishads.

The Beginnings of Indian Philosophy, by Franklin Edgerton (Cambridge, MA: Harvard University Press, 1965), is the summary of a great scholar's lifetime's work on early Indian thought.

The Mandukya Upanishad and the Agama Sastra: An Investigation into the Meaning of the Vedanta, by Thomas E. Wood, Monograph of the Society for Asian and Comparative Philosophy, no. 8 (Honolulu: University of Hawaii Press, 1990), is a careful study of the *Mandukya Upanishad*, comparing it with other Upanishads and with the *Agama Sastra* and its Vedanta commentaries.

CHAPTER 3

The Jain Vision

BRIEF OVERVIEW

Jainism has had a major influence on all of Indian thought. Its philosophical explanations of how *karma* shapes the lives of living beings, its stress on virtuous conduct, and its emphasis on human experience and reason have helped shape the Indian philosophical tradition. The fundamental aim of Jainism is to awaken human beings to the plight of their suffering and to help them achieve liberation from this suffering.

Rather than relying on God for salvation, Jains look to the example and teachings of those human beings who have conquered suffering. These spiritual heroes are called Conquerors *(Jinas)*. They are also called Ford-makers *(Tirthankaras)* because they show others how to cross over the stream of suffering caused by bondage. This Jain spirit of self-reliance, and the consequent emphasis on the need to understand the conditions of bondage and the way of release from bondage, led the Jains to develop sophisticated philosophical explanations of existence and a rationally based ethics.

According to Jainism, the fundamental cause of human suffering is bondage of the soul by karmic matter. The only way to liberate the soul from its karmically determined body is to stop the further accumulation of *karma* and to exhaust the karmic forces already accumulated. To accomplish this a person needs to follow a path of purification incorporating knowledge, moral conduct, and ascetic practice.

HISTORICAL CONTEXT

The beginnings of Jainism are lost in the dim reaches of antiquity, perhaps rooted in the Indus culture that existed more than a thousand years prior to the Vedic age. Mahavira, twenty-fourth and most recent Ford-maker *(Tirthankara)* of the present age, was born at Kundagram (near Patna) in 599 BCE. After his enlightenment in 557 BCE, he taught the way of liberation through the practices of nonhurting, asceticism, and the attainment of true knowledge until his final liberation in 527. His predecessor, Parsva, the twenty-third Ford-maker, lived in the middle of the ninth century BCE. But the twenty-two previous Ford-makers claimed by tradition have so far not been discovered by historical scholarship.

India was experiencing a cultural revolution in Mahavira's time, with exciting new developments occurring in philosophy and religion. By the fifth century BCE, this revolution had culminated in the establishment of the great and enduring ways of Jainism, Buddhism, and devotional Hinduism.

Perhaps the most impressive evidence of vigorous religious and philosophical debates in the sixth and fifth centuries BCE comes from the *Digha Nikaya,* one of the oldest Buddhist texts. Here King Ajatasatru, a renowned seeker of wisdom, describes to the Buddha the different doctrines of the six famous teachers whom he has consulted. This diversity of views among these teachers suggests that this was a time of great intellectual ferment.

Unfortunately, there is little surviving literature from this period to which we can turn to piece together and describe the origins, developments, and arguments of these different views of life and reality. But it appears that the main ideas that shaped the major Indian traditions were already being debated between 800 and 500 BCE.

Mahavira

Although twenty-three Ford-makers are said to have preceded Mahavira, he is the great teacher of the present era. Little is known about his personal life, for the biographical facts that were deemed important concerned only his practice and his teachings. It was his accomplishments in overcoming samsaric bondage and his presentation of a path to be followed by other persons that were important to his followers. The tradition embellishes his biography with all sorts of achievements and accomplishments to illustrate important Jain attitudes and teachings, but most of these accounts are legend rather than fact.

The outline of Mahavira's personal life appears to be this: He was born in 599 BCE at Kundagram (near modern Patna), as noted previously. At thirty, upon the death of his parents, he renounced all worldly ties. For the next twelve years, he lived a severely austere life, until in the thirteenth year he achieved omniscience *(kevalajnana)* and came to be recognized as a Conqueror *(Jina)* and Ford-maker *(Tirthankara)*. For the next thirty years, he led the community through teaching and example, gathering around him a great many monks, nuns, and devoted laypersons. According to one tradition, his disciple, Indrabhuti, collected and compiled Mahavira's words into the twelve collections *(Angas)* constituting the Jain scriptures.

BONDAGE

To understand the ideas of bondage and liberation, we must explore Jain views of reality, knowledge, and morality. How does ignorance create the bondage that manifests itself in suffering and death? The Jain answer places the responsibility on human beings themselves. It is human thought, speech, and action that create and perpetuate this bondage. And it is human virtue and wisdom that can provide liberation from karmic bondage.

The Man in the Well

There is probably no better illustration of the Jain conception of the human condition than the parable of the man in the well. This story, focusing on the bondage of karma, is not unique to Jainism, although the version that follows is told by the great seventh-century Jain writer, Haribhadra. He tells of a man, greatly oppressed by poverty, who decided to find a new life in another land. After several days, he lost his way in a thick forest. Hungry and thirsty, surrounded by wild animals, stumbling along the steep paths, he looked up to see a mad trumpeting elephant charging straight at him with upraised trunk. Simultaneously, a hideous and wicked demoness, laughing madly and brandishing a sharp sword, appeared in front of him. Trembling with fear, he searched for a way to escape. Seeing a great banyan tree off to the east, he raced across the rugged terrain to its refuge. But when he reached it, his spirits sank, for it was so high that not even the birds could fly over it, and its great trunk was unscalable.

Finally, looking all around, he saw an old grass-covered well nearby. Frightened of death and hoping to prolong his life, even if for only another moment, he leaped into the dark hole, grasping a clump of reeds growing from its wall to support himself. As he clung to these reeds he saw beneath him terrible snakes, enraged by the sound of his falling, while hissing at the very bottom was a huge black python, thick as the trunk of a heavenly elephant, mouth wide open, looking at him with its terrible red eyes. More frightened than ever, the man thought, "My life will last only as long as these reeds hold."

But raising his head, he saw two large rats, one white and one black, gnawing at the roots of the clump of reeds. In the meantime, the enraged elephant charged the great banyan tree overhanging the well, battering its trunk with his mighty head, dislodging a honeycomb swarming with bees. While the angry bees were stinging the poor defenseless man, a drop of honey chanced to fall on his head and roll down his face to his lips, giving him a moment's sweetness. Forgotten were the python, elephant, snakes, mice, bees, and the well itself, as he became possessed by the craving for still more drops of sweet honey.

Haribhadra interprets the parable with forceful clarity. The journeying man is the soul or life-principle *(jiva)*, and his wanderings are the four types of existence in which the life-principle dwells: divine, human, animal, and hell-beings. The wild elephant is death, the wicked demoness old age. The banyan tree represents salvation, for it is out of reach of death, the elephant. But no person attached to the senses can achieve this refuge. The well is human life itself, and the snakes are the passions that craze and confuse, preventing a person from knowing what to do. The clump of reeds is a person's allotted lifetime during which the soul is embodied in this form. The rats are the fortnights (bright and dark phases of the moon) that destroy the support of life, and the stinging bees are the many afflictions that torment a person, destroying every moment of joy. The terrible python at the bottom of the well is hell, which seizes the person ensnared by sensual pleasure and imposes pains by the thousandfold. The few drops of honey are the pleasures of life that bind one to terrible suffering. "How," concludes Haribhadra, "can a wise person want them in the midst of such peril and suffering?"

View of Reality

To Haribhadra, it is clear that human suffering is caused by ignorance and wrong conduct. But how do ignorance and immoral conduct cause bondage? And how can knowledge and moral conduct achieve liberation? To answer these questions, we must investigate the Jain vision of reality. According to Jainism, reality consists of two fundamentally different kinds of substances, souls and matter. Each has its own distinctive qualities and modes.

The essence of the soul *(jiva)* is life, and its chief characteristics are perception, knowledge, bliss, and energy. In its pure state, when it is not associated with matter, its knowledge is omniscient, its bliss is pure, and its energy is unlimited. But the matter that embodies the soul defiles its bliss, obstructs its knowledge, and limits its energy. This is why matter is seen as a fetter binding the soul.

The word for matter, *pudgala* (mass-energy), is derived from *pum,* meaning "coming together," and *gala,* meaning "coming apart," and it reveals the Jain conception of matter as that which is formed by the aggregation of atoms and destroyed by their disassociation. Matter refers both to the mass of things and to the forces or energy that structure this mass, making and remaking it in its diverse forms.

The word *karma* means "to make," and in Jainism it refers to the making and remaking of the karmic matter that embodies the soul. But this making and remaking is not something separate from the mass and energy of the body, which is constantly being made and remade.

The mass of karmic matter embodying the soul is constituted by an infinite number of invisible and indivisible atoms, each possessing the qualities that make possible seeing, tasting, touching, and smelling when the atoms are aggregated to constitute a person's body and mind. Most significantly, these material atoms also constitute the senses, mind, and speech that form the subtle body of the soul through which experience is possible. The matter constituting the senses, mind, speech, and volitional faculty is thought to be especially subtle and fine, as distinct from the coarse matter making up the physical objects in the world. This view of *karma* as a material force distinguishes the Jain view from other Indian views that take *karma* to be only a psychological or metaphysical force. Jains do not deny the moral, psychological, and metaphysical dimensions of *karma,* but they insist that the primary dimension is that of a subtle material force. Thus, Jains share with other Indian thinkers the idea of *karma* as a determinant of future existence, agreeing that each action leaves a residual force that inevitably expresses itself as a determinant of existence at a future time. They also accept the common analogy of this residual karmic force as a seed that, given the right conditions, will grow and bear fruit according to its own nature. The implication is that each person will reap the results of his or her every action, in the form of either reward or retribution, either immediately or in the future. This is the inexorable law of *karma* as understood by nearly every Indian thinker.

The uniqueness of the Jain view of *karma* is in the insistence on the material basis of this law of life. According to Jains, the universe is filled with tiny imperceptible particles of karmic matter, indistinguishable from one another and floating about freely until attracted to an embodied soul. In a way, the Jain view of *karma* is similar to the scientific view of the atmosphere as pervaded by tiny indistinguishable molecules of air that can be felt only when aggregated and set in motion as wind.

It is important to understand that the Jains view embodiment as karmic: the body, senses, mind, intelligence, and volitional faculty are all constituted by karmic matter and are not part of the soul itself. Instead, they obscure the omniscient knowledge, defile the pure bliss, and limit the energy—all of which are the soul's natural qualities—thereby constituting the bondage that obscures and limits the expression of these qualities.

Real knowledge is obtained not from the senses or the mind but from the soul's inherent luminosity. The difference between a wise person and an ignorant person is that a wise person's mind blocks out less of the soul's natural knowledge than does the ignorant person's mind. A popular analogy suggests that just as when the fog and clouds are cleared away, the light of the sun illuminates the entire world, when the karmic obstacles are removed from the soul, its natural omniscience will reveal everything.

Karmic Bondage

But why, if the soul is inherently pure and omniscient, did it come to be embodied in matter and thereby subjected to the bondage of repeated births and deaths? The Jain assumption is that souls have always been embodied in karmic matter, just as gold has always been embedded in ore. Indeed, this analogy is taken a step further: just as gold can be separated from the ore containing it by a refining process, so can the soul be liberated from *karma* by a process of purification. Even as the nature of gold is different from the ore in which it is embedded, so the nature of the soul is different from the matter in which it is embodied.

In order to remove *karma,* it is important to understand what causes the inflow of *karma* and how to prevent these inflows. Bondage is not limited to the human condition, but human embodiment is special because it represents a unique opportunity to achieve liberation.

Elaborate theories of how karmic bondage works have been developed, describing the karmic process in great detail, for understanding the process of bondage is the first step toward eliminating it. Bondage begins with embodiment, a beginningless process that defiles the inherent bliss of the soul. Because of this defilement, the soul's natural energy, flowing out through the body by the conduits constituted by thoughts, speech, and actions, is obstructed and forms an energy field around the soul that attracts the freely floating particles pervading the universe. When the soul is infected with the passions of desire and hatred, these particles stick to it, like dust sticks to a moist jewel, obstructing its natural brilliance. Fettered by these new accumulations of *karma,* all of the actions of living beings, whether mental acts, such as thought or speech, or physical acts, accumulate a certain amount of additional karmic matter. Those actions prompted by desire or hate and those that hurt other living beings attract the greatest amount of defiling and obstructing *karma.* It is a difficult cycle to break, for the initial impurity leads to actions producing yet additional impurities in the soul, which lead to still more *karma*-producing actions, which, in turn, even further obstruct the knowledge, limit the energy, and defile the purity of the soul.

Kinds of Karma

Although the subtle karmic particles pervading the universe are indistinguishable from one another in their free condition, when they are attracted to the soul, they take on the characteristics of the acts that attract them. This makes possible a classification of the many different forms of *karma* into eight major kinds, according to the actions producing them and the effects that they will have on a person. Four of these are known as destructive *karmas* because they have a directly negative effect, the other four as nondestructive because they bring about particular kinds of embodiment.

The worst kinds of *karma* are those that are attracted to the soul by actions proceeding from ignorance and a desire to hurt others. These are said to be destructive *karmas,* for they destroy the soul's insight into its own nature, generating false views of itself and the material world, and causing the passions of craving and hatred. Both craving, which is expressed as greed, dishonesty, and pride, and its opposite, hatred, which is expressed as anger and violence, destroy pure conduct and lead to further karmic entanglement. Because the destructive *karmas* defile the soul's purity, limit its energy, and obscure its knowledge, they allow the entry of a variety of secondary *karmas* to surround the soul, producing additional bondage. These secondary *karmas* produce the feelings of pleasantness and unpleasantness that help to direct one's actions along the paths of craving and hatred. They determine the particular birth of a soul and the life span of a particular incarnation. Finally, they also determine the particular circumstances that will either promote or hinder the quality of spiritual life in a particular incarnation.

It is not necessary to go into the minute details of karmic classification to appreciate the main point: all karmic bondage is earned by the actions producing it. Furthermore, the specific characteristics and effects of the attracted *karma* are determined by the nature of the act attracting it.

The length of time the attracted *karma* will bind a person is determined by the intensity of the passions motivating the act as well as the nature of the act itself. Once the *karma* has produced its full effects, it falls away and returns to a free and undifferentiated state.

But those *karmas* that have not yet produced all their effects continue to adhere to the soul, constituting a subtle body within the physical body. When the karmically determined life span is up, the soul departs from the physical body and, embodied by the unspent karmic matter, is reborn into another physical body of precisely the kind merited by the accumulated *karma*. This is why Jains recognize all living things as equal, treating them as members of the same global family. This is also why the goal of liberation dominates Jain life, for karmic bondage means not only the life of a human being, but also the untold lifetimes spent embodied in other forms of life.

WAY OF LIBERATION

For a devout Jain, the quest for liberation is the central focus of life. The four restraints of body, senses, speech, and mind, along with the five great vows of nonhurting, nonstealing, sexual purity, truthfulness, and nongrasping, are willingly undertaken to check the inflows of *karma*. In addition, every Jain undertakes a variety of penances to burn up the karmic forces already accumulated.

The Fourteen Stages of Purification

Liberation, a process of stopping the influx of new karmic matter and eliminating existing bondage, can be seen as a path of progressive purification. Traditionally, fourteen stages on this path have been distinguished.

Stage One. The first stage marks the beginning of the path. At this stage, the soul is spiritually asleep, ignorant of its own karmic bondage, characterized by uncontrolled passions and wrong views.

Stage Two. At the second stage, a small amount of faith, which quickly disappears, triggers a slight movement toward insight. The unusual characteristic of this stage is that it is a stopping place for the soul on its way down from the fourth stage, where it had achieved its first glimpse of enlightenment. It is called the stage of "lingering vision" because the soul retains a motivating impression that will make it easier to again experience the flash of enlightenment that marks stage four.

Stage Three. At stage three, there is stronger faith, but because of powerful doubt the soul cannot yet achieve true insight. At this stage, however, the soul's innate capacity to throw off its karmic burden enables it to see, for the first time, the ignorance and the passions that bind it to the sufferings of the body and mind. This awareness makes it possible for the soul to confront and resist its bondage, enabling it to achieve a momentary flash of true insight. When this occurs the soul undergoes a series of purifications that dramatically reduces the power and duration of the bondage of old *karmas* previously accumulated, as well as new *karmas* that will be accumulated in the future. If the karmic burden is too great to be resisted at this time, however, the soul will fall back to stage one, rather than advancing to the fourth stage.

Stage Four. At stage four, the soul experiences its first genuine awakening, a brief, but true and joyous glimpse into its real nature. Because this vision is due to the suppression, rather than elimination, of the deluding *karmas*, however, it lasts only a brief moment, after which the soul invariably slides back to stage two. Gradually, as further purification removes more and more bondage-producing *karmas,* there will be more experiences of enlightenment, and of longer duration, as the soul makes its spiritual journey toward final liberation.

Stage Five. At stage five, one experiences the power to control the passions and is able, at least partially, to restrain them. At this stage, one takes the vows to abstain from violence, falsehood, stealing, possessiveness, and improper sexual activity, as part of the effort to cultivate right conduct.

Stage Six. At the sixth stage, one's moral discipline makes it possible to achieve greater restraint of the passions.

Stage Seven. At the seventh stage, self-restraint is perfected, and anger overcome. Here carelessness and moral laxity are overcome and meditative powers increased, allowing one to live in greater awareness, restraining the actions that perpetuate karmic bondage. A person at the fourth, fifth, sixth, or seventh stage who reexperiences a temporary enlightenment, either by partially suppressing and partially eliminating the vision-obscuring *karmas* or by completely eliminating them, can then enter the eighth stage.

Stage Eight. With carelessness overcome and self-restraint perfected, a deeper enlightenment is experienced, and one attains the stage of unprecedented spiritual progress. Here pride is overcome, harmful *karma* diminished, and the power of beneficial *karma* increased through positive motivation.

Stage Nine. The spiritual progress of stage eight leads to advanced spiritual activity and greater purification of the soul. More conduct-obscuring and vision-obscuring *karmas* are eliminated at this stage, and deceit is overcome.

Stage Ten. The tenth stage of spiritual development is called "complete self-restraint with flickering greed," because moral purification reaches the stage where even gross greed is eliminated. The subtlest form of greed, however, the greed to possess a body, is not yet eliminated, but merely restrained.

Stage Eleven. At the eleventh stage, one moves beyond restraint to at least the partial elimination and total suppression of even the subtlest form of greed.

Stage Twelve. Stage twelve is called "complete self-restraint with eliminated passions," because all of the obscurations of the passion-producing *kar-*

mas have been removed with the elimination of these deluding *karmas.* With the complete elimination of even the passion known as "subtle greed for a body," all of the *karma*-producing passions have been eliminated.

Stage Thirteen.   At stage thirteen, the perception, knowledge, bliss, and energy of the soul are full, pure, and unlimited. *Karmas* are still accumulating, however, because the soul is still embodied. That is why this stage is called "omniscience with physical activity."

In order to enter stage fourteen, the final stage of "omniscience with no activity," the soul must stop all activities, gross and subtle, of the body, speech, and mind. This is accomplished through deep meditation.

Stage Fourteen.   In the final stage, with the last residue of karmic matter eliminated, the soul is free of all activity. Here, in the last instant before death, the soul has completed its spiritual development. The next instant it experiences *moksha,* perfect freedom, attaining disembodied eternal liberation.

FAITH, KNOWLEDGE, AND CONDUCT

Progress through the stages of purification is achieved by a combination of deep faith, right knowledge, and pure conduct—the "three jewels" of Jain practice by which the influx of destructive karmas, caused by delusion, false views, and the passions, can be halted.

Deep faith is traditionally considered the first of the three jewels because its realization marks the moment in life that decisively turns the individual away from the path of further bondage and toward liberation. We will consider the Jain view of knowledge first, however, in order to appreciate both the nature of, and the need for, faith.

Knowledge

Ignorance produces *karmas* that destroy the soul's insight into its own nature and generate false views of itself and the world. This ignorance, caused by the soul's initial defilement, obscures its omniscient knowledge and makes it dependent on perception, reason, and the authority of others for its knowledge. But these kinds of knowledge are extremely limited, obscuring more of reality than they reveal.

According to Jain metaphysics, reality is constituted by innumerable material and spiritual substances, each of which is the locus of innumerable qualities. Not only are there innumerable substances, each with innumerable qualities, but each quality is susceptible to an infinite number of modifications. Clearly ordinary knowledge (nonomniscient) cannot fully comprehend this complex reality, for it is limited by the senses and reason, the perspectives adopted by the knower, and by the conditions of space, time, light, and so on.

Recognizing the incredibly rich and complex nature of reality, Jains developed the notion of the "many-sidedness" *(anekanta)* of existence, in opposition to the Vedanta claims that *Brahman* alone, because it is permanent and unchanging, is ultimately and absolutely real. The notion of *anekanta* is also opposed to the Buddhists' claim that nothing is permanent, and that changing processes are the only reality. This concept of the many-sidedness of existence enabled Jain thinkers to affirm both permanence and change. What things are in themselves, as substances, is permanent. But the forms or modes of these substances are continuously changing.

Emphasizing the limits of ordinary knowledge, Jainism developed the theory that truth is relative to the perspective *(naya)* from which it is known. Furthermore, because reality is many-sided and knowledge true only from a limited perspective, all knowledge claims are only tentative *(syat)*, having the form "X *may be* Y," rather than "X *is* Y."

Limiting Perspectives. The limitations of knowledge are illustrated with a popular Jain story involving five blind men and an elephant: A king once brought five blind men into his courtyard, where he had fastened a large elephant, and asked them to tell him what it was. Each man touched the elephant and, on the basis of his perceptions, told the king what he knew this thing to be. The first felt the trunk and declared that it was a huge snake. The second touched the tail and said that it was a rope. The third felt the leg and called it a tree trunk. The fourth took hold of an ear and called it a winnowing fan, whereas the fifth felt the side of the elephant and declared it to be a wall. Because each insisted that his claim was correct and truly described the object in question, the five men were soon in the middle of a heated argument, unable to resolve the dispute because they failed to recognize that each of their claims was true only from a limited perspective.

Like the blind men, each person perceives things only from his or her own perspective. When it is understood that knowledge is limited by the particular perspectives from which it is achieved, it becomes easy to see that knowledge claims are conditioned by the limitations of the perspective that is assumed and should always be expressed as only tentatively true. For example, in the Jain story, the blind men should have been more circumspect, saying, for example, "Standing here, touching the object with my hands, it feels like a winnowing fan. It *may be* a winnowing fan." Likewise, because all knowledge is from limited perspectives, everyone should understand that knowledge claims should be asserted only conditionally.

Conditional Predication. Analyzing the logic of conditional assertion, the Jains came up with a sevenfold schema for making a truth claim about any particular object. For example, the following assertions are possible with respect to, say, the temperature of a glass of water:

1. It may be warm (to someone coming in from the cold).
2. It may not be warm (to someone coming from a very warm room it will feel cold).
3. It may be both warm and not warm, depending upon certain conditions.
4. Independent of all conditions, the water is indescribable (all knowledge rests on certain conditions).

5. Indescribable in itself, the water may be said to be warm subject to certain conditions (a combination of 1 and 4).
6. Indescribable in itself, the water may be said not to be warm, subject to certain conditions (a combination of 2 and 4).
7. Indescribable in itself, the water may be said to be warm and not warm, depending upon certain conditions (a combination of 3 and 4).

The reason why the last three assertions all begin with the claim "indescribable in itself" is that every substance known and described possesses an infinite number of qualities, each of which also possesses an infinite number of modifications. Although ordinary knowledge reveals some of these qualities and modifications, it cannot reveal them all. Thus, all descriptions of reality are only partial. The substance itself, with its infinite qualities and modifications, can be fully known only when all the limitations to knowledge are overcome. The sevenfold schema of conditional assertion enables us to recognize the partial and incomplete nature of ordinary human knowledge.

Awakening Vision.   Understanding the partial nature of ordinary knowledge makes Jains more appreciative of the knowledge of the Ford-makers. It encourages faith in their teachings and motivates effort to emulate their lives in the hope of achieving similar omniscience, purity, and bliss. This, in turn, awakens a deep longing for true insight and knowledge that may serve as a catalyst to activate the soul's natural inclination toward freedom and to direct its energies toward recovery of its omniscience, making possible the momentary flash of insight *(samyak darshana)* that marks the beginning of the way out of bondage. Although this initial awakening experience is only the fourth stage on the path of liberation, it is extremely significant. It is this momentary flash of insight that directs the energies of the soul to overcoming bondage, setting it on its way toward liberation. This momentary illumination of the soul is thus the critical turning point in the quest for liberation.

Most important, this momentary vision of the true nature of the soul enables a person to cease identifying with the body-mind and its actions, bringing the realization that the soul's only pure and proper activity is that of knowing. This realization brings an inner peace that fosters the pure conduct needed to overcome the tendencies toward anger, hatred, pride, deceitfulness, and greed.

This flash of insight also reveals the universal community of souls, engendering a strong feeling of brotherhood for all beings. This realization generates a pure compassion, which expresses itself in the inclination to avoid hurting any beings and, more positively, in the inclination to help all beings to salvation.

Faith

Faith *(darshana)*, awakened in a momentary flash of insight, is constituted by a vision of reality and an affirmative attitude toward life and liberation. It replaces skepticism about the teachings of the *Jinas* with a positive, though critical, outlook that affirms the truth of these teachings and eliminates desires for gain and profit as sources of motivation. Aversion to ordinary kinds of evil and suffering are replaced with a deeper feeling that regards as unpleasant only that which produces bondage. Faith provides security in Jain beliefs and practices and motivates one to act in a way that will illuminate and exemplify the Jain teachings and, ultimately, to follow the example of the *Jinas*. Faith also moves a person to become protective of the Jain order.

It must be emphasized that although faith is indispensable to the Jain way, this faith is a vision of reality, not a blind faith in scriptures or persons. The basis of faith is an experience of a momentary flash of insight into the true nature of the soul, which introduces a positive approach to life and motivates one to work for liberation.

Furthermore, the understanding provided by faith needs to be clarified and tested carefully by experience and reason. Jainism has placed great emphasis upon philosophical vision and reasoning as means of salvation and has placed equally great emphasis on personal effort and right conduct as means to salvation. The vision provided by faith gives direction for life and releases the soul's energies needed to stop the karmic accumulations, but only prodigious human efforts of moral and ascetic practice can eliminate bondage.

Conduct

Although faith and knowledge prepare the way and provide the necessary direction, it is right and pure conduct that brings a halt to the passions causing karmic bondage and achieves the progress toward liberation marked by stages five, six, and seven. This understanding has resulted in a strong Jain commitment to moral principles and practice. Not only is the honesty of Jain businessmen proverbial, but the high moral standards of the entire Jain community have affected and influenced all the peoples of India and many outside the subcontinent.

Pure conduct means living a virtuous life. Every Jain vows to practice the five primary virtues of nonhurting, truthfulness, nonstealing, sexual purity, and nongrasping as the core of right conduct. Many Jains, especially those advanced in their practice, also vow to practice a long list of secondary virtues.

The Primary Virtues

Nonhurting. Ahimsa, or nonhurting, is the basis of Jain morality, for ultimately all questions of good and evil and right or wrong come down to whether or not the thought, speech, or action in question hurts any life-form. Although Buddhists and Hindus also recognize the principle of nonhurting as a fundamental rule of life, the Jains have developed this principle most fully and have carried its application the furthest. The term *nonhurting* is negative, but the principle is entirely positive, being rooted in a philosophy that recognizes the community of all living organisms and that sees love as the basis of a relationship between all the members of this community. It embodies the realization that all life belongs to the same global family and that to hurt others is to destroy the community of life, which is the basis of all sacredness. Umasvati, the great Jain teacher of the second century, defines the purpose of souls as that of helping each other: "Souls exist to provide service to each other" (Tattvartha Sutra, 5.21).

Ahimsa implies both action and intention. Hurting is defined as harming other living organisms either deliberately, or by carelessness or neglect, or through actions motivated by pride, greed, hatred, prejudice, or desire. But the very intention of harming others, even if the physical action is not carried out, is regarded as hurting them. All actions rooted in anger, pride, hatred, greed, and dishonesty are regarded as forms of violence and must be renounced and abandoned.

Truthfulness. The second great vow is that of truthfulness *(satya)*, which requires that great care be taken to ensure that speech is always used to promote the well-being of the community of life. The virtue of truthfulness is closely related to that of *ahimsa,* for the rule is that speech resulting in hurting is to be avoided.

Truthfulness requires complete honesty in all business and professional activity, encouraging the scrupulous behavior of Jain businessmen that has earned them the respect of nearly everyone. Also precluded by truthfulness are speech acts that might hurt others through unkindness, harshness, rudeness, gossiping, breaking confidences, slander, or even idle chatter.

Nonstealing. The third vow, nonstealing *(asteya)*, requires that a person refrain from taking what belongs to another, whether in the form of outright theft or in more subtle forms, such as adulterating a product, tax evasion, black marketing, providing improper weights and measurements for exchanged products, failing to provide full value of goods or services exchanged, and so on. One must not accept stolen or lost goods or buy goods at a lower price if they were obtained wrongfully in the first place. The general rule is not to take anything that is not offered to one. Stealing, in any form, is regarded as hurtful activity stemming from greed, and the positive virtue of nonstealing consists in being completely satisfied with what you have so there is not the slightest desire for somebody else's possessions.

Sexual Purity. The fourth vow is that of sexual purity *(brahmacarya)*. The rationale for this vow is that sexual activity proceeds from the desires that create bondage. The Jain ascetic abstains not only from all sexual activity, but from all thought about sex as well. For laypersons, celibacy means that no sexual activities or thoughts are allowed outside the relationship between husband and wife.

Nongrasping. The fifth vow taken by every Jain is that of nongrasping *(aparigraha)*. An attitude of nonattachment must be cultivated to put an end to action that seeks identification with the external world of karmic bodies. Thus, *aparigraha* is much more than simply nonpossession, though this is the most obvious external sign and the first requirement. The mendicant is required to give up all wealth and possessions upon joining the order, and the layperson must observe numerous restrictions and conditions on wealth and possession and their means of acquisition. But physical renunciation by itself is not the goal. The goal is to get completely rid of all thoughts and attitudes that are the agents and vehicles of the desire and the aversions proceeding from a perspective distorted by karmic accumulations. The vow to eliminate thoughts and actions rooted in desire or aversion is based on the insight that this is an effective way of eliminating the desires and aversions themselves.

These five basic vows are strengthened and expanded by a series of secondary vows that (1) curtail travel; (2) prohibit drinking unfiltered water, eating certain kinds of food, and using certain methods of preparing foods; (3) proscribe brooding, mischief making, giving harmful advice, and watching or listening to unedifying events or performances; (4) obligate fasting; (5) require meditation; (6) enjoin almsgiving; (7) temporarily restrict one's activities to a given location; and, finally, (8) commit one to a holy death through meditation and fasting.

IMPACT OF JAIN THOUGHT

Finally, it should be pointed out that the Jain way of liberation has made important cultural contributions to Indian life. Jain emphasis on the importance of human knowledge led to important accomplishments in philosophy, logic, literature, architecture, art, mathematics, and the sciences, encouraging non-Jains to develop and refine their own systems and methods. The contributions of Haribhadra (seventh century), Hemacandra (twelfth century), and Mallisena (thirteenth century) to Indian logic were impressive enough to stimulate the thinking of major Buddhist and Hindu philosophers and to result in important conceptual breakthroughs.

Using the vernacular languages to create stories, narratives, and poems to present Jain teachings to the lay community, Jain monks contributed a great deal to the development of literature in the vernacular languages. The Jain penchant for writing and collecting texts resulted in impressive libraries that served the larger community and saved many ancient texts on astronomy, mathematics, and grammar from destruction. Hemacandra's poetic history of the world as contained in myth and legend, his Sanskrit and Prakrit dictionaries and grammar, and his science textbooks, for example, contributed much both to the ongoing study of these subjects and to their preservation.

But perhaps the greatest contributions to Indian life were made by Jain exemplars of moral virtue and careful reasoning. Their migrations from the Ganges Valley to the southern tip and over the western borders of the subcontinent allowed them to spread the best of Indian culture to these parts of India through their exemplary lives. Jain adherence to the rule of nonhurting has been a major factor in the importance that this moral principle has assumed in Buddhist and Hindu life over the centuries. Mahatma Gandhi, the Hindu saint whose adherence to nonhurting in his successful efforts to throw off the yoke of British colonial rule, bringing the principle of nonviolence to the admiring attention of the whole world, gratefully acknowledged the great impression made on him by the virtuous Jains he knew as a youth.

REVIEW QUESTIONS

1. How does Jainism conceive of karmic matter? Discuss its mass aspect, its force aspect, and its atomic constituency.
2. What is the soul? What are its principal characteristics?
3. What is bondage? How does bondage occur? How is it constituted?
4. In what does liberation consist and how is it achieved? Discuss how faith, knowledge, and conduct work together to enable a person to attain the various levels of purification.
5. What is the Jain theory of knowledge? Explain the conditional nature of knowledge *(syadavada)*.

FURTHER READING

Collected Papers on Jaina Studies, by Padmanabh S. Jaini (Delhi: Motilal Banarsidass, 2000), is a collection of essays on important topics, including *ahimsa* and *karma*, by one of the world's foremost Jain scholars.

Tattvartha Sutra: That Which Is, by Umasvati, translated and introduced by Nathmal Tatia (San Francisco: Harper Collins, 1994), is an excellent translation of this foundational Jain text and its three most important commentaries.

The Jaina Path of Purification, by Padmanabh S. Jaini (Berkeley: University of California Press, 1979), is by far the best book on Jainism. Sympathetic but unbiased and scholarly, it is written in clear, straightforward English, simple enough for the beginning student of Jainism, yet accurate and profound enough to help the more advanced student.

Central Philosophy of Jainism (Anekantavada), by Bimal Krishna Matilal (Ahmedabad: L.D. Institute of Indology, 1981), is an excellent comparative philosophical analysis of Jain theory of knowledge showing the basis of conditionality *(syadavada)*.

Jainism Explained, by Paul Marett (Leicester: Jain Samaj, 1985), is a careful explanation of the basic features of Jainism.

The Scientific Foundations of Jainism, by K.V. Mardia (Delhi: Motilal Banarsidass, 1990), discusses the basic concepts of Jainism in terms of modern science.

Studies in Jaina Philosophy, by Nathmal Tatia (Varanasi: Jaina Cultural Research Center, 1951), is a work of solid scholarship, based on the most important Jain texts and commentaries. Throughout, Jain philosophies are compared with Hindu and Buddhist views and arguments on each topic. This volume is appropriate for the advanced student.

Sources of Indian Tradition, 2d ed., vol. 1, edited by Ainslie T. Embree (New York: Columbia University Press, 1988), contains translated Jain texts and explanations by the great scholar A.L. Basham (pp. 43–92). Topics covered include cultural background, ideas of bondage and liberation, and philosophical and political thought.

Philosophies of India, by Heinrich Zimmer (Cleveland, OH: World, 1961), contains a long, illuminating chapter on Jainism.

CHAPTER 4

Society and the Individual

What are my duties? What are the fundamental values of human life? What is righteous conduct *(dharma)*? To answer these questions, providing guidance to society and its members, India produced a variety of texts that explained the basic aims of life and the ways of achieving these aims. This literature, composed largely between about 400 BCE and 200 CE, includes the two great epics, the *Ramayana* and the *Mahabharata*; the *Bhagavad Gita*; and the treatises on right conduct *(dharma shastras)* that defined the right way to live. These texts combine the early Vedic emphasis on religious ritual and moral duty with the Upanishad's emphasis on self-discipline and meditative knowledge, as they seek to integrate the worldview of the *Rig Veda* with that of the Upanishads.

BHAGAVAD GITA

The most important synthesis of Vedic, Upanishadic, and theistic visions is the *Bhagavad Gita*, the "Song of the Lord." In the *Gita*, which is a portion of the great epic *Mahabharata*, both the identification of the individual person with *Atman* and the identification of *Atman* with the ultimate reality of the universe are taken over from the Upanishads. But in the *Gita, Atman/Brahman* is symbolized by God, and the divine teacher of the *Gita*, Krishna, describes himself as a finite form of the infinite, claiming to be both God and the *Brahman* of the Upanishads.

When *Brahman* was given concrete form in the person of Krishna, the gap between the finite and the infinite was bridged. This was the solution offered by the *Gita* to the problem of how to realize the infinite, a solution offering hope and inspiration to the ordinary people who could not spend their lives pursuing the liberating knowledge extolled by the sages. The concrete forms of religious worship were now seen as a means to the realization of that ultimate Self taught in the Upanishads.

The *Gita* not only offered hope and inspiration but also provided a guide to life, leading to the fulfillment of that hope and inspiration. The two important questions taken up by the *Gita* are (1) What is the relation between the ordinary, empirical self and the ultimate Self *(Atman)*? (Or looked at from the point of view of things, What is the relation between ordinary things and the ultimate reality [*Brahman*]?); and (2) By what means can a person come to realize or experience that ultimate Self, the *Atman*?

It is significant that these questions are considered in the context of a moral decision. As the *Gita* opens, Arjuna finds himself unable to determine the right thing to do. The specific question concerns the decision to fight or not to fight to regain the kingdom that rightfully belongs to him. The answer, given by Krishna, disguised as Arjuna's charioteer, is provided in general terms so that it can be adapted to any specific moral choice. The answer turns on the nature of human existence, the nature of reality, and the purpose of life.

The *Gita* accepts the view of the Upanishads that reality, though it appears to be an ever-changing set of diverse processes, is, at its core, ultimately unchanging and permanent, without multiplicity. According to the *Gita*, the ultimate Self *(Atman)* is also unchanging, identical with the ultimate reality. But because of ignorance about his true nature, Arjuna mistakes himself for a changing self, living in a world of changing objects. Having identified himself with the impermanent and changing self, he seeks satisfaction in the world of change, always without success, because the whole quest is fundamentally misguided.

But why does Arjuna make this mistake? According to the *Gita*, it is the failure to distinguish between the lower self and the higher Self. The lower, empirical self is constituted by the *gunas*, the strands of energy-matter *(sattva, rajas,* and *tamas)* that are the basis of all psycho-physical existence. This empirical self covers and obscures the ultimate Self, the *Atman*, leading Arjuna to mistake the empirical self for the true Self. That is why Arjuna, who suggested that it would be wrong to engage in the great war that he is preparing to fight because of the destruction and killing that would occur, is instructed by Krishna to shift his attention to the eternal *Atman*:

> Arjuna, when a man knows the Self
> to be indestructible, enduring, unborn
> unchanging, how does he kill
> or cause anyone to kill?[1]

But if the individual person mistakenly identifies with the empirical self constituted by the *gunas* because the real Self is obscured, how can the obscuring veil of the *gunas* be removed so that the real Self might be seen? This is the all-important practical question about the way to the realization of the *Atman*.

The *Gita*'s answer to this question is that the empirical self must be disciplined and brought under control so that it is no longer capable of confusing a person. But this short answer is insufficient, for the starting point on the path to *Atman*-realization is always occupied by the ignorant self, who regards the self and world constituted by the *gunas* as ultimate. Krishna needs to present ways to the ultimate liberating knowledge that begin where the individual actually is, but progressively lead to higher understanding, until gradually one is freed entirely from ignorance.

Nonattached Action

What is fundamental to every way of liberation, according to the *Gita*, is the discipline that enables a person to engage in action without becoming attached to the results of action. It is attachment to the *guna*-self that constitutes the bondage from which Arjuna should seek liberation, according to Krishna.

The empirical self constituted by the *gunas* is a combination of three kinds of matter with different tendencies that combine in varying proportions. The first kind of matter, *sattva*, is the tendency that inclines one to intellectual activity. The second kind of matter, *rajas*, is the tendency that inclines one to vigorous action. The third *guna, tamas*, inclines one to devotional activity. These three *gunas*, in their varying combinations, account for the different kinds of persons that exist, each kind with its own forms of attachment.

The recognition that different kinds of persons are bound by different kinds of attachment according to differing proportions of the three *gunas* led to the recognition of three basically different paths leading to the realization of *Atman*. These three paths, which correspond to the kinds of attachment generated by the *gunas* of *sattva, rajas*, and *tamas*, are the paths of knowledge, work, and devotion, respectively. Common to these three paths is the self-discipline leading to nonattachment, which progressively frees the real Self from the *guna*-self. These three ways of disciplined nonattachment are the three famous *yogas* that are taught in the *Gita*; the *yoga* of knowledge, the *yoga* of work, and the *yoga* of devotion. Because of the nature of the *guna*-self, one cannot avoid engaging in action. But it is possible to discipline oneself, no matter what kind of action is involved, so that one can disassociate from the action itself, which belongs to the *guna*-self, not to the *Atman*. This is the essence of the way of nonattachment[2] taught in the *Gita*.

Underlying these three ways of nonattachment are (1) a goal of achieving independence of the *gunas*; (2) a method, namely, self-discipline in action, feeling, and thought; and (3) a principle stating that in order to free oneself from the *gunas* through self-discipline, it is necessary to cooperate with and work through the *guna*-self, progressively transcending it.

HUMAN AIMS

The principle of attaining freedom from the *gunas* through cooperation with them underlies a variety of practices and ideals constituting the everyday life and social practice of the person who aims at *Atman*-realization. How can the life of the individual and the institutions of society be ordered to ensure progress toward Self-realization? This is a question that India took very seriously. The answer has three parts. First, the fundamental purposes of life, the basic human aims, must be understood and achieved. Second, the essential functions of society must be fulfilled by the persons best suited to perform these functions. Third, each person's life should be divided into progressive life-stages aimed at fulfilling the basic human aims, including the aim of liberation.

To order the life of the individual and the institutions of society, one must first be clear about the fundamental aims of human life and the essential functions of society. According to Indian philosophy, there are four fundamental aims of life, corresponding to basic human needs. The organization and institutions of society are intended to make it possible to attain these four aims. The word for these fundamental aims is *purushartha*, which means "aim of a person." Everyone has four basic aims in life, according to Indian tradition. The first three, virtuous living *(dharma)*, means of life *(artha)*, and enjoyment *(kama)*, were already recognized in Vedic times, more than three thousand years ago, and are common to all societies. The fourth, self-liberation *(moksha)*, was added as a result of the insights of the sages of the Upanishads. Together, these four aims have constituted the basis of Indian values since the time of the Upanishads. The tension between the first three aims, which emerge from a worldview that embraces the value of human life in this world, and the aim of liberation, which emerges from a worldview that celebrates the value of a spiritual existence beyond life in this world, has been recognized since at least the time of the *Gita*. Indeed, creative attempts to deal with this tension have contributed much to the vitality of Indian tradition.

Essentially, the theory of human aims represents an attempt to divide the basic rules concerning possible courses of action into four categories corresponding to the four aims of life. Thus, the rules concerning how one should act with respect to other persons are included under the heading of *dharma*. The rules concerning how one should act with respect to wealth and power are included under *artha*. The rules concerning how one should act with respect to pleasure and enjoyment are included under *kama*. Finally, the rules concerning how one should act with respect to self-realization are grouped under the heading of *moksha*. Looked at in this way, the human aims are essentially an answer to the question, How should life be lived?

Dharma

Although the word *dharma*, which refers to what ought to be done, is used in a variety of ways, there is a common notion of a rule of action running through the different uses of the term. The word *dharma* is derived from the root *dhri*, which means "to support" or "to maintain," and the reason for a rule is that it maintains or supports certain activities. Consequently, *dharma* came to mean that which one should do because it supports the individual and society and is therefore the right thing to do. *Dharma* is thus the moral guide to action.

With respect to the individual, one's *dharma* is one's moral duty, which is determined by one's place in the family, one's social class, one's stage in life, and the variety of roles one assumes in life. But with respect to society, *dharma* provides rules for settling disputes and possible conflicts between individuals, for only when conflicts of interest between individuals and groups are kept to a minimum can society be well maintained. Thus, *dharma* has a social sense and significance, for it represents possible rules for action in society that enable self-fulfillment of the individual and that at the same time make a contribution to the self-fulfillment of others.

Artha

The word *artha* is derived from the root *ri*, which means, literally, "that which one goes for." From this basic meaning of "aim," *artha* comes to refer to the thing or state of affairs at which one aims. Because everyone aims at advantage and success, success became a common meaning of *artha*.

The following statements from the *Mahabharata* and the *Panchatantra*, two of India's most popular sources of values, reveal the common attitude toward *artha*. In the *Mahabharata*, in a passage that not only encourages the seeking of wealth, but also condemns as morally wrong actions depriving others of their wealth, it is said:

> What is here regarded as *dharma* depends entirely upon wealth *(artha)*. One who robs another of wealth robs him of his *dharma* as well. Poverty is a state of sinfulness. All kinds of meritorious acts flow from the possession of great wealth, as from wealth spring all religious acts, all pleasures, and heaven itself. Wealth brings about accession of wealth, as elephants capture elephants. Religious acts, pleasure, joy, courage, worth, and learning; all these proceed from wealth. From wealth one's merit increases. He that has no wealth has neither this world nor the next.[3]

The collection of stories known as the *Panchatantra* contains the following observations:

> The smell of wealth *(artha)* is quite enough to wake a creature's sterner stuff. And wealth's enjoyment even more. Wealth gives constant vigor, confidence, and power. Poverty is a curse worse than death. Virtue without wealth is of no consequence. The lack of money is the root of all evil.[4]

Sometimes the remark that "poverty is a curse worse than death" is misunderstood to say that the poor are cursed. But the point that the text is trying to make is that poverty is such a terrible thing that anyone causing the poverty of another is cursed. The securing of success and power is advocated as a primary aim in life subject only to the important restriction that no *artha* be pursued in violation of *dharma*.

Kama

Since wealth and power are not valuable primarily for their own sake, but mainly for the enjoyment they make possible, the human aim of enjoyment, *kama*, is included as one of the basic aims in life. The classic definition of *kama*, which includes sexual enjoyment, but which extends beyond that narrow meaning to enjoyment of all kinds, is found in the teachings of Vatsyayana:

> Kama is the enjoyment of the appropriate objects of the five senses of hearing, feeling, seeing, tasting, and smelling, assisted by the mind, together with the soul. The ingredient in this is a peculiar contact between the organ of sense and its object, and the consciousness of pleasure that results from the contact is called *Kama*.[5]

Moksha

The fourth basic human aim is *moksha*. The word derives from the root *muc*, meaning "to release" or "to free." In accord with the literal meaning of the word, *moksha* means freedom of the higher Self, the *Atman*, from body, mind, and the world. This aim reflects the emphasis put on the spiritual nature of human life in India. According to the teachings of the Upanishads, the true Self, the *Atman*, is beyond the physical and mental realms. In agreement with this conception of human nature, the ultimate perfection of a person is seen to lie in Self-realization, in realizing one's true identity with *Brahman*, the ultimate source and power of all reality. Because of India's integral view of human existence, it was held that the fulfillment of a person's biological and social nature is a necessary, though not sufficient, condition for the fulfillment of one's spiritual nature. Thus, achievement of the first three human aims, *dharma*, *artha*, and *kama*, was seen as necessary to achieving the final aim of *moksha*.

SOCIAL CLASSES

To provide opportunities for members of society to achieve the basic human aims of *dharma*, *artha*, *kama*, and *moksha*, the Indian tradition recommended specific forms of social organization. All of the various social functions that these achievements require, such as education, health care, family, security, and so forth, must be provided. One aspect of this social organization is a basic scheme of social classification that ensures adequate personnel to provide the various basic social functions. A fourfold class system called *varna*, with each class further subdivided into numerous *jatis* or castes, provides the basic class structure of Indian society.

Varna divides all persons into four classes according to their fundamental characteristics. It is possible that initially *varna* referred to a system of social classification of persons according to their qualifications, tendencies, and dispositions. But lacking a system to classify persons according to their own natures, the *varnas* soon became hereditary, determined by birth. Apparently, the *varnas* soon subdivided into castes according to social functions. For example, the *vaishya varna* was divided into separate castes such as farmer, trader, carpenter, and so on. Every person belonged to the caste of his or her parents. Thus, although there are only four fundamental classes of people (*varna*), with membership determined, ideally, by a person's nature, in fact there are more than two thousand separate castes, constituting the Indian social class structure. These castes or *jatis* are distinguished from one another not by the qualifications of the individual, but primarily by heredity, dietary regulations, rules of marriage, occupation, and rank.

According to the ideal, each of the four social classes *(varnas)*, which in practice is constituted by hundreds of castes *(jatis)*, is expected to provide its share of the required social functions. The theory behind *varna* is that the good of society will be furthered if there are distinct classes of individuals who are especially well qualified to perform the different tasks requisite for a good life in society. Furthermore, this classification will be to the advantage of the individual in that it will prove easier to fulfill oneself and reach the true self if one is engaging in those activities for which one is peculiarly well suited by temperament, disposition, and natural ability. According to ancient theory, and reiterated in the *Gita*, each *varna* is distinguished from the others according to the characteristics of its members and according to the social functions they should perform because of those characteristics.

Indian tradition views moral duties as grounded in the very order of the universe. The universe is regarded as essentially moral. Everything happens according to a rule for the benefit of the whole. Each class of beings in the universe, by functioning according to their nature, contributes to the order and well-being of the whole.

The *brahmana varna*, characterized by excellent intelligence and speech, consists of the priests and teachers, whose primary function is to maintain the cultural traditions. They are responsible for preserving knowledge and culture, performing rituals, and safeguarding morality.

The *kshatriya varna*, characterized by strength, valor, and courage, consists of the protectors and administrators of society. They are the guardians of the rest of society, providing for their security, and enforcing the various rules required for the necessary social functions. According to the *Gita*, fiery energy, resolve, skill, refusal to retreat in battle, charity, and majesty in conduct are intrinsic to the action of a *kshatriya* (18.43).

The *vaishya varna* is characterized by practical intelligence and initiative, and it consists of the traders and producers in society. Their chief function is to produce society's economic goods. The *Gita* says that engagement in agriculture, raising cattle, and trading are the duties of a *vaishya*, born of his own nature (18.44).

The *shudra varna*, characterized by lower intelligence, lack of initiative, and ability to take on huge burdens, consists of society's workers and servants. According to the *Gita*, the *dharma* (duty) of a *shudra*, born of his own nature, is action consisting of service (18.44).

According to the principle of *varna*, certain rights and duties accrue to an individual by virtue of belonging to a certain class in society. For example, *kshatriyas* have a duty to protect society, and other classes have a right to this protection. *Shudras* have a duty to serve society, whereas the other classes are entitled to their service. Because the specific duties and rights are predetermined for each of the four classes, once an individual's class is known, so are his or her duties and rights. The rights and duties of the four *varnas* do not exhaust a person's *dharma*, however, because there are certain duties that a person has simply as a human being and as a member of society, regardless of class. Thus

Bhisma, in the *Mahabharata*, says that all persons have the duties of controlling their anger, telling the truth, forgiving others, maintaining pure conduct, avoiding quarrels, and acting justly (*Shantiparva*, 60.7).

Traditionally, until it was made illegal by India's new constitution in 1947, when persons violated serious *varna* and *jati* rules of behavior, they could be cast out of their social class, thereby becoming outcastes, without the usual rights of other members of society. Since children of outcastes were automatically also outcastes, the number of outcastes grew to the point where British census takers estimated that one out of every four persons in India was an outcaste. This problem has attracted a great deal of attention on the part of Indian leaders over the past one hundred years, and great strides have been made in solving the problem and correcting past injustices.

LIFE-STAGES

Whereas the theory of social classes addresses the issue of how to maintain the social order while acting in accord with one's own nature, the theory of life-stages *(ashrama)* responds to the question, How should the individual's personal life be ordered to maximize progress in achieving the four basic aims of life while maximizing contributions to society? The institution of *ashrama* consists of a series of four stages in life, classified according to the activities proper to each stage.

The first life-stage, the student stage, enables the individual to learn about life in all of its various aspects. It is here that one learns the duties of religion, class, life-stages, and so forth and is introduced to the art of self-discipline.

The second stage of life is that of the householder. All the texts recognize the central importance of this stage, for the entire society is dependent upon the goods and services the householder provides. To maintain and support society, the householder must uphold *dharma*, secure the economy, and support the values of the culture. Although raising children and taking care of the old and the needy are primary duties enjoined on the householder, this is also the period in life when worldly success and life's pleasures are to be enjoyed.

The third stage, ideally the third quarter of one's life, is that of the forest-dweller. Here one withdraws from society, giving up the aims of success and pleasure, preparing oneself for the spiritual life of the fourth stage, in which *moksha* is the only goal.

The fourth stage, that of the recluse seeking *moksha*, is characterized by complete renunciation of worldly objects and desires. Having already achieved the first three aims of life, one is now concerned only with attaining the complete freedom of liberation from this body-mind and this world—known as *moksha*.

Underlying the institutions of life-stages and social classes, and the theory of human aims in which these institutions find their justification, is the perennial Indian concern to participate fully in life while fulfilling one's spiritual nature through *Atman*-realization. According to Indian tradition, although these goals may appear opposed to each other, they do not exclude each other. Both participation in the life of this world and liberation from it are necessary components of the ideal life.

REVIEW QUESTIONS

1. What is Arjuna's dilemma in the *Bhagavad Gita*?
2. What is the relation between the ultimate Self *(Atman)* and the *guna*-self? Why is this distinction important?
3. What are the basic aims in life *(purusharthas)*? Explain each aim and how each is related to the others.
4. Why is life ideally divided into four life-stages *(ashramas)*?
5. What are the four *varnas*? How are they distinguished from the castes *(jatis)*?

FURTHER READING

Dharma Sutras: The Law Codes of Apastamba, Gautama, Baudhyayana, and Vasistha, translated by Patrick Olivelle (Delhi: Motilal Banarsidass, 2000), is a fresh translation of these important texts on *dharma*, with excellent introductions.

Transcreation of the Bhagavad Gita, by Ashok Kumar Malhotra (Upper Saddle River, NJ: Prentice Hall, 1999), was prepared especially for students.

Hindu View of Life, by Sarvepalli Radhakrishnan (New York: Macmillan, 1964), presents Hinduism as a practical philosophy, guiding and directing daily life.

The Evolution of Hindu Ethical Ideals, by S. Cromwell Crawford (Honolulu: University of Hawaii Press, 1982), is a systematic examination of the ethical philosophies of the main philosophical systems of India.

Hindu Ethics: Purity, Abortion, and Euthanasia, by Harold G. Coward, Julius J. Lipner, and Katherine Young (Albany: State University of New York Press, 1989), consists of three essays, each focusing on what the Hindu tradition has to say regarding the three issues indicated in the title.

The Bhagavad Gita, translated by Barbara Stoler Miller (New York: Bantam Books, 1986), is an excellent translation that retains the power of the original. It is inexpensive and convenient to use.

The Mahabharata: A Film, by Peter Brook, 1989, Parabola Video Library, Dept. 13, 656 Broadway, New York, NY 10012, is a contemporary dramatization that makes the central events of the epic accessible to students.

Dilemmas of Life and Death: Hindu Ethics in a North American Context, by S. Cromwell Crawford (Albany: State University of New York Press, 1994), applies Hindu ethical principles to important moral issues.

NOTES

1. *Gita*, 2.21. Translation by the author.
2. See Chapter 5 for a discussion of the *gunas* and the practice of *yoga* as a way of overcoming attachment to them.
3. *Mahabharata, Shantiparva*, 12.8.11 (Poona: Bhandarkar Oriental Research Institute, 1927–54).
4. *The Panchatantra*, trans. by A.W. Ryder (Chicago: University of Chicago Press, 1925), p. 210.
5. *The Kama Sutra of Vatsyayana*, trans. by R. Burton and F.A. Arbuthnot (London: Panther Books, 1963).

CHAPTER 5

Self and the World:
Samkhya-Y*oga*

The ethical, social, political, and religious philosophies of the epics, *Dharma Shastras,* and the *Gita* presuppose certain relationships between the empirical self that is the social organism and the ultimate Self that is pure subject. This presupposition is obvious from the emphasis placed on the various prescriptions for life in society in order to realize the ultimate Self. Unless there were a connection between the empirical self and the ultimate Self, the activities of the empirical self would be irrelevant to self-liberation.

SAMKHYA: A DUALISTIC THEORY OF REALITY

The oldest philosophical school to focus on the relation between the self and the not-self was the school of Samkhya. Historians disagree on whether Samkhya grew out of certain portions of the Upanishads or whether it developed independently as an alternative philosophy. But everyone agrees that Samkhya is dualistic, recognizing two kinds of ultimate reality. Samkhya focuses on the analyses of the relationship between the empirical and the ultimate and on the relation between the self as knowing subject and the things that it knows as objects of knowledge. Indeed, the word *samkhya* that gives this school its name means the "enumeration" or "discrimination" that results from the analysis of reality.

As a result of its analysis of reality, Samkhya gives an evolutionary explanation of the empirical world and self, explaining how they evolved from the constituent strands (*gunas*) of *prakriti*, the ultimate substrate of the empirical world. According to Samkhya, the ultimate Self of each person is a *purusha*, a

54

spiritual monad of pure consciousness that in its own nature is separate from the *gunas* that constitute the empirical world and the empirical self.

The starting point for any analysis of world and self must be one's experience of the self and the world. This experience reveals the existence of a knowing self in a changing world. Obviously, we and the world around us are changing. It is with this obvious fact that the Samkhya philosophers begin, and from which they derive the conclusion that all that is experienced is fundamentally of the same nature, though basically different from the Self that is the ultimate experiencing subject.

CAUSALITY

The analysis of causality provides the main reasons for the claims made about the world and the self by Samkhya. The orderliness and regularity of the experienced world cannot be dismissed as the result of chance. Changes are caused. Whatever is or will be, is or will be due to various causes.

The theory of causality adopted is called *satkaryavada*, which means that the effect "preexists" in the cause rather than being something completely new. Now, if it is the case that nothing can occur without a cause and it is also the case that every effect preexists in its cause, then the effect cannot be a new reality, completely different from its cause. This means that causality is simply a matter of transforming a reality that already existed, although in a different form.

The Samkhya theory of causation is summed up by Ishvara Krishna, a leading Samkhya thinker, as follows:

> The effect exists before the operation of cause: (A) because of the nonproductivity of non-being; (B) because of the need for an [appropriate] material cause; (C) because of the impossibility of all things coming from all things; (D) because something can only produce what it is capable of producing; and (E) because the effect is nondifferent from the cause. (*Samkhya Karika*, 9)

The reason for claiming that effects exist is that they are the observable world that is experienced. To deny the existence of effects would be to deny the existence of the world. The reason for claiming that causes exist is that something must have produced the effects that constitute the world. To be a cause is to produce an effect. Therefore, if there are effects, there must be causes. Furthermore, according to the Samkhya analysis, the effect is as real as the cause, for the effect is simply a transformation of the cause.

The claim that the effect is of the same essence as the cause is crucially important to Samkhya. It is the main support for the claim that all objective reality is ultimately of the same nature because it is simply the result of various transformations of *prakriti*, the primordial matter from which everything evolves.

An objection to the Samkhya view is that the effect is a new whole, different from the constituent parts because no effect can be known before it is produced. But if it were essentially the same as its cause, it should be possible to know the effect even before it is produced just by knowing the cause.

According to Samkhya, this objection is not valid, for it makes no sense to say that a whole is different from its material cause. For example, the pieces of wood that are the material cause of the table when arranged in a certain way are not different from the table. If it were different, one could perceive the table independently of its parts. But this is clearly impossible. Samkhya claims that perceiving an effect is simply perceiving the cause in transformation. To go on from this to say, "and therefore seeing the effect is seeing a new entity," is not to present an objection at all, but simply to presume that to perceive something being transformed is to perceive a new entity.

Another objection to the Samkhya view is that if causality is simply a matter of transformation and not the production of something new, then the activity of an agent, the efficient cause, is unnecessary, because the effect already exists. Samkhya philosophers address this objection by considering the contrary assumption, namely, that the effect does not preexist in the cause. If the effect does not preexist in the cause, then causality would bring something into existence out of nothing—hence the claim, "because of the nonproductivity of nonbeing." But causality cannot produce existence out of nonexistence. An agent is required to transform something into something else, not to produce something out of nothing. To claim that what exists can be caused by what does not exist is not to provide an alternative theory of causation but to deny causality completely.

Furthermore, according to Samkhya, if you do not admit that the effect preexists, then you have to say that it does not exist until it is caused. This is equivalent to claiming that the nonexistent effect belongs to the cause. But since the effect does not exist before it is caused, there is nothing to belong to the cause, for a relation of belonging is possible only between existing things. Thus, if the effect can be said to belong to the cause, it must be admitted that it preexists.

But then what of the objection that if the effect preexists no cause is needed? The Samkhya answer is that the agent or efficient cause simply manifests what was unmanifest in the cause and does not actually create something new.

Another Samkhya reply to the objection that cause and effect are distinct entities is that the preexistence of the effect can be seen from the fact that nothing can be obtained from a cause that was not in the cause. For example, curd is gotten from milk because it preexisted in the milk. It cannot be gotten from water or oil because it did not preexist in them. Indeed, if it were not the case that the effect preexisted in the cause, then it would be possible for any effect to proceed from any cause. But this is obviously not the case; curd cannot be produced from water.

But if it is the case that only certain causes can produce certain effects, then obviously some causes are potent with respect to some effects but not with respect to others. This shows that the effect preexists in the cause; otherwise it would make no sense to say that a cause is potent with respect to a given effect. A cause is potent only if it has power related to the effect. Without the preexistence of the effect, however, there is nothing for the power to be related to, and then it makes no sense to talk about potent causes or potential effects.

To clinch their case for the preexistence of effects in their causes, Samkhya philosophers argue that the very concept of causal production requires the pre-existence of the effect in the cause. Non-being, the nonexistent, requires no cause. So if the effect were nonexistent at any time, there would be no question of locating its cause. But it does make sense to talk about the possibility of effects that do not yet exist and to try to determine what will cause these effects to come into existence. This makes sense, however, only upon the assumption that the effect preexists in some sense, for that which is absolutely nonexistent cannot have a cause.

The foregoing Samkhya arguments are all designed to support the claim that causes and effects are the same in essence, differing only in their form or manifestations. It is important to note that Samkhya philosophers are primarily concerned with material causes, the stuff out of which something is made. An example frequently used is a piece of gold that can be pressed into many shapes and pieces. But changing its shape does not make the effect something totally new. The flower made of gold is basically gold, as is the earring that is made of gold; the difference involves only name and form, and not the stuff out of which these things are made.

EVOLUTION OF THE WORLD

Having established that the effect necessarily preexists in the cause, the Samkhya philosophers proceed to argue that this implies a single ultimate material cause of the world. This primordial material cause, through a process of evolutionary transformation, is transformed into the effects that we experience as the world.

The claim that the whole world evolved from a single material cause is a logical conclusion from two premises that the Samkhya philosophers have established. The first premise is that the present world exists as the result of previous changes. The second is that change is not the production of something radically new, but only the transformation of something that existed previously. If these two premises are accepted, then in order to avoid infinite regress, it must be admitted that there is one ultimate material cause, which in its various transformations constitutes the world of experience. From this, it follows that the entire world of experience is of the same fundamental nature as this ultimate material cause, for everything is basically only a transformation of this first cause. Despite their differences, all the various things that exist in the world, from bodies and minds to stones and stars, have the same nature because they arise from *prakriti*, the primordial matter from which everything evolves. Thus, Samkhya concludes that the entire experienceable world is of the nature of *prakriti*, the primordial material cause.

This conclusion raises another question, however. How does the pluralistic world of experience evolve from this basic reality called *prakriti*? If there are no effects except those that preexisted in the cause, then all of the effects that constitute the experienced world must have preexisted in *prakriti*. Consequently, *prakriti* itself must have different characteristics that account for its ability to transform into different kinds of things.

Samkhya accepts this analysis, claiming that the tendencies to transform into different kinds of things are rooted in the three strands or *gunas* that constitute *prakriti*. Just as a multicolored rope is constituted by weaving together three strands, each of a different color, so *prakriti* is constituted by three *gunas*, namely, *sattva*, *rajas*, and *tamas*, each with its own characteristics.

Sattva, described as buoyant and shining, is responsible for the self-manifestation and self-maintenance of *prakriti*. *Rajas*, said to be active and stimulating, energizes *prakriti*, moving it to transform itself unceasingly. *Tamas*, the heavy and enveloping, is the *guna* responsible for constancy and endurance. From a psychological perspective, *sattva* produces pleasure, *rajas* produces pain, and *tamas* produces indifference.

Through an evolutionary process, the varying combinations of the *gunas* produce the different types of persons and the various kinds of things. The order of evolution of *prakriti* regards the first transformation as an illumination of *prakriti* by *purusha* (pure consciousness). This illumination is called *buddhi* (intelligence) or *mahat* (the "great one"). This intelligence becomes aware of itself as the "I-maker" *(ahamkara)*, leading to the evolution of distinct individual beings. Next, as *prakriti* continues to evolve, it produces the mind and the organs of sensation as well as the organ of actions and the subtle essences of the things that are sensed and acted upon. Finally, the various objects of the world evolved.

But what caused the evolution of *prakriti*? If the world is looked at as evolving, then, according to Samkhya philosophers, it is implied that there was a logical time when the *gunas* constituting *prakriti* were in a quiet state of equilibrium. If this is the case, it is necessary to suppose that there is another principle of reality in the world, a principle responsible for disturbing the equilibrium of the *gunas*, thereby setting in motion the evolution of *prakriti*. This second reality is the pure consciousness called *purusha*.

Although it is the existence of *purusha* that accounts for the evolution of *prakriti*, it is not that *purusha* actually is involved with *prakriti*. Rather, simply because of the presence of *purusha*, the equilibrium of *prakriti* is upset and the evolutionary process begins.

How do we know that *purusha* exists? Ishvara Krishna, author of the foundational text of the Samkhya tradition, summarizes the arguments for the existence of *purusha* as follows:

> The *Purusha* exists because: (A) aggregations or combinations exist for another; (B) this other must be apart or opposite from the three; (C) this other must be a superintending power or control; (D) there must be an enjoyer; and (E) there is functioning for the sake of isolation or freedom. (*Samkhya Karika*, 17)[1]

Arguments A and B rest on the premises that (1) all experienced objects consist of parts, these parts being ordered in such a way as to serve the purposes of other objects or beings so that all of nature holds together as an ordered whole, and that (2) unless there is that which is not composed of parts, for the sake of which those things composed of parts exist, we are caught in an infinite regress. For example, earth serves the purpose of grass, grass serves the purpose of cows, and cows serve the purpose of people. But unless there is some ultimate purpose for all of these things, a final end that is itself not a means to some further end, then the whole chain of means has no end or purpose. Since we see that in nature many things exist for the sake of others, and these others exist for the sake of yet others, Samkhya concludes that *prakriti*, the world of nature, must exist for the sake of another that is not of the nature of *prakriti*. This ultimate other, different from the *gunas*, is *purusha*.

Argument C assumes that material objects, the objects constituting the world of *prakriti*, could not work together, each being directed to its proper end, unless there is some principle of intelligence guiding this world. The conclusion is that *purusha* must exist as the controlling intelligence of the world.

Argument D claims that from the psychological point of view, all the objects of the world are of the nature of pleasure, pain, or indifference. But pleasure and pain cannot exist without an experiencer. The conclusion is that the world of *prakriti* must exist for some experiencer, and therefore *purusha* as the principle of experiencer must exist.

Argument E claims that *purusha* must exist because of the desire for self-transcendence. In an ordered universe, it could not happen that the universal tendency toward the infinite—toward self-realization—would be self-frustrating. Consequently, *purusha* must be there to be realized, since it is being sought.

In addition to establishing its existence through arguments, Samkhya regards the existence of *purusha* as put beyond question or doubt by the experience of those who have transcended the world of *prakriti*.

Purusha is different from, and independent of, *prakriti*. The text says, "Because the *purusha* is the opposite of the unmanifest *prakriti*, it is established that *purusha* is witness, isolated, indifferent, a spectator, and inactive" (*Samkhya Karika*, 19, author's translation). This means that the opposition between *purusha* and *prakriti* is total: (1) *Purusha* is never something observed; it is only an observer (witness). (2) *Purusha* is of the nature of freedom, isolated from the bondage of *prakriti*. (3) *Purusha* is indifferent, not moved by pleasure and pain. (4) *Purusha* is simply a spectator, observing the play of *prakriti*, whereas *prakriti* is the spectacle being observed. (5) *Purusha* is inactive and unmoved, whereas *prakriti* is unceasing movement.

But if *purusha* is independent of *prakriti*, then the questions of how they are related and how *purusha* can be realized appear more problematic than ever. The Samkhya response is that bondage is rooted in ignorance and only the knowledge that discriminates between *purusha* and *prakriti* can dissolve ignorance and thus free the *purusha*. Ignorance confuses *prakriti* and *purusha*, seeing *purusha* as an aspect of *prakriti*, as the self constituted by the *gunas*. Because *purusha* is really different from and independent of *prakriti*, when the ignorance constituting its bondage is removed, the *purusha* is revealed to be the free, self-shining, ultimate subject. The supposed relation between the *purusha* and the *guna*-self is actually an illusion created by ignorance.

In order to explain how an illusory connection between *purusha* and *prakriti* can cause the real evolution of *prakriti*, it is necessary to see how the mere existence and presence of *purusha* affects *prakriti*. The Samkhya analogy is to imagine that *purusha* is a shining light and *prakriti* a pool of water reflecting the light. Without *purusha* doing anything more than shining by its own light, it is reflected in *prakriti*. Now this reflected light mistakes itself for *purusha*.

But this is not the true light of *purusha*; it is only a reflection in *prakriti* and therefore essentially of the nature of *prakriti*, rather than *purusha*. In this reflection, which is the reflection of *purusha* in *prakriti*, *purusha* is lost sight of, and *prakriti* is taken to be the ultimate reality. Due to this mistake, the illumination of the empirical self that enables a person to see, hear, feel, think, desire, and so forth is not recognized to proceed from the great light that is *purusha*. Consequently, as *prakriti* continues to evolve, *purusha* is not discriminated from *prakriti* but is identified with the evolutes of *prakriti*. This is how bondage to the *gunas* is generated by ignorance of the true nature of *purusha*.

YOGA: THE WAY OF DISCIPLINE

The preceding account of the nature of the empirical self and world, and their relation to *purusha*, the ultimate Self, provides a rational basis for the techniques of discipline known as *yoga*. The basic question of *yoga* is, How can that wisdom be achieved wherein *purusha*, the ultimate Self as pure subject, realizes that it is simply the spectator of *prakriti*, not actually a part of it or connected to it?

How the relationship between *purusha* and *prakriti* results in suffering, as explained by Samkhya, can be pictured by imagining a person in a room surrounded by audiovisual devices. A film projector runs, showing someone being picked up out of the sea, wafted to the peak of a jagged cliff high over the water, and plummeted down to be dashed against the rocks below. The viewer who identifies with the victim of this horrible fate suffers. But when the viewer realizes that this suffering self is an illusion created out of mere film and sound, freedom from suffering is achieved.

The point is that *purusha*, like the viewer, is really free from suffering, but ignorance prevents this realization. To overcome this suffering, something must be done to remove the ignorance leading to the mistaken identification of the true Self with the not-self.

To this end, a kind of self-discipline called *yoga* is prescribed. The first four aphorisms of Patanjali's *Yoga Sutra* indicate that nature and purpose of *yoga*:

> Now the exposition of yoga. Yoga is the restriction of the fluctuations of the mind-stuff *(citta)*. Then the Seer [that is, the Self] abides in himself. At other times it [the Self] takes the same forms as the fluctuations [of mind-stuff].[2]

By "mind-stuff," Patanjali means the consciousness embodied in the psychophysical manifestations of *prakriti*. The consciousness of mind-stuff must be distinguished from the pure consciousness that is *purusha*, which is eternally distinct from *prakriti*.

To help us understand what Patanjali is saying, we might think of *purusha* as a shining light reflected in the rippling waters of a clouded pond. Seeing only the light reflected in the pond, we think that the light itself is clouded and rippled. But when the pond is calm and the dirt allowed to settle, the light appears clear and still. The contrast between the two images leads us to discriminate between the light itself and its reflection in the pond. In a similar way, the disciplined activities of *yoga* calm the mind and the body, stopping the movements of embodied consciousness so that *purusha*, the pure consciousness, can be seen.

Forces of Bondage

Realizing the separation of pure consciousness from the *gunas* of *prakriti* is no easy task, however. Because of ignorance, the embodied consciousness mistakes itself for the ultimate Self of *purusha* and resists the disciplined efforts of *yoga* to isolate its operations. To understand the basic techniques of *yoga*, we must first understand these forces through which the embodied consciousness functions to maintain itself.

Patanjali describes five such forces or agencies. The first force is ignorance, the lack of awareness that ultimately the self is of the nature of *purusha* rather than *prakriti*. As a result of this ignorance, the embodied self strives to maintain its existence as a prakritic being, "forgetting" that its ultimate nature is that of pure consciousness.

The second force is the incessant urge to create and maintain an ego. This ego-force (*asmita*) is experienced as the will to survive as a psycho-physical being. It transforms everything into "mine" and "not-mine," as the ignorant self tries desperately to maintain its prakritic existence.

The third force, *raga*, is an infatuation with things that expresses itself through grasping and attachment. To maintain its prakritic existence, the ignorant self grasps at the objects of experience, attaching itself to their ephemeral existence. Afraid to let go, the embodied self desperately hangs on to every pleasurable experience.

The fourth conditioning force, *dvesha*, is the counterpart of the third. It is the dislike of, and aversion to, everything that threatens the prakritic self. It operates through hatred and fear, seeking to avoid or destroy whatever threatens the embodied self. Together, the forces of attachment and aversion drive a person. Pushing and pulling against each other, they leave the individual in a constantly agitated state of being.

The fifth force, the will to live forever as a prakritic being (*abhinivesha*), is deeper than aversion and attachment and overrides them when they jeopardize life. This force conditions the individual to fear death and everything associated with death. Rooted in ignorance, it supports the ego-drive of the embodied self, holding out a false promise of psycho-physical immortality.

Because these five forces condition how the embodied self acts and thinks, they must be clearly understood and counteracted. They are the basic forces that underlie the "fluctuations of the mind-stuff" that *yoga* seeks to stop. By stopping these movements and eliminating the driving forces behind them, consciousness becomes clear and can be differentiated from *prakriti*. Thus, *yoga* is essentially a process of "deconditioning" the self of embodied consciousness.

Techniques of *Yoga*

The techniques for yogic deconditioning are divided into eight groups by Patanjali, proceeding from the more superficial and external to the inner and more profound. The earlier groups of techniques are regarded as necessary conditions for the later groups and are incorporated into the more advanced techniques of the later stages.

Moral Restraints. *Yoga* begins with a set of moral restraints designed to reorient a person's will and actions. Rather than acting out of a sense of attachment or aversion, motivated by blind ego forces, a person is expected to act out of sympathetic compassion for the well-being of others.

The first restraint is *ahimsa*. Although literally the word means "nonhurting," *ahimsa* is essentially the expression of compassionate love for all living creatures. Developing this universal love is recognized as an effective means for getting rid of the selfish drives of the ego.

The second moral restraint prohibits words and intentions that hurt others, including empty talk, mindless chatter, and lying. Since the principle is that speech should promote the good of others, any intentions or words that hurt others are to be avoided.

Nonstealing, the third moral restraint, rules out taking what belongs to another. But it goes much deeper, for it also aims at eliminating the state of mind that desires what someone else possesses.

The fourth restraint, nongrasping, carries the prohibition against stealing to a more profound level. Nongrasping means eliminating even the desire for possessing goods.

The fifth moral restraint is directed against wrong sexual activity. To the extent that sexual activity proceeds from and nourishes the ego, it constitutes a hindrance to self-awareness.

Taken together, these five moral restraints have as their goal both the elimination of the proscribed activity and the elimination of the drives that give rise to them. Because these drives bind a person to the forms of prakritic existence that obscure the light of pure consciousness, they must be eliminated by the yogin.

Spiritual Observances. The second set of disciplinary techniques, known as *niyama*, are intended to dispose one toward a more spiritual existence. They are essentially the cultivation of good habits.

First, one must observe purity in action, thought, and word. The body must be kept clean. More important for the yogin, however, is inner purity, for if the mind is impure, it is impossible for actions to be pure. Consequently, the yogin must eliminate all impure and unwholesome thoughts, striving also to eliminate the residual effects of previous unwholesome thoughts and actions, for these will give rise to future unwholesome thoughts.

The second rule of spiritual practice is to be satisfied with whatever one has, unperturbed by events and circumstances. By not allowing oneself to be agitated by desires for things one does not have, a calmness conducive to spiritual activity is introduced into life.

The third spiritual discipline is that of asceticism. Here one practices self-control aimed at self-denial. The idea behind ascetic practice is to free oneself from the pushes and pulls of likes and dislikes by generating a sense of independence of the body.

The fourth rule is to study. In the first place, this rule refers to the initiate's attitude, which must be one of humility and openness to the teaching. In the second place, it refers to the teachings themselves, directing one to the wisdom of the master, the Vedas, or the texts on *yoga*.

The fifth rule calls for devotion. This may include ritualistic devotion to one or more of the gods and goddesses, or it may refer to an attitude of service on behalf of the greater powers of the universe. It may also include an attitude of reverence to one's teacher.

Postures. Established in moral and spiritual discipline, the student is now ready to practice the exercises and postures *(asanas)* designed to discipline the body and bring it under control. The importance of practicing these various postures lies in the control over the body they provide, control making it possible to tap the deeper powers of life. Because embodied consciousness is not really distinct from the body, the control of the body that the different postures make possible increases the yogin's control over consciousness as well. This is important, because the whole point of *yoga* is to bring the psycho-physical activities under control so that they can become means of liberation rather than of bondage.

Disciplined Breathing **(Pranayama).** Controlling the breath is essential to yogic practice, for breath makes available the vital energy that sustains and nourishes life. This vital energy, the *prana*, is given to every person at birth and is nourished and purified by breath. Since a high level of vital energy is needed to purify and free consciousness, it is important to control the breathing process in order to maximize *prana*.

In addition to increasing the amount of vital energy available, breath control is important for meditation. All of one's psycho-physical functioning is dependent upon the rhythm and flow of breath energy. In meditation, it is the calm period between inhalation and exhalation that allows the deepest entry into consciousness. Inhalation fragments the conscious stream of feelings and ideas into noisy confusion. Exhalation scatters the energies of consciousness in all directions. But between inhalation and exhalation is a calm where the mind can concentrate all of its energies and contents in self-revealing vision.

Withdrawing the Senses. The fifth set of yogic techniques *(dharana)* is designed to shut off sensory input into consciousness. Sensory input is regarded as a kind of noise, obscuring the pure signals of the internal and self-sufficient consciousness. To eliminate this unwanted input, the yogin practices withdrawing the senses, just as, the texts say, a tortoise withdraws its legs and head into itself, shutting out the world.

Sense withdrawal must be practiced at various levels. Not only must contact with external colors, sounds, tastes, odors, and tactile objects be stopped, but also contact with the internal sensory objects of memory and imagination (generated by prior contact with external objects) must be eliminated.

Concentration. With the practice of concentration or *dharana*, one enters the meditative stage of *yoga*. With the body and senses under control, the yogin can focus on controlling the mind. The agitations of the mind must be brought under control through the practices of concentration in order to reveal the deeper consciousness of *purusha*.

Meditation. Because concentration employs a meditative object, it is incapable of completely overcoming the subject-object duality of consciousness. Therefore, in the seventh stage, the yogi practices *dhyana*, the meditation that leaves behind all objects of meditation. Here, consciousness confronts itself not in the guise of any object, but as it is in its pure, self-shining nature. The one-pointed awareness of concentration is deepened until its object becomes transparent, revealing the underlying consciousness. Here, all the agitations of the mind-stuff have been quieted, and nothing blocks out the light of *purusha*, pure consciousness.

Samadhi. With the movements of embodied consciousness stilled, the *purusha* is revealed by its own light. This is the perfect fulfillment in which *yoga* culminates. Since it goes beyond all subject-object duality, this state of being is beyond description. But the word *samadhi*, used to refer to this ultimate awareness, refers to the self's perfect placing of itself in the pure consciousness called *purusha*. This, of course, represents the ultimate goal of *moksha*, perfect freedom.

The relation between *prakriti* and *purusha* and the nature of the mistake causing bondage and suffering, which is to be remedied by the discipline of *yoga*, is nicely summed up in an old and favorite Indian story. A little tiger raised by wild goats came to mistake itself for a goat. Only when provided with the right kinds of experience did he realize his true nature——that of a tiger.

The tiger's mother had died, and the poor little tiger was left all alone in the world. Fortunately, the goats were compassionate and adopted the little tiger, teaching him how to eat grass with his pointed teeth and how to bleat like they did. Time passed and the little tiger assumed that he was just a little goat.

But one day an old tiger came upon this little band of goats. They all fled in terror, except for the tiger-goat, now about half-grown, who for some unknown reason felt no fear. As the savage jungle beast approached, the cub began to feel self-conscious and uncomfortable. To cover his self-consciousness he began to bleat and nibble some grass. The old tiger roared at the little tiger in amazement and anger, asking him what he thought he was doing eating grass and bleating like a goat. But the little tiger was too embarrassed by all this to answer and continued to nibble grass. Thoroughly outraged by this behavior, the jungle tiger grabbed him by the scruff of his neck and carried him to a nearby pond. Holding him over the water he told him to look at himself. "Is that the pot face of a tiger or the long face of a goat?" he roared.

The cub was still too frightened to answer, so the old tiger carried him to his cave and thrust a huge chunk of juicy, red, raw meat between his jaws. As the juices trickled into his stomach the cub began to feel a new strength and a new power. No longer mistaking himself for a goat, the little tiger lashed his tail from side to side and roared like the tiger he was. Having achieved Tiger-realization, he no longer took himself to be a goat.

REVIEW QUESTIONS

1. Why is causality a central topic in Samkhya philosophy?
2. Samkhya presents five arguments to show that the effect exists (preexists) in the cause. What does it mean to say that the effect exists in the cause, and what are the arguments to show that this is the case?
3. The fundamental categories of Samkhya are *prakriti* and *purusha*. What are these, and how are they related to each other?
4. What are the forces that according to *yoga* constitute the bondage of the Self?
5. Explain the eight groups of yogic techniques described by Patanjali for overcoming bondage.

FURTHER READING

Yoga Mind, Body and Spirit: A Return to Wholeness, by Donna Farhi (New York: Henry Holt, 2000), is a comprehensive, illustrated guide to the teachings and practice of *yoga*. It is an excellent place to begin.

The Yoga Tradition: Its History, Literature, Philosophy and Practice, by Georg Feuerstein (Prescott, AZ: Hohm Press, 1998), is a comprehensive survey of *yoga* in some 600 pages by one of the great *yoga* scholars of our time.

Integrity of the Yoga Darsana, by Ian Whicher (Columbia, MO: South Asia Books, 2000), is a new translation and study of Patanjali's *Yoga Sutras* that points out many common misinterpretations of this foundational text.

Yoga and the Hindu Tradition, by Jean Varenne and translated by Derek Coltman (Chicago: University of Chicago Press, 1976), covers both the techniques of *yoga* and its underlying philosophy.

Classical Samkhya: An Interpretation of Its History and Meaning, by Gerald Larson (Delhi: Motilal Banarsidass, 1979), contains a translation of the *Karika,* a history of its interpretations by modern thinkers, and an interpretation of the historical development and meaning of Samkhya.

Encyclopedia of Indian Philosophies, Vol. 4: Samkhya, A Dualist Tradition in Indian Philosophy, by Gerald James Larson and Ram Shankar Bhattacharya (Princeton, NJ: Princeton University Press, 1987), is the standard reference work on Samkhya. It contains an overview of the tradition as well as outlines of the major Samkhya literature.

Yoga: Immortality and Freedom, 2d ed., by Mircea Eliade and translated by W.R. Trask (Princeton, NJ: Princeton University Press, 1969), is a classic study.

Yoga: The Technology of Ecstasy, by Georg Feuerstein (Los Angeles: J.P. Tarcher, 1989), focuses on the *yoga* techniques for transforming consciousness.

NOTES

1. *Samkhya Karika*, 17. See Gerald James Larson, *Classical Samkhya: An Interpretation of Its History and Meaning*, 2d ed. (Delhi: Motilal Banarasidass, 1979), p. 255. Unless noted otherwise, all translations of the *Samkhya Karika* are from this work.
2. *The Yoga Sutras of Patanjali*, I. 1–4, trans. by James Haughton Woods, Harvard Oriental Series, XVII (Cambridge, MA: Harvard University Press, 1914).

CHAPTER 6

Knowledge and Reality: Nyaya-Vaisheshika

As we have seen, the Upanishads emphasize the ultimate nature of reality as the identity of *Atman* and *Brahman,* while Samkhya emphasizes the dualistic nature of reality in order to explain both our experience of the ordinary world and the experience of the ultimate Self, the *purusha.* The Nyaya tradition, however, focuses on the nature of knowledge, asking, What is knowledge? and What are the valid means of knowledge? Vaisheshika is a tradition closely linked to Nyaya. It borrows the Nyaya theory of knowledge and goes on to ask, What exists? In answering this question, it develops an atomistic view of existence, a view of existence adopted also by Nyaya.

THE PROBLEM OF KNOWLEDGE

The basic problem of knowledge is that of ascertaining whether or not what is claimed as knowledge is actually knowledge, rather than just mistaken opinion. Mistakes are easily made in matters of perception and inference. For instance, in dim light, a discarded rope appears to be a snake; it could cause someone to claim knowledge of a snake on the path. But if there were only a rope on the path, obviously no one could have *knowledge* of a snake on the path. As examples such as this are considered, it becomes possible to speculate that perhaps what appears to us is always different from what is really there. It might be that the eyes always present things as red, yellow, and blue, whereas all things are really orange, black, and green. It might be that the ear presents sounds differently from what they really are, and that the other senses equally distort the reality with which they come in contact. Skeptical considerations of this sort push philosophers in the direction of trying to analyze what knowledge is and when it can be claimed to be valid.

In Nyaya, the analysis of knowledge is taken up in terms of the knowing subject, the object to be known, the known object, and the means of coming to know the object. Analysis of claims to knowledge reveals that these four factors are involved in all knowledge, for there is no knowledge except when someone knows something. The one who knows is the subject; the something known is the object. The object is either the object to be known or the object that is known. The whole point of coming to know things is to pass from ignorance, in which case the subject is separated from the object, to knowledge, in which case the subject, by various means, comes to be related to the object in certain ways. These relations constitute knowledge of the object. Consequently, anyone wishing to come to an understanding of what knowledge is must inquire into these four topics: (1) the knowing subject, (2) the object to be known, (3) the object as known, and (4) the means of knowledge whereby the object comes to be known.

THE MEANS OF KNOWLEDGE

According to Nyaya, the main characteristic of knowledge is that it illumines and reveals what exists. If we had no eyes to illumine and reveal the green grass, we would not know that it exists or that it is green. The means of knowledge are distinguished according to the different causes responsible for the revelation of the object in knowledge. This principle of distinction yields perception, inference, analogy, and testimony as the four basic means, or sources, of knowledge. The reason for distinguishing between these sources is that a person is doing four basically different things in coming to know something in each of the different ways. We begin our discussion of the Nyaya theory of knowledge with an analysis of these four valid means of knowledge, showing how they constitute different ways of knowing.

Perceptual Knowledge

Perceptual knowledge is defined as the true and determinate knowledge arising from the contact of the senses with their proper objects. It is known, by means of perception, that these words appear on a piece of paper because of the contact of the eyes with the words. If one were a considerable distance from the paper and perceived only dark spots on the paper, it would not be a genuine case of perception, for the object perceived would not be determinate. If one were to mistake these words for logic symbols, this would not be a case of genuine perception either, for it would not be true knowledge, since there were no symbols there to be perceived.

Even in the case of mistaken perception, an external object is actually perceived, though it is wrongly identified as something other than what it really is. If the words on this page are mistaken for symbols, the ink marks that constitute the words are actually perceived, though they are mistaken for symbols. Unless the senses made contact with an external object, there would be nothing revealed. To assume that perception can occur without perceiving an external object is to assume that the perceptive act creates the object, rather than revealing it. If the senses created their objects, rather than revealing them, asks Nyaya, how could mistaken perceptions be detected or corrected? There would be no external object to which the perceptions could be compared.

But how can genuine perceptions be distinguished from perceptual mistakes? The Nyaya explanation of this point rests on a distinction between two kinds of perception. Determinate perception—perception of words on this paper—is preceded by the indeterminate perception of sense contact with the marks on the paper prior to the recognition and classification of them as words. To talk about a perceptual mistake in reference to the indeterminate perception does not make any sense, for nothing is taken to be anything, and therefore it cannot be taken for something other than what it is. Indeterminate perception is simply the contact of the sense with its object. It is the most elementary sensory experience, limited to precisely what is given by sense contact. Since it is not determinate, mere sensory contact is not classified as perceptual knowledge.

Perceptual knowledge requires determinate perception in which the basic sensory experience of the indeterminate perception is determined to be some kind of thing with various qualities and relations. Determinate perception is, in principle, nameable. Thus, a distinction is made between an immediate sensory experience and perception, though the latter always includes the former. Consequently, there is also a distinction between ignorance and error.

Ignorance may be due either to a lack of the immediate sensory experience or to a lack of determinate perception. Error, on the other hand, results from mistaking what is given in immediate sensory experience for something other than what it is. In terms of the example of erroneously perceiving a snake instead of a rope, the immediate sensory experience reveals a dark-colored, elongated, and twisted shape. But in perception, this content of sensory experience is seen as a snake when it is, in fact, a rope. The result is the erroneous claim that a snake has been seen. From this it is evident that true perceptual knowledge is the perception of what is perceived as it really is, and error is the perception of something as other than what it really is.

But now the question may be raised as to how a particular perceptual judgment can be known to be true. Obviously, it is impossible to directly test the correspondence between the perception and the reality being perceived, for this would mean knowing what is true knowledge by going outside of knowledge itself. But to know something outside of knowing is impossible. If, however, the correspondence is tested within the framework of knowledge, all we get is another knowledge claim about the claimed correspondence. And this can go on indefinitely without ever revealing anything about the actual correspondence between the knowledge claim and reality.

This is why Nyaya suggests that mistaken knowledge claims are detected, ultimately, in terms of the successfulness of practice. If one's perception of the finely granulated white stuff in the bowl on the table as sugar is erroneous because the bowl in reality contains salt, it will not help to take another look at it. Rather, it is necessary to take some action based on the perception and see how the action turns out. If the perception is nonerroneous, a spoonful of the contents of the bowl will make the coffee a pleasant drink. If the perception is erroneous because the bowl contains salt, a spoonful in the coffee will make the contents of the cup undrinkable. Expanding this pragmatic principle of verification of perceptual claims, the position is reached that whatever works—in the sense that it provides for successful activity, and eventually, human happiness and liberation—is true because it is seen to correspond to reality as attested to by the successful activity. In this way, the Nyaya philosophers define true perception in terms of correspondence to reality. But they advocate practice as the means of testing this correspondence.

Different kinds of perceptual knowledge can be distinguished according to the ways in which contact is established between the senses and their objects. Ordinary perception occurs when the eye sees colors, the ear hears sounds, the nose smells odors, the tongue tastes flavors, the body feels resistance, or the mind comes into contact with physical states and processes. The first five kinds of perceptual knowledge yield indeterminate perception, or merely the basic sensory experience itself. The sixth kind of perceptual knowledge, which is internal, is a matter of becoming aware of the sensory experiences and perceiving them to be something or the other. It corresponds to ordinary determinate perception.

In addition, Nyaya admits extra-ordinary perception. Not only are there basic sensory experiences and perceptions of individual things, but there are also perceptions of the natures of things. Visual experience of certain color shapes is not simply perceived to be an individual thing called Rama, but is perceived to be that *man,* Rama. Since the perception of the *nature* of the individual, that by virtue of which the individual can be recognized as a member of a class (e.g., the class "man"), is not given in ordinary perception, it is regarded as one of the three kinds of extra-ordinary perception.

The second kind of extra-ordinary perception accounts for how what is proper to one sense organ can become the object of another sense. For example, it is often said that ice looks cold, or that flowers look soft. But coldness and softness are not the proper objects of sight. Consequently, these kinds of perceptual experiences are regarded as extra-ordinary.

The third kind of extra-ordinary perception recognized by Nyaya refers to the perception of things in the past or future, or hidden, or infinitely small in size by one who possesses unusual powers generated by disciplined meditation, or *yoga.*

Inference

Although perception is the basic kind of knowledge, three other means of knowledge are recognized by Nyaya. *Inference,* the second means of valid knowledge, is regarded as an independent means of valid knowledge that is defined in the *Nyaya Sutra* as producing "a knowledge that comes after other knowledge" (I.5). For example, from perceptual knowledge, it is possible to infer something about reality that has never actually been perceived. We know that dinosaurs existed because of certain fossil remains that have been seen.

Inference proceeds from what has been perceived to something that has not been perceived by means of a third "something" called a *reason,* which functions as a middle term in syllogistic reasoning. For example, in the syllogistic inference, "there is fire on the hill because there is smoke on the hill, and wherever there is smoke there is fire," the universal connection between smoke and fire is the reason (the third "something") for affirming fire on the hill, even though the fire was not actually perceived.

The full syllogistic form of this commonly used example of inference is, according to Nyaya, as follows:

1. Yonder hill has fire.
2. Because it has smoke.
3. Whatever has smoke has fire, for example, a stove.
4. Yonder hill has smoke such as is always accompanied by fire.
5. Therefore yonder hill has fire.

The essential part of the inference in this example is the coming to know that there is fire on the hill on the basis of (1) the perceived smoke and (2) the reason constituted by the invariable connection between smoke and fire. The first proposition represents the new knowledge claim. The second proposition gives the perceptual grounds for the new claim. The third proposition asserts the reason for moving from a claim about smoke to one about fire. The fourth proposition asserts that the reason applies in this case. The fifth proposition repeats the claim, now not as a matter for testing, but as a valid knowledge claim, as established by the reasons provided.

Clearly, the most crucial part of the inferential process is establishing the invariable connection between two objects or events. Nyaya philosophers regard the enumeration of individual objects or events as an important part of the establishment of universal connections between events or objects. If ten black crows and no nonblack crows are seen, some probability exists that there is a universal connection between being a crow and being black. But if thousands of crows have been observed, all of them black, the probability is increased. Even if a million crows, all black, have been observed, however, and the next crow observed is white, the probability that there is a universal connection between being a crow and being black is zero, even though we might want to say that the probability is very high that the millionth-and-second crow will be black.

But if this is the case, it would seem that no number of confirming instances would ever establish a necessary connection between events or objects, for it would always be possible that the very next observed case would refute the necessity of the connection. In light of this possibility, even though Nyaya places much emphasis upon presence of confirming experience and absence of disconfirming experience, the matter is not left here. After all, they argue, there is a difference between claims such as, Wherever there is smoke there is fire, on the one hand, and All crows are black, on the other. The difference is that nothing in the nature of a crow requires blackness. But something about the nature of smoke invariably connects it with fire.

Nevertheless, even if there really is a difference between these cases, the question still arises as to how it is possible to determine that in some cases the connection is universal and necessary because it is causal, while in others the connection is mere coincidence, without any causal basis. Since inference proceeds from perceptual knowledge, if knowledge of a universal and necessary connection between events or objects is possible, it must be that this necessity is perceived, and not inferred. Accordingly, Nyaya includes in perceptual knowledge the perception of the class-nature of the individual. This is a kind of extra-ordinary perception whereby the individual is perceived not merely to be this particular thing or event, but as both this particular thing and a thing of a certain *kind,* or class, of things.

Inferences involving universal connection are of two kinds. Either (1) the unperceived effect can be inferred from the perceived cause, or (2) the unperceived cause can be inferred from the perceived effect. All other inferences depend upon a noncausal and nonnecessary uniformity and cannot be shown to be necessarily true.

Inferential Fallacies. To aid in avoiding certain common mistakes in drawing inferences, the Nyaya philosophers have listed a number of fallacies to be avoided. A *fallacy* is defined as that which appears to be a valid reason for inference, but which is really not a valid reason. In the inference, "There is fire on the hill because there is smoke on the hill and where there is smoke there is fire," the inferred knowledge is that there is fire on the hill. The assertion "There is fire" is being made about the hill. Technically, the term "fire" is called *sadhya.* The term "hill" is called *paksha.* The reason for the assertion, namely, "there is smoke," is called *hetu.* Unless what is taken to be a reason for connecting the *sadhya* with the *paksha* is really a reason, the inference will be invalid. To ensure that the given reason will really be a reason, several rules must be observed: (1) the reason must be present in the *paksha* and in all other objects having the *sadhya* in it; (2) the reason must be absent from objects not possessing the *sadhya;* (3) the inferred claim should not be contradicted by valid perception; and (4) the reason should not make possible a conclusion contradicting the inferred claim.

Comparison

The third means of valid knowledge recognized by Nyaya philosophers is knowledge by comparison based on similarity. For example, if you knew what a cow was, and were told that a deer was like a cow in certain respects, you might come to know that the animal you met in the woods was a deer. This is different from being told what name to apply to a certain object. If, for example, one were to see a deer for the first time and be told "that is a deer," the knowledge would be due to testimony, not to comparison. Knowledge by means of comparison is attained when the association of the name of an unknown object is made by the knower on the basis of experiencing the similarity of the unknown object with a known object. The crucial aspect of this means of knowledge is the observation of the similarity. Nyaya thinkers hold that similarities are objective and perceivable. Accordingly, knowledge of the nature of a new object on the strength of its similarity to a known object constitutes a separate means of knowledge. While comparative knowledge involves both perception and inference, it cannot be reduced to either of them, and therefore is to be counted as a third means of knowledge.

Testimony

The fourth means of valid knowledge recognized in Nyaya is technically called *shabda*. Literally, it means "word," and it refers to the knowledge achieved as a result of being told something by a reliable person. Opinion is not the same thing as knowledge, for opinion might be erroneous, but knowledge cannot be. Consequently, simply hearing the opinion of another person is not a means of knowledge. But when the knowledge claims of another person are heard and understood, then genuine knowledge is attained.

The three criteria of knowledge based on the testimony of another person are (1) the person speaking must be absolutely honest and reliable; (2) the person speaking must actually *know* that which is communicated; and (3) the hearer must understand exactly what is being heard.

THE OBJECTS OF KNOWLEDGE: THE VAISHESHIKA CATEGORIES

Having analyzed the means of valid knowledge, the next step is to consider the objects of valid knowledge, the kinds of things that exist and can be known. According to the *Nyaya Sutra,* the things that we can know include the self, the body, the senses, the objects of the senses, mind, knowledge, action, mental imperfections, pleasure and pain, suffering, and freedom from suffering (I.9). It is important to note that not all of these objects of knowledge are physical objects. Knowledge itself becomes an object of knowledge if, as Nyaya does, we inquire about knowledge, seeking to know what it is.

As objects of knowledge, all these kinds of things depend upon the relation between a knowing subject and a world of objects. If we consider the kinds of things that exist and that can become objects of knowledge from the viewpoint of their own independent existence, we come up with the categories of the Vaisheshika system. These categories are (1) substance, (2) quality, (3) motion, (4) generality, (5) particularity, (6) inherence, and (7) nonexistence.

These categories are the types of things that correspond to the different types of knowable objects. Since knowledge is due to revelation of objects by a knowing self, the differences in known objects must be due to different real objects. Thus, classification of the kinds of objects that can be known yields a classification of the different kinds of existing things.

Substance

The first kind of existing thing is *substance*. This refers to that which exists independently of other kinds of things, but which is the locus of existence for other kinds of things. Something real in itself, a substance can be thought of as the substratum of qualities and actions. The category of substance includes nine kinds of things: (1) earth, (2) water, (3) light, (4) air, (5) ether, (6) time, (7) space, (8) self, and (9) mind. Earth, water, light, air, and ether are regarded as physical elements because each of them is known by a particular external sense: earth by smell, water by taste, light by sight, air by touch, and ether by sound.

These substances can be considered in two ways. First, they can be thought of as eternal and indivisible atoms. Second, they are the results of combinations of atoms, in which case they are temporal, composite, and destructible, being produced by the combination of atoms. That substances in the sense of composite things, such as a jar, are made up of atoms is known on the basis of inference. If the jar is broken, it is reduced to several parts. Each of these parts can again be broken, being reduced to more parts. But no matter how long this process continues, it is impossible that every part should be destructible, for that would mean that even the smallest part is composite. But if composite things exist, it is necessary that their ultimate constituents be simple, or else composite things would never be produced, according to Vaisheshika. Therefore, the ultimate constituents of gross substances must be atomic.

The substances space and time are known to exist because of our perceptions of here and there, far and near, and past, present, and future. The existence of *space* is inferred on the grounds that sound is perceived and since sound is a quality, there must be that in which it inheres or that to which it belongs, namely, space. Similarly, *time* is inferred on the grounds that change is perceived as a quality of things and this quality must inhere in some substance, namely time. *Knowledge* is a quality of the knower, and therefore it must exist in a substance called the *self*, which is the ground of consciousness. *Mind* is inferred on the grounds that feeling and willing are known, but since they are not known by the external senses they must be known by the mind. In addition, there is that which directs the senses and collects their contacts into experience. Mind is the substance in which sense contacts reside as qualities.

Quality

The second category of objects is that of the qualities of things. *Quality* refers to the various qualifications of the substances, and it includes color, odor, contact, sound, number, measure, difference, connection, separation, duration, distance, knowledge, happiness, sorrow, volition, hatred, effort, heaviness, fluidity, potency, merit, and demerit. This list of qualifications is a way of saying that things or substances can be, for example, red or blue, pungent or fragrant, touching or apart from, soft or loud, one or many, large or small, the same as or different from, separate or together, long or short, far or near, knowing or ignorant, happy or sorrowful, desiring to or desiring not to, loving or hating, trying or not trying, light or heavy, mobile or immobile, able or not able, and good or bad, respectively. There are many divisions of some of the qualities, but the previous list includes all the basic kinds of qualifications of substances.

Motion

The third kind of basic and irreducible reality is *motion*. The different kinds of motion are (1) upward, (2) downward, (3) contraction, (4) expansion, and (5) locomotion. The kinds of motion are the kinds of reality that account for the changes that substances undergo.

Universals

The fourth category is that of *universal essences*. It accounts for sameness found in substances, qualities, or actions. Four cows, four red objects, and four upward motions are each of them the same in that they are cows, reds, or upward motions. This sameness is regarded as objective, belonging to the individual things just as truly as do qualities. The reason that the four cows can all be recognized as cows is that they share in the same essence or nature of *cowness*. This essence is the universal that enables one to form class concepts and to assign individual things to their proper class.

Particularity

The ability to perceive particular and distinct objects is due to the category of *particularity* that belongs to the objects perceived. From a continuous field of sensing and mental activity, particular objects are perceived. If things did not have the character of being different from other things, there would be no reason why they should be perceived as particular things. But since they are perceived as different particular things, there must be some foundation for this difference in reality. Hence, particularity must exist in reality.

Inherence

The category of *inherence* reflects the fact that different things, such as substance, quality, action, and so forth, appear as one whole. Thus, the size of the object, its color, its nature, and its particularity as this object, all appear so unified that we think of one thing appearing, rather than a collection of things appearing to us. Thus, the whole inheres in its parts: the jug in the clay, the pencil in the wood, and so forth. The basis for the unity of different kinds of things in one substance must, like the other categories, have a foundation in reality. And since inherence cannot be reduced to any other kind of thing it is recognized as an independent kind of reality.

Nonexistence

In addition to these kinds of knowable objects, Vaisheshika recognizes a category called *nonexistence*. Although nonexistence may seem to be a strange kind of reality, its existence cannot be questioned, according to Vaisheshika, for to question it is to suggest that it does not exist, which is to affirm the category of nonexistence. The main argument for claiming nonexistence as a category is that without it, negation would become impossible.

These categories of existence constitute an inventory of the various kinds of things that exist, according to Nyaya and Vaisheshika. Nyaya places special emphasis on the self as knower, whereas Vaisheshika emphasizes the kinds of things that exist as objects of knowledge.

The Knower

Nyaya argues that the self that is the knowing subject is a unique substance. The qualities of the substance that is the self are knowledge, feeling, and volition. Accordingly, the self is defined as the substance in which the qualities of desire, aversion, pleasure, pain, and so forth inhere, for these follow upon knowing, feeling, and volition. None of these are physical qualities, because they cannot be perceived as physical qualities by any of the senses. Therefore, they must belong to a substance other than a physical substance, according to Nyaya.

Furthermore, the self must be distinct from physical objects, sensations, consciousness, and the mind, for the self experiences all of these as objects of knowledge. One may ask, who knows reality, who perceives, who is conscious, and so forth? In every case, the answer is given, the self. Since everything else can become an object for the self, but objects—as objects—require a subject for whom they are objects, it follows that the self cannot be an object. Nor, for the same reason, can it be identical with anything that becomes an object, such as the mind or the body, for self is defined as subject.

Since the self is a unique substance and consciousness belongs to it as a quality, the self does not depend for its existence upon consciousness. In fact, according to Nyaya, ultimate liberation, or freedom, will also be freedom from consciousness. The reason for this is that consciousness is seen as consciousness of something or other. But that presupposes a duality between subject and object. And when there is duality, suffering and bondage are possible, for the subject can be bound by the object and caused to suffer. But to eliminate suffering and bondage, duality must be eliminated. This can be done by eliminating consciousness. But if the self were essentially consciousness, this would mean the extinction of the self. Since consciousness is only a characteristic of the self, however, the self is not destroyed when consciousness is eliminated. This self is neither derived from, nor reducible to, anything other than itself. All that can be said about the self in the state of liberation is that it simply exists as self.

REVIEW QUESTIONS

1. What are the four valid means of knowledge, according to Nyaya? Are any of these means of knowledge completely reducible to the others?
2. Define perception. What is the distinction between determinate and indeterminate perception, and why is it important?
3. Valid inference is possible because of the invariable connection between objects or events. How is this invariable connection known?

4. According to Vaisheshika, there are seven fundamental kinds or categories of existence. What are these? What categories would you add to, or eliminate from, this list? Why?

5. What is the Nyaya view of the self? What are the arguments for regarding the self as a unique substance?

FURTHER READING

On Being and What There Is: Classical Vaisesika and the History of Indian Ontology, by Wilhelm Halbfass (Albany: State University of New York Press, 1992), is an excellent analysis of Vaisheshika metaphysics in the context of the entire Indian metaphysical tradition.

The Logic of Gotama, by Kisor Kumar Chakrabarti, monograph no. 5 of the Society for Asian and Comparative Philosophy (Honolulu: University of Hawaii Press, 1977), discusses the Nyaya theory of inference or deductive logic.

The Nyaya Theory of Knowledge, 2d ed., by Satischandra Chatterjee (Calcutta: University of Calcutta Press, 1950), is a classic account of Nyaya. It contains lucid discussions of each of the four valid means of knowledge and compares Nyaya theories to other Indian theories of knowledge.

Indian Metaphysics and Epistemology: The Tradition of Nyaya-Vaisheshika up to Gangesa, edited by Karl H. Potter (Princeton, NJ: Princeton University Press, 1977), is the most complete book on Nyaya available. The first 200 pages introduce the reader to the important concepts, and the remaining 400 pages contain summaries of major Nyaya works. This material is difficult for beginners but invaluable for serious students of Nyaya.

Perception: An Essay on Classical Indian Theories of Knowledge, by Bimal Krishna Matilal (Oxford: Clarendon, 1986), is a careful study of Nyaya epistemology in its larger philosophical context by an outstanding contemporary Indian philosopher.

Indian Realism: A Rigorous Descriptive Metaphysics, by Pradyot Kumar Mukhopadhyay (Calcutta: K.P. Bagchi, 1984), is an interpretive study of Vaisheshika metaphysics.

Epistemology, Logic and Grammar in Indian Philosophical Analysis, by Bimal K. Matilal (The Hague: Mouton, 1971), is an excellent analysis of Indian theories of knowledge by an outstanding Nyaya scholar. It is intended for the advanced student.

CHAPTER 7

Self and Reality: Mimamsa and Vedanta

$\mathbf{M}$imamsa and Vedanta are both philosophical traditions that attempt to establish the truth of the Vedas and Upanishads. But they do this not by relying on the authority of the Vedas themselves, but by means of philosophical arguments based on reason and experience. Mimamsa takes the early portions of the Vedas, the injunctions to perform rituals and to fulfill duties as authoritative, and argues for the truth of these injunctions. Vedanta takes the later portions of the Vedas, the Upanishads, to be authoritative and argues for the truth of their knowledge claims, particularly the claims that *Atman/Brahman* is the ultimate reality and that by coming to know this ultimate reality one would experience final liberation *(moksha)*.

MIMAMSA

It was a common belief in the Vedic age that the pronouncements of the Vedas, taken to be infallible, free from error in every way, were the ultimate authority for how to live. But questions naturally arose, What makes the Vedas infallible? and How are the Vedas known to be error-free? These questions became serious challenges to the authority of the Vedas as a result of the development of philosophical traditions such as Samkhya, Buddhism, Jainism, and Carvaka that rejected claims to knowledge that went beyond possible human experience. To defend their belief in the authority of the Vedas, it became necessary for believers in the Vedic tradition to respond to these challenges. The Mimamsa tradition developed as a philosophical response to these challenges, arguing that these objections are not valid. In the process of philosophical response, it developed a theory of knowledge that supports belief in the authority of the Vedas as well as a theory of language.

The cornerstone of Mimamsa theory of knowledge is its understanding of the self-validity of knowledge. Unlike other theories of knowledge that maintain that knowledge claims are known to be true when they correspond with reality, or when they lead to successful action, or when they cohere together in a consistent system, Mimamsa maintains that it is the very nature of knowledge to be self-certifying. Our belief in the truth of the claim that knowledge makes (e.g., "There is a snake in the corner") arises naturally as a feature of knowledge itself.

But if all knowledge is true because this is the nature of knowledge, how is it possible that sometimes knowledge claims turn out to be false? Mimamsa admits that sometimes knowledge claims are mistaken, but it argues that not only is this the exception, but that even to know that a given knowledge claim is false we must accept other knowledge claims to be true. For example, if someone claims to see a snake but then, upon closer approach, sees that it is merely a piece of rope that appeared to be a snake because of the poor light and its distance from the knower, the first claim can be known to be false only when the second claim, that it is a rope, is assumed to be true. And this is the case with every knowledge claim that is discovered to be false; its known falsity depends upon the assumed truth of the correcting knowledge. Unless the correcting knowledge can be accepted as being true, it cannot be used as evidence that the prior knowledge claim was false. It is only by accepting the correcting knowledge to be self-certifyingly true that we can correct another knowledge claim.

Furthermore, upon the discovery of a false knowledge claim by means of new knowledge, it is possible to discover the cause of the original mistaken claim. Perhaps the person's eyesight was defective, or the light was poor, or something else interfered with the normal process of knowing. Where no defect in the knowing process is detected, we assume the knowledge to be true and act on it.

On the basis of these arguments, Mimamsa concludes that (1) the truth of knowledge is given with the knowledge itself, and not through any external conditions or processes, and (2) belief in what is known arises with the knowledge itself, and not as the result of verification by some other knowledge. This view of knowledge, that truth is self-evident and inherently justifies belief in its truth *(svatahpramanyavada)*, applies not only to perceptual knowledge, but to all kinds of knowledge, including verbal testimony, the means of knowledge by which the truth of the Vedas is known.

If testimony is a valid means of knowledge, then like all other means of valid knowledge, it is ultimately self-certifyingly true. And if the Vedas provide knowledge about right action and rituals by means of testimony, then they can be accepted true and authoritative. It is important to note that it is through a process of reasoning that Mimamsa attempts to establish that the norms of right action are not determined by reason but are revealed in the Vedas. Perhaps Mimamsa argued that the norms of ritual and moral action were established by the revelations of the Vedas, and not by reason, in order to shield these norms from rational analysis.

That testimony *(shabda)* is a separate and valid means of knowledge is accepted by many of the Indian philosophical traditions, including Nyaya. Testimony is knowledge derived from words or sentences. But as a valid means of knowledge, testimony refers only to verbal claims that issue from a reliable source and that are truly understood. Given the self-certifying nature of knowledge claimed by Mimamsa, a sentence that is understood as intended is taken to provide knowledge except in cases where the source is unreliable. Where the source of testimony is a person, reliability means that the person really knows what she is testifying about, that she knows how to communicate her knowledge, and that she tells the truth. Mimamsa is more interested in impersonal testimony, the testimony of the Veda that is claimed to be impersonal *(aparurusheya)* or authorless. And the sentences of the Vedas that are all-important are its claims about how to perform ritual and moral actions. According to Mimamsa, everything said in the Vedas, even the songs, theoretical reflections, and existential claims, are for the sake of actions to be performed.

Unlike some of the other systems, Mimamsa does not believe in any Creator of the world or a divine author of the Vedas. Rather, the Vedas are the direct and eternal revelation of reality itself. That these sounds can be heard by humans is possible because the basic sounds of reality are the sounds that constitute the basic sounds of the letters of the alphabet, like the sound of the letter *a* ("uh") or the sound of the letter *k* ("kuh"). The letter *a* can be pronounced by different persons at different times and in different ways, but it is the same, unspoken, unchanging letter *a* that is pronounced differently, by different people, at different times. It is possible for wise persons to hear the sounds of reality and give human voice to these sounds, creating the sentences of the Vedas. But it is the eternal sounds of reality that are the true Veda, even though these sounds are given voice in different ways, at different times, by different people. The recited texts of the Veda that exist to provide knowledge of right action were the original sounds of reality itself. These sounds were first heard by the ancient seers who expressed them in human voice to their students, who carefully preserved them and handed them down to their students, who did the same, thus transmitting these teachings in an unbroken line down to the present.

Because the true Veda, existing beyond the human sentences that express this wisdom through a human voice, is eternal and authorless, it cannot be erroneous the way human testimony can be. There can be no unreliability of source, for the source is not human but is the voice of the self-existent reality itself. Nor, according to Mimamsa, can it be called into question by perception or reason, because it refers to matters beyond the realm of ordinary knowledge. The other possibility of detecting error in the knowledge of the Veda would be if the Veda contradicted itself, internally. But when the Veda is properly understood, according to the rules of interpretation spelled out by Mimamsa, it is found to be internally self-consistent.

This interesting view of the self-validity of knowledge and the validity of the Vedas was challenged repeatedly by philosophers of the other systems, including the Vedanta philosophers. Indeed, it was these repeated challenges that stimulated some of the most sophisticated developments within Mimamsa.

VEDANTA

As noted earlier, Vedanta, like Mimamsa, accepts the Vedas as the highest truth and as authoritative for life. But the Vedanta tradition regarded the knowledge claims, not the injunctions to action, as the crucial part of the Vedas. There are three principal schools of Vedantic philosophy, differing from one another in the way they account for the relations between persons, things, and ultimate reality *(Brahman)*. The oldest of these schools, that of *Advaita* (nondualism), is often referred to as the Shankara school, being named after Shankara, one of its important early philosophers, who lived in the eighth century CE. The second school, that of *Vishistadvaita* (qualified nondualism), claims the eleventh-century philosopher Ramanuja as its principal figure and is therefore sometimes called the Ramanuja school. The third school, *Dvaita* (dualism), has as its central figure the thirteenth-century philosopher Madhva.

These three schools of Vedanta represent the three basic ways of looking at the relations between the world and *Brahman,* and thus they constitute the three basic interpretations of the Upanishads. According to Shankara, *Brahman* alone is real, the world being mere appearance. Ramanuja claims that the world is real but is not different from *Brahman,* since *Brahman* is the unity of differences that constitute the world. Madhva argues that the world and *Brahman* are eternally distinct. Reality is of the dual nature of *Brahman* plus the world, with *Brahman* always remaining distinct and different from the world of selves and things.

According to Vedanta, the Upanishads taught that the ultimate reality is Brahman, and that the way to realize this ultimate reality was through liberating the innermost Self, the *Atman,* from its embodiment in mind and body. Some of the great teachings of the Upanishads that Vedanta thinkers based their teachings on are *Chandogya* 7.25.2: "All this is *Atman*"; *Brihadaranyaka* 4.5.6: "*Atman* being known . . . everything is known"; *Chandogya* 6.2.1: "There was only Being at the beginning, it was one without a second"; *Mundaka* 2.2.11, *Chandogya* 3.14.1: "All this is *Brahman*"; *Brihadaranyaka* 2.5.19: "This Self is the *Brahman*"; and *Brihadaranyaka* 1.4.10: "I am *Brahman.*"

The very fact that the ultimacy of *Brahman/Atman* was taught in the Upanishads was sufficient for the tradition to accept it as true, for the Upanishads are regarded as errorless revealed truth. Nevertheless, for the critical mind, it is important to show that this teaching does not conflict with reason or experience. A significant step in this direction could be taken by showing that opposing claims about reality were self-contradictory and implausible. Consequently, the critical examination of the other systems became an important part of the Vedanta agenda.

Showing that other views were unsatisfactory was not sufficient, however. It was also necessary to show that the view of reality claimed by the Vedantic interpretation of the Upanishads was in accord with the Upanishads themselves and that this view was not subject to the same kinds of criticisms aimed at the other systems. Therefore, the Vedanta philosophies came to provide rational criticisms of the other philosophies and also to provide rational defenses of their own interpretations and systems.

SHANKARA'S NONDUALISM

Shankara's view of reality is that there is one absolute and independent reality that alone exists as real and unchanging. This reality is the *Brahman* of the Upanishads. This view rules out theories according to which the world is thought of as the product of material elements, the transformation of unconscious matter that evolves, or the product of two kinds of independent reality, such as *Brahman* and matter.

According to Shankara, *Brahman* is the reality that underlies the appearances that constitute the empirical world. *Brahman,* however, should not be confused with these appearances, for it goes beyond these appearances, not being limited by them. From the empirical and conceptual point of view, *Brahman* is in the world as its foundation. From the absolute point of view, however, *Brahman* is beyond the empirical reality that can be known through the senses or by the mind.

The nature and existence of *Brahman* cannot be proved from perception or reasoning but are to be taken either on the basis of scriptural testimony (the Upanishads) or by direct and intuitive experience of the kind made possible by yogic concentration. Nevertheless, reason can be used to justify these means of knowing *Brahman.*

To reconcile the perceived plurality and objective reality of the world with the nondual conclusions of the Upanishads, Shankara regards the world of appearance as ultimately unreal. Perception is ultimately illusory; the world it reveals, though it exists, is only an appearance, not ultimately real. *Brahman* alone is ultimately real and the Self as pure subject, *Atman,* is identical with *Brahman.*

To refute conflicting dualistic and pluralistic claims about the nature of reality, Shankara considers first the Samkhya view and then the pluralistic Vaisheshika view. According to Samkhya, the world is the result of the spontaneous evolution of unconscious matter, or *prakriti,* which is composed of the three *gunas: sattva, rajas,* and *tamas.* Samkhya includes within its view the existence of purpose in the world, for the world is such that it fits reborn selves and enables them to be liberated. But how, asks Shankara, can one suppose that the world is the accidental result of an unconscious cause, when it is experienced as a harmonious system of related objects and ordered events? Shankara argues that it is unintelligible to attribute purpose to unconscious nature, and therefore the Samkhya view is untenable.

The Vaisheshika view is that the world is caused by the combination of atoms. But again, how can unconscious atoms produce out of their combinations the order that makes possible the moral law claimed by the Vaisheshika philosophers? Further, how or why should unconscious atoms first begin to move around and join together to produce the world? If atoms were incessantly in motion and joining together because of their very nature, then neither the beginning of the world nor its dissolution would be explicable. Because the Vaisheshika philosophers claim that the world is both produced and destroyed, their view is inconsistent, and therefore unsatisfactory, according to Shankara's analysis.

Thus, the explanations of Vaisheshika and Samkhya are seen to be inconsistent within the framework of their own assumptions. But their basic assumptions are not satisfactory either. Nyaya, Vaisheshika, Samkhya, and Mimamsa all accept as a basic assumption the fact of real change and causation. That is, they all admit that various real changes occur in the world and that these changes are caused. How, asks Shankara, do these systems view causality?

Concerning the relation between cause and effect, only two views are possible. Either the effect preexists in the cause or it does not. If the effect does not preexist in the cause, then the effect is totally new. This view is called *asatkaryavada* (nonexistence of the effect). If the claim is that the effect preexists in the cause *(satkaryavada),* then two alternative explanations are possible, neither of which recognizes the effect as a new reality. On the one hand, causal change can be explained as a matter of making explicit what was implicit in the cause. On the other hand, the explanation can claim that there is no difference between cause and effect.

Nyaya and Vaisheshika held the *asatkaryavada* view of causality, as did some of the Mimamsa philosophers. They argued that effects are experienced as something totally new and that this experience is valid. Some Mimamsa philosophers and all Samkhya philosophers held the *satkaryavada* view, admitting change in the sense of making explicit what was implicit in the cause, but denying that effects were new realities.

Shankara, in critically examining these two views of causation, found them both logically unacceptable. Nothing can show an effect to be different from its material cause. Clay pots are clay, gold rings are gold, and so forth. Furthermore, the clay pot cannot exist apart from the clay, nor the gold ring apart from the gold. Consequently, it is incorrect to say that an effect is something new that has been produced and that it did not exist before. In terms of its material cause, it has always been there. Furthermore, we have no experience of things coming into being out of nothing. Our experience of change is always of something being transformed into something else. To conceive of something coming into existence out of nothing is impossible; all we can think is the transformation of something into something else.

Samkhya also argues vigorously against *asatkaryavada,* pointing out that if the effect were something totally new, without prior existence in any form, then we would have to admit that existence is produced from nonexistence. But if this is possible, why can't nonexistence produce everything? Since curds are nonexistent in water, why can't water produce curds? Since gold is nonexistent in clay, why can't gold rings be produced out of clay? Water can't produce curds, and clay can't produce gold rings, because curds have no prior existence in water and gold has no prior existence in clay. In contrast, curds can be produced from milk because they preexist in milk, and gold rings can be produced from bars of gold because they preexist in the bars of gold. Clearly, nonexistence does not produce effects; only the preexistent produces effects, concludes Samkhya.

Shankara accepts these arguments of Samkhya against *asatkaryavada* but goes on to argue against the Samkhya view that the effect actually preexists in the cause. If the effect actually preexists, he asks, how can there be genuine change? If the effect already exists, then it is impossible for the material to become the effect. It makes no sense to talk of the coming to be of that which already exists. The Samkhya reply that Shankara considers is that though matter does not come into existence, the form does, and that this admits that something not preexisting comes to be, namely, the new form. But this, says Shankara, is just another form of *asatkaryavada,* which claims the effect as something new that did not previously exist. This, however, is self-refuting because it contradicts Samkhya's own rejection of *asatkaryavada.*

Since the Samkhya position is self-contradictory, it is unacceptable to Shankara. The challenge he faces is to set out a consistent view of causality based on the preexistence of effects in their causes. In meeting this challenge, he must be sure that, unlike Samkhya, he does not implicitly assume the *asatkaryavada* view. Since it cannot be denied that changes in form are perceived, the crucial question for Shankara is, Is a change in form a *real* change?

Shankara's solution is to show that though changes in form are perceived, this does not imply a change in reality unless a form has reality of its own. But, of course, form has existence only in dependence upon matter, for there is no form except in formed matter. For example, there is no form of a cup except the cup made of clay (or other matter). If a change in form were a change in reality, a person sitting down would be a different reality from a person standing up, since the form is different. But, of course, a person standing up or sitting down is the same person. Therefore, form has no independent reality.

Another argument is that if substances are distinct from their forms, then it is impossible to explain the relation between the form and the substance. If the form is distinct from the substance, it cannot be related to the substance except in terms of a third reality that relates them. But then, in order to relate this third reality to the other two, another distinct reality is needed. And to relate this reality to the others, still another is needed. This is the gist of Shankara's argument: if form is distinct from substance and is related externally through a third thing, causality, then it is impossible to account for change.

To help understand the argument, imagine that A is a lump of clay and B is its gray color. Suppose that A and B are related only through inherence of the gray color in the clay. Inherence is a third thing, C. Although C (inherence) is supposed to account for the relation between A (clay) and B (color), what accounts for the relation between A and C? If yet a fourth thing, D, is required to relate C to A, then it would seem that a fifth thing, E, would be required to relate C to D. But if there is no end to this regress, then A and B have not been successfully related. If the substance, clay, and its color are unrelated, then a change in color cannot be a real change in the clay. Indeed, Samkhya cannot even make sense of the notion of "a change in form."

Appearance. These arguments, if valid, lead to the conclusion that it is impossible for causation to bring about real change. How, then, does Shankara explain our experience of change? Because changes are perceived, it is impossible to deny that change exists. Shankara's solution to the dilemma is to suggest that since the perceived changes cannot rationally be accepted as real, they must exist only as appearances, similar to the existence of things in a dream.

If the objects of the world are like the illusory objects of dreaming experience, then it becomes possible to reconcile the existence of *Brahman* alone as ultimately real with the existence of the empirical world. The snake perceived in the dream exists in the dream, but it is not real. That it exists must be admitted, for otherwise there would be no dream. But that it is real cannot be admitted, for its unreality is what marks this particular experience as dreaming experience. In a similar way, the objects of the empirical world exist, for they are perceived. To deny the existence of the objects of the empirical world is to deny ordinary perceptual experience. But the analogy between dream objects and the objects perceived in waking experience suggests that the objects of waking experience, although they exist from the perspective of ordinary waking experience, are seen to be unreal when one awakens to the higher reality of *Brahman.*

This analogy draws on the fact that while one is dreaming, it is impossible to regard the objects of the dream as unreal. It is only possible to regard the dream objects as unreal when a different level of experience is attained. Only from the vantage point of waking experience can the dream objects be said to be unreal. In a similar way, from the vantage point of another level of experience—the higher experience of *Brahman*—the objects of ordinary waking experience can also be seen to be unreal.

If the analogy between dreaming and waking experience works, then it is possible to reconcile the existence of the perceptual and empirical world with its unreality in the way that we reconcile the existence of dream objects with their unreality. When we wake up, we realize that the things that existed in the dream were unreal in comparison to the things experienced in waking experience. In a similar way, when we "wake up" from ordinary waking experience to the experience of *Brahman,* then we can realize that the things that exist in waking experience are unreal in comparison to the experience of *Brahman.*

To understand Shankara's view that the whole world of ordinary experience is only an appearance, like the appearance of dream objects, it is important to understand the nature of appearance. An example of an appearance that is unreal, as considered in Vedanta, is that of the rope mistakenly seen as a snake. The rope is claimed to be a snake because of ignorance that it is a rope. If it were known that it is a rope, the appearance of a snake would not be mistaken for a real snake.

But ignorance in itself is not enough to produce the illusion of a snake. After all, there are many things of which one is ignorant, but one does not say that these are snakes. The ignorance that produces an illusion must have two aspects. First, it covers up the reality actually present, for example, the rope. Second, it actually distorts what is really there, presenting it as something other than what it is, in this case, presenting the appearance of a snake as a real snake.

Now, if the nature of the world is merely an appearance, like an illusory object, then the world must also be a product of ignorance. The underlying reality is not simply obscured and hidden from view, but is actually distorted into something other than what it is. Because of this distortion, the true reality, *Brahman,* is mistaken for the world of ordinary empirical objects. But these objects are not real; they are simply the concealing distortion of *Brahman,* which alone is real.

Of course, it is only from the standpoint of the ignorant that there is any ignorance. It is only from this ignorance that the world appears, covering up the true reality of *Brahman,* causing us to mistakenly see the world, rather than *Brahman,* as real. Just as an illusion is created when a magician makes one coin appear to be many (though there is no illusion for the magician; the illusion exists only for the ignorant observers), so from the point of view of absolute reality there is no illusion of plurality. There is only *Brahman,* the one true reality, just as for the magician there is only the one coin. For the wise, who succeed in seeing through the illusion of the magician, there do not appear many coins. Similarly, for the wise who experience *Brahman,* the world of empirical objects does not appear as the ultimate reality.

For Shankara, what is ultimately real, *Brahman,* does not change. What changes, the empirical world, cannot be ultimately real. It is only a world of appearance wherein things appear to change as the result of causes. Consequently, Shankara's theory of causal change must be a theory of *apparent* change. Although things appear to change, at the deepest level of reality—the level of *Brahman*—nothing changes. In the final analysis, at the level of *Brahman,* the appearance of change is mere appearance.

By regarding change as appearance rather than reality, Shankara can explain those passages in the Upanishads that speak of the world being produced out of *Brahman.* On the face of it, the production of the world out of *Brahman* is a change that contradicts the claim that reality is ultimately changeless. Using the theory of apparent change, Shankara argues that the world can be produced out of *Brahman* just as snakes are produced out of ropes and bent sticks are produced by water (by refraction). There is existence inasmuch as there are objects for experience. But there is no reality because the objects are illusory, being the result of ignorance.

Shankara's explanation of the world as an appearance produced by ignorance depends for its success largely upon the analogy of illusory perception. To make the analogy work, Shankara must do two things. First, he must show that perception is, at least in principle, illusory. Second, he must show that the analogy of perceptual illusion is appropriate for explaining the appearance of the world.

Nyaya admits that perceptual error is possible but regards it as an unusual kind of perception. What happens when a snake is perceived as a rope is that this perception sets up the memory image of a snake perceived in the past so sharply that one becomes immediately aware of that image, mistaking it for the perceived object.

If the Nyaya account of perceptual error is correct, then the idea that the world is an illusion is mistaken. To say that the world we now perceive is an illusion makes sense only upon the assumption that a real world was perceived in the past and is being substituted now for the world presently being perceived. But this argues for the reality of the empirical world and not for the Vedantic view of the world as unreal.

Shankara's first objection to the Nyaya theory of perceptual error is that it is not possible that something that existed at some other time and in some other place should be perceived now. What is perceived is *this,* and a memory is always of *that,* no matter how vivid. Thus, on the Nyaya account, the presence of the illusory object would be unexplainable. To suppose that a memory idea could actually transfer objects from one time and place to another is implausible.

Shankara's second objection is that the Nyaya view is unsatisfactory because what does not exist here now can appear to exist here now, and this is due to ignorance of what is here now.

Having examined competing theories of perceptual error, Shankara is prepared to set forth his own view. In simplest terms, his view is that perceptual error occurs when the object actually present is not perceived and the mind constructs another object, substituting it for the actual object. In terms of the snake-in-the-rope example, Shankara would say that the rope is not perceived, but the mind creates a snake and substitutes it for the rope, thereby generating the illusion that the snake is actually present.

The illusory object, though created by ignorance, exists, for it is present to consciousness. When the rope is mistaken for a snake, it cannot be denied that the snake exists. Its presence is why one screams and runs away. It is not real, however, for it is merely a construction. This snake, though it may be frightening, cannot bite. Furthermore, when the ignorance generating the construction is removed, the constructed object disappears. Upon realizing that what was seen was only a rope, the snake no longer exists and cannot frighten you.

Ordinarily we say that what exists is real. But we do not say that what exists merely as a construction in the mind is real. Thus, though we admit that various objects exist in our dreams, we deny that they are real. In a similar way, although Shankara denies the ultimate reality of the world, he does not deny its existence.

To appreciate Shankara's distinction between existence and reality, we need to consider his classification of reality according to four levels. At the first level, nothing can exist; this is the level of things that are logically impossible, such as square circles. At the second level are the objects of dreams and illusions. Although these objects exist in our minds, their reality is repudiated by normal waking experience. At the third level, we find the objects of normal waking experience—which the realist takes to be the ultimate reality. But these objects are not ultimately real, for they are repudiated by experience of *Brahman*. At the fourth level is the ultimate reality, *Brahman,* which cannot be repudiated by anything.

Thus, Shankara does not deny the existence of the world or any objects of experience. Rather, he adds another level of reality by recognizing a higher reality beyond the levels of dreaming and waking reality. Recognition of this higher level of reality enlarges our conception of reality. It is only from the standpoint of this higher reality that the rest of existence can be seen to be ultimately unreal. In this respect, the matter is similar to waking and dreaming. Unless one wakes up, it is impossible to regard dreaming objects as unreal. Within the dream, they can be regarded only as real. But when one wakes up, the existence of dream objects is not denied. One simply now recognizes that dream objects were merely dream objects. Only now it is seen that there is a higher level of reality, namely, waking reality. In a similar way, through enlightenment one might wake up to the higher reality of *Brahman* and discover that until now one has been having merely ordinary waking experience and not experience of true reality (*Atman*-realization).

Shankara's view of the nature of reality provides explanations for both the reconciliation of the perceived plurality in the world with its absolute oneness and the identity of the Self with this absolute oneness. He can say, "All this is that," where "this" refers to the empirical world and "that" refers to *Brahman,* because the world is merely the misperception and the misconception of *Brah-*

man. It is like saying that the many coins of the magician are really the one coin displayed before performing the magic. But due to our ignorance, we mistake the one coin for many. In a similar way, due to ignorance, we mistake the world for *Brahman.*

In an analogous way, we mistake the psycho-physical self to be the true reality, whereas in fact this self is ultimately illusory and unreal. To say, "thou art that," is to say that "thou"—the self one takes oneself to be in ignorance—is, not in its appearance but only in its true reality, that *Brahman.* For the ignorant, the self is only potentially *Brahman,* and this potentiality is realized by overcoming the ignorance. From the viewpoint of *Brahman,* however, it is not possible that the Self is only potentially *Brahman.* It is one thing to regard the snake as potentially a rope and quite another thing to suppose that, from the viewpoint of what things really are, a snake is a rope.

Because of ignorance of our true nature as *Atman,* we tend to confuse the Self that is the subject of experience with the self that is experienced. The self that is experienced belongs to the world of objects. From the standpoint of the experiencing Self that is always the subject of experience, the self experienced as object is not-self. In ordinary experience, Self and not-self are confused.

For Shankara, realizing *Brahman* is a matter of removing the ignorance that results in mistaking the appearance of the not-self for the reality of the Self. *Brahman,* identical with *Atman,* the true Self, alone is ultimately real. Ignorance veils this truth, but a practical realization of the ultimate Self will destroy the ignorance.

Theoretical knowledge of the ultimate reality is, of course, impossible. Such knowledge is ruled out by the fact that the ultimate reality is pure subject, one without a second. Knowledge of *Brahman* is practical knowledge; it is a matter of direct and immediate personal experience. Since ultimately the universe is identical with the Self, realizing *Brahman* is a matter of being completely oneself and experiencing one's ultimate reality.

The real Self, the *Atman,* is not an appearance and is therefore not subject to the laws of appearances. The laws of causation apply to the world of appearance, not to the world of reality, or *Brahman.* Self cannot be said to be causally related to the world of appearances, for it is neither cause nor effect, since these relations belong only to the lower level of appearances.

And if the *Atman* is not related to the appearances constituting the empirical world in any ways that are knowable, it becomes impossible to know *Brahman* except by an intimate experience that will be ineffable and incommunicable. The realization that one is the Self of pure consciousness, free from change and suffering, is certified by its own illumination. As Shankara, in his commentary on the *Brahma Sutra,* asks, "How can one contest the fact of another possessing the knowledge of *Brahman;* vouched as it is by his heart's conviction?" (IV.I.15).

THE QUALIFIED NONDUALISM OF RAMANUJA

Ramanuja, the eleventh-century Vedantic thinker who interpreted the Upanishads as teaching a qualified nondualism *(vishishtadvaita),* agrees with Shankara that ultimate reality is one rather than many. But he disagrees concerning the nature of the one. Ramanuja's view is that *Brahman,* as the ultimate reality, is not distinct from the empirical world, but that this world is a constituent part of *Brahman. Brahman* is a unity made up of the differences that constitute the experienced world as well as its ground.

Ramanuja argues that identity and difference are correlative and dependent upon each other. To posit one without the other is to posit an empty nothing. Unity is the unity of different things; identity is an identity of parts. When the different things or parts are denied there can be no unity or identity. The unity constituting *Brahman,* according to Ramanuja, is the union of the different selves and things making up the world. The identity is the identity of these parts in their substrata as existing.

Ramanuja also argues that the self cannot be identified with knowledge, for knowledge requires a known and a knower. Where there is no known, there is no knower, and so to regard the self as pure knower without a known is to eliminate the self. Rather, it should be said that consciousness is the substratum of the self, wherein the self can come to know the unity of reality.

Thus, Ramanuja's view is that *Brahman* is an organic unity constituted by the identity of the parts. It is not abstract, but concrete, being made up of the various objects of consciousness as well as consciousness itself. This organic unity Ramanuja calls *Brahman,* or the Lord *(Ishvara).*

His view is that things and selves are distinct from *Brahman* in the way the body of a person is distinct from the self of a person. On this view, unity of reality is maintained because the person is one thing, but plurality is also maintained because a person consists of both self and body. Furthermore, on this analogy *Brahman* is superior to selves and things, just as a person's self is superior to the body, with the body belonging to the self as the self's qualifications. The position is stated by Ramanuja as follows:

> The supreme *Brahman* is the self of all. The sentient and nonsentient entities constitute its body. The body is an entity and has being only by virtue of its being the mode of the soul of which it is the body. The body and the soul, though characterized by different attributes do not get mixed up. From all this follows the central teaching that *Brahman,* with all the nonsentient and sentient entities as its modes, is the ultimate.[1]

According to this explanation, reality is one, like a person, with the many things and selves in the universe constituting the body of reality and *Brahman* constituting the Self of reality. The body is real, although real not independently, but as a mode of *Brahman*'s being. Thus, individual selves and individual things are the real qualities or modes of *Brahman.*

According to the metaphysics underlying this account of the relation of *Brahman* to selves and things, substance alone is independently real, and whatever exists as a characteristic or quality of a substance exists as a mode of that substance and can be identified with the substance of which it is a mode. The teaching, "All is *Brahman*" should not be taken to affirm the existence of *Brahman* alone without qualification, for on that interpretation there is no "All" that can be identified with *Brahman.* Rather, the "All" should be taken to refer to the various things and selves in the world, because these are the real qualifications of *Brahman.* The mode of their existence is that of the body of *Brahman.* Just as a body does not exist except as the body of a self, so things and selves do not exist except as belonging to *Brahman.*

Ramanuja supports his metaphysical view with a theory of meaning according to which the terms referring to the qualities of a substance refer also to the substance that the qualities qualify. For example, if we say, "The teacher is white-haired," then "white-haired" refers to the color of the teacher's hair, but it also refers to the teacher whose hair is white, for having white hair qualifies the teacher. But the reference does not stop there, for being a teacher is a qualification of the person who is the teacher, and thus "white-haired teacher" refers to a qualification of a person and to the person who is so qualified. Being a person, in turn, is a qualification of matter and self, and so the term "white-haired-teaching-person" refers beyond merely the person to that reality of which person is a qualification. Continuing in this way, the term "white-haired" is seen to ultimately refer to the absolute reality upon which everything else is dependent for its existence as a mode of the ultimate. This ultimate is, of course, *Brahman,* and therefore all terms refer ultimately to *Brahman.* If *Brahman* did not exist as the ultimate reality to which all terms refer, there would be nothing for terms to refer to, just as if there were no ultimate substance there would be nothing of which qualifications would be qualifications of, and then there would be no qualifications. Thus, if there are qualifications—and this cannot be denied, for qualities are the primary objects of perception upon which knowledge rests—there must also be *Brahman* as the ultimate possessor of these qualities.

Ramanuja puts the point this way:

> This is the fundamental relationship between the Supreme and the universe of individual selves and physical entities. It is the relationship of soul and body. . . . That which, in its entirety depends upon, is controlled by and subserves another and is therefore its inseparable mode, is called the body of the latter. Such is the relation between the individual self and its body. Such being the relationship, the supreme Self, having all as its body, is denoted by all terms. (*Vedarthasamgraha,* para. 95)

In this way, Ramanuja maintains the reality of both selves and *Brahman* by admitting differences within the identity that is *Brahman.* Selves are real as differentiations within (rather than from) the ultimate reality.

THE DUALISTIC VEDANTA OF MADHVA

A third school of Vedanta, that of Madhva, who lived in the thirteenth century, differs from the positions of the Shankara and Ramanuja schools in claiming a fundamental dualism in the world. According to Madhva, the world as it is experienced empirically, and its foundation as *Brahman,* are eternally and fundamentally distinct. And the self that experiences the world and *Brahman* is distinct from both *Brahman* and the empirical world.

Madhva's basic argument for his position is that perception is essentially a matter of becoming aware of the uniqueness of something. Since perception is the basis of all *knowledge,* and since perception depends upon realizing differences, to claim nonexistence of differences is to repudiate the very basis of the arguments for the nonexistence of difference. Objects are perceived as distinct from the self, and the basis of things and self is perceived to be different from either the things or the self. No possible evidence suggests that these perceived differences are mistaken, as they constitute the very possibility of knowledge. Therefore these basic differences must be admitted.

Furthermore, individual selves must be distinguished from *Brahman* if they are said to be caught up in suffering and bondage, for *Brahman* does not suffer. Because it is with the individual suffering self that every attempt to achieve liberation must begin, the existence of individual selves cannot be denied. But if individual selves are admitted, they must be admitted as different from *Brahman*. It will not do to say that as suffering the individual self is different from *Brahman,* but that as released from suffering it is identical with *Brahman,* for two things that are really different cannot at any time be said to be the same. Being released from suffering does not change the nature of something, making it something else. What is not *Brahman* does not become *Brahman* merely by being released from suffering. But if this is the case, and an initial difference is postulated, then individual selves and *Brahman* must remain eternally different.

Madhva argues in the same way for the eternal difference between *Brahman* and matter. Along the same lines, arguing also for a real difference between selves and matter, between one self and another, and between one thing and another, he arrives at his "five differences." These are the differences between (1) *Brahman* and matter, (2) *Brahman* and selves, (3) selves and matter, (4) one self and another, and (5) one thing and another.

The epistemological basis for Madhva's claim that these five basic differences exist consists in his analysis of knowing as a simultaneous revealing of both the subject who knows and the object that is known. According to this analysis, there is no denying that subject is different from object, for knowledge is always knowledge of something, and it is always knowledge for someone. Furthermore, to know one particular thing is to know it as that thing rather than another, and this is to be aware of its differences from other things. But if this is true, and the differences between subject and object and between one object and another are known, they must be revealed in knowledge. Thus, knowledge in its very nature reveals differences in reality. These differences cannot be denied without denying the very basis and nature of knowledge. And if this is attempted within the limits of knowledge, the attempt is self-defeating, for it requires rejecting that upon which a stand must be taken in order to do the rejecting.

Since knowledge reveals things to be different from one another and different from the self, and since it is acknowledged that both selves and things depend upon *Brahman* for their existence, Madhva claims a real difference between *Brahman,* selves, and things.

Unlike Ramanuja, Madhva does not account for these differences in terms of the qualifications of *Brahman,* thereby maintaining the unity of reality, but he claims they are different substances. But if they are different substances, then it is hard to see how things and selves—as ultimate substances—could depend for their existence upon a third substance, for to be a substance means to exist independently and in itself.

In fact, it is difficult to see why a third substance would need to be postulated as the ultimate reality. Of course, Madhva is reluctant to give up the dependency of selves upon *Brahman,* for then all traditional teachings about salvation must be abandoned. And if he were to give up not only dependency, but also *Brahman* as the ultimate reality, he would be giving up the whole tradition. But Madhva argues that while things and selves are substances, they are different kinds of substances than *Brahman. Brahman* alone is completely independent; other substances are real and exist separately, but ultimately depend on *Brahman.*

REVIEW QUESTIONS

1. Shankara supports his claim that only *Brahman* is real by arguing against the possibility of real change. What are his arguments? Are they sound?
2. To explain the perception of a plurality of things while maintaining that *Brahman* alone is real, Shankara analyzes the concept of appearance. What does Shankara mean when he describes the world as an appearance?
3. How does Shankara's theory of perceptual error differ from the Nyaya theory? How does it differ from the Mimamsa theory? How would you argue for or against Shankara's theory of perceptual error?
4. How do Shankara, Ramanuja, and Madhva differ in their interpretation of the relations between selves, things, and *Brahman?*
5. How would you argue for or against Ramanuja's view that the world is the body of Brahman?

FURTHER READING

Advaita Vedanta: A Philosophical Reconstruction, by Eliot Deutsch (Honolulu: East-West Center Press, 1966), is clearly written, with a minimum of technical terminology, managing to make sense out of subtle and complicated concepts and arguments in a way that beginning students appreciate.

A Thousand Teachings: The Upadesasahasri of Sankara, translated, with introduction and notes by Sengaku Mayeda (Albany: State University of New York Press, 1992), is a valuable guide for both students and teachers. The *Upadesasahasri* ("Thousand Teachings") is the most accessible of Shankara's work and constitutes an excellent introduction to his thought. Mayeda provides a comprehensive introduction to Shankara's work.

Shankara and Indian Philosophy, by Natalia Isayeva (Albany: State University of New York Press, 1992), is a study of Shankara's life and philosophy in its historical context.

A Source Book in Advaita Vedanta, by Eliot Deutsch and J.A.B. Van Buitenen (Honolulu: University of Hawaii Press, 1971), provides excellent translations of the important texts as well as a useful introduction to the philosophical context in which *Advaita* philosophers worked. The introduction is suitable for both beginning and advanced students.

Advaita Vedanta up to Sankara and His Pupils, edited by Karl H. Potter (Princeton, NJ: Princeton University Press, 1981), contains a good introduction to Advaita and reliable summaries of the major works of Gaudapada, Shankara, and some of Shankara's pupils. This reference book is for the serious student.

The Six Ways of Knowing: A Critical Study of the Vedanta Theory of Knowledge, 2d ed., by D.M. Datta (Calcutta: University of Calcutta, 1960), is a comprehensive analysis of Vedantic theories of knowledge, comparing the views of Shankara, Ramanuja, Madhva, and other thinkers. It is suitable for the serious student.

Consciousness in Advaita Vedanta, by William H. Indich (Columbia, MO: South Asia Books, 1980), is a systematic and critical study of the Advaita view of consciousness; it includes comparisons with Husserl, Jung, and Freud.

Purva Mimamsa in Its Sources, by Ganganatha Jha (Benares: Benares Hindu university, 1942), remains the single most important study of Mimamsa in English. It contains an analysis of the thought not only of Jaimini, whose *sutras* are the earliest text, and of Sabara, who wrote the first commentary on Jaimini's sutras, but also of Kumarila Bhatta and Prabhakara, the two most famous Mimamsa philosophers.

Epistemology of the Bhatta, by Govardhan P. Bhatt (Varanasi: Chowkhamba Sanskrit Series Office, 1962), is a detailed analysis of the Mimamsa theory of knowledge that examines both Prabhakara's and Kumarila's arguments for their theories of knowledge.

NOTE

1. *Vedarthasamgraha of Shri Ramanujacarya,* para. 81, trans. by S. Raghavachar (Mysore: Sir Ramakrishna Ashrama, 1956), p. 67.

CHAPTER 8

Theistic Developments

In the previous chapter we saw how Vedantic philosophers conceived of ultimate reality *(Brahman)* in abstract terms. Shankara conceived of it as absolutely nondual, Ramanuja as nondual, but with differences, and Madhva as twofold. They all recognized that *Brahman*, as the ultimate reality, could not be defined in any literal way. It could be approached conceptually by describing it in terms of the most perfect qualities conceivable. But since *Brahman* is beyond conception, ultimately even these highest qualities—being, knowledge, and bliss—must be denied. This is the famous *via negative*, characterized in the Indian tradition as *neti, neti*, an expression that means, literally, "not thus, not thus." *Neti, neti* clearly reveals the philosophical understanding that *Brahman* could not be comprehended in conceptual terms.

Reality can be approached in nonconceptual ways, however. Indian thinkers thought of *Brahman* in personal, as well as conceptual, terms, making use of a great deal of sensual imagery in the process. The senses stimulate feelings and faith as well as thoughts, and India has prized this religious understanding as highly as the understanding achieved through abstract thought. This religious understanding is active, leading a person to embrace or avoid reality in its immediate, concrete forms. With this approach, the knowledge, bliss, and being that describe *Brahman* abstractly take on flesh and personality as a God who can be loved and feared, seen and touched.

In the *Bhagavad Gita*, Krishna, an incarnation of Lord Vishnu, who appears as Arjuna's chariot driver, declares that he is, indeed, the ultimate *Brahman*. The worshipers of Shiva regard the Shiva *linga* they adoringly garland with flowers as the reality that goes beyond being and non-being, that both

94

destroys and creates existence. But what is important for them is its concrete presence in the Shiva image, not its abstract conception. Similarly, the Bengali devotees of Kali worshipping her fearsome image know that this great Goddess can help them overcome their fear of change and death.

This chapter focuses on three concrete, personal images of the ultimate reality that have dominated Hinduism: Vishnu, Shiva, and Kali. Each of these deities represents a different dimension of reality. Vishnu is its power to sustain and nourish life; Shiva is both the destructive power that clears away the old to make room for the new, and the transcendent mystery that lies beyond creation and destruction; Kali is the divine energy that underlies the transforming power of change. As we shall see, just as there are many symbols of the ultimate, so are there many forms of each of these deities, each representing a significant function or power of reality.

VISHNU

Vishnu nourishes and sustains life through his own greatness and generosity. He personifies the love, beauty, and goodness of reality. In Vedic times, Vishnu was not a major deity, though already then he was seen as measuring out, with three world-covering strides, the space for life to dwell. It seems that with the decline of Indra and Agni, Vishnu grew in importance. In part, this was accomplished through identification with other popular deities, such as Narayana, Vasudeva, and Gopal Krishna. Through this process of identification, the devotional approach to Vishnu came at least partially to replace the ritualistic approach of the Vedas.

In the Hindu conception of trinity, wherein Brahma creates and Shiva destroys, Vishnu's function is to sustain the world. Since it is nearly universal human experience that life is nourished and sustained by love, it is natural that as the sustainer of existence, Vishnu should be seen as the embodiment of love, an embodiment most obvious in his incarnation as Krishna. But Krishna is only one of Vishnu's incarnations. His function of sustaining existence is manifested in many different forms.

Forms of Vishnu

Two of the most popular forms of Vishnu are Rama and Krishna. Rama, the hero of the *Ramayana* epic, is the living embodiment of goodness. He represents the ideal man, even as his wife, Sita, represents the ideal woman. Indeed, they are paradigms of human virtue, providing time-honored exemplars of right action. The Krishna manifestation of Vishnu is the most popular and beloved of all the deities, for he is the very embodiment of love and beauty.

While this examination of Vishnu will focus primarily on Krishna, it must be remembered that Vishnu assumed many other forms in his efforts to protect and sustain the world. The Hindu tradition recognizes ten major incarnations of Vishnu. As Krishna tells Arjuna in the *Gita*,

> Whenever righteousness declines and unrighteousness flourishes, O Son of India, then I send forth myself. For the preservation of good, for the destruction of evil, to establish a foundation for righteousness, I come into being in age after age. (4.7–8)

In his first incarnation, Vishnu appeared as Matsya, a huge fish, to save Manu during the great flood. Manu, a kind of Indian Noah, is the first man, the ancestor of all human beings. When the flood waters threatened to destroy him, and thereby the whole human race, Vishnu incarnated himself as a great fish so that he could protect the human species from the deluge.

Another time, when the gods and demons were churning the ocean to obtain the elixir of immorality, they threatened to submerge the whole earth and destroy it. So Vishnu appeared in the form of a giant tortoise, Kurma, supporting the earth on his back, thereby saving it from destruction. At yet another time, after the earth had become flooded by the oceans, Vishnu incarnated himself as a huge boar, Varaha, raising the earth above the waters. As before, Vishnu had assumed a form appropriate to the need at hand, saving the world from destruction.

Vishnu's incarnation as Narasimha, half man, half lion, was for the sake of destroying a demon threatening the world with his mischievous evil. Because the demon was convinced that he was invulnerable to attack from gods, humans, and beasts, both day and night, no fear held his evil in check. So Vishnu, knowing the secret of his vulnerability, appeared in his lion form on the demon's porch at twilight (when it was neither day nor night) and tore him to pieces.

Vamana, the dwarf incarnation of Vishnu, rescued the world from an evil demon by the name of Bali. The demons, under Bali's command, managed to gain control of the entire earth through their deceitful and cunning ways, allowing no room for the gods. Vishnu, taking form as a dwarf, begged Bali to give him only as much of the earth as he could cover in three strides. Thinking the amount this little fellow could cover with three strides insignificant, Bali agreed. But suddenly the dwarf grew to gigantic size, and with three strides covered the entire earth, winning it back for the gods.

Paraushrama, the fierce mustached *brahmana* incarnation of Vishnu, put an end to the *kshatriya* attempt to usurp the place and power of the *brahmana* class, returning them to their proper place, subordinate to the *brahmanas*.

The next three incarnations are Rama, hero of the *Ramayana* epic; Krishna, the divine teacher of the *Gita*; and Buddha, the enlightened founder of Buddhism. That even the Buddha is included as an incarnation suggests that every manifestation of goodness was seen as originating from Vishnu. It also suggests that the devotees of Vishnu were trying to absorb the other religious movements of the day.

The tenth incarnation, Kalkin on his white horse, will be the next descent of Vishnu, a descent that will occur at the end of the present age. He is seen as a kind of savior, coming to punish the wicked and to reward the good, ushering in a new age of bliss. Whether the inspiration for this incarnation comes from the Buddhist teachings of future Buddhas, or from Zoroastrian ideas of a savior who will triumph over evil, is not clear. In any event, Kalkin has not played a significant role in Hinduism. Indeed, the influence of Krishna on the tradition is so much greater than any of these other manifestations that the rest of this examination of Vishnu will focus exclusively on his manifestation as Krishna.

Krishna

It is in the eighteen chapters of verse known as "The Song of the Lord" *(Bhagavad Gita)*, that Krishna is most fully presented to the world. Here, in the guise of Arjuna's charioteer, Krishna delivers his stirring message to humankind, teaching a way of devotion to God that incorporates the ways of knowledge and action. Making sure that Arjuna understands who he really is, Krishna announces that although he is now present in human form, as a charioteer, he is truly the supreme reality, the source, ruler, power, and in-dwelling unity of all existence. As the supreme God, all things are present in him, and he is present in all things:

> All beings emerge from it [My Nature].
> Know that of all of them
> And of the whole world
> I am the origin and the dissolution.

> Nothing higher than Me exists,
> O Arjuna.
> On me this [whole universe] is strung
> Like pearls on a string. (7.6–7)

This vision of God's presence in all things is not pantheistic, however. It does not equate God's reality with the reality of existing things, for as Krishna proclaims, "Whatever being has glory, majesty or power, know that in every case it has originated from a fraction of my glory" (10.41). And in the next verse, he again emphasizes that though he is present in all things, his being far surpasses them, saying, "I support this whole world with a single fraction [of Myself]." In another verse, Krishna proclaims that though the world depends on Him, His existence is independent of the world, saying, "My Self is the source of all beings and sustains all beings but does not rest in them" (9.4).

The eleventh chapter of the *Gita* eloquently demonstrates the Hindu understanding that the fullness of God's being is beyond ordinary human understanding. To see God, Arjuna must be granted a divine vision by Krishna, for which he must be given a divine eye. Even then, the vision of God in all His glory dazzles and overwhelms Arjuna, leading him to beg Krishna to assume a lesser form.

Krishna's devotees know that in his own being, Vishnu surpasses all forms, remaining incomprehensible to humans. But they also know that in his goodness and by his grace he appears in forms that they can relate to in their humanness. Thus, they take the reality of his incarnations seriously, knowing that God is truly present in his various manifestations. But by the same token, they know that these various manifestations are but symbols of the supreme reality, not to be mistaken for the supreme reality itself. It is this knowledge that enables Hindus to acknowledge the existence of many deities, for all are simply different forms of the one supreme reality. But when God takes on human form, appearing, for example, as Krishna, then human beings can relate to him in a direct and personal way. In his personal form, Krishna invites humans to come to Him in loving devotion, surrendering themselves to his loving care.

Krishna of Vrindavana   The Krishna revealed to Arjuna in the *Gita* is perhaps so terrifying in his awesome splendor and power that it is difficult to approach him in devoted love. The gap between the Supreme Lord, as he appears to Arjuna, and human beings is too vast to be bridged. The human condition requires a humbler, more human form of God to love, a form like that found in the Krishna of Vrindavana.

Thus, though the Krishna of the *Gita* is of great importance to the followers of Vishnu, it is the cowherd God, Krishna of Vrindavana, who fires the Hindu devotional imagination. This Krishna is revealed as an adorable little baby, a playful young boy, and a beautiful, amorous youth. In the simple pastoral setting of Vrindavana, Krishna, a humble cowherd boy, reveals the divine beauty, joy, and love of ultimate reality. Here his exuberant and carefree play is an invitation to his devotees to share the joys of existence with him.

This pastoral setting symbolizes God's approachability. The low-caste peasants who live there are the most ordinary of people, barred from Vedic scripture and ritual by caste. They do not practice asceticism or meditation. Instead they rejoice in the beauty and sacredness of the ordinary reality they find all around them. Ordinary, everyday experience is sacred; the divine presence shines forth everywhere. If the people of Vrindavana are special, it is only because they recognize the sacredness of ordinary reality and open their hearts to the divine love radiating through all existence.

This Krishna is as ordinary as the Vrindavana setting. As a child, he plays with the other cowherd children, and as a youth, he makes love to the cowherd girls. He is approached not as lord, but as an equal with whom to share one's love and joy. Storytellers delight in describing little Krishna's wondrous beauty and grace. His playfulness and lovingness are the topic of hundreds of stories. Even his childish mischief is precious, for it symbolizes the exuberance of the divine play and the joy of existence.

This vision of God as a little child playing, freely and exuberantly, enables Hindus to emphasize the importance of spontaneity, play, and joy in human life; it affirms that life is to be celebrated. Krishna, the divine child, announces to the world that the very essence of the divine is a playful, exuberant joy. And because he is a little child, he can be approached directly and openly, without formal rituals and careful circumspection.

As an amorous youth making love to the cowherd girls, Krishna reminds his devotees that the ecstatic fulfillment of the deepest human longings in the embrace of the beloved symbolizes the loving relationship to God that is ultimate human salvation. Loving devotion, *bhakti*, enables the devotee to break out of the confining walls of self-centeredness. Through loving surrender to Krishna, the devotee's love is allowed to provide a new ground for existence that leaves behind the pettiness of selfish concerns and worldly troubles. The devotee is transported to the realm of divine ecstasy, symbolized by Krishna's love-making on the banks of the Jumna river in Vrindavana. Krishna's actions declare not only that love is the fullest and most joyous expression of life that human beings can experience, but also that God's love is the very perfection of human love. Showing the way, Krishna invites humankind to come to him through love, play, and beauty, for these are the most profound dimensions of human life and the divine attributes of God Himself.

KALI

Like Vishnu and Shiva, the Goddess Kali presents different faces to her devotees. As the personification of death and destruction, her appearance is hideous and terrifying. But as the divine mother, she offers her children the comfort and security of maternal love. As the personification of the terrifying dimensions of existence, she helps her devotees come to grips with the violence, suffering, and death that enter into every human life. To encounter Kali in any of her fierce and gruesome manifestations is to come face to face with the instability and disorder of the world, to feel its hidden terrors. As the great mother, however, she not only rescues her children from the terrors of the world, but affirms that love is more fundamental than violence, providing a way out of life's terrors.

Kali's origins are obscure. As the great goddess, the earth mother, she may well have roots in a distant past, going back to the Indus valley civilization of 2000 BCE. The Vedic goddesses may also have contributed to her nature, for as the energizing power of consciousness and speech, the goddess reminds us of Vac, the Vedic goddess of speech. Other traditions, since lost, may also have contributed features of this popular goddess. The Puranas and Tantric texts give Kali a mythic history accounting for her origins and explaining her features and functions. Sometimes she is seen as a particular manifestation of Durga, one of the names by which the great goddess was well known in medieval India.

According to one well-known story, she came into existence as a terrible demon-destroying force to rescue the gods and preserve the world. A race of demons had grown so strong that they were successfully challenging the supremacy of the gods, threatening to destroy the very foundations of order in the world. Unable to defeat these demons themselves and, indeed, on the very brink of defeat, the gods called upon the terrible power of their shared anger. Issuing forth from their faces as a blinding light, this force manifested itself in the form of a goddess who, in various guises, came to the gods' rescue on numerous occasions when the demons appeared certain of victory.

Born of the gods' anger, Kali is a force greater than that possessed by the gods themselves. They depend on her for their survival. The gods represent the forces of good, but when these forces are threatened by evil, only a power great enough to destroy the forces of evil can save them. That Kali is such a great power is clear not only from the account of her origins as the savior of those gods, but also from the fact that she is often called simply Shakti, which means energy or force. Hinduism conceives of the throbbing energy of existence as female, as *shakti*, whereas the substance of things is thought of as male, passive and inert. In one of the fundamental polarities characterizing Hinduism, that of

Shiva-Shakti, the male and female principles are seen cooperating in energizing and structuring the world.

Even though Kali is the embodiment of terror and anger, black with rage and covered with the blood of her victims, she is not the embodiment of evil, but rather of the power to overcome and destroy evil. Thus, despite her fearsome appearance, she is ultimately benevolent, coming to the rescue of her devotees just as she came to the rescue of the gods. Although at the proper moment she takes the form of the great destroyer, she is also the primordial, unborn being who becomes this entire existence and sustains the world. That is why some of the texts go on to describe her as the divine mother *(Mata)* and the beautiful Lakshmi, goddess of happiness and fortune. The implication is that the goddess takes form as the terrifying Kali, death personified, precisely in order to overcome terror and death, thereby making room for life and joy.

This duality of Kali is a common theme of the literature and art that has grown up around the goddess. For example, there are popular paintings showing her dancing on her husband's corpse. Surrounded by bones and skulls, jackals and vultures (symbols of death), the black Kali does her eternal dance of destruction. As usual, the bloody tongue protrudes between her gleaming fangs, and her garland of severed heads sways to the rhythm of the dance. But the paintings show clearly that she is much more than the power of death and destruction. Her multiple hands, symbolizing her divine power, grasp the symbols of life as well as of death. In her two right hands, she brandishes sword and scissors, symbolizing her power to destroy and cut the cord of life. One of her left hands offers a bowl, symbol of nourishment, while the other displays a lotus, the symbol of life and purity. Like the hands simultaneously offering life and death, so the dancing feet reveal both destructive and life-giving powers. Two bodies are shown beneath her dancing feet. The lower Shiva, a bearded, naked ascetic, out of touch with Kali's life-giving energy, is completely lifeless *(shava)*. But the upper Shiva, young and beautiful, is stirring into life as a result of the divine energy he has received from her dance. So the dance is simultaneously the dance of death and the dance of life.

This painting recalls a well-known story told by one of the attendants at the Kali temple in Kalighat. According to this story, the world was being threatened by a horrible blood-seed monster who appeared totally invincible because from every drop of blood he shed, a thousand new demon monsters, equally ferocious and wicked, sprang forth. Frustrated by the monster's invincibility, the gods and goddesses called upon Kali. Ever ready to do battle with the forces of evil and destruction, the ferocious Kali swept down upon the monster and his hordes. Leaping and whirling among them, her flashing sword cut them down by the thousands, her thirsty tongue lapping up their blood before it could touch the ground and generate thousands of new monsters. Having destroyed his hordes, the blood-thirsty Kali finally swallowed the blood-seed monster himself.

Then she started her victory dance, dancing herself into a state of frenzy, oblivious to everything around her. She was time gone crazy, totally out of control, threatening all creation. The earth trembled and quaked as the tempo of her frenzied dance increased. Fearing the destruction of the very universe, the gods appealed to her husband, Shiva, begging him to intercede and stop this wild dance of destruction. Deaf to his pleas, Kali continued to dance. Finally, in desperation, he threw himself under her feet. Oblivious to her husband under her feet, she now danced on his body, threatening to bring death to him as well as to the rest of the world. Finally, however, she became aware that she was dancing on her husband's body and stopped, thus saving the universe from the ravages of time's mad dance. Interpreting the story, the attendant commented that Kali's terrible dance is really the dance that destroys evil. All those who come to her for refuge, throwing themselves at her feet, she rescues. She destroys evil for them just as she did for the gods and goddesses when Shiva threw himself at her feet.

Why, if Kali is ultimately a beneficent protector, does she appear in such gruesome and terrifying forms? The Hindu answer is clear: these images help us recognize the presence of evil in life, of fear, terror, despair, suffering, and death. To confront the Goddess in her fearsome forms is to confront our own fears of loneliness, terror, and death and to see the suffering present in all existence. Kali refuses to allow us to pretend that everything is really all right, that it is okay to suppress our fear and hurt. She insists that we face up to the fearful aspects of existence, for fear cannot be conquered until it is recognized. Thus, the aim of Kali is not to terrorize and frighten her devotees, but to face life as it really is—beauty, peace, and joy mixed with ugliness, violence, and sorrow. To those who accept her, coming to her feet in refuge, she gives the strength and courage to conquer fear, allowing them to accept the full richness of life, participating wholeheartedly in its total expression in every moment of existence.

SHIVA

Shiva is a paradoxical God. He is simultaneously the lord of death and of creation; the cosmic dancer and the immobile yogi. He is symbolized by the male phallic symbol, the *linga*, but he is also the great ascetic. In addition to these images, he is also regarded as transcending all polarities, beyond all images.

As the "great God," beyond all polarities, Shiva is not merely the lord of destruction functioning in partnership with Brahma, the lord of creation, and Vishnu, the lord of sustaining life. He is the one Supreme God, performing all of these functions. Furthermore, he provides the grace whereby the impurities that defile the self, appearing as imperfections and defects in the bound self, can be removed.

Shiva can combine the functions of all the other deities because he is the primordial consciousness present in all existence. His being is coterminous with all existence. But he goes beyond this, for he is also the original undifferentiated whole out of which existence is created, transcending all forms and expressions of existence. In his own mysterious being, he not only comprises everything that exists, but he also transcends existence. As the great yogi, he guards and protects the undifferentiated wholeness of the uncreated; as the great lord of creation, the dancing Shiva, he is the energy and rhythm that bring forth existence from the womb of *Brahman*.

The fundamental symbol of Shiva, the *linga*, is the axis of the universe. Extending infinitely beyond the universe, it declares the transcendence of the infinite/finite polarity in Shiva's being. Symbolizing the deep stillness of the absolute prior to creation, the *linga* simultaneously symbolizes the throbbing potency of the creative power of life, suggesting the reconciliation of the opposition between manifested existence and the unmanifested *Brahman*. That Shiva is both lord of the dance and the great yogi shows that he also overcomes the opposition between immanence and transcendence.

Lord of the Dance

To get a sense of how Shiva combines the functions of world creation, maintenance, and destruction while at the same time transcending these polarities, it is helpful to examine his image as Lord of the Dance *(Nataraja)*. Dancing within the ring of fire, Shiva embodies the primordial creative energies of existence. The rhythm of his dance and the energy of his movements transform the primordial energy into life. The entire universe is the effect of Shiva's eternal dance, which simultaneously creates and destroys the world in a never-ending process.

In the palm of his upper left hand, Shiva holds a tongue of flame, representing the destructive forces that have long been associated with this deity. The flickering flame marks the changes brought about by the destructive forces. In his upper right hand is the drum that furnished the dance's rhythm, the rhythm of creation. It symbolizes the eternal sound vibrating in the ether of space to create the first stirring of revelation and truth, and the first forms of existence. These two polar forces, the creativity embodied in sound and the destruction embodied in fire, complement each other. In their harmonious balance, they constitute the continuous creation and destruction that characterizes all existence.

His lower right hand, displayed in the traditional "fear not" gesture, shows that this cosmic dance of creation and destruction is not to be feared. Indeed, his lower left hand points to his upraised left foot, which shows that this is really a dance of liberation. His devotees know that by worshipping the raised foot of Shiva, they will find refuge and salvation. The other foot is planted firmly on the infant form of the demon of ignorance, showing that ignorance must be stamped out in order to attain the pure wisdom that brings liberation from bondage.

As Shiva dances the world into existence, maintains it, and dances it out of existence, he removes the veil of illusion that misleads us into taking existence to be the fundamental reality. The movements and symbols of the dance are revealed to be none other than the manifestations of Shiva himself: creation, destruction, maintenance, concealment, and divine favor or liberation. The hand with the drum represents creation, the hand with the flame represents destruction, and the "fear not" gesture represents maintenance. The foot planted on demonic ignorance symbolizes the concealment of reality, and the upraised foot signifies the divine favor that makes liberation possible.

While the energy of the dance immediately captures our attention, when we begin to see the dance as a whole, rather than in terms of its various motions, our attention is drawn to the center of the image. There we see the wonderfully calm face of the Lord, seemingly independent of the dance. This blissfully calm face, and the balanced immobile head, symbolize Shiva's transcendence of space and time and the frenzied dance of existence. The beautiful inward smile suggests the peace of absorption into that deeper reality where all polarities are reconciled in a harmony.

The sacred ring of fire that surrounds the dancer symbolizes both the sacredness of existence and the destruction of ignorance. With the destruction of ignorance comes release from bondage to time and change. Thus, the ring of fire also suggests a purification process whereby the dancer is released from the dance.

Shiva, as lord of the dance, is the embodiment of the total energy of manifested existence in all its forms. But his face, which is the face of the ascetic, embodies the peace and tranquility of self-fulfillment that transcends the dualities of manifested existence. Because Shiva is both his dancing body and his peaceful face, however, this image informs us that energy and substance, manifest and unmanifest, transcendent and immanent, are ultimately one and the same reality. In Shiva, all polarities are reconciled in a greater unity.

Shiva as Symbol of the Unmanifest

The fundamental pair of opposites reconciled in Shiva is that of created, manifested reality on the one hand, and uncreated, unmanifested reality on the other. Hinduism tends to see the original, uncreated reality as primary; creation or manifestation is a kind of degeneration of the primordial undifferentiated wholeness, and it is therefore relegated to a lower level of reality. If we see the Rudra of the Vedas as a kind of proto-Shiva, then there is a very ancient myth that presents Shiva as both the guardian of the ultimate, uncreated reality and, because he allowed it to degenerate, guardian of created existence as well.

According to this story, Rudra, the fierce archer, was guarding the original, uncreated reality, protecting it from any efforts to transform it into manifested existence. Suddenly he saw the Father, the Creator, preparing to plant the seed of the uncreated reality into the womb of the mother of existence so that created existence could issue forth. Rudra let fly an arrow to destroy the Father before he could complete the act. But he was too late; the seed of creation had already been planted. Because his arrow, the arrow of time itself, provided the dimension needed for creation to occur, Rudra unwittingly became a cause of the very creation he was trying to prevent. Though originally, as the guardian of the uncreated, he tried to prevent creation from occurring, now that reality had passed over into created form, his task as guardian was to protect the reality embodied in the various forms of existence. Shiva's cosmic dance, as we have seen, destroys old forms of existence even as it creates the new. In this dual act of destroying and creating, he maintains the existence that he allowed to be created. Although originally the guardian of the uncreated, he now becomes the protector of the creation he dances into existence, the Lord and protector of all creatures *(Pashupati)*.

Shiva's primary symbol, the *linga*, reaching from the very womb of created existence to the invisible realm of the primordial, uncreated reality, encompasses both dimensions of his being, the transcendent and the immanent, the uncreated and the created. As the lord of the dance, he symbolizes the energies of creation. As the great yogi engaged in ascetic practice, he goes beyond to the undifferentiated consciousness that reaches the primordial, uncreated reality, recalling his function as guardian of the uncreated.

When it became popular, in later tradition, to think of the creative energy of existence as female, as the divine *shakti*, Shiva was frequently visualized with a divine consort, often Parvati. Here Shiva symbolized the uncreated wholeness of *Brahman* and Parvati, his inseparable spouse, the creative energy of existence. But because Shiva is actually both, he also comes to be portrayed as combining in his own person both the eternal male and the eternal female. As half male and half female *(ardhanaraishvara)*, he visibly reconciles the male/female polarities of existence in his own being.

The many myths and images and the innumerable names that belong to Shiva barely begin to describe this great god, however. As the life of all beings and the ground of existence beyond all names and forms, the names and forms that describe him can never define him. The eternal Shiva is always unmanifest and invisible in his highest being.

REVIEW QUESTIONS

1. What are the main differences between the philosophical approaches to the understanding of ultimate reality by the Vedanta philosophers and the devotional understanding of the ultimate in the religious traditions?
2. How does Vishnu's incarnation as Krishna reveal his essential functions?
3. According to Krishna of Vrindavana, what is the ultimate nature of reality, and how should one approach the ultimate?
4. Why does Kali appear in terrifying forms? How do these forms help her devotees?
5. What are the fundamental polarities that are reconciled in Shiva?

FURTHER READING

Devi: Goddesses of India, edited by John S. Hawley and Donna M. Wulff (Berkeley: University of California Press, 1996), is a collection of essays by scholarly experts exploring Kali and other forms of the Goddess.

The *Sword and the Flute*, by David R. Kinsley (Berkeley: University of California Press, 1977), is a good place to begin one's study of Hindu devotionalism. Focusing on Krishna and Kali, this little book brings these deities to life, enabling one to appreciate their influence on Hindu religious life.

The Presence of Siva, by Stella Kramrisch (Princeton, NJ: Princeton University Press, 1981), is a rich, scholarly account of the myths, images, and meanings of Shiva. Kramrisch weaves the many myths of Shiva into a tapestry that displays the vitality of this great god and reveals the significance of his paradoxical nature for understanding not only the Indian tradition, but ourselves as well. The thirty-two plates of Shiva sculptures from Elephanta provide rich materials for visual contemplation.

Love Song of the Dark Lord: Jayadeva's Gitagovinda, edited and translated by Barbara Stoler Miller (New York: Columbia University Press, 1977), is an excellent translation of one of India's greatest devotional poems. Celebrating Krishna as the embodiment of love, the *Gitagovinda* offers an inspiring glimpse into the beauty and power of the way of love as a form of worship.

The Divine Hierarchy: Popular Hinduism in Central India, by Lawrence A. Babb (New York: Columbia University Press, 1975), provides a good account of the practice of Hinduism. The last chapter, on the Hindu pantheon, is particularly helpful.

A Brief Introduction to Hinduism, by A.L. Herman (Boulder, CO: Westview Press, 1991), is an excellent brief survey of Hinduism, starting with three modern thinkers, Gandhi, Maharshi, and Bhaktivedanta, and working back to the foundations of the religion.

A Survey of Hinduism, 2nd ed., by Klaus K. Klostermaier (Albany: State University of New York Press, 1994), is a highly recommended comprehensive overview of Hinduism.

The Bhagavad-Gita, translated by Barbara Stoler Miller (New York: Bantam Books, 1986), is a fine contemporary translation that captures the beauty and the power of the original.

CHAPTER 9

Islam

Islamic thought has flourished in India since early in the thirteenth century. Although the first Muslim conquests occurred as early as the eighth century (General Qasim's first victory came in 712 CE), it was after the armies of the Chinghis Khan had ravaged Muslim lands that Muslim culture really took hold in India. With the destruction of major Muslim centers of culture and learning at Samarqand, Balkh, Gahznin, and finally, in 1258, Baghdad itself, many Muslim scholars, poets, artists, scientists, and historians fled to India. Soon the Delhi sultanate and the Mughal courts in India became more than merely centers of political rule; they became distinguished centers of Islamic learning as well.

Islam had great influence on Indian thought and culture during the five hundred years of Muslim rule. This chapter examines the basis of Islam and some of the developments of Islamic thought in India. It begins with the fundamentals of Islam as a way of life, for all Islamic thought is ultimately rooted in these fundamentals. Then, inquiring into the interaction between Muslim Sufis and Hindus, the philosophical roots of Sufi thought in Al-Ghazali and Ibn Sina (Avicenna) are explored. This is followed by an examination of the thought of Kabir, Dadu, and Guru Nanak, three thinkers profoundly influenced by Sufi thought. Finally, because both Islam and Hinduism view religion and politics as inseparable, the interaction between religious and political thought at Akbar's court and thereafter is explored.

BASIC TEACHINGS OF ISLAM

According to the faithful, Islam is the way that brings peace to those who commit themselves to God's way and submit to His will. The word *Islam* means "peace through submission" and comes from the root word *sim*, meaning "peace." One who submits to God's will and seeks peace by following His way is called a Muslim. For Muslims there is no god but God (Allah) and no religion but Islam. God sent His Messengers to all the corners of the earth to make known His message of life and salvation. When the world was ready, God revealed His full and final message in the form of the Holy Qur'an through his Messenger, Muhammad, who lived from 570 to 632 CE. That is why Muhammad is known as the seal of the prophets and Islam as the complete and perfect religion. This conviction that their God is the only true God and that their religion is the only full and true religion underlies the Muslim zeal for propagation of the Faith.

To understand Islam, we must ask what a Muslim is expected to believe, do, and realize, for faith, action, and spiritual realization define the way a Muslim commits to God and submits to His will.

The Five Pillars

1. *Faith,* the first pillar, the very foundation of Islam. Through Faith a Muslim believes:
   i. God alone is real. Everything else is His creation and exists in dependence upon Him.
   ii. All creation exists as a manifestation of God's power and glory, and its purpose is to reflect the power and glory of God. Therefore, the proper relationship of a human being to God is that of a servant to his Lord. To serve God is the fundamental purpose of life for a Muslim.
   iii. The way to serve God is revealed in God's message transmitted through the prophets, especially Muhammad, for he is the seal of the prophets.
   iv. Muhammad is the final and most perfect Messenger of God. This entails belief in the Qur'an as the word of God in its fullest and most complete form, and in Muhammad as the most perfect example of human relationship to God. Muhammad is the ideal servant, and his life as embodied in his saying and practice *(Hadith and Sunnah)*, constitutes a norm of faith and action for all Muslims, providing guidance for life and the most important clues to the meaning of the Qur'an.

The remaining four pillars are requirements of action. They include the following:

2. *Prayer,* at least five times a day, to recall human dependence on God and to sustain and nourish life in service to God.

3. *Fasting,* for one month each year, to realize inner spirituality and develop a closer relationship with God. Eating, drinking, smoking, and sexual intercourse are forbidden from dawn until sunset every day during the month of Ramadan, and every effort is made to avoid all evil thoughts, actions, and words during this time.

4. *Sharing,* requiring that all people donate a percentage of their income and savings every year, to help the needy. The underlying assumption is that everything belongs to God and that all wealth is held in trusteeship for the well-being of all God's creatures. Everyone is entitled to share in the community's wealth according to their need, and everyone is required to share with those who are less fortunate.

5. *Pilgrimage,* to Mecca, symbolizing the unity of the Muslim community, the equality of all persons, and the oneness of humankind. Here one effectively suspends all worldly activities in order to foster the realization that the essential concern of life is that of developing the right relationship between the soul and God.

Spiritual Realization

These five pillars of faith and action define the essential duties of every Muslim. According to the holy Qur'an, each person is free to submit to God's will and to live the life of righteousness delineated in the Qur'an. One is also free to reject God and to live in defiance of the way He has ordained. But life does not end with death, and all will face the judgment of God on the Day of Judgment. The righteous, who have submitted to His way, will reap God's blessings in Heaven, but those who do not submit will go to Hell to suffer eternal punishment.

Although every Muslim is motivated by the promise of Heaven and the threat of Hell, a deeper motivation is provided by love of God. Out of love for God, a true Muslim strives to make his or her will an instrument of the Divine Will, bringing it into harmony with God's will. The divine spark within each person that constitutes the likeness of God enables one to enter into a spiritual relationship with God, bringing the human will into harmony with the Divine Will, thereby making one a perfect instrument of the Creator.

This spiritual realization of the right relationship between God and the individual sanctifies all of life. It also becomes the basis of righteous action, guiding and directing one's life in the holy way of submission to God. The whole world, material and spiritual, body and soul, is created by God, and every sphere of human action has a moral and spiritual dimension. The secular cannot be separated from the religious within Islam; everything is ultimately religious, because everything proceeds from God and belongs to Him. This means that Muslim Holy Law *(Shari'ah)* extends to every sphere of human action, individual and collective, social, political, and economic. The modern inclination to separate state and religion is entirely foreign to Islamic tradition. A Muslim cannot say, "Give to Caesar what is Caesar's and to God what is God's," because everything is God's. Life is an integrated whole, and all of it must be lived as an act of service to God.

DEVELOPMENT OF SUFI THOUGHT

Within Muslim India, the main tension was between the orthodox Sunni and the Sufi ways. Since the attempt to reconcile these tensions in a creative way gave rise to yet a third response, we can distinguish between three different attitudes toward religion among Indian Muslims. The first attitude, frequently regarded as orthodox (Sunni) Islam, stresses the accumulated tradition of the Muslim community in the understanding of the Qur'an. The Qur'an and Muslim tradition form the basis of Islamic Law that regulates social and political life that governs the life of the individual.

The second attitude, characteristic of the Sufis, stresses the spiritual experience and fulfillment of the individual. Sufis see the community and tradition as a natural outcome of intense personal experience of the reality of God and the truth of His revelation. This attitude modifies the rigidity of the accumulated tradition through personal experience and accommodation of the needs of the individual. In turn, the orthodox attitude modifies the sometimes whimsical and idiosyncratic impulses of the individual by stressing the more normal experiences and needs of the entire community. An almost continuous tension exists between these two attitudes within the history of Islam, a tension that for the most part has been healthy, promoting both stability and personal spiritual growth.

The third attitude arises from this tension between the previous two attitudes. It emphasizes the need to coordinate personal experience and belief with the laws and practices of the larger community. This attitude resulted in the movement of thought that helped to transform the inherent tensions between the orthodox (Sunni) and Sufi ways into a healthy and mutually enriching complementarity. In a way, this third attitude amounted to a continuous reformation of Islam that helped to keep the tradition and the law from becoming sterile or dead, and that restricted the extravagances of the personal mystic way. The religious thinkers who embodied this attitude went beyond the letter of the Holy Law to the spirit on which it was based. For the orthodox majority, Islam was simply submission to the Holy Law as interpreted and enforced by the political system that the leaders of the community accepted and insisted upon. For the religious thinker, it was necessary to go beyond blind acceptance and dogmatic adherence of the Holy Law. The Holy Law had to be interpreted and applied to particular circumstances in a creative way according to the underlying spirit.

Al-Ghazali

Of all the thinkers who experienced this tension and tried to accommodate both dimensions of Islam, perhaps the greatest was Al-Ghazali. His work gave respectability to Sufism while curbing its excesses. He also gave orthodoxy a lasting theology, framing its spiritual basis and insights in doctrinal formulations consistent with scripture and tradition, yet defensible by reason.

Al-Ghazali (1059–1111) grew up in an environment dominated by Sufism. But deeply interested in philosophy, theology, and jurisprudence, he began a serious study of these subjects in his late teens. Still in his twenties, he was recognized for his brilliance and was appointed to the most famous university in Baghdad, the center of Islamic scholarship at the time. Despite his fame as the unequaled authority of Muslim theology and law, however, he felt his scholarship was destroying his faith and his life.

Near despair, Al-Ghazali returned again to the Sufi way. Here he found the inner peace he was seeking and discovered that reason cannot illuminate the divine likeness that abides in the heart. On the contrary, reason, taking itself as the ultimate criterion of truth, can reduce everything to absurdity, destroying faith and life in the process.

Convinced of the priority of faith and intuition over reason, and of the need to employ reason in its proper sphere of clarifying, interpreting, and defending the insights of faith and the knowledge of the heart, he wrote his masterpiece, *Revival of Religious Sciences,* through which he gave Islam a lasting theology. Quickly embraced by almost the whole Islamic community, it has served both Sunnis and Sufis well over the intervening centuries, providing a commonality sufficient to keep them within the same house of faith—even though in separate rooms.

Revival of Religious Sciences maintains that ultimately God is the only real object of knowledge and that God can be known only through faith. It responds to a challenge constituted by the philosophers' emphasis on reason. Inspired by translated works of Plato, Aristotle, and the Neoplatonists, Arab philosophers developed philosophical systems that took reason—rather than the Qur'an—as the ultimate criterion of truth. Ibn Sina (Avicenna) (981–1037), for example, had taught that the world was uncreated, existing eternally, because although the scriptures taught that the world was created by God out of nothing, reason can make no sense out of something being created out of nothing. Therefore, he concluded that creation was really a transformation of something existing previously. Even though it might be a radical transformation, it was not creation out of nothing.

In a similar way, Ibn Sina had argued that since all knowledge is of universal intelligible forms rather than of concrete existence, it follows that God's knowledge, too, is not of particular things in their concreteness but only of universals. This conclusion, however, runs contrary to the scriptural teaching in the Qur'an that God knows all things in every detail.

In a corollary argument, Ibn Sina claimed that because the soul is the knowing part of a person, and because knowledge is only of forms, the soul itself is a form. If the nature of the soul were different from that of knowledge, knowledge would be impossible. But if the soul is a form, then it is universal and indestructible. The body, however, is naturally destructible. Although from this it follows that the soul is indestructible, it also follows that there can be no eternal resurrection of the body—a conclusion that contradicts the Qur'anic teaching of the eternal resurrection of the body after the Last Judgment. It thus repudiates the teaching that the resurrected person will either suffer eternal punishment in Hell or enjoy eternal rewards in Heaven.

In light of such contradictions between philosophical conclusions and the teachings of scripture, it is easy enough to understand why the orthodox believers felt threatened by philosophers who, like Ibn Sina, relied on reason rather than God's word as the criterion of truth. No wonder Al-Ghazali's *The Nonsense of Philosophers,* in which he showed that reason could be used to defeat the arguments and conclusions of reason just as easily as it could be used to defeat the doctrines of faith, was warmly received by the orthodox and enshrined, along with his positive theology in the *Revival of Religious Sciences* as "official" teaching. Although Al-Ghazali's attack on philosophy was subjected to a brilliant criticism by Ibn Rushd (Averroes) in a book aptly titled *The Nonsense of Nonsense,* Al-Ghazali had already convinced the orthodox that reason by itself was an unreliable and dangerous tool.

It is interesting to speculate whether, if Al-Ghazali had not won the day and convinced Muslim orthodoxy that rational thought was a great danger to the Faith, modern science might have developed in the medieval Muslim world rather than during the Enlightenment in Europe. The Arab philosophers were acquainted with Greek logic and science. They recognized causal connections between all natural things, connections that could be known through a combination of experimentation and reason. Their sense of the capability of reason and the value they placed on knowing God through rational knowledge of His creation might well have inspired Muslim thinkers to have developed something akin to what we call the scientific attitude and method. But like Thomas Aquinas in Europe a century later, Al-Ghazali insisted that the proper employment of reason is not in speculation about the natural world, but rather in defense of scripture and orthodox theology. And just as Thomas Aquinas gave enduring shape to Christian theology, so Al-Ghazali provided the theological foundation for Islam—both in its orthodox (Sunni) form and in its mystical (Sufi) form.

Ibn Sina's Metaphysics of Divine Love

Although Ibn Sina's natural theology was rejected because it clashed with the Qur'an, his metaphysics of Divine Love fared much better. It became the philosophical basis for the Sufi way of devotion to God through love. Starting from the philosophies of Plato and Aristotle, Ibn Sina gave reason an honored and highly respected place, regarding it as the last word in matters of science and logic and as the ultimate criterion of truth for our knowledge of nature. But religious experience told him that the human heart has a more direct and immediate access to the ultimate truth. Through the soul's intuition, the light of God is reflected in the mirror of the human soul, illuminating the entire universe in the process.

God, the ultimate reality, is eternal beauty, according to Ibn Sina, as demonstrated by the beauty of nature. It is the very nature of beauty to be self-expressive, he says, and nature is simply the self-expression of God. In God, this self-expression, not different from His Being, is the supreme love, for love is nothing other than the expression and appreciation of perfect beauty. In other words, beauty is the ultimate being of the universe, while love is its ultimate energy, causing all beings to seek their original perfection. But being and energy are simply different aspects of the same reality. It is through love, therefore, that a person can turn away from imperfection and return to full perfection in the eternal beauty that is God. This is possible because God is love and humans are created in His image, having a spark of the Divine Love in their own souls, a spark that can ignite the whole being and reveal the eternal oneness with God.

Although Ibn Sina's metaphysics is abstract, Sufi life is not. The supreme love for God experienced in the Sufi's heart is manifested typically through sharing the concerns and sorrows of others and is frequently given literary expression through the images of human love. Sufis usually lived extremely simple, sometimes ascetic, lives. Indeed, Sufism began as an ascetic movement to prepare the way for direct personal experience of the human relationship to God.

Although asceticism continued to be a Sufi hallmark, the increasing emphasis on personal experience led to the development of devotional practices aimed at facilitating spiritual experience. Love for God and adoration of His name and presence ruled Sufi life. But Sufis rarely became hermits. The bonds of God's love for them and their love for Him reached out to embrace their fellow humans. Most Sufis understood that one of their urgent purposes in life was to provide spiritual guidance for the people. This meant guidance in worldly affairs as well as spiritual affairs, for in Islam these realms are not really separate.

To provide this guidance, it was necessary for Sufis to discover the innermost heart of those who came for guidance, and to open their own hearts. This "discovery and sharing" required keeping in close touch with the daily lives of the people. It also meant staying out of the political fray because political involvement would hinder the Sufis' personal quest for a deeper spiritual relationship with God and would get in the way of their efforts to comfort the troubled hearts of their fellow human beings. Only by staying out of politics and government could they come to know and share the trouble in the hearts of those who came to them in need of solace. As an old Sufi saying has it, "Though there are as many paths to God as there are particles in the universe, none is shorter than that of bringing comfort to troubled hearts."

Sufi disdain of administrative service and professional work was based on the conviction that such work required allegiance to a ruler or professional goals rather than to God, resulting in ego gratification rather than spiritual fulfillment of one's relation to God and humanity. Perhaps the best definition of the Sufi ideal is given by Shaikh Fariduddin in advice to his disciples about how to live. Men of God, he advised them, are like this: "First, anxiety as to what they shall eat and what they shall wear does not enter their heart.... Secondly, in private and in public they remain absorbed in God: that is the essence of all spiritual striving. Thirdly, they never utter anything with the idea of pleasing people and attracting them toward themselves."[1]

Sufis who were able to put this advice into practice were distinguished by their serenity and holiness. Their spiritual greatness prompted many stories about their extraordinary powers. For example, once the opponent of a blind saint came to the saint hoping to cast doubt upon his saintliness. Thinking that the external flaw of blindness was certainly mirrored in an internal spiritual flaw, the opponent, hoping to trip up the saint in some way, asked him, "What is the sign of a saint?" While asking the question a fly settled on the opponent's nose. Though he brushed it away, the fly returned. Again he brushed it away, but when the fly landed a third time, the blind saint said, "One of the signs of a saint is that no fly lands on his nose!"[2]

Another story tells how a very old spiritual master, Badr-ud-Din, would get up and dance with great joy whenever he heard a devotional song. Music and dance were forbidden in orthodox Islam, but they became an important means of inspiration and attainment in Sufism. Sufis, of course, regarded music and dance not as profane, human creations, but rather as expressions of the Divine Love to which the human soul responded through its body. Even when very old and scarcely able to move, Badr-ud-Din would become so filled with ecstasy by the sound of a devotional song that he would get up and dance like a young man. When asked, "Shaikh, how can you dance like this when you cannot even walk?" he replied, "Where is the Shaikh? It is only Love that dances!"

This Love, of course, is the Divine Reality. Though transcending all created existence, it is nonetheless present everywhere in all existence. According to the Sufi theory of the oneness of existence worked out by Ibn Arabi (1165–1240), transcendence and immanence are simply two different aspects of the same reality. God is both transcendent and immanent, for in Him, being and existence are one and inseparable. Although it is impossible to become God, because He is the Creator and we are the created, it is possible for the mystic to realize that his existence is eternally contained in God's existence—even as a drop of water in the ocean is contained in the ocean—for God's creation is part of His existence.

This philosophy, though by no means identical to yoga, is certainly compatible with it, and the Sufi stages of preparation for this realization often resemble the eightfold path of Buddhism and the eight aids to yoga enunciated by Patanjali. Indeed, many Sufis studied and practiced yoga to aid their efforts at realizing their existence in God.

THE SUFI PATH

The spiritual preparation required to achieve this realization constitutes the very heart of Sufism. It is the path to God, a path marked by a series of stages. These stages are often described in different ways, but the following is a typical description:

1. *Repentance.* An awakening to the heedlessness and sinfulness of life accompanied by a repentant attitude and the resolve to live virtuously, according to God's law.
2. *Abstinence.* Possessions and enjoyments are abandoned in recognition of the truth that nothing belongs to oneself; everything belongs to God, and only God is to be sought.
3. *Renunciation.* Not only must pleasures and possessions be abandoned, but even the desire for them must be renounced.
4. *Poverty.* Everything that can distract the mind from God must be rejected so that it cannot stand between the soul and God. Although poverty begins with non-ownership, it requires abandoning not merely property, but wishes and thoughts that separate the soul from God.

5. *Patience.* Any misfortune must be accepted as part of God's way, and one must be willing to follow His way even when human inclinations run in a contrary direction.
6. *Trust in God.* Complete confidence in God's grace is required to overcome all obstacles on the path, including the traveler's sinfulness.
7. *Satisfaction.* At this stage, nothing satisfies the pilgrim except following God's will. But accepting and following the Divine Decree is completely satisfying.

These seven stages are achieved primarily by the individual's own efforts. To progress farther along the path requires Divine help. Indeed, even as the pilgrim makes his or her way along the first stages of the path, God provides (1) the power to meditate, (2) the sense of closeness to Him, (3) love for Him, (4) fear of separation, (5) hope and longing for the Divine embrace, (6) intimacy with Him, (7) inner peace, (8) the ability to contemplate the Divine, and (9) confidence in salvation through God's help.

These divine gifts, in conjunction with the achievements of self-effort, prepare the traveler on the path to receive the Divine Light from God Himself. Through this Divine Light, the likeness of the soul to God is recognized, and all passions, desires, and conscious thoughts are utterly extinguished. The individual soul is now like a drop of water in the great ocean that is God's Being. Subsisting in this wonderful condition allows the Truth to be seen and the soul to be reunited with God.

Although some of the Sufis, speaking from the ecstatic rapture of their vision, declared themselves identical to God, the more sober, like Al-Ghazali, recognized that the experience was beyond the limitations of thought and language and refrained from misleading statements that might confuse the religious seeker and scandalize the orthodox. Since the instruments of power were always in the hands of the orthodox, Sufi excesses could prove dangerous. In 922 CE, Al-Hallaj was executed for heresy in Baghdad. His "crime" was to give expression to his rapturous experience of the Divine Reality by declaring that God was incarnate within him. But for the most part, the Sufis built upon the foundations of orthodoxy rather than attempt to destroy those foundations. In the spirit of Jesus, a thousand years earlier, they saw their work as fulfilling the Holy Law rather than destroying it.

INTERACTION BETWEEN MUSLIMS AND HINDUS

Although the Muslim ruling class in India was almost exclusively Orthodox Sunnis, the Sufis exerted the most influence on Hindu thought. They also received the most from Hindu culture, for these sincere spiritual seekers interacted freely with spiritual persons whatever their background or allegiance.

The Sufis were concerned almost exclusively with realizing a personal inner relationship with God. Striving to find the living presence of Allah in their personal experience, they abandoned the wealth, luxury, and material distractions of urban civilization in favor of an ascetic and rural existence. Because nothing mattered so much as spiritual experience, and because the very restrictions of Muslim orthodoxy were rejected, the Sufis were open to spiritual practices and ideas wherever they found them. They were influenced by Christianity, Buddhism, and Hinduism and inspired by the ideas of the Upanishads and Plotinus, as well as by the scriptures and traditions of Islam. The basis of Sufi thought and practice remained Islam, of course, but there was considerable borrowing, adapting, and adopting in the encounter of mystic Islam with Hinduism.

Considerable interaction occurred between Muslims and Hindus. Millions of Hindus converted to Islam, and a new religion, the Sikh, was born of the encounter between Islam and Hinduism. Many converts were Hindus influenced by the saintly examples of the Sufis, whose piety and religious devotion were extremely attractive to Hindus, prepared by their culture to venerate saints—indeed often to honor them as incarnations of gods or goddesses. If Islam could produce saints of the holiness and stature of the great Sufis who wandered into the provinces and villages where the powerful arm of government hardly ever reached, then surely it must be a worthy way that could be safely followed in the quest for liberation and perfection by any sincere spiritual seeker.

Even among those Hindus who did not convert to Islam, the piety and devotion of the Sufis had an impact, and among the many devotional sects and movements that flourished in the fifteenth and sixteenth centuries, a Muslim influence can be traced. The great Hindu devotional poet from Maratha, Namadeva (Namdev), for example, blended Islamic worship of God with Upanishadic monism in his verses. Using many Persian and Arabic words, he showed great respect for the one, omnipotent God.

His compatriot, Tukaram, who lived perhaps a hundred years later and is one of the greatest devotional poets of medieval India, was also deeply influenced by Islam. In a typical verse he says,

> First among the great names is Allah, never forget to repeat it.
> Allah is verily one, the prophet is verily one.
> There Thou art one, there Thou art one, there Thou art one, O! friend.
> There is neither I nor Thou.[3]

No hostility toward Islam is found in the poems and songs of Namadeva, Tukaram, and other devotional poets of the time. They sing the praises of Allah along with those of the Hindu deities, seeing all as manifestations of the supreme unmanifest reality uniting and pervading all existence.

Sometimes hostility did exist, of course, as in the case of Shivaji (1627–1680), one of the fiercest enemies of the Muslim rulers in India. He expressed his hostility in political opposition. But even in this case we detect an earlier feeling of respect and goodwill, for Shivaji's father, Shaji, was named after the great Sufi saint, Shah Sharif of Ahmadnagar, suggesting that Shivaji's grandfather was a great admirer of this saintly Muslim.

Of course, many of these influential Muslim saints went very far in the direction of admitting the validity of Hinduism, urging their followers to follow what was best in both of these great religions, encouraging them to see what they had in common at their spiritual core rather than emphasizing their differences and antagonisms at the periphery of spiritual belief. Three of the most notable examples of this tendency are Kabir, Guru Nanak, and Dadu.

Kabir

Kabir, born near the beginning of the fifteenth century, was a disciple of both the Sufi Shaikh Taqi and Ramananda, the great Hindu *bhakta* (devotee) who was instrumental in spreading devotional Hinduism across northern India. Although he is frequently claimed by Hindus as a Hindu mystic and reformer, it is almost certain that Kabir was born into a Muslim family and that he never renounced Islam. But he certainly denounced both the narrowness of Islam and the rigid sectarianism of Hinduism.

Kabir's Hindu guru, Ramananda, may also have been influenced by Islam, though this is not certain. In any event, Ramananda himself protested against the caste system, admitting all persons equally into his following. But since the best of the Hindu devotional leaders emphasized that true devotion and spiritual realization surmounted the distinctions of sect and caste, the fact that Ramananda accepted people of all castes, as well as outcasts and even Muslims, certainly does not prove Islamic influence. Undoubtedly, however, Kabir accepted both Islamic and Hindu ideas and practices, attempting to reconcile these two religions on the basis of what he recognized as a deeper unity. His most trenchant criticisms of Islam were directed at the rigid formalism and the exclusive absolutism that refused to recognize as true or spiritual any idea or practice that had not been so defined and accepted by previous Islamic authority. He saw formalism and absolutism suffocating spiritual life under the external wrappings of required beliefs, observances, practices, and laws.

In criticizing Hinduism, he was unsparing in his denunciation of Hindu caste system, polytheism, and idolatry. No one, he said, should be denied a full measure of both human dignity and access to spiritual practice simply because of birth into a low caste or outcaste family. Idolatry he condemned for directing the energies of devotees away from what is truly spiritual, while polytheism was seen to detract from devotion and service to the Supreme.

Kabir was embraced by later Hindus as a great saint and reformer and was given a thoroughly Hindu biography. That he was actually a Muslim reformer did not initially matter to Hindus nearly as much as his spiritual message, which offered hope to millions of poor and oppressed persons. Hinduism has always been able to accommodate radicals and reformers, enfolding them into its lifestream even as it has absorbed Aryans, Ajivakas, Buddhists, and countless other religious movements and persons over the ages. But the formalism of Islam, against which Kabir militated so vigorously, was too rigid to allow him to be accepted as a Muslim saint, except by a handful of admirers.

Guru Nanak

Guru Nanak (1469–1539), founder of the Sikh religion, was in the same spiritual tradition as Kabir. He may also have been a Muslim, although both Hindu and Sikh traditions regarded him as Hindu. Like Kabir, he sought to transcend the differences between Islam and Hinduism, uniting Hindus and Muslims on the basis of the great underlying spiritual truths that these two religions held in common. He also denounced the idolatry and polytheism of Hinduism, insisting on the pervasive Will of a single omnipotent and omniscient God. But his insistence on the uniqueness and absoluteness of God was based not on the Islamic tendency to exclude from God what was not of His own nature, but rather on the ancient Indian tendency to include all things in a greater unity, thereby admitting opposites as corollaries and complementarities.

The way of Sikhism is to find salvation through union with God by realizing, through love, the in-dwelling Person of God. Union with God is the ultimate goal. Apart from God, life has no meaning. As Guru Nanak says, "What terrible separation it is to be separated from God and what blissful union to be united with Him!"[4]

Separation from God causes the suffering experienced as the usual human condition. Although human beings and the world are created by God, human perversity and pride, stemming from self-centeredness, lead to attachment to the pleasures and concerns of this world. According to Sikhism, this attachment separates us from God, resulting in all forms of human suffering, including the seemingly endless round of deaths and rebirths.

It is God, one without a second, formless and eternal, who created all existence, and it is God who sustains all forms of existence by dwelling within them. Through His will we are sustained, and through His grace God reveals Himself to us through His creation. This divine revelation calls forth recognition of our separateness and sparks the response that can bring salvation through union with Him in love, according to Guru Nanak.

Only when God's voice is heard within the human heart and the heart responds is salvation possible. Worship of images and asceticism are pointless, as are yoga and ritual actions. Only through love for the Person of God can the bliss of union be achieved. As Divine Guru, God declares His message directly to the heart of those who will hear. In the message of Guru Nanak and the other gurus, as recorded in the scripture called *Adi Granth* (or *Guru Granth Sahib*), is to be heard the message of God, the Original Guru.

Dadu

Dadu (1544–1603) was another Muslim reformer whose combination of Muslim and Hindu ideas influenced many Hindus. The inspiration for his reform efforts was found in the teachings of Kabir, for he was a member of a Kabir sect. But as they did with other great saints, later Hindus gave Dadu a Hindu biography and accepted him as a strictly Hindu saint.

It is, of course, part of the traditional Indian way to accept as saints those great spiritual persons whose ideas are worthy of belief and whose practice is worthy of emulation. Most of the religions and sects that developed on Indian soil began as small groups of followers of a holy person. If the following grew sufficiently large, it became a separate sect or even, as in the case of Buddhism and Jainism, an independent religion. In other cases, the following was small or did not endure long enough to achieve independent or semi-independent status. But at any particular time in history, including in contemporary India, what we call Hinduism is made up of many sects, distinguished on the basis of different deities, different saint leaders, or differences in practice and belief—sometimes despite common deities or a common saint leader.

No person or institution has ever defined Hindu orthodoxy, and no exclusive doctrine or practice has ever become the basis for orthodoxy. And in the absence of orthodoxy, unorthodoxy is undefinable and heresy quite impossible. Hinduism is rather like a large family of practices and beliefs in which there is no central authority or head. As long as all members live under one roof or on the same soil, they accept one another as members of the same family, despite considerable differences among them. When Muslims on Indian soil were perceived as true spiritual seekers and genuinely devout, holy persons, they were accepted as part of the religious family, to be honored as saints.

Later, in the seventeenth and eighteenth centuries, when opposition between Hindus and Muslims grew intense—primarily for political reasons—Hindus often conveniently forgot the Muslim ancestry of some of these saints and in some cases, almost certainly in the case of Dadu, deliberately falsified the historical record to blot out Muslim origins. But the saint was not forgotten or pushed into oblivion, for in Hinduism sainthood essentially has nothing to do with politics or nationality or religious sect; it is simply a matter of holiness and spiritual realization.

Of course, the movement of religious influence was not only from Muslim to Hindu, but also from Hindu to Muslim. Because of the rigid structure and formalism of Islam, however, there was little perceptible change in orthodox Islam. Nevertheless, there was considerable Hindu influence on the lives of individual Sufis and, through them, on the lives of many Indians whom the Sufis converted to Islam. Indeed, Hinduized Muslims had their own caste system and observed Hindu sacraments and holy days along with their observance of the five pillars of Islam. Although it shocked the Muslim orthodoxy, many Hindu converts to Islam, influenced by the culturally inclusive attitude, saw no inconsistency between being a Muslim and observing Hindu practices. It is as though they recognized that both the ultimate reality and the ultimate religious practice go beyond all names and forms, beyond all rules and conventions, and beyond proclamations of doctrine and definitions of orthodoxy.

RELIGION AND POLITICS

This urge toward religious unification was felt even by one of India's greatest rulers, and religious interaction promised to develop at the very center of the imperial court during Akbar's reign (1556–1605). Out of deep personal interest in religion and dissatisfaction with the narrowness of Islam and the continuous theological and juridical haggling of his two chief religious advisers, Akbar invited Muslim mullahs, Hindu pandits, Jaina sadhus, Jewish rabbis, Parsi mobeds, and Jesuit priests to religious discussions in the imperial court.

Although scholars disagree over whether Akbar actually promulgated a new religion, the *Din-i Ilahi,* there is no doubt that he encouraged religious dialogue and openness among people of different faiths and sects. It is also clear that he accepted disciples and that as emperor of India, he saw himself responsible for the well-being of all the people, Hindus, Jainas, and Parsis, as well as Muslims. In this concern, he promulgated decrees against the involuntary cremation of widows, child marriages, and the taking of multiple wives.

But the promise of interaction and unification at the imperial level was unfulfilled because historical forces were against the attempt. Although Akbar's spirit of tolerance and sense of fairness in allowing all classes and creeds to participate in the Mughal administration became a regular part of the Mughal policy—and, by any measure, a great success in political integration and tolerance—the same cannot be said about his efforts to secure religious tolerance and integration.

Part of the reason is that a great Hindu religious revival, initiated by Chaitanya, among others, spread across India and became strongly established at Mathura, almost within earshot of the Mughal court. This had two important effects. On the one hand, it alarmed the orthodox Muslims, for it threatened both their religion and their security and drove them to repudiate the tolerance that they felt had encouraged this revival of Hinduism. This reaction of the conservative Muslims at the imperial court touched off a wave of protectionism and intolerance that threatened to destroy the existing basis for cooperation and mutual toleration between Hindus and Muslims. On the other hand, this strong revival of Hinduism led to a greater pride in Hinduism and a defiance of the felt need to submit to rulers who practiced a foreign faith and who falsely regarded themselves as the only truly religious people.

Half a century after Akbar's death, his grandson, Aurangzeb, began his fifty-year rule as emperor of India. Aurangzeb's reign began in 1658, when he imprisoned his father, Shah Jahan, builder of the beautiful Taj Mahal, and ended with his death in 1707. Aurangzeb's religious policy was almost directly opposite to that of his great-grandfather's. In place of Akbar's emphasis on equality of religions and toleration of all creeds and practices, Aurangzeb insisted that his kingdom was Muslim and that it be governed and administered strictly according to Muslim law. Orders were given to collect the military support tax from non-Muslims, to destroy non-Muslim places of worship, and to prohibit the teachings and practices of the "infidels." He also greatly decreased the scope of service for non-Muslims in his administration.

It is hard to judge to what extent these orders and their subsequent enactment flamed the fires of Hindu political rebellion and encouraged the ongoing Hindu religious revival. But they certainly added to the deepening rift between the Muslim and the Hindu communities that was to eventually make it impossible for them to cooperate to defeat the British, and that later would lead to the carving of the subcontinent into the two separate Muslim states of Pakistan and Bangladesh and the secular, but Hindu-dominated, state of India.

Aurangzeb's reactionary religious policies seem to follow the lines indicated by Shaikh Ahmad's open letters to the Muslim court. Shaikh Ahmad (1564–1624) was a disciple of Khwaja Baqi Billah, who established the Naqshbandi movement in India to exert religious influence on the political rulers. Up to this time the various Islamic spiritual orders in India had not gotten directly involved in purely political affairs. Shaikh Ahmad, following his teacher, believed that everything that involved the well-being and welfare of Muslims was a religious concern. No activity was excluded, of course, and political activity, because of its far-reaching effects, became a central area of religious concern and a target for religious influence.

Unlike Akbar, Ahmad regarded India as a Muslim state. He complained that "non-Muslims carried out aggressively the ordinances of their own religion in a Muslim state and the Muslims were powerless to carry out the ordinances of Islam; if they carried them out, they were executed."[5] Although Ahmad may be referring to only scattered incidents, his observations are rooted in facts that were upsetting to many other orthodox Muslims as well. He complained in other letters that Hindus destroyed Muslim mosques and tombs in order to replace them with temples. He made it clear that he felt that Akbar's imperial policy had weakened the positions of Muslims and had strengthened the position of Hindus. He lamented that "during the sacred month of Ramadan, they [the Hindus] openly prepare and sell food, but owing to the weakness of Islam, nobody can interfere. Alas, the ruler of the country is one of us, but we are so badly off!"

Aurangzeb did attempt to institute Muslim reforms that would strengthen the position of Islam and curb the power and practices of non-Muslims. But the fact that many new Hindu temples were constructed in Bengal in the seventeenth and eighteenth centuries, that Krishna and Kali worship flourished, and that many Hindus were powerful enough to refuse to pay the *jizya* (military support tax) or to negotiate a lower tax rate, suggests that although Muslims ruled India, they by no means controlled the people. And this is understandable, considering the Muslim political principle that so long as non-Muslim communities paid their taxes and did not interfere with the practice of Islam, they should be allowed to manage their own affairs. This meant that throughout most of India, caste organizations and village councils were the real governing powers, almost totally immune from Muslim rule.

The near immunity from the influence of political rule helps to explain how, despite a generally conservative attitude, exciting developments in Indian logic, yoga, metaphysics, and religion occurred under Muslim rule. Lively and imaginative debates and careful study marked the continuing development of philosophy.

REVIEW QUESTIONS

1. How do the five pillars of Islam encompass the faith, action, and spiritual realization that define the way of Islam?

2. What are the three basic attitudes toward religion found among Indian Muslims?

3. What is the proper role of reason in relation to faith, according to Al-Ghazali? Explain your answer in terms of the dispute between Al-Ghazali and Ibn Sina over creation, knowledge, and the soul.

4. How does Ibn Sina argue for love as the basis of life and knowledge?

5. Explain the stages on the Sufi path to God.

6. How do Kabir and Guru Nanak differ? What do they have in common?

FURTHER READING

The House of Islam, 3d ed., by Kenneth Cragg and R. Marston Speight (Belmont, CA: Wadsworth, 1988), is an excellent introduction to the meaning and message of Islam. It combines an emphasis on fundamental ideas and practices with a good sense of historical development.

Muslim Civilization in India, by S.M. Ikram, edited by A. Embree (New York: Columbia University Press, 1964), is a very good general survey of Indian Muslim life, emphasizing the broad cultural and religious dimensions of Islam in India.

The Indian Muslims, by M. Mujeeb (London: Allen and Unwin, 1967), is a comprehensive explanation of the life of Islam in India.

Kabir, by Charlotte Vaudeville (London: Oxford University Press, 1974), is a comprehensive and reliable work on the life and ideas of this great apostle of Hindu-Muslim unity.

Sufis of Bijapur, 1300–1700: Social Roles of Sufis in Medieval India, by Richard Maxwell Eaten (Princeton, NJ: Princeton University Press, 1978), emphasizes the great variety of ideas, attitudes, and practices that characterized Sufi relationships with orthodox Islam (the *Ulama*) and with the Hindus, giving us a rich picture of the Sufi life and influence in India.

A History of Sufism in India, 2 vols., by S.A. Rizvi (Philadelphia: Coronet Books, 1983) is the definitive work on Sufism in India.

Iqbal, Poet-Philosopher of Pakistan, edited by Hafeez Malik (New York: Columbia University Press, 1971), is a collection of essays on Iqbal's life and poetry and contains discussions of his philosophical, religious, and political thought by distinguished authorities in the field. It is probably the best introduction to Iqbal's thought.

"The Faith of the Sikhs," in *The Indian Way,* by John M. Koller, chap. 15, pp. 328–47 (New York: Macmillan, 1982), is a succinct explanation of the fundamentals of Sikh thought.

"The Teachings of Guru Nanak," in *Guru Nanak and the Sikh Religion,* by W.H. McLeod, chap. 5, pp. 148–227 (New York: Oxford University Press, 1968), is an outstanding study of Guru Nanak's thought.

NOTES

1. Quoted in M. Mujeeb, *The Indian Muslims* (London: Allen and Unwin, 1967), p. 146.
2. Ibid., p. 123.
3. Quoted in Tara Chand, *The Influence of Islam on Indian Culture* (Allahabad: Indian Press, 1954), p. 228.
4. *Adi Granth,* p. 1, as quoted by W.H. McLeod in *Guru Nanak and the Sikh Religion* (New York: Oxford University Press, 1968), p. 148.
5. All quotations from Ahmad are from S.M. Ikram, *Muslim Civilization in India* (New York: Columbia University Press, 1964), pp. 171–72.

CHAPTER 10

Continuing Tradition

Throughout the centuries, new ideas and ways of thinking have been introduced into India, catalyzing philosophical thinking. As a result, traditional philosophical positions have been interpreted and reinterpreted in a variety of ways. Modern Western influence provoked a vigorous intellectual response by Indian thinkers and renewal of philosophical activity in the nineteenth and twentieth centuries. This chapter focuses on the thought of four philosophers who typify, each in his own way, the renewal of traditional philosophy in modern India.

Mohandas Gandhi (1869–1948) brought together the traditional values of *ahimsa* (nonhurting) and *satya* (truth) as a basis for social and political thought and action, providing a basis for social reform. His philosophy is a renewal of the ancient vision of *dharma* or moral order. It is informed, however, by his understanding of Christianity and modern Western thought and shaped by his involvement in contemporary political events in South Africa and India.

Aurobindo Ghose (1872–1950) presents a philosophical vision that is based on the ancient Vedic and Yoga traditions but that incorporates his understanding of Western thought, especially the ideas of evolution and progress.

Mohammed Iqbal (1877–1938), national poet of Pakistan, is widely regarded as one of the subcontinent's most profound modern philosophers as well as the greatest Urdu poet of his time.

Sarvepalli Radhakrishnan (1888–1975), late president of India, was essentially a Vedantist of the *Advaita,* or nondual, school. But he was sensitive to and influenced by Western thinkers, especially Kant and Hegel.

GANDHI

Gandhi saw the moral order of the universe as a fundamental dimension of its reality, a part of the eternal truth, discoverable by participation in the processes of everyday existence. Most important for his philosophy were the lessons contained in the two maxims that dominated family and community life in his childhood. The first of these, "There is nothing higher than truth," reflects a wisdom already taught in the *Rig Veda* three thousand years ago, where the normative functioning of existence *(rita)* is regarded as its truth. The second, "*Ahimsa* ('nonhurting'; 'love') is the highest virtue," also incorporates moral wisdom that has shaped the Indian tradition for thousands of years. The Jain community in which Gandhi grew up is noted for its strict adherence to the principle of *ahimsa,* providing an example that made a great impression on young Gandhi.

In his *Autobiography,* Gandhi tells us that Tolstoy's book *The Kingdom of God Is Within You* and Ruskin's *Unto This Last* made lasting impressions on him. Tolstoy convinced him that the Sermon on the Mount represents the essential teachings of Christianity. These teachings, that hatred should be conquered by love, and evil overcome by nonresistance, seemed to Gandhi to echo the Jain, Buddhist, and Hindu teaching of *ahimsa,* which had inspired India's ethical life for thousands of years.

Ruskin's book impressed Gandhi with the dignity of manual work, and it reinforced the *Gita's* teaching that the highest life is a life of service, helping him to see that the fulfillment of both the individual and society are to be achieved through one's chosen work. Here also, as Ruskin pointed out, lies a natural bond between educated and peasant classes, a bond that needed to be formed to give India unity in its efforts to achieve freedom.

Gandhi's use of "truthfastness" *(satyagraha)* as a means of active, but nonviolent, resistance to British rule was based on the conviction that all evils could be conquered by love if one adheres firmly to the truth. But to adhere to the truth and apply love to the injustices of the world is an extremely difficult challenge, as Gandhi clearly saw.

According to Gandhi, the reason for our ability to overcome the difficulties of this challenge is that we, along with all other beings, are enveloped by truth, and move according to its power. This is implied, he says, by the first verse of the *Isha Upanishad,* which declares: "All this, whatever moves and changes in this changing world is enveloped by the Lord." This is the basis of the principle of "truthfastness" *(satyagraha),* for holding fast to the truth expressed in the divine law of existence means acting in accord with one's own nature and purpose, and at the same time acting in accord with the nature and purpose of all other beings.

Although Gandhi recognized that the truth from which all existence issues is present in every being, he also recognized that it is obscured by ignorance and vice. Self-purification, self-sacrifice, and critical reflection are needed to realize this inner truth.

For Gandhi, Truth is the God that dwells in all beings, and love is the soulforce by which they move. The word Gandhi used for love was *ahimsa,* which, as we have seen, literally means nonhurting. But he recognized that this negative sense of the word was too narrow to express his meaning, explaining that he was using the term in its broadest sense to refer to a pure and perfect love. This is a love that expresses itself in kindness, compassion, and selfless service to others.

This broader sense of *ahimsa* underlies Gandhi's abhorrence of violence. Violence is an expression of fear and anger, growing out of weakness that only calls forth more violence. Love, however, calls forth love, which explains why Gandhi was completely convinced that the truth and love expressed in nonviolent resistance to wrongdoing was bound to succeed.

AUROBINDO

Sri Aurobindo, the great philosopher-yogi of Pondicherry, gained his initial fame as a leader of a Bengal revolutionary group advocating violent overthrow of British rule. After a brief term of imprisonment for conspiring to overthrow the government, however, he abandoned revolutionary politics in order to devote himself to revolutionizing the life of the Spirit. This led him into explorations of metaphysics and social philosophy. It also led to an intense life-long involvement in yoga and meditation.

Emphasizing the spirituality of human existence, Sri Aurobindo identified the greatest problem of our times as the problem of how to transform our present lowly and ignorant condition into the greatness of which human beings are capable. To this end, he worked out a theory of social organization based on the traditional ideals contained in the theories of *purusharthas, varnas,* and *ashramas.* His major works, *The Life Divine* and *Synthesis of Yoga,* are attempts to show the type of life we can achieve by a total and comprehensive discipline, or *yoga.* The "life divine" is, of course, the life lived in full realization of *Brahman,* and *yoga* is the chief means to this life. Sri Aurobindo emphasizes that *yoga* must be practiced by people in their present condition as a means of changing this condition, for therein lies the secret of transformation into ideal human being.

Aurobindo's conception of the task of philosophy and the nature of reality is indicated in the following statement:

> The problem of thought therefore is to find out the right idea and the right way of harmony; to restate the ancient and eternal spiritual truth of the Self, so that it shall re-embrace, permeate and dominate the mental and physical life; to develop the most profound and vital methods of psychological self-discipline and self-development so that the mental and physical life of man may express the spiritual life of man through the utmost possible expansion of its own richness, power and complexity; and to seek for the means and motives by which his external life, his society and his institutions may remold themselves progressively in the truth of the spirit and develop towards the utmost possible harmony of individual freedom and social unity.[1]

According to this view, the reality constituted by things and selves is the manifested power of the Spirit. Spirit provides the unity of reality, and the manifested power of Spirit provides the manifoldness of the universe. The various levels of existence—matter, life, mental life, supramental life—are distinguished insofar as the fullness of spirit emerges through these manifestations of its powers.

The main problem for Aurobindo is that of explaining how all the many things experienced—both at the conscious level of the empirical and rational, and at the supraconscious level of mystic intuition—came to be, and why they are different. His solution is to explain that the absolute existence that makes it possible for anything whatsoever to exist is itself pure existence, complete, and perfect. This existence—*Brahman*—for no reason whatsoever, simply out of the sheer exuberance of its being, manifests its *maya,* or power, in the manner of creative play. The manifestations of this power constitute the universe of existing things. The universe exists, therefore, as the creative play of pure existence. But it is not simply capricious, for this play is directed by the Being-Consciousness-Joy *(sat-chit-ananda)* that constitutes the absolute Spirit of the universe. The evolution of the universe as a whole and of particular species within the universe is seen as the returning of the manifested powers of *Brahman* to their source. As these powers move toward their source, evolution moves to higher and higher forms of life and consciousness.

According to this explanation, the differences between levels of reality are due to the evolution of Spirit. As the Spirit evolves, higher life-forms come into existence. But this is not the evolution of one kind of thing to another kind of thing, such as matter becoming Spirit. Rather, it is the evolution of one thing—Spirit—from its many lower forms and manifestations to its higher forms, the aim being to reach the fullness of being, consciousness, and joy that constitutes Spirit.

The usual problems attending evolutionary accounts of existence, the problem of blind matter groping impossibly to evolve beyond itself, into something quite other than itself, and the problem of blind matter being lifted beyond itself by some other reality without any effort on its own part, do not arise for Aurobindo. According to his explanation, the lower is ever evolving into the higher, but these are not absolutely different. The higher is making itself felt in the lower, and the lower is struggling to express itself according to the higher laws of the Spirit within, and this is the mutual effort that constitutes the play of *Brahman* manifesting itself through its powers, but always remaining *Brahman.*

Seeing evolution as involving the mutual activity of both the lower and higher forms of Spirit has important consequences for human life, for it means not only that it is possible to evolve to a higher kind of being, but also that we can, at least in part, direct this evolution. The aim of human experience—in its self-consciousness higher than the existence of matter and nonconscious life-forms—is not to remain at its present level, but to transcend itself, moving on to higher levels of existence just as previously lower levels of existence have moved up to the level of human existence. This is possible, Aurobindo points out,

> for the evolution proceeded in past by the upsurging, at each critical state, of a concealed power from its evolution in the inconscient, but also by a descent from above, from its own plane, of that power already self-realized in its own higher natural province.[2]

How are human beings to direct their own evolution? Aurobindo's answer is that we must practice self-discipline (*yoga*) that is all-inclusive, not ignoring any part of our being. We must integrate the various aspects and faculties of our being so that the lower comes under the control and direction of the higher, allowing us to gradually come to live according to the laws of the spirit dwelling within us, at the very center of our being. This requires, among other things, the material and social conditions that will enable people in their present state successfully to reach beyond themselves, elevating their existence until it becomes the "Life Divine."

In his social philosophy, Aurobindo argued that justice and freedom are to be provided for and guaranteed by society as necessary conditions for the higher evolution of humanity. His view of the purpose of society is

> first to provide the conditions of life and growth by which individual Man—not isolated men according to their capacity—and the race through the growth of its individuals, may travel towards its divine perfection. It must be secondly, as mankind generally more and more grows near to some figure of it—for the cycles are many and each cycle has its own figure of the Divine in man—to express in the general life of mankind, the light, the power, the beauty, the harmony, the joy of the Self that has been attained and that pours itself out in a freer and nobler humanity.[3]

IQBAL

Mohammed Iqbal, lawyer, philosopher, and world-renowned poet, was one of the leaders of the twentieth-century Muslim renaissance and India's independence movement. (The division of the subcontinent of India into the two separate countries of India and Pakistan did not occur until 1947.) His two most important philosophical works, *The Reconstruction of Religious Thought* (prose) and *The Secrets of the Self* (poetry), reveal that although he was influenced by Western thought (particularly by Kant, Fichte, Bergson, Hegel, and Nietzsche), Iqbal was deeply inspired by traditional Islamic thought.

His exposure to the best and the worst of life in both India and Europe left Iqbal with a strong desire to understand and address the problems of life in modern society. Political oppression under British rule in India was clearly a major problem, but Iqbal recognized the oppression of poverty and the oppression of the spirit by life-negating ideas as equally serious problems. Where will we get the strength to overcome the political and ideological oppression responsible for India's major problems? What principles will guide the human struggle to regain our freedom and dignity? These are the questions Iqbal put to himself, to the people of India, and to the world.

Although he is remembered largely for his poetry and philosophy, his political contributions were also significant. In 1930, he formally enunciated the theory of two nations, calling for the creation of a separate nation for the Muslims of Bengal and northwest India. In 1937, just a year before his death, he persuaded Jinnah, the founder of Pakistan, to insist on a separate Muslim state.

But his greatest influence on politics and society in India—and later, in Pakistan—came through his poetry and philosophy, which were a source of hope and confidence among the masses. It is hard to separate Iqbal's poetry and philosophy. Many of his most profound insights came through poetic intuition and are powerfully expressed in verses known to hundreds of millions of people in India and Pakistan.

Iqbal's most significant philosophical contribution was his reinterpretation of religion. According to him, only religion can reach the profound truth at the very core of life, and therefore only religion can guide the effort of the individual and society to realize the full human potential.

At the core of Iqbal's understanding of religion is a vision of the self-affirmation of the individual *(khudi).* A person's individuality is sacred, never to be given up or subordinated to some supposedly higher, universal reality. Rather, it is precisely one's individuality that the religious way seeks to realize more and more fully. Thus, he describes the ultimate aim of religious life as "the reconstruction of the finite ego by bringing him into contact with an eternal life-process, and thus giving him a metaphysical status of which we can have only a partial understanding in the half-choking atmosphere of our present environment."[4]

Iqbal's view of the individual is clearly opposed to the view that devalues the individual in favor of some supposedly higher abstract reality, requiring renunciation of self and the world and resignation to the sufferings of life. According to Iqbal, this latter view dominated life in India. His own view, he says, "is opposed to . . . all forms of pantheistic Sufism which regard absorption in a universal life or soul as the final aim and salvation of man."[5] His view is, of course, equally opposed to pantheistic Vedanta and the Hindu view that *moksha,* liberation from the ego's participation in life and society, is the highest aim of religion.

Iqbal sees the main function of religion to be the nurturing and fulfilling of the ego's potential. He says, "The moral and religious ideal of man is not self-negation but self-affirmation, and he attains to this ideal by becoming more and more individual, more and more unique."[6]

According to Iqbal, the main problem of modern society is that personal and social life is not lived in accord with the fullness of the individual. To solve this problem, it is necessary to replace life-negating religious ideas with an affirmative view of the individual and the world. Science, however, cannot provide this affirmative view because the full reality of the individual goes beyond the reaches of conceptual thought. The modern world, dominated by the rule of reason, fails to recognize the full reality of individual beings. Instead, it regards the individual merely as a class member, as a type that functions according to a conceptual classification.

Like everything else that is real, religious life is also a living process with its own stages of growth. In the first stage, which he labels the stage of Faith, the emphasis is on obedience to divine command. Here life is disciplined in accord with the demands of faith without concern for understanding the ultimate meaning and purpose of these demands. In the second stage, the stage of Thought, the emphasis is on achieving a rational understanding of the demands and authority of faith. At this stage, science, theology, and philosophy provide a rational foundation and interpretation of faith. The third stage of religious life, the stage of Discovery, is its mature stage. This stage is characterized by the discovery of the ultimate source of the divine command within the depths of one's own being. Here, Iqbal says, "religion becomes a matter of personal assimilation of life and power; and the individual achieves a free personality, not by releasing himself from the fetters of the law, but by discovering the ultimate source of the law within the depths of his own consciousness."[7]

Because religion in its highest form, the third stage of Discovery, is the path to the realization of the fullness of being, it takes precedence over politics, economics, science, and philosophy. In its second stage, that of Thought, the intellectual tools and resources of the sciences and philosophy are properly used in the service of religion. Despite its importance for self-preservation and growth, however, intellectual understanding is too limited to guide human beings into their full growth, into the perfection of which they are capable. According to Iqbal:

> Infinity is not amenable to our intellect,
> "One" in its hand becomes a thousand,
> As it is lame, it likes rest [immobility];
> It does not see the kernel; therefore it looks toward the shell.[8]

Intellectual understanding, however, must be incorporated in a deeper understanding at stage three. Here, at the level of self-discovery, thought proceeds beyond the limits of merely logical understanding. Here, the self directly encounters itself in its many-faceted, concrete individuality, in its deepest levels. In describing the discovery that characterizes the third stage of religious life, Iqbal says:

> Strictly speaking, the experience which leads to this discovery is not a conceptually manageable intellectual fact; it is a vital fact . . . which cannot be captured in the net of logical categories. It can embody itself only in a world-making or world-shaking act; and in this form alone the content of this timeless experience can diffuse itself in the time-moment, and make itself effectively visible to the eye of history.[9]

For Iqbal, God is the ultimate source of value, through the creative action of the individual. Only through creative action can the individual and society be infused with the divine energy that sustains all things. A verse from a poem entitled "God's Talk with Humans" proclaims the greatness of human deeds by comparing them to the acts of God:

> You created the night—I lit the lamp
> You created clay—I molded the cup.
> You made the wilderness, mountains and forests
> I cultivated flower-beds, parks and gardens.[10]

In the last analysis, according to Iqbal, it is what the individual does that matters; the fullness of being that religion seeks can be attained only through one's own efforts. A couplet from his greatest work, *Asrar-i Khudi (Secrets of the Self),* reveals his conviction that individual effort is the key to success:

A whole ocean, if gained by begging, is but a sea of fire;
Sweet is a little dew gathered by one's own hand.[11]

RADHAKRISHNAN

Sarvepalli Radhakrishnan, the recent president of India, wrote many philosophical articles and books. By and large, he can be classified as a Vedantin, like Shankara. He agrees with Shankara that the empirical is not the ultimate reality, but he is aware that just as the criteria of logic and experience demand that philosophy admit an ultimate reality, so also do they require inclusion of the empirical and practical. For him there is no inconsistency in a philosopher actively participating in social and political affairs, for these are *appearances* of Brahman, and thus they are means to be utilized in the effort to achieve the experience of the ultimate reality.

One of Radhakrishnan's main projects was to work out a satisfactory philosophy of religion. The task of a philosophy of religion is to develop a theory of the nature of things in the world, selves, and the ultimate ground of things and selves that will explain the interrelations between these three realities. This theory must account for the facts of religious experience and at the same time accommodate reason. Granted rational consistency, the theory must have its basis in religious experience itself. The experience and statements of religious persons must be explained—not repudiated or ignored—by a philosophy of religion.

Radhakrishnan sees theology, dogma, ritual, and institutions as secondary, not the essence of religion. The essence of religion is the attempt to discover the ideal possibilities of human life. This quest is personal and necessarily involves the whole person. Experience that involves merely an aspect of a person, such as feeling, thinking, or volition, is not religious. What distinguishes religious experience from aesthetics, science, philosophy, and morals is that these are guided primarily by feeling, reason, and volition, respectively. Religion includes feeling, reason, and volition, but it goes beyond them to the innermost center of the person, to the very source of these aspects of humanity, integrating these faculties and directing them from the wholeness that is their source, using this wholeness to transform the life of the person into something complete and whole. The substance and essence of religion, according to Radhakrishnan, is experience of the life of the Spirit as it joins together self and other in a whole that is complete and perfect.

Although a philosopher of religion could hardly proceed except by giving primacy to religious experience—that is, by considering the data of religious experience to be the basic material out of which one fashions a theory of religion—to do so is exceedingly complicated because of the great difficulty in describing religious experience. Religious experience is unlike the ordinary experience that provides the foundations for thinking and talking about ourselves and the reality around us. Ordinary experience presupposes that the something experienced is always distinct from the experiencer; that the subject is never the object, and vice versa. But in religious experience, subject and object are integrated; there is nothing outside of the unified experience. Radhakrishnan explains religious experience as follows:

It is a type of experience which is not clearly differentiated into a subject-object state, an integral, undivided consciousness in which not merely this or that side of man's nature but his whole being seems to find itself. It is a condition of consciousness in which feelings are fused, ideas melt into one another, boundaries broken and ordinary distinctions transcended. Past and present fade away in a sense of timeless being. Consciousness and being are therefore not different from each other. All being is consciousness and all consciousness being. Thought and reality coalesce and a creative merging of subject and object results. Life grows conscious of its incredible depths. In this fullness of felt life and freedom, the distinction of the knower and the known disappears. The privacy of the individual self is broken and invaded by a universal self which the individual feels as his own.[12]

Granted this view of religion and religious experience, what theory of selves, things, and ultimate reality will serve to adequately accommodate, in a rationally acceptable way, the facts of religion? If the ultimate reality, *Brahman,* is taken to be alone real, it is difficult to see how religion is possible, for the self striving to realize *Brahman* would have to be regarded as unreal. And without a self striving to achieve ultimate reality, there can be no religion. If, however, selves and *Brahman* are taken to be distinct and different realities, it is difficult to see how the self could ever successfully identify itself with *Brahman,* without self-repudiation or self-annihilation.

Radhakrishnan's solution to this dilemma is to interpret *Brahman* not as static but as dynamic being. *Brahman* is the absolute reality, providing the ground of all existence and giving the universe unity. All things are united in *Brahman,* which is the source and ground of all being. As the source and ground of all being, *Brahman* is ever active, by its function expressing its substantial nature. It is this functioning of *Brahman,* which is the expression of its being, that manifests itself in the various things and processes that make up the universe of selves and things. Thus, things and selves are not unreal, for they are the expression of *Brahman's* functions. But as expressions of *Brahman,* they are not totally distinct and separate from *Brahman* either.

This explanation provides for distinctions between individual things and selves, for the functions of *Brahman* are dynamic, ever new. Since no one of *Brahman's* functions (nor any one aspect of the functioning of *Brahman*) totally exhausts the nature of *Brahman,* any given expression of *Brahman's* function lacks the total reality of *Brahman* wherein all functions and all expressions of those functions are united.

Radhakrishnan regards the self as the locus where *Brahman,* as absolute Spirit, and the world, as the functioning of this absolute Spirit, come together, for the person combines Spirit with matter. He makes this point by distinguishing between the empirical or lower self and the higher or spiritual Self, which in its purity is one with the absolute Spirit. The essence of the religious quest is interpreted to be the lower self striving to return to its source in the higher Self.

In explaining the relations between selves and things, and both of these to *Brahman,* Radhakrishnan abandons the static view of reality, according to which the world is thought to be made up of a great many independent beings or substances, each attended to by a greater or lesser number of characteristics or qualities. Instead, he views the world as constituted by processes. The structure of reality is not due to the relations that qualities have to their substances, but to the inner structure of the activities making up reality. Thus, the world is essentially dynamic, with all of the various processes interconnected.

To explain the diverse structures found in the processes corresponding to the various gradations of existence, Radhakrishnan postulates unceasing activity of the absolute Spirit. Spirit is the source and ground of all the various grades of existence encountered on the empirical level. But these various distinctions do not imply absolute differences; they merely serve to mark out modes of spiritual activity. Even matter, finally, is spiritual activity. It is merely a different mode of the Spirit than consciousness or life. But regardless of the mode of manifestation, Spirit means Spirit, and insofar as it is Spirit, there is no denial of its reality. The various grades of matter and life are real because they are expressions of *Brahman,* the absolute Spirit. But no one mode in itself is the totality of *Brahman,* and no single mode can be equated with the absolute reality.

The main purpose of religion is to help a person rise above the limits imposed by matter, life, and consciousness—to realize that the innermost self is identical with the absolute Spirit, completely free from the limitations inherent in identification with simply one particular mode or function of Spirit. This realization is possible only in terms of practical activity—an activity of being rather than knowledge. It is the spiritual realization of Uddalaka's teaching to his son, Shvetaketu, "Thou art that *[Brahman],*" in the *Chandogya Upanishad,* according to Radhakrishnan.

REVIEW QUESTIONS

1. What are the fundamental principles of Gandhi's philosophy? How do they figure in his lifestyle and his role in Indian life?
2. How would you defend Gandhi's principle of nonviolence? What do you see as the weaknesses of nonviolence as the basis of social and political action?
3. How would you defend Aurobindo's view of the ideal life? What are your main objections to this view?
4. What are the three stages of religious life, according to Iqbal? Do you agree?
5. What is Radhakrishnan's view of religion? How does he distinguish between the externals and the essence of religion? Is he right?

FURTHER READING

Probably the best way to begin a study of Gandhi is to see the 1982 film *Gandhi,* directed by Richard A. Attenborough (distributed by Columbia Pictures). It shows the unity of thought and action in Gandhi's life, the primacy of *ahimsa* and truthfastness in his thought, and his identity with the people of India.

The Philosophy of Mahatma Gandhi, by Dhirendra Mohan Datta (Madison: University of Wisconsin Press, 1953), is an excellent book with which to begin. Small and nontechnical, it conveys the essentials of Gandhi's philosophy, whetting the appetite for more detailed studies, such as *The Moral and Political Thought of Mahatma Gandhi,* by Raghavan N. Iyer (New York: Oxford University Press, 1973). Gandhi's autobiography is available under the title, *The Story of My Experiments with Truth,* in many editions.

The Mind of Light, by Sri Aurobindo, introduction by Robert A. McDermott (New York: E.P. Dutton, 1971), is an excellent, brief introduction to Aurobindo's thought.

The Life Divine, The Synthesis of Yoga, and *The Human Cycle* contain Aurobindo's most significant writings. They are available in various editions, easily obtainable almost anywhere in the world.

The Secrets of the Self (a translation of *Asrar-i Khudi*), by Muhammad Iqbal, translated by R.A. Nicholson (Lahore: Muhammad Ashraf, 1961), is Iqbal's major collection of verse dealing with the self, originally published in 1915.

Iqbal: Poet-Philosopher of Pakistan, edited by Hafeez Malik (New York: Columbia University Press, 1971), is a collection of first-rate essays on Iqbal by a variety of scholars. It contains four essays on philosophy and three on Islamic mysticism.

Radhakrishnan: A Religious Biography, by Robert N. Minor (Albany: State University of New York Press, 1987), is a very useful biography that chronicles the development of Radhakrishnan's understanding of religion. It contains an excellent bibliography and a full list of Radhakrishnan's writings.

The Philosophy of Sarvepalli Radhakrishnan, edited by Paul Arthur Schlipp (New York: Library of Living Philosophers, 1952), contains essays on Radhakrishnan's philosophy by distinguished philosophers and a reply by Radhakrishnan to his critics.

Radhakrishnan: Centenary Volume, edited by G. Parthasarathi and D.P. Chattopadhyaya (Delhi: Oxford University Press, 1989), is a collection of papers by international scholars presented in a seminar commemorating the birth of Radhakrishnan.

NOTES

1. *Arya,* July 15, 1918, pp. 764–65; reprinted in Sarvepalli Radhakrishnan and Charles A. Moore, eds., *A Sourcebook in Indian Philosophy* (Princeton, NJ: Princeton University Press, 1957), p. 577.
2. Sri Aurobindo, *The Life Divine,* p. 853, reprinted in *A Sourcebook in Indian Philosophy,* p. 604.
3. Sri Aurobindo, *The Human Cycle* (Pondicherry: Sri Aurobindo Ashram, 1962), pp. 83–84.
4. From the essay "Is Religion Possible?" in *Reconstruction of Religious Thought* (London: Oxford University Press, 1954), reprinted in John M. Koller and Patricia Koller, *Sourcebook in Asian Philosophy* (New York: Macmillan, 1991), p. 153.
5. Mohammed Iqbal, *The Secrets of the Self,* translated by R.A. Nicholson (Lahore: Muhammed Ashraf, 1961), p. xviii.

6. Ibid., pp. xxiii, 57–58.
7. In Koller and Koller, *Sourcebook in Asian Philosophy,* p. 145.
8. From *Gulshan-i Raz-i Jadid,* p. 23, as quoted by B.A. Dar, in Malik, *Iqbal,* p. 200.
9. In Koller and Koller, *Sourcebook in Asian Philosophy,* p. 147.
10. Quoted by N.P. Anikeyev in Malik, *Iqbal,* p. 274.
11. Iqbal, *Secrets,* pp. 39–42. Quoted by N.P. Anikeyev in Malik, *Iqbal,* p. 272.
12. Ibid., pp. 617–18.

PART II

BUDDHIST PHILOSOPHIES

Buddha. (Asia Society, New York: Mr. and Mrs. John D. Rockefeller 3rd Collection. Photo by Lynton Gardiner)

BUDDHIST CHRONOLOGY

BCE	**Events and Thinkers**
600–400	Siddhartha Gautama, the Buddha (563–483); first Buddhist Council (483)
400–200	Second Buddhist Council (383); King Ashok (r. 269–232) supports Buddhism; Alexander invades India; Buddhism enters Sri Lanka; Third Buddhist Council (240)
200–0	Beginnings of Mahayana Buddhism; Theravada Buddhism established as state religion in Sri Lanka (101–77); Pali canon written down in Sri Lanka (25–17)
CE	
0–200	Buddhism enters Central Asia and China first century. Sarvastivada tradition develops; Nagarjuna born; Perfection of Wisdom tradition reaches high point; Madhyamaka begins as a correction of Sarvastivada.
200–400	Nalanda University founded; Buddhism goes to Burma, Cambodia, Laos, and Indonesia; Buddhism enters Korea
400–600	Asanga and Vasubandhu develop the Yogacara; Candrakirti develops Madhyamaka; Bodhidharma goes to China (520); Chinese Buddhism develops T'ien T'ai, Hua Yen, Ch'an, and Pure Land schools
600–800	Buddhism enters Japan; the golden Buddhist age in China; Padmasambhava brings Buddhism to Tibet (760); Saicho (767–822) founds Tendai in Japan; Kukai (774–835) founds Shingon in Japan
800–1000	Persecutions of Buddhism in China (845); first Chinese Buddhist canon printed
1000–1200	Atisha initiates new Buddhist developments in Tibet; Son develops in Korea under Chinul; Honen establishes Jodo-shu in Japan; Rinzai flourishes under Eiasai
1200–1400	Nalanda destroyed by Muslim armies; end of Buddhism in India; Dogen (1200–1253) establishes Soto Zen in Japan; Tibetan canon compiled; Tsong kha pa (1357–1419) in Tibet; Theravada becomes state religion of Thailand (1327)
1400–1600	Beginning of Dalai Lama lineage
1600–1800	Buddhism is state religion of Japan during Tokugawa (1603–1867); Dalai Lamas begin ruling Tibet (1617)
1800–2000	Buddhism enters the West (Pali Text Society founded 1881); Dalai Lama forced to flee Tibet (1959); Buddhism decimated in Cambodia (1975); Thich Nhat Hanh establishes Plum Village monastery in France

CHAPTER 11

Historical Perspectives

The Buddhist tradition began in India, in approximately 528 BCE, with the enlightenment of Siddhartha Gautama (563–483 BCE). After his enlightenment, he was known as the Buddha (the "Enlightened One") because he had awakened to the truth of suffering *(duhkha)*, its causes, and the way to eliminate suffering by removing its causes. His way of understanding and overcoming suffering, presented in the Buddha's first teaching in the Deer Park at Sarnath, caught on quickly. By the time of his death in 483 BCE, it had already spread throughout the kingdoms of Magadha and Kosala. Within a few hundred years, especially under the patronage of King Ashoka (who ruled 269–232 BCE), Buddhism had spread throughout the Indian subcontinent and beyond. Ashoka had provided the model for later Buddhist missionary efforts that successfully spread Buddhism throughout all of Asia by 700 CE.

CENTRAL TEACHING

The central teaching of Buddhism is contained in the Noble Fourfold Truth presented by the Buddha in his first teaching after attaining enlightenment. According to the first part of this fourfold truth, life as it is usually lived is *duhkha,* profoundly unsatisfactory.

But according to the second part of the Noble Fourfold Truth, the Buddha saw that *duhkha* arises because of ignorance about existence. What the Buddha saw was the truth that existence is dynamic, ever-changing, consisting of interrelated processes. But if the very nature of existence is change, then the crav-

137

ing for permanence will inevitably be frustrated. And if the nature of existence is interrelatedness, then the craving for separateness will also be inevitably frustrating. This insight leads to the third part of the Noble Fourfold Truth, that giving up craving for separate and permanent existence will eliminate *duhkha*.

The fourth part of the Noble Fourfold Truth constituting the central teaching of Buddhism is the practical way of eliminating the ignorance and selfish grasping that causes *duhkha*. This eightfold path to the elimination of *duhkha* consists in the acquisition of right views and wholesome intentions, moral practice (right speech, right actions, and right livelihood), and meditative practice (right effort, mindfulness, and concentration).

INDIA AT THE TIME OF THE BUDDHA

What was India like twenty-five hundred years ago, during the Buddha's lifetime? The answer to this question provides a sense of the various influences that shaped the Buddha's life and teachings. Overall, India was one of the world's great civilizations at this time. It was a civilization with a rich culture, advanced science and technology, sophisticated intellectual traditions, and flourishing industry and trade. A major social transformation from agrarian life to urban trade and manufacture was underway in India at this time, leading to a questioning of the old values, ideas, and institutions. Without a doubt, the Buddha grew up in intellectually exciting times, with stimulating discussions about new ideas an important part of daily life.

From a religious perspective, new ways of faith and practice challenged the older, established religions. The main concern dominating Indian thought and practice at the time of the Buddha was the problem of suffering and death. Fear of death was an especially acute problem in India, because death was seen as an unending series of deaths and rebirths. Although the Buddha's solution to the problem of suffering was unique, most religious seekers at the time of the Buddha were engaged in the search for a way to obtain freedom from suffering and repeated death.

Philosophically, the quest for liberation from suffering and death led to reflection on the nature of self, action, and knowledge, resulting in an atmosphere that encouraged critical discussion, producing a great variety of philosophical views. What most of these views had in common was a tendency to seek an absolute ground of self and reality, an unchangeable foundation of truth and certainty. There was a sense that a unified, unchanging self—a self beyond the ever-changing mental and physical processes ordinarily experienced as self—was needed to account for human experience. There was also a sense that an independent, permanent reality—a reality beyond the conditioned flux ordinarily experienced as reality—was needed to account for the objectivity of the world. Without any absolute self or reality, it was feared that there would be no ground for truth or values. And without truth or values life would be meaningless. Thus, for most thinkers at the time of the Buddha, the choice appeared to be either to accept that self and reality were grounded in some absolute reality, beyond suffering and death, or to admit that the problem of suffering and death has no solution. The Buddha was unique among Indian thinkers in seeing a middle way that would solve the problem of suffering and death without postulating any absolutes.

AFTER THE BUDDHA

Although the oldest available written Buddhist texts are relatively late, tradition assures us that the texts known as *Nikayas* contain an early and reliable record of the Buddha's actual teachings, for immediately after the Buddha's death a council of monks was called in order to recall and collect his teachings. These basic Buddhist texts reflect the experience and vision of the historical Buddha as he engaged in his own quest for freedom from the restrictions and sufferings experienced in life. The Buddha's quest for freedom belongs to a tradition already hundreds of years old at this time, as do the meditative techniques constituting the foundation of this quest. But genuinely new were the Buddha's way of appropriating these meditative techniques, his way of integrating them with morality and wisdom, and his vision of existence as interdependently arising.

In the historical development of Buddhist thought, there was continuous interaction both with the older visions of life and meditative traditions that had influenced the Buddha and with other new visions and ways of life. These interactions provided much of the stimulus for the analysis and reasoning that shaped the Buddhist philosophical tradition. It was natural that questions of interpretation and orthodoxy should arise after the Buddha's death, because during his lifetime he established neither criteria for interpreting his teachings nor bases for defining orthodoxy in the practice of these teachings. Even on his deathbed, in about 483 BCE, he refused to appoint a leader to succeed him. Instead, he advised the assembled monks, "let the teaching *(dharma* [P: *dhamma])* be your teacher," and "be diligent in your efforts."

It was natural for the Buddha's followers to emphasize those aspects of the Buddha's teachings that they found most helpful. They also interpreted the Buddha's teachings in different ways, following their own experiences and reflections. So it is not surprising that despite general agreement on the central teachings and main practices, many different versions of the teachings and practice developed.

It should also be emphasized, however, that despite their differences, monks from the different traditions often lived together in the same monastery and engaged in the same practices during the early centuries. What the monks had in common far outweighed the differences among the traditions with which they were affiliated.

MAHAYANA AND THERAVADA

The major split in Buddhism, that between the Theravada and Mahayana traditions, occurred some three to five hundred years after the death of the Buddha. Historians are unsure of what caused the split, or precisely when it occurred. Most likely it was a gradual process that occurred sometime between 200 BCE and 100 CE. By the second century, there was already a significant Mahayana lit-

Historical Sketch of the Early Development of Buddhist Schools

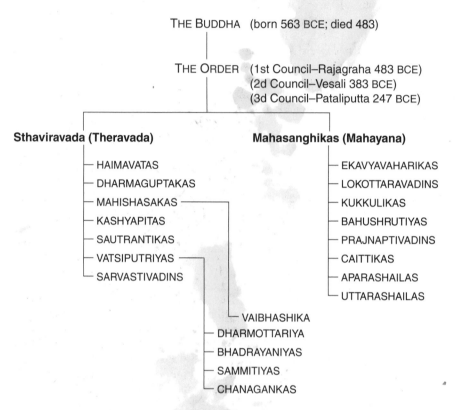

THE BUDDHA (born 563 BCE; died 483)

THE ORDER (1st Council–Rajagraha 483 BCE)
(2d Council–Vesali 383 BCE)
(3d Council–Pataliputta 247 BCE)

Sthaviravada (Theravada)

— HAIMAVATAS
— DHARMAGUPTAKAS
— MAHISHASAKAS
— KASHYAPITAS
— SAUTRANTIKAS
— VATSIPUTRIYAS
— SARVASTIVADINS

Mahasanghikas (Mahayana)

— EKAVYAVAHARIKAS
— LOKOTTARAVADINS
— KUKKULIKAS
— BAHUSHRUTIYAS
— PRAJNAPTIVADINS
— CAITTIKAS
— APARASHAILAS
— UTTARASHAILAS

— VAIBHASHIKA
— DHARMOTTARIYA
— BHADRAYANIYAS
— SAMMITIYAS
— CHANAGANKAS

erature, some of which clearly expressed a sense of superiority over the Theravada tradition.

The Mahayana initially developed in India but then spread to Central Asia, Tibet, and China. From China, it spread to Korea, Vietnam, and Japan, bringing most of East Asia under its influence. Although there are significant differences between Mahayana and Theravada Buddhism, they share much in common, namely, their commitment to the central teaching of the Noble Fourfold Truth and the Noble Eightfold Path; their emphasis on establishing mindfulness as the heart of their practice; and their acceptance of the Buddha, the teaching, and the community as the triple refuge of practice.

Differences Between Mahayana and Theravada

The major differences between Mahayana and Theravada can be categorized according to their answers to seven important questions: (1) Who is the Buddha? (2) Which are the essential teachings? (3) Who is a member of the Buddhist community? (4) At what ideal should one aim? (5) What path should one follow? (6) In what does one have faith? (7) What is the nature of reality?

The Buddha. According to Theravada, the Buddha is first and foremost the historical person Siddhartha Gautama, who achieved enlightenment in the sixth century BCE. Mahayana, in contrast, emphasized the timeless nature of Buddha as the in-dwelling truth and enlightenment of reality. Siddhartha, the historical Buddha of our era, is merely one of innumerable manifestations of the eternal Buddha, according to Mahayana.

Essential Teachings. The Theravada scriptures emphasize the instructions given by the historical Buddha regarding the Way and its practice (as recalled and recited by trusted senior monks shortly after the Buddha's death) as the essential teachings. Mahayana accepted the Theravada scriptures as authentic but placed much greater emphasis on the Buddha's teaching by example, stressing, for instance, the importance of compassion as shown by his efforts to alleviate the suffering of all beings after his enlightenment. Furthermore, seeing the Buddha as the timeless embodiment of truth and enlightenment, Mahayana saw the teachings as being presented in different forms at different times according to the needs of the people. In this vein, the Mahayanists created a whole new literature, embodying the essential teachings of the way to enlightenment, suited to the needs and circumstances of the new age, some 200 to 600 years after the historical Buddha's death. They did not claim, however, that they had created these new scriptures; rather, they attributed them to the historical Buddha, claiming that they had been lost and now were recovered. By claiming this new literature as the actual teachings of the historical Buddha, the Mahayanists were able to claim the same authentic status for these writings that the Theravada claimed for their scriptures.

Buddhist Community. Early Buddhism and the continuing Theravada tradition regarded the monastic community of monks and nuns as the primary members of the Buddhist community. Laypersons were considered inferior, incapable of attaining nirvana. Mahayana elevated the status of laypersons, regarding them as fully capable of attaining enlightenment.

Ideals. The ideal at which Theravada aimed was that of an *Arhant,* a person worthy, because of personal attainment, of attaining the ultimate goal of nirvana, the complete elimination of suffering. To the Mahayana, this ideal seemed small and selfish. Looking to the example of the Buddha, they declared that the ideal at which Buddhists should aim is that of becoming a *Bodhisattva,* an enlightened being dedicated to ending the suffering of all others.

The Path. The Theravada emphasized the practice of morality, meditation, and knowledge, constituting the Noble Eightfold Path as the way leading to the overcoming of suffering by the practitioner. While the Mahayana also accepted the Noble Eightfold Path as the way to this goal, they reformulated it as the path of the *paramitas,* the surpassing virtues that will carry all beings beyond the world of suffering. The six surpassing virtues *(paramitas)* are generosity, morality, patience, vigor, meditation, and wisdom.

Faith. In early Buddhism and among the Theravada, Buddhists had faith in the Buddha, the truth of his teachings, and the power of the community to help one progress on the path. To this, the Mahayana added a host of celestial beings who had attained sovereignty over the world. In the devotional practices dedicated to these celestial beings, often faith in, and devotion to, one of these Buddhas or Bodhisattvas was regarded as sufficient to attain the final goal of nirvana.

Reality. Although both Theravada and Mahayana saw interdependent arising to be the true nature of reality, Mahayana philosophers emphasized the "emptiness" *(sunyata)* of all things and persons, whereas the Theravada thinkers emphasized the reality of what was experienced in profound meditative insight as the ultimate truth.

Analysis of these seven differences reveals that the Mahayana did not reject the basic teachings and practices of the Theravada; rather, they added practices and teachings that provided a new emphasis on becoming Buddha-like.

PHILOSOPHICAL TRADITIONS

From the perspective of practice, the major Buddhist division was into Theravada and Mahayana. From a philosophical perspective, however, the rise of the Sarvastivada, Madhyamaka, and Yogacara philosophies was the major development. It should be emphasized that these philosophical traditions were never divorced from the practice traditions.

The basic Buddhist teachings of *duhkha,* no-self, impermanence, and *nirvana,* or enlightenment, encapsulated the Buddhist understanding of the Middle Way, as taught by the Buddha, and gave rise to a number of philosophical problems. One group of problems pertains to the self: (1) If there is no self, then who experiences *duhkha* and who experiences nirvana? (2) If the impermanence of existence means that there are no permanent beings, then what reason is there to think that the same person who at one time experiences *duhkha* can, at another time, experience nirvana? (3) If existence is simply the interrelated functioning of the groups of existence, without a self, then what holds these groups together and gives them continuity? (4) How, in the face of the denial of a self that can be reborn, can rebirth take place? (5) If a self is denied, then what sense does it make to ascribe moral responsibility to a person?

Another group of problems pertains to external reality: (1) If things are said to lack being, then are not the things themselves denied? (2) If all things lack being, then how can the Buddha's existence be real? (3) Unless real beings are admitted, how can there be causes and effects? (4) Without causes and effects, how can there be causal transformation, including the transformation from *duhkha* to nirvana that practicing the Noble Eightfold Path is supposed to achieve?

A third group of problems concerns knowledge: (1) How, if the reality of both self and things is denied, can there be knowledge? (2) But without knowledge, how can the ignorance that causes *duhkha* be overcome? (3) If the knowledge that destroys ignorance is said to be immediate, nondual knowledge, then what role does conceptual knowledge play in overcoming ignorance? (4) If conceptual knowledge is regarded as incapable of grasping the true nature of reality, then is it completely irrelevant to insight and transformation? (5) If conceptual knowledge is relevant, how is it relevant and what is the relation between conceptual understanding and the meditative knowledge that liberates one from *duhkha?*

The three major Buddhist philosophies, Sarvastivada, Madhyamaka, and Yogacara, answered these questions differently and gave different reasons for their answers. Sarvastivada held that although self and ordinary things are unreal because they are constructions, the ultimate units out of which they are constructed, the *dharmas,* are ultimately real, not dependent on or reducible to anything else. Madhyamaka analysis showed that Sarvastivada claims about *dharmas* as independently existing realities were inconsistent and incoherent. Arguing that reality at every level is empty *(sunya)* of separateness and permanence, Madhyamaka insisted that interdependent arising is the true nature of reality. Yogacara accepted the Madhyamaka analysis of existence but focused on the nature and functions of consciousness in the process of attaining liberating knowledge.

Sarvastivada

The Sarvastivadins were a strong philosophical force in northwest India from the first to the ninth centuries, excelling in their development of Abhidharma philosophy, a rigorous metaphysical analysis of the phenomena of experience. Disagreements, particularly over the comparative importance of the *sutras* (P: *suttas*), the core teachings regarded as containing the Buddha's own words, and *abhidharma* analysis, and over how past and future exist in the present moment, resulted in the emergence of the Sautrantika and the Vaibhasika as the two main branches of Sarvastivada thought. But after the ninth century, Sarvastivada declined in importance and gradually disappeared as a living tradition. Today, as has been the case for hundreds of years, there are no Sautrantikas or Vaibhasikas.

Madhyamaka

The Middle Way philosophy called Madhyamaka argues for a view of reality as interdependent process, constantly changing, a view that is midway between existence and nonexistence. The Sarvastivada claim that the essences of things *(dharmas)* had independent existence was already rejected by the new wisdom *(Prajnaparamita)* texts that began appearing shortly before the beginning of the common era. But it was Nagarjuna, the founder and principal philosopher of the Madhyamaka tradition, who launched a devastating attack against the essentialism of the Sarvastivada philosophy early in the second century CE. His analysis was accepted by the entire later Mahayana tradition and underlies the

Mahayana repudiation of the Sarvastivada claim that *dharmas* have inherent, independent existence and that they possess unique defining characteristics.

Madhyamaka is best known for its teaching that reality is empty *(shunya)* of separateness and permanence. Clearly, one of the principal aims of the teaching of *shunyata* (emptiness), a teaching set out clearly in Nagarjuna's main work and a hallmark of Mahayana thought, is to establish that because *interdependent arising* is the very nature of existence, it makes no sense to postulate self-existing, self-defining *dharmas* as the ultimate kinds of existence.

The Madhyamaka philosophy continues to shape Tibetan Buddhist thought and practice to this day and is an important part of the curriculum in Tibetan Buddhist universities. Absorbed in the T'ien T'ai and Hua-yen Chinese Buddhist traditions, Madhyamaka became an important foundation of Ch'an thought and practice, spreading to Korea, Japan, and Vietnam, where it continues to be an important influence.

Yogacara

The origins of the Yogacara School are obscure, though tradition regards a third-century thinker by the name of Maitreyanatha as the founder. Yogacara was likely already several centuries old by the time it reached its definitive formulation by the brothers Asanga and Vasubandhu in the fourth century.

Asanga's fame, first in India, then later in China and Tibet, was secured by his monumental work *Stages of Yoga Practice (Yogacarabhumi),* sometimes attributed to Maitreyanatha. Asanga refuted the charge that emptiness *(shunyata)* was a nihilistic teaching and established that it provided a basis for Buddhist practice by distinguishing between the three natures of things. First, there is what the mind imposes on things as it attempts to know them. This is the mentally constructed and illusory nature, recognized by the wise to be empty of intrinsic reality. The second nature refers to the relative nature of things as dependent on one another and on mind. When this nature is recognized, things are seen to be relatively real (although devoid of separate and independent reality). Finally, the third nature, the absolute perfection of things, is precisely their interdependent existence, seen with the eye of wisdom when the meditational insight of yoga practice has gone beyond all conceptual dualities. In the chapter on knowledge, Asanga explains how the different kinds of knowledge correspond to the three natures of things, offering a bridge between rational knowledge and the wisdom of meditational insight that sees things just as they are.

Vasubandhu, a great Sautrantika thinker and expert in abhidharma, was converted from Sarvastivada to Yogacara by his brother Asanga, probably in the late fourth century. His summary of Sarvastivada in *A Treasury of Metaphysics* is the principal surviving source for study of the Sarvastivada. His *Twenty Verses with Commentary (Vimsatika Karika)* is one of Vasubandhu's later works, and it reveals him at his philosophical best, vigorously advancing his own views and refuting those of his opponents. Although frequently interpreted as a work advocating philosophical idealism, the text itself makes no claims that the things of the world are the creations of consciousness. Rather, it argues against the assumption that we can adopt a perspective beyond our actual experience, emphasizing that whatever is experienced is known only to the extent that it affects consciousness in some way at some level. The *Thirty Verses (Trimsika Karika)* is Vasubandhu's famous attempt to relate the motivating dispositions to the six stages of consciousness that evolve from the seed consciousness.

BUDDHISM IN CHINA

Buddhism arrived in China during the first century, but its main development began in the fourth century, and its full flowering occurred during the Sui and T'ang dynasties (589–906 CE). Indeed, Buddhism proved so attractive to the Chinese that it became the dominant Chinese way of thought in the Sui and T'ang Dynasties (589–906), temporarily eclipsing both Confucianism and Taoism.

Although all of the various schools of Indian Buddhism found their way to China, it was the Madhyamaka and Yogacara traditions of Mahayana that eventually provided the basis for the Chinese transformation of Buddhism into the highly successful Hua-yen, Fa-hsiang, T'ien-t'ai, and Ch'an schools. Middle Way thought was introduced to China by Kumarajiva, who arrived in Ch'ang-an from his native Kucha in 402. Kumarajiva, assisted by a large team of scholars, translated most of the important Sanskrit Mahayana texts into Chinese. One of the most creative Chinese developments of Buddhism was to transform the idea of *shunyata* (emptiness), the core idea of Middle Way thought, from what appeared to be an essentially negative idea, namely, the denial of separateness and permanence to beings, into an essentially positive notion, namely, the omnipresence of Buddha-hood as the true reality of all things, realizable when separation and permanence were overcome.

The Chinese acceptance of Buddhism from the fourth century onwards occurred at a time when political and military disarray, the near collapse of traditional Confucian norms and virtues, and the Neo-Taoist attitude of retreat and seclusion from public life combined to create a kind of spiritual vacuum. The Mahayana Buddhism that attracted the Chinese glorified the ideal of Buddhahood, assuring the faithful that they already possessed the beginnings of this perfected condition of being. Furthermore, by accepting the help of innumerable celestial and heavenly Bodhisattvas, who for countless eons have been working tirelessly in all the regions of this vast universe, they too could attain Buddha-hood.

BUDDHISM IN KOREA AND JAPAN

All of the Chinese Buddhist traditions were brought to Korea beginning in the fourth century, but they became an important cultural force only in the seventh century, in part because of the prodigious efforts of the great Korean Buddhist scholar Wonhyo (617–686 CE). Ch'an, the most influential tradition, was probably brought to Korea, where it is known as Son, by Pomnang in the middle of the seventh century. But it was Chinul (1158–1210) who established the Chogye-chong school of Son as Korea's dominant Buddhist tradition.

Buddhism came to Japan from Korea in the early seventh century, and from the late seventh century on, directly from China as well. Ch'an, known in Japan as Zen, also became the dominant form of Buddhism in Japan, penetrating deeply into its culture, especially from the time of the great Zen master Dogen (1200–1253). But other Chinese Buddhist traditions were also influential. Tendai (T'ien-t'ai), established at Mount Hiei by Saicho (767–822), was dominant during the Heian period (794–1185). Shingon, the tantric tradition of Chen-yen, brought back from China by Kobo Daishi (774–835), was also important during the Heian period. Later, Honen (1133–1212), attempting a reform, broke from the Tendai tradition to establish the extremely popular Pure Land Buddhism in Japan. Tendai also gave rise to the Nichiren school, founded by Nichiren (1222–1282) as a reform movement aimed at saving the nation through a return to "true Buddhism." In both Korea and Japan, as in China, Mahayana forms of Buddhism dominated, and the underlying philosophy was provided by the Madhyamaka and Yogacara traditions.

BUDDHISM IN THE WEST

Although the West had encountered and had been influenced by Buddhism in previous centuries, it was only in the twentieth century that Buddhism became a living presence in Europe and the Americas. While Zen has captured the most attention, various other forms of Chinese and Japanese Buddhism are also now practiced in the West. More recently, various Tibetan and Southeast Asian Buddhist traditions have also taken hold in the West. As they mature, most of these traditions take on the characteristics of the culture in which they are practiced, producing, for example, a uniquely American Zen.

REVIEW QUESTIONS

1. What concerns dominated religious and philosophical thought in the Buddha's time?
2. What is the central teaching of Buddhism?
3. What are the main differences between Mahayana and Theravada Buddhism?
4. What are the three main philosophical traditions that developed in India, and what are the main differences between them?
5. What are the main Buddhist traditions that developed in China, and how do they differ from one another?

FURTHER READING

A Concise History of Buddhism, 2d ed., by Andrew Skilton (Birmingham, England: Windhorse Publications, 1997), is a well-informed and highly readable history of Buddhism containing a good bibliography on Buddhist history.

A Concise Encyclopedia of Buddhism, by John Powers (Oxford: Oneworld Publications, 2000), is a well-organized digest of important information about almost every facet of Buddhism, and it has a good, though brief, bibliography.

A History of Buddhist Philosophy, by David J. Kalupahana (Honolulu: University of Hawaii Press, 1992), is an excellent historical introduction to Buddhism. The first half deals with the history of early Buddhism from a philosophical perspective. The second half deals with the development of the Mahayana, with special attention to Nagarjuna, Vasubandhu, and Dignaga.

A History of Indian Buddhism from Sakyamuni to Early Mahayana, by Hirakawa Akira (Honolulu: University of Hawaii Press, 1990), focuses on the first five centuries of Indian Buddhism.

Theravada Buddhism: A Social History from Ancient Benares to Modern Colombo, by Richard F. Gombrich (London and New York: Routledge & Kegan Paul, 1988), explains the early development of Buddhism in India and Sri Lanka.

An Introduction to Buddhist Thought: A Philosophic History of Indian Buddhism, by Arthur L. Herman (Lanham, MD: University Press of America, 1983), provides a good philosophical overview, set up in problem-solving terms.

Mahayana Buddhism: The Doctrinal Foundations, by Paul Williams (London and New York: Routledge & Kegan Paul, 1989), is probably the best introduction to the development of Mahayana thought.

Buddhism in China, by Kenneth Ch'en (Princeton, NJ: Princeton University Press, 1964), is the standard history of Chinese Buddhism. The same author's *The Chinese Transformation of Buddhism* (Princeton, NJ: Princeton University Press, 1973) is probably the best explanation of the transformations that Buddhism underwent in China.

The Awakening of the West: The Encounter of Buddhism and Western Culture, by Stephen Batchelor (Berkeley, CA: Parallax Press, 1994), is a highly readable history of Western encounters with Buddhism.

The History and Culture of Buddhism in Korea, edited by the Korean Buddhist Research Institute (Chae, Taeg-su) (Seoul: Dongguk University Press, 1993), is the best book available on Korean Buddhism.

The Korean Approaches to Zen: The Collected Works of Chinul, by Robert Evans Buswell Jr. (Honolulu: University of Hawaii, 1983), contains an excellent early history of Korean Buddhism.

CHAPTER 12

The Life and Teachings of the Buddha

Buddhism is a way of life that provides freedom from the deepest forms of human suffering. Sometimes the Buddhist way of life is interpreted as a religious way, a quest for salvation predicated on faith in the Buddha and his teachings. Others deny that Buddhism is a religion, claiming that it is a philosophy of life, emphasizing human insight and effort. Perhaps instead of insisting that it be exclusively one or the other, it should be recognized that in Asia, where Buddhism originated and has been practiced for twenty-five hundred years, religion and philosophy are not seen as separate and opposed activities. Rather, they are viewed as components of a total way of life aimed at achieving the greatest possible human perfection. Buddhism has always been regarded by its practitioners as a way of life, specifically, a way of life based on the life and teachings of its founder, Siddhartha Gautama, the Buddha. This chapter focuses on the Buddha's life and on his basic teachings, because they provide the core of the Buddhist way of life and the foundation for further Buddhist developments.

THE BUDDHA

We begin with the question, Who was the Buddha? This is an important question because not only was the Buddha the founder of Buddhism, but his life exemplified the Buddhist way of life. The Buddha's example of how to practice the way leading from suffering to enlightenment and peace has inspired Buddhists everywhere. Indeed, his example has been regarded as the core of his teaching, fully

148

as important as his teaching through words. As exemplar, the Buddha showed the world how to practice the Noble Eightfold Path, which combines moral conduct, mental discipline, and wisdom. This path, the path of right view, right intention, right speech, right action, right livelihood, right mindfulness, right effort, and right concentration, constitutes the core of the Buddhist way of life.

According to a widely accepted tradition, the person who became the Buddha, Siddhartha Gautama, was born in 563 BCE at Kapilavastu in what is today Nepal. Shielded by his father from the distressing scenes of suffering to be found all around, Siddhartha led the easy pleasure-filled life of a prince of leisure until he was twenty-nine years old. Then, encountering the suffering of old age, sickness, and death, he began to reflect deeply on the unsatisfactoriness of life as it is usually lived.

The Four Signs

The experiences that set Siddhartha off on his quest for a way of life that would eliminate suffering is recorded in the legend of the four signs. The first three signs that the Buddha-to-be encountered were an old man, a sick man, and a corpse. These were signs of suffering in three of its many forms. The fourth sign was a recluse, at peace with himself and happy. This was a sign of the possibility of life free from suffering.

First Sign. According to the legend of the four signs, the young prince, who had been protected from the sights and sounds of human suffering for the first twenty-nine years of his life, was out riding in his chariot one day when he saw an old man, "bent like a roof-beam, broken, leaning on a stick, tottering, sick, his youth all vanished."[1]

Upon seeing this old man, Siddhartha asked his charioteer why this man was not like other men. The driver told him that it was because this man was old. According to the legend, Siddhartha did not understand what this meant because he had never had any experience with old age. The driver patiently explained that being old meant that this man could hardly function, that he was nearly finished, that he was soon to die. As understanding of old age began to trouble his spirit, Siddhartha asked his driver, "But am I too liable to become old, and not exempt from old age?" The answer that startled and upset Siddhartha was, "Both you and I, Prince, are liable to become old, and are not exempt from old age."

Deeply disturbed at the prospect of everyone, himself included, having to endure life in the miserable condition of the decrepit old man he had just seen, Siddhartha returned to the palace. How, he wondered, can anyone find happiness in the comforts and gaiety of palace life knowing how temporary they are? The suffering of old age lies in wait for everyone.

Second Sign. Many days later, Siddhartha was once again setting out for the park, when he encountered "a sick man, suffering, very ill, fallen in his own urine and excrement, and some people were picking him up and others putting him to bed." Upon seeing this sick man, Siddhartha asked his chariot driver what this man had done that he was not like other men. The driver explained that the man was ill, and that this meant that he was not far from being finished, that he might not recover.

Wondering whether the sick man he had seen was a rare exception or whether everyone becomes ill, Siddhartha asked again,

> But am I too liable to become sick, and not exempt from sickness?

The answer that sent him back to his palace reflecting on the suffering of illness was,

> Both you and I, Prince, are liable to become sick, and not exempt from sickness.

Back at the palace Siddhartha thought to himself,

> I too am subject to sickness and cannot escape it. If I, who am subject to sickness without escape from it, should see another who is sick, and should be oppressed, beset, and sickened, it would not be well with me.[2]

Third Sign.   Some days later, when Siddhartha was again driving to the park, he saw "a large crowd collecting, clad in many colors, and carrying a funeral bier." Curious about this extraordinary scene, he asked his chariot driver what these people were doing. Upon being told that a man had died, Siddhartha asked to view the corpse in order to see this thing called "death."

Distressed by this sight, he asked for an explanation. His driver explained that death meant that this person's life was over and that the remains would be burned on the funeral pyre. Siddhartha now asked,

> But am I too then subject to dying, not exempt from dying?

The driver's answer was that death, like old age and illness, afflicts everyone:

> Both you and I, Prince, are subject to dying, not exempt from it.

Reflecting on this encounter with death, Siddhartha thought to himself:

> I, too, am subject to death, and cannot escape it. If I, who am subject to death without escape from it, should see another one who is dead, and should be oppressed, beset, sickened, it would not be well with me.[3]

Fourth Sign.   Sometime later, after reflecting on the suffering that old age, illness, and death bring to all human beings, Siddhartha was once again driving to the park. On the way he saw a shaven-headed man, a recluse, wearing a yellow robe, looking contented and at peace with himself. Wondering how despite the presence of old age, illness, and death, this man could be free of suffering, Siddhartha asked his driver what sort of person this was. Upon learning that this recluse is one who is said to have "gone forth," Siddhartha was curious to learn what this meant. Approaching the recluse, he asked,

"You, master, what have you done that your head is not as other men's heads, nor your clothes as those of other men?"

"I, my lord, am one who has gone forth."

"What, master, does that mean?"

"It means, my lord, being thorough in the life of truth, thorough in the peaceful life, thorough in good actions, thorough in meritorious conduct, thorough in not harming, thorough in compassion to all living beings."[4]

Reflecting on his encounter with the contented recluse who had freed himself from suffering, Siddhartha realized that suffering is not inevitable, that it is possible to live a life of peace and contentment, free from suffering, despite the inevitability of sickness, old age, and death. He now decided that he, too, would go forth on a religious quest, seeking to discover a way to eliminate life's sufferings. He told his chariot driver to return to the palace, saying:

But I shall stay here and shave off my hair and beard, put on the yellow robes, and go forth from the household life into homelessness.

Moved by compassion and stirred by the recluse's example, Siddhartha left his palaces and family in order to become a recluse. For the next six years, he devoted himself to the search for a way of overcoming suffering.

Symbolic Meaning of the Four Signs

Before going on to examine the Buddha's quest for enlightenment, a word about the legend of his encounter with the four signs is in order. Are we to believe that he had never encountered an old person or a sick person? Surely he himself had been sick occasionally, and undoubtedly other people that he knew had also been sick. And even though it is possible that for twenty-nine years he had been protected from the sight of a dead person, it is hardly possible that he had never seen an old person. Most likely the truth of the legend of the four signs is symbolic rather than literal. In the first place, they may symbolize existential crises in Siddhartha's life occasioned by experiences with sickness, old age, death, and renunciation. More important, these four signs symbolize his coming to understand the true reality of sickness, old age, death, and contentment.

The legend of the four signs tells us that the Buddha came to a deep and profound understanding of the reality of sickness, old age, and death as forms of human suffering. The legend also tells us that he came to understand that suffering is not inevitable, that peace and contentment are possible despite the fact that everyone experiences old age, sickness, and death.

QUEST FOR ENLIGHTENMENT

For the next six years Siddhartha lived the life of a seeker of truth, free from the pursuit of pleasures, from family duties, from social responsibilities, and from political concerns. What did Siddhartha do during these six years of truth-seeking?

What ways did he follow? What methods and techniques did he employ? What truth did he experience? While we have no detailed account of Siddhartha's life during these six years, we know that he tried the leading ways of spiritual transformation available in his society, seeking out the most highly esteemed teachers of his day.

Practice of *Yoga*

First Siddhartha sought out the famous *yoga* teacher Arada Kalama, with whom he studied until he had attained the same level of meditational attainment as his teacher, the level described as the attainment of nothingness. But when Siddhartha reflected on these yogic accomplishments, he realized that he was seeking something more. Although the trance described as nothingness provided temporary relief from suffering, it did not bring the knowledge, peace, and well-being that he sought. Arada's way produced only a temporary trance that blocked the awareness of suffering through the suspension of consciousness. But Siddhartha was seeking a conscious understanding of life that would *eliminate* suffering; he sought a continuing sense of well-being and inner peace through increased awareness. To temporarily suspend awareness, as Arada taught, was not an adequate solution to Siddhartha's problem.

Having found his first teacher's way unacceptable, Siddhartha then turned to a second teacher, Udraka Ramaputra. Udraka's yogic practice led to a state that is described as "neither conscious nor unconscious." When he had attained this state in his own practice, Siddhartha realized that this too was merely a temporary suspension of awareness that did not illumine suffering, its conditions, and the way to eliminate suffering. Udraka's way was also inadequate; it was not the way to knowledge that would bring peace through the elimination of suffering.

Practice of Asceticism

Having tried the way of yogic meditation as practiced by two of its most illustrious teachers, Siddhartha then decided to try the other highly acclaimed religious way of his time, that of asceticism. Through extreme forms of self-mortification, he disciplined his body, hoping to control and eliminate the passions that the ascetic way regarded as the source of human suffering.

Finding that he could not eliminate the feelings in his body through stopping the breath, Siddhartha decided to starve the body, eating no more than a handful of food per day. Even though he nearly died from lack of food, however, Siddhartha discovered that he could not eliminate his feelings by starving the body.

Reflecting on the fact that he had carried the practice of asceticism to its furthest extreme, Siddhartha realized that the way of asceticism did not calm the passions, did not produce knowledge and insight, and did not lead to peace and well-being. Like the extreme of indulgence in pleasures that he had tried as a young man, the extreme of ascetic self-mortification was an extreme to be avoided. It was time to try a middle way.

Finding a Middle Way

Having tried the ways of the most famous teachers of his day, and having found them inadequate, Siddhartha realized that he would have to find his own way to solve the problem of suffering. Taking what was of value from each of the ways he had tried, Siddhartha resolved to follow a "middle way." Knowing how to focus his consciousness and how to observe his feelings, and no longer afraid of the happiness that is not coupled with evil and depravity, the Buddha-to-be practiced a form of reflective meditation in which he investigated the arising of suffering in life, its conditions, and the way to remove these conditions.

Enlightenment

Unlike the meditation of his teachers, which merely led to a temporary state in which all awareness disappeared, Siddhartha's meditation proceeded beyond the focusing and quieting of the mind. With passions calmed, mind focused and alert, he reflected on his existence, seeing deeply into the various conditions that had shaped his life. The insight, the meditative knowledge he acquired through this reflection, was that a person's life is not self-contained and unchanging at its core. Rather, human life is a continuous process of change, rising and falling through interdependence with numerous other processes. This insight into existence as a continuous process of change as a result of interaction with other processes became one of the most important teachings of Buddhism. Known as *interdependent arising (pratitya samutpada* [P: *paticca samuppada]),* this was the key insight of the Buddha's enlightenment, providing him with a basis for understanding what suffering is, how it arises, and how it can be eliminated.

Continuing with his reflective meditation, the Buddha saw that although a person has no control over most of the factors that shape life, those factors that can be controlled are of great significance. The important insight he attained through this reflection was that the immediate conditions that produce suffering are thoughts, words, and actions motivated by the selfishness embodied in greed and hatred. Focusing his energies, he saw deeply into the dispositional conditions that give rise to greed and hatred and saw how to eliminate these conditions.

As he eliminated his own greed and hatred by removing their dispositional conditions, he saw how selfish greed and hatred can be controlled and transformed. By controlling and transforming one's greedy and hateful thoughts, words, and actions into thoughts, words, and actions of compassion and love, suffering can be overcome. This insight into the moral dimension of action provided the foundation for the Buddha's emphasis on morality and discipline in the Noble Eightfold Path he taught for overcoming suffering.

The Buddha's enlightenment had provided insight into interdependent arising, the ever-changing, interrelated nature of existence, and into how ignorance of this truth gives rise to the dispositional influxes that produce greed and hatred, thereby producing suffering. As the Buddha reflected on the knowledge he had attained through meditational insight, he realized that this knowledge was experiential and direct. As the Buddha, in concluding his first public teaching after enlightenment, said about what he had experienced,

> This suffering, as a noble truth, has been fully understood.... This origin of suffering, as a noble truth, has been abandoned.... This cessation of suffering, as a noble truth, has been realized.... This Path leading to the cessation of suffering, as a noble truth, has been followed: such was the vision, the knowledge, the wisdom, the science, the light, that arose in me with regard to things not heard before.[5]

Unlike a set of beliefs rooted in faith, or a set of "facts" derived from theoretical assumptions, or a philosophical view justified by subtle reasoning, no claims of universal or eternal truth could be made for the Buddha's experiential knowledge. In contrast, the claims of truth that are based on faith, on theories, or on philosophical views provide no real guarantee: beliefs vanish when faith is lost; so-called facts become merely mistaken claims when new theories are embraced; and philosophical views have to be abandoned when undermined by new reasonings. The truth of the Buddha's knowledge, while restricted to the experiential context, was solidly grounded in experience. Furthermore, because the Buddha was a human being, what he had experienced can be experienced by any other human being who attains the requisite discipline, moral purity, and wisdom.

The Buddha's Optimism

Before turning to the Buddha's teaching of the way, we need to consider two questions that are frequently raised about his starting point and the experiential basis of the way that he taught. His starting point was his recognition of the pervasiveness of suffering in human life and his determination to find a way to eliminate this suffering. Was the Buddha's preoccupation with suffering unduly pessimistic? Why not be more optimistic and focus on life's happiness, even though some suffering is inevitably mixed in with the happiness?

In truth, the Buddha was not a pessimist at all, but an optimist. Although he certainly encouraged efforts to reduce suffering, his solution to the problem of suffering was much more radical and optimistic. He was convinced that life could be lived without suffering, that suffering could actually be eliminated, not merely reduced. Indeed, the way to a joyous and peaceful life that he taught is one of the most optimistic teachings that the world has ever heard.

What was the basis for the Buddha's optimism? In presenting his teachings on the way of overcoming suffering, the Buddha repeatedly insisted that these teachings were based on his experience. It was not because of what he had heard, nor because of faith, nor because of some theory, that he knew that suffering could be overcome. Rather, it was because of his own experience of overcoming suffering that he *knew* that it could be overcome. Furthermore, his experience showed him *how* it could be overcome. Thus, the basis for the Buddha's optimistic teaching was experiential; he himself had experienced both the truth and the way he taught. Furthermore, the joy and peace that he had experienced could be experienced by anyone else who chose to practice the way that he taught.

THE BUDDHA'S TEACHINGS

After his enlightenment, in approximately 528 BCE, Siddhartha, now called the Buddha (the "Enlightened One") by his followers, devoted his life to teaching the way of overcoming suffering that he had discovered. These teachings, in simplest form, consist in the Noble Fourfold Truth and the Noble Eightfold Path. During its twenty-five hundred year history, Buddhism has undergone many changes. But in all of the different forms of Buddhism that have developed, the teaching of the Noble Fourfold Truth and the Noble Eightfold Path has always been the heart of Buddhism.

The Noble Fourfold Truth taught by the Buddha in his first sermon, delivered in the Deer Park at Banaras shortly after his enlightenment, has four components:

1. The truth of what suffering *(duhkha)* is;
2. The truth of the conditioned arising of suffering;
3. The truth that suffering can be eliminated by eliminating its conditions; and
4. The truth that the way to remove the conditions that give rise to suffering is to follow the Middle Way, constituted by the Noble Eightfold Path.

This fourfold truth is called "noble" *(arya),* meaning that it is worthy of assent and respect because it is supremely valuable in the human effort to understand and eliminate suffering. In describing the Noble Fourfold Truth as the teaching of the Middle Path, the Buddha emphasized its value, saying that "it gives vision, it gives knowledge, and it leads to calm, to insight, to enlightenment, to *Nibbana [Nirvana]*."[6]

The First Noble Truth

Having given a general description of the Middle Path, the Buddha went on to explain each component of the Noble Fourfold Truth that constituted the Middle Path. Concerning the truth of suffering, he said,

> The Noble Truth of Suffering *(duhkha)* is this: birth is suffering; aging is suffering; sickness is suffering; death is suffering; sorrow and lamentation, pain, grief and despair are suffering; association with the unpleasant is suffering; dissociation from the pleasant is suffering; not to get what one wants is suffering—in brief, the five aggregates of attachment are suffering.

Because the way of life taught by the Buddha, the Noble Eightfold Path, is essentially a remedy designed to cure the fundamental human illness of *duhkha,* it is important to understand the truth of suffering. To this point, we have been using the standard translation of *duhkha* as suffering. But the Buddhist conception of *duhkha* goes well beyond the ordinary meaning of suffering, as is clear from the inclusion of birth as suffering, as well as from the statement that "the five aggregates of attachment are suffering." Indeed, as the following analysis shows, ordinary suffering is only the first, and shallowest, meaning of *duhkha*.

Duhkha has a deeper meaning of "unsatisfactoriness," as for example when it is used to refer to a wheel's worn-out axle hole, a condition that enables the wheel to function only poorly, if at all. If the true nature of existence is that of interrelated and constantly changing processes, then the usual human attempt to achieve a separate and permanent existence for oneself is totally at odds with reality. The deepest meaning of *duhkha* is the inability to live well when at odds with the truth of interdependent arising. In order to avoid the temptation to think of *duhkha* only as ordinary suffering, I will frequently leave the word untranslated.

Looking at the Buddha's description of *duhkha* in terms of traditional Buddhist understanding, we see that birth, the arising of existence, is equated with aging and death as a form of *duhkha*. Old age and death are easily understood as forms of suffering. But how is birth a form of suffering? When Buddhists think of birth as suffering, they do not deny that the arising of life is a joyous event. Rather, they see that the joyous event of birth also has the form of suffering in two ways. First, the act of birth not only involves the mother's suffering, but is painful and traumatic for the infant as well. Second, Buddhists view birth and death as part of a beginningless cycle, where each birth is followed by death and rebirth.

After identifying birth, aging, and death as forms of suffering, the Buddha went on to say that "sorrow and lamentation, pain, grief and despair are suffering." "Sorrow" refers to the feelings that arise from misfortune and loss as well as the worry and anxiety that one feels when anticipating loss and misfortune. "Lamentation" refers to the expression of sorrow through crying and self-pity. "Pain" refers to the hurt and pain experienced in one's body. "Grief," in contrast to pain, refers to mental hurt and anguish. "Despair" refers to the distress and desperation one feels in extreme loss or misfortune.

The next forms of suffering identified by the Buddha are "association with the unpleasant, dissociation from the pleasant," and "not to get what one wants." This statement has two meanings, an obvious meaning and a deeper meaning. The deeper meaning shows that beings are caught up in the cycle of rebirth and re-death. They find their unpleasant association with this cycle a form of suffering.

What did the Buddha mean when he concluded his description of suffering by saying, "in brief, the five aggregates of attachment are suffering"? This is the most profound part of the statement. It reflects an important distinction between the kind of being we usually take ourselves to be and the kind of being we really are. Most people think of themselves in terms of a continuous, permanent self that has certain physical and mental characteristics that are constantly changing. Not only do most people think that the core of their being is an unchanging self, but they think that this self is separate, not only from other beings, but also from their own body and mind.

The Buddha regarded this kind of thinking as ignorance. In truth, there is no existence that is either permanent or separate. All existence is of the nature of interdependent arising; all things are constantly changing and interrelated with all other forms of existence. Looking carefully at what a person is, the Buddha found no separate and permanent self; he discovered only five interrelated groups of processes:

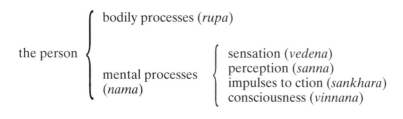

1. *Physical processes,* giving all kinds of bodies their solidity, their liquidity, their ability to transform various kinds of energy, and their ability to move and act.
2. *Processes of sensation,* producing pleasant, unpleasant, and neutral feelings.
3. *Perceptual processes,* which produce perceptions of material and mental objects through the senses and the mind.
4. *Volitional processes,* producing impulses to action that enable a person to act in the world.
5. *Processes of consciousness,* which enable one to be aware of the presence of various objects.

A person is simply the interrelated functioning of these five groups of constantly changing processes. Nowhere is there found a separate and unchanging self to whom the processes belong. But in their ignorance, people construct a separate and permanent self to which they attempt to attach the material and mental processes constituting these five groups. This is why they are called attachment groups. They are the most basic form of suffering because the attempt to create and maintain a separate and permanent self through attachment to the five groups of processes is doomed to failure. Body and mind are constantly changing processes that are interrelated with other processes; a separate and permanent self can never be found through attachment to constantly changing, interrelated processes. Attachment can only produce suffering.

Furthermore, attachment to the various pleasures of life ensures that the desire for these pleasures will be not only self-perpetuating, but also self-accelerating. Deriving pleasure from an activity or object to which one is attached does not diminish the drive for that pleasure, but rather serves to strengthen the drive. The more pleasures one achieves, the more are sought. This cycle goes on unendingly, catching one up in its increasing tempo, with no escape. Granted that attachment to pleasure does not bring fulfillment and contentment, but rather leaves one even more dissatisfied and unhappy, it is clear that grasping at the pleasures of life ultimately increases suffering.

This does not mean that a person should not care about anything, or that a follower of the Buddha should not engage in worldly action. It means, rather, that there should be no attachment of a separate and permanent self to the various groups of existence. Putting it slightly differently, the *Dhammapada*'s advice is to detach oneself from the mistaken belief that there is a separate and permanent self. Without the craving for a separate and permanent self, attachment to the groups of existence is impossible.

Thus, there are three levels of *duhkha*. At the first level is the ordinary suffering of pain and sorrow associated with birth, sickness, death, the presence of the unpleasant, the absence of the pleasant, separation from loved ones, and unsatisfied desires.

At the second level, it is the resistance to change that characterizes the experience of suffering. Even the pleasant and happy moments in life are only temporary, eventually giving way to unhappiness and suffering. Knowing that friendship can turn into enmity; that good health can quickly be replaced by illness; and that life itself will sooner or later give way to death, the joys of life, health, and friendship are tinged with the sorrow of their temporariness.

The third level of suffering, underlying and giving rise to the first two levels of suffering, is the attachment of a self to the processes of existence. What the Buddha awakened to was the truth that existence consists of interrelated processes. Nothing exists separately, by itself, and nothing is permanent. When this became clear to him, then it also became clear that *duhkha* is the human attempt to construct and maintain a separate and unchanging self that goes against the very nature of existence and is therefore doomed to frustration. Attachment of a self to the groups of existence is a futile effort to achieve separate and permanent existence. This is the deepest level of *duhkha,* underlying and giving rise to all the forms of suffering.

The Second Noble Truth

In explaining the conditioned arising of suffering, the Buddha said,

> The Noble Truth of the origin of suffering is this: It is this "thirst" (craving; *trishna*) which produces re-existence and re-becoming, bound up with passionate greed. It finds fresh delight now here and now there, namely, thirst for sense-pleasures; thirst for existence and becoming; and thirst for nonexistence (self-annihilation).[7]

What is the thirst or craving that the Buddha says is the cause of suffering, and how does it cause suffering? Craving is a strong, desperate form of desire that moves a person to extremes in trying to attain or avoid something. For example, a starving person may crave food so desperately that he may steal. Or a person might crave relief from the suffering of an illness so much that he or she would ask a physician to terminate his or her life. It is important to note that the Buddha did not say that all desire causes suffering. After all, there is nothing wrong with desiring food when you are hungry or desiring relief from pain when your head aches. But when desire is a function of greed and selfishness, then it becomes a problem, a source of *duhkha*. That is why the Buddha says that the origin of suffering is the craving that is bound up with passionate greed and that produces re-existence.

What is this selfish craving, bound up with greed, that produces re-existence? Ultimately, it is the craving for a separate and permanent self to be attained through attachment to the various processes of existence. In trying to satisfy the craving for separate and permanent existence, a person grasps for wealth, power, fame, and health. But none of these things can satisfy the craving for separate and permanent existence.

The principle underlying the second noble truth is that suffering is caused by craving what one cannot have or craving to avoid what cannot be avoided. Thus, craving freedom when incarcerated in prison and craving immortality in the face of the inevitability of death produce suffering. But these cravings are ultimately forms of the deeper craving *to be or have a separate and permanent self.*

If craving for separate and permanent selfhood is the origin of all forms of suffering, what is the origin of this craving? The primary originating condition is ignorance of the true nature of existence as constantly changing and totally interconnected processes. In place of this truth, to which it is blind, ignorance constructs a false reality of separate and permanent selves and things. Mistaking this false reality for the truth, people take themselves to be permanent and separate selves, separate from other selves and the world of changing processes. As a result, they are engulfed in the loneliness and anxiety created by the chasm that separates their existence from the other on all sides. Now either they desperately crave the other, grasping at it, trying to bring it into themselves in order to maintain their selfhood, or else, when the other is seen as a threat to the self, they desperately create defenses to keep the other from destroying their selfhood. In either case, it is this volitional misdirection of life arising from ignorance, this craving, that gives rise to *duhkha* in its various forms.

The Third Noble Truth

The truth that freedom from suffering is possible follows upon analysis of the conditioned arising of *duhkha.* If selfish craving gives rise to suffering, then freedom from suffering can be achieved by eliminating that craving. This is precisely what the Buddha said,

> The Noble Truth of the Cessation of Suffering is this: it is the complete cessation of that very thirst (craving), giving it up, renouncing it, emancipating oneself from it, detaching oneself from it.[8]

The elimination of suffering through the extinction of craving is called *nirvana,* a word that literally means "extinguished." What is extinguished is the craving for separate and permanent selfhood that is at odds with the truth of interdependent arising. When this craving is extinguished, suffering is pulled up by the root. Thus, though the term *nirvana* is negative, the Buddhist goal of nirvana is positive, for it refers to the peaceful and joyous life free from suffering that is achieved by extinguishing craving for permanence in one's own separate life.

It is a long way, however, from the recognition that eliminating craving will eliminate suffering to actually eliminating craving. That is why the Buddha, good physician that he was, did not stop with a diagnosis of the fundamental illness of life, or with a statement of what was required for its cure. Knowing that the question of *how* craving could be eliminated by ordinary human beings was crucial, he went on to prescribe a method of treatment that would actually eliminate the craving that gives rise to suffering. The prescribed method of treatment constitutes the fourth noble truth, which teaches the famous Middle Path of Buddhism.

The Fourth Noble Truth

The way to eliminate *duhkha* is to practice the Noble Eightfold Path that leads to the cessation of suffering. In the words of the Buddha,

> The Noble Truth of the Path leading to the cessation of suffering is this: It is simply the Noble Eightfold Path, namely, right view; right thought; right speech; right action; right livelihood; right effort; right mindfulness; right concentration.[9]

THE NOBLE EIGHTFOLD PATH

The Noble Eightfold Path is the Buddhist guide to life. Recognizing that suffering originates in ignorance and craving, the Noble Eightfold Path sets out a practical way to eliminate ignorance and craving. The heart of this way is the cultivation of the wisdom, moral conduct, and mental discipline required to eliminate ignorance and craving. If we look at the eight components of the path, we see that the first two cultivate wisdom, the next three provide moral guidance in the conduct of life, and the last three provide the insight and mental discipline needed to live in accord with the true nature of existence. Schematically, the Noble Eightfold Path can be set out as follows:

1. Right view 2. Right intention	Wisdom
3. Right speech 4. Right action 5. Right livelihood	Conduct
6. Right effort 7. Right mindfulness 8. Right concentration	Mental Discipline

The Noble Eightfold Path should not be thought of as a set of eight sequential steps, with perfection at one step required before advancing to the next. Rather, these eight components of the path should be thought of as guiding norms of right living that should be followed more or less simultaneously, for the aim of the path is to achieve a completely integrated life of the highest order. Underlying the eight guiding norms that make up the path are the three basic principles of the path, namely, wisdom, moral conduct, and mental discipline.

Wisdom, in seeing things as they really are, as interrelated and constantly changing processes, sees what *duhkha* is, how it originates, and how it can be eliminated. In overcoming ignorance, wisdom shows how to overcome craving and provides the resolve to live in accord with the truth of interdependent arising. Wisdom includes both right view and right intention.

The purpose of moral conduct is to purify one's motives, speech, and action, thereby stopping the inflow of additional cravings. The principle of moral conduct includes the norms of right speech, right action, and right livelihood.

Mental discipline works to attain insight and to eliminate the bad dispositions and habits built up on the basis of past ignorance and craving. It also works to prevent the development of additional bad dispositions and habits and to develop wholesome dispositions and habits. It includes right effort, right mindfulness, and right concentration.

The three principles of wisdom, moral conduct, and mental discipline are interdependent and mutually supporting. A person who sees that the lives of all people and all beings are intertwined will be moved to love and compassion for others by this wisdom. Thus, moral conduct is based on love and compassion and springs from wisdom. But mental discipline is required to achieve both wisdom and moral conduct. Mental discipline, however, requires moral conduct and wisdom. As moral conduct improves, mental discipline improves and wisdom deepens. Then, as wisdom deepens, moral conduct improves and mental discipline becomes stronger. Better mental discipline, in turn, further increases wisdom and moral conduct. Gradually, as one puts the norms of the path into practice, wisdom becomes deeper, moral conduct purer, and mental discipline stronger, and all traces of ignorance and craving are eliminated.

Because the Noble Eightfold Path is the basic Buddhist guide to life, following the path of wisdom, moral conduct, and mental discipline has remained the constant core of Buddhist practice, despite the significant changes that occurred in Buddhism as it spread throughout Asia almost two millennia ago, and as it has expanded throughout much of the rest of the world in the past two centuries. Therefore, we need to understand each of the path's eight norms.

Right View

As we have seen, wisdom includes both the correct understanding of things as they are and the resolution to act in accord with this understanding. Having the right view consists in seeing things as they are. This includes, on a lower level, intellectual understanding of things. But intellectual knowledge takes place within a system of concepts and principles resting on underlying assumptions which necessarily reflect limited perspectives. Because intellectual knowledge is determined by the concepts, principles, and assumptions of the system, its truth is relative to the system in which it occurs. Consequently, intellectual knowledge is considered a lower kind of understanding than the understanding that results from seeing things just as they are by direct insight. This direct seeing is the complete illumination of things just as they are in themselves and not as limited by concepts and theories. This direct insight into things reveals that all things are of the nature of interdependent arising, and that *duhkha* is caused by craving for separate and permanent existence. This is why right view is usually defined as seeing the truth of interdependent arising and as understanding the Noble Fourfold Truth.

Right Intention

Having a wrong view of reality, seeing things as separate and enduring, a person wrongly thinks that grasping for what appears to contribute to a separate and permanent self, and avoiding what appears to threaten the self, will bring happiness. But this way of thinking, rooted in ignorance, gives rise to craving, hatred, and violence. On the other hand, a person with the right view, seeing that all things are interdependent processes, thinks rightly that cultivating love and compassion for all beings will bring happiness. This right thought is expressed in the intention to free oneself from all craving, ill will, hatred, and violence. Positively, it is the intention to act only out of love and compassion.

Right Speech

Right view and right thought provide a basis for moral conduct, which includes right speech, right action, and right livelihood. Right speech means generally to avoid all talk that will hurt either oneself or others, and to speak pleasantly in ways that will help overcome suffering. In its negative form, the norm of right speech prohibits (1) lying; (2) slander, character assassination, and talk that might bring about hatred, jealousy, enmity, or discord among others; (3) harsh or rude talk, malicious talk, impolite or abusive language; and (4) idle or malicious gossip and foolish chatter. In its positive form, right speech means telling the truth, speaking in a kindly and friendly way, and using language meaningfully and usefully. It means knowing the time and place for which certain talk is appropriate, implying that sometimes one should maintain "noble silence."

Right Action

In its negative form, right action means not killing, hurting, stealing, cheating, or engaging in immoral sexual activity. Positively, it means that one's actions should aim at promoting peace and happiness, respecting the well-being of all living things.

It is obvious how the principal of moral conduct rests upon compassion and love for others. But further, this compassion and love are the natural result of a recognition of the interrelatedness of all beings. If no beings have independent existence *(svabhava)*, then all are dependent upon one another. When this is understood, there is no longer any basis for selfishness. Consequently, ignorance and selfishness must be replaced by wisdom and compassion.

Right Livelihood

Right livelihood extends right action and right speech to one's way of earning a living. This norm prohibits careers that bring harm to others. Specifically, it prohibits careers that involve (1) drug dealing; (2) using and dealing in weapons; (3) making and using poisons; (4) killing animals; and (5) prostitution and slavery. Positively, the norm of right livelihood requires that one's living is earned by means that are honorable, useful, and helpful. In explaining right livelihood to a banker, the Buddha emphasized the importance of (1) attaining sufficient means of life through one's own efforts without engaging in fraud, trickery, or other kinds of wrongdoing; (2) enjoying one's rightfully acquired wealth; (3) enjoying freedom from debt; and (4) enjoying the happiness of being free of blame.[10]

Right Effort

The development of wisdom and moral conduct require discipline, which includes the practice of right effort, right mindfulness, and right concentration. Practicing right effort includes (1) preventing evil and unwholesome states of mind from arising, (2) getting rid of evil and unwholesome states of mind that may already exist, (3) bringing about good and wholesome states of mind, and (4) developing and perfecting good and wholesome states of mind already present.

Right Mindfulness

Right mindfulness consists in being aware of and attentive to all of one's activities. This includes (1) the activities of the body, (2) sensing and feeling, (3) perceiving, and (4) thinking and consciousness. Being aware of and attentive to one's activities means understanding what these activities are; how they arise; how they disappear; how they are developed, controlled, and gotten rid of; and how they are linked together.

Right Concentration

Right concentration refers to a focusing of consciousness that enables one to see deeply into something. Both ignorance and enlightenment, which produce suffering and happiness, respectively, have their root in one's mental activities. The first two verses of the *Dhammapada* emphasize the importance of right concentration:

Mind is the forerunner of all actions.
All deeds are led by mind, created by mind.
If one speaks or acts with a corrupt mind, suffering follows,
As the wheel follows the hoof of an ox pulling a cart.

Mind is the forerunner of all actions.
All deeds are led by mind, created by mind.
If one speaks or acts with a serene mind, happiness follows
As surely as one's shadow.[11]

Because one's mental states determine everything one does, it makes sense to concentrate on purifying one's mental activities as a means of achieving happiness.

Four stages of concentration are distinguished. In the first stage, one concentrates on getting rid of lust, ill will, laziness, worry, anxiety, and doubt. These unwholesome mental activities are replaced by feelings of joy and happiness. In the second stage, one concentrates on seeing through and getting beyond all mental activities while retaining an awareness of joy and happiness. In the third stage, one goes beyond the mental activity responsible for the feeling of joy and achieves an equanimity pervaded by happiness. In the fourth and final state of concentration, complete equanimity and total awareness, beyond both happiness and unhappiness, is achieved.

REVIEW QUESTIONS

1. What is the significance of the four signs that Siddhartha saw during his chariot rides outside the palace grounds?
2. The core of the Buddha's enlightenment was his insight into *interdependent arising* as the true nature of existence. What does this term mean? How would you argue for the truth of this insight?
3. What are the Noble Four Truths taught by the Buddha in his first sermon? How would you argue that they do [or do not] constitute an adequate analysis of *duhkha*, its arising and its elimination?
4. According to the second noble truth, craving gives rise to suffering. What did the Buddha mean by *craving*, and how does craving give rise to suffering?
5. What are the components of the Noble Eightfold Path? How are they related to one another?

FURTHER READING

The Feeling Buddha: A Buddhist Psychology of Character, Adversity and Passion, by David Brazier (New York: Fromm International, 2000), is an interesting interpretation of the basic teachings of the Buddha in terms of common sense. This is highly recommended to students curious about how Buddhism might be relevant to their own lives.

An Introduction to Buddhist Ethics: Foundations, Values and Issues, by Peter Harvey (Cambridge: Cambridge University Press, 2000), is a comprehensive systematic introduction to Buddhist ethics. Of special interest is the lucid discussion of the relevance of Buddhist ethics to a wide range of contemporary issues.

Ethics in Early Buddhism, by David J. Kalupahana (Honolulu: University of Hawaii Press, 1995), shows how practicing the moral way is at the heart of Buddhist practice. This study is solidly grounded in the discourses of the Pali canon.

Being Peace, by Thich Nhat Hanh (Berkeley, CA: Parallax Press, 1987), is an excellent brief introduction to Buddhism in terms of both teachings and practice by one of the world's most respected Zen Buddhist teachers.

What the Buddha Taught, 2d ed. by Walpola Rahula (New York: Grove Press, 1978), is an excellent introduction to Buddhism by a practicing Theravada Buddhist monk.

Old Path White Clouds: Walking in the Footsteps of the Buddha, by Thich Nhat Hanh (Berkeley, CA: Parallax Press, 1991), is the life story of the Buddha. This compelling biography is drawn from Pali, Sanskrit, and Chinese sources.

Understanding Buddhism: Key Themes, by Heinrich Dumoulin, translated by Joseph S. O'Leary (New York and Tokyo: Weatherhill, 1994), is a succinct presentation of the fundamental teachings of Buddhism from the perspective of encouraging Buddhist-Christian dialogue.

A Living Buddhism for the West, by Lama Anagarika Govinda, translated by Maurice Walshe (Boston: Shambala, 1990), is a comprehensive summary of Buddhism in its three main forms, Hinayana, Mahayana, and Vajrayana.

Rationality and Mind in Early Buddhism, by Frank J. Hoffman (New Delhi: Motilal Banarsidass, 1987), provides a clear analysis of the nature of mind and the role of reason in early Buddhism.

On Being Buddha: The Classical Doctrine of Buddhahood, by Paul J. Griffiths (Albany: State University of New York Press, 1994), is a careful analysis of the meaning of Buddha-hood within the classical Buddhist tradition.

Buddhism in Practice, edited by Donald S. Lopez Jr. (Princeton, NJ: Princeton University Press, 1995), is a wide-ranging collection of texts dealing with the practice of Buddhism.

A Sourcebook in Asian Philosophy, by John M. Koller and Patricia Koller (New York: Macmillan, 1991), contains more than 200 pages of important Buddhist texts in English translation.

Recently several CD-ROMs have become available, with the likelihood of more in the near future. *BUDSIR,* created at Mahidol University, contains the Pali canon. It is available from American Academy of Religion at 819 Houston Mill Rd., Atlanta, GA 30239.

Hanazono University in Kyoto has recently produced a CD-ROM on Zen. In addition, the *Buddhajayanti Tripitika* is available for downloading at the Journal of Buddhist Ethics web site in Goldsmith and Penn State University. For more information on electronically available texts, consult the journal *Electronic Bodhidharma,* produced by Urs Upp at Hanazono University, Kyoto, Japan.

NOTES

1. This account of Siddhartha Gautama's encounter with the four signs is found in *Digha Nikaya,* 14.2. Translation by Maurice Walshe, in *The Long Discourses of the Buddha: A Translation of the Digha Nikaya* (Boston: Wisdom, 1995), pp. 207–10.
2. *Anguttara Nikaya I* , 145.
3. Ibid.
4. Author's translation, based on Walshe, *The Long Discourses* .
5. John M. Koller and Patricia Koller, *A Sourcebook in Asian Philosophy* (New York: Macmillan, 1991), pp. 195–96.
6. Ibid., p. 195. All quotations from the Buddha's first sermon are from this source.
7. Ibid.
8. Ibid.
9. Ibid.
10. *Anguttara Nikaya,* 2.69–70. See David J. Kalupahana, *A History of Buddhist Philosophy* (Honolulu: University of Hawaii Press, 1992), p. 107.
11. Translated by Ananda Maitreya, in *The Dhammapada* (Berkeley, CA: Parallax Press, 1995), p. 1.

CHAPTER 13

Interdependent Arising

The Buddha's teaching of the Noble Fourfold Truth, examined in the previous chapter, was based on his insight into interdependent arising *(pratitya samutpada)* as the nature of existence. *Interdependent arising* means that everything is constantly changing, that nothing is permanent. It also means that all existence is selfless, that nothing exists separately, by itself. And beyond the impermanence and selflessness of existence, interdependent arising means that whatever arises or ceases does so dependent upon conditions. This is why understanding the conditions that give rise to *duhkha* is crucial to the process of eliminating *duhkha.*

PRINCIPLE OF CONDITIONED EXISTENCE

The general principle of the conditionedness of existence is expressed in a classic fourfold statement in the *Samyutta Nikaya,* 2.28: (1) "When this is, that is; (2) this arising, that arises; (3) when this is not, that is not; (4) this ceasing, that ceases."[1]

The first part of the statement, "When this is, that is," declares that only because of these conditions ("this") can something else ("that") exist. The second part of the statement, "this arising, that arises," expresses this principle dynamically, declaring that only from the arising of these conditions will that state of affairs arise. The third part of the statement, "when this is not, that is not," expresses the principle with respect to the absence of existence, declaring that when these conditions do not exist, then that state of affairs does not exist.

167

Finally, the fourth part of the statement, "this ceasing, that ceases," dynamically expresses the principle of the absence of conditions, declaring that from the ceasing of these conditions, that state of affairs will cease.

A classic twelvefold formula applies this principle of conditionality to the arising and ceasing of the conditions of *duhkha.* The *Samyutta Nikaya* goes on to say,

> Ignorance conditions volition; volition conditions consciousness; consciousness conditions the mind-body; the mind-body conditions the six senses; the six senses condition contact; contact conditions feeling; feeling conditions craving; craving conditions grasping; grasping conditions becoming; becoming conditions birth; birth conditions aging and death. In this way all of duhkha arises.[2]

THE WHEEL OF BECOMING

This twelvefold set of conditions of the arising of *duhkha* came to be symbolically portrayed as the wheel of becoming. The wheel, shown grasped in the clutches of impermanence, has three components. In the hub, which drives the wheel, are depicted ignorance, grasping, and aversion. Between the hub and the rim of the wheel, the six types of samsaric existence are depicted, namely, human, animal, ghosts, demons, deities, and beings in hell. On the rim of the wheel are depicted the conditions that give rise to *duhkha* listed in the twelvefold formula: ignorance, volition, consciousness, body-mind, the six senses, contact, feeling, thirst, grasping, becoming forces, birth, and suffering.

Ignorance, grasping, and aversion are shown as the primary driving forces of *duhkha* at the center of the wheel. But because grasping and aversion arise in dependence on ignorance, it is ignorance that is considered the root condition of *duhkha.* To see how ignorance functions as the root cause of suffering, we need to answer the question, How do these twelve conditions depicted on the wheel explain how *duhkha* arises from ignorance? It is helpful to first examine how ignorance has the power to determine human life, using an ordinary example of ignorance that reveals the interconnectedness of the twelve conditions depicted on the wheel. Then it can be shown how ignorance as understood by Buddhism determines a life of *duhkha* and how this whole mass of suffering arises due to these twelve conditions, beginning with ignorance.

Ignorance of a Garden Hose

Ignorance *(avidya)* has two aspects. First, it is an absence or lack of true knowledge. Second, ignorance is the imposition of a false view on the object in question. For example, when you mistake a garden hose for a snake, not only do you lack knowledge of the hose that is present, but you also impose the false view that it is a snake. This example of ignorance of a garden hose can help us see how ignorance can give rise to a certain kind of life through the twelve conditions depicted on the rim of the wheel of becoming.

Suppose you are afraid of snakes. One evening you get out of your car and see a snake coiled up in the grass at the edge of the driveway. You become

Wheel of Becoming.

frightened and attempt to escape. Actually what you see as a snake is just a piece of old garden hose, which you mistake for a snake. The ignorance is your lack of awareness of the garden hose. But it is more than that; it is also your seeing a snake where none exists. As long as you think that the hose is a snake you will be afraid. This fear will in turn give rise to volition, a choice of action.

The volitional factor has two aspects, a previous disposition and a present urge to act. Because of previous conditioning, you are afraid of snakes and disposed to flee from them. Now, seeing a snake, you have an immediate urge to flee. This decision to escape the dangerous snake will in turn affect your consciousness.

Seeing the snake and wanting to escape, your consciousness will be shaped in such a way that it sees the world as a series of escape routes and obstacles to escape. What, under different circumstances, would be seen as beautiful roses are now only seen as thorny barriers to escape.

This consciousness conditions your whole person, both body and mind. Now, in terms of the mental and physical phenomena constituting your personal existence, you are a frightened person, frantically trying to escape the snake.

Your senses are thereby conditioned to perceive the world in terms of snakes and escape from snakes. You hear the rustling of leaves as the sounds of a snake getting ready to strike. You may think that you see the snake moving toward you as you try to escape between the rose bushes.

The strong, unpleasant feeling of being threatened by the snake arises as a result of sensory contact with the object of your fear, the snake. This unpleasant feeling, in turn, gives rise to a desperate craving to escape the danger. Driven by fear, this desperate grasping generates the becoming forces by which you become a terrified person, desperately clinging to the hope of escape.

It is these becoming forces, produced by your grasping, that give birth to your present existence as a terrified person. Perhaps, you could die on the spot of heart failure, your death being conditioned by the existence of terror.

In this way ignorance conditions all of the eleven other conditions depicted on the wheel, including the suffering of the present moment, which in the case of a heart attack could coincide with death. Clearly, ignorance (even of a garden hose) can have real effects.

Ignorance of Interdependent Arising

What is the ignorance that gives rise to the deepest kinds of human suffering? Because the fundamental insight of Buddhism is that the true nature of existence is that of interdependent arising, it sees the most basic ignorance as the lack of awareness of the true nature of existence as interdependent arising. But this ignorance is not merely lack of awareness, it is also the obscuring of the true nature of existence through the imposition of a false view on it. The false view is that existence—our own existence as well as the existence of other things—consists of permanent, separate beings. This false view prevents a person from seeing the truth of interdependent arising, from seeing that, in truth, existence is of the nature of ever-changing, totally interrelated processes. The twelve conditions represented on the wheel of becoming show how this ignorance of interdependent arising gives rise to *duhkha*. (In most artistic representations of the wheel, the artist vividly depicts the various elements—as described in what follows.)

Ignorance.   Ignorance is depicted on the outer rim by a blind woman feeling her way with a stick, for just as a blind person cannot see where she is going, so a person blind to the truth of interdependent arising cannot see how to live. When, because of ignorance of interdependent arising, a person takes herself to be an independent and separate self, separate from all other beings, she becomes engulfed in the loneliness and anxiety created by the chasm that separates her existence from the other on all sides.

Volition.   Because ignorance construes existence to be of the nature of separate and permanent selves and things, the ignorant person attempts to live as a separate and permanent being. This volitional direction of life, rooted in ignorance, which disposes a person to act as though he really is a separate and permanent self, is depicted on the rim of the wheel by a potter with pots. Just as the guiding hand of the potter shapes the clay on the wheel into a pot, so does a person's choice of responses to the world constructed out of ignorance shape his or her life. Taking his existence to be separate from everything else, a person desperately craves the other, grasping at it, trying to bring it into himself; or else, seeing the other as threatening his existence, he desperately creates defenses that will keep the other from destroying him. Furthermore, because he falsely views himself as permanent, all the changes in life threaten to diminish and destroy his life. Good looks, money, friends, health, youth, and even life itself will all disappear in time. For a person living in the illusion of permanence and separateness, life is but a brief and frustrating moment of anxiety.

Consciousness. This volitional urge—to shape ourselves to live in an illusory world of separateness and permanence constructed out of ignorance— shapes our consciousness so that it sees everything in terms of separate things to be grasped or things to be avoided. Consciousness, conditioned by volitional choices, is depicted on the rim of the wheel by a monkey, for just as a monkey restlessly jumps from branch to branch, so consciousness moves from one object to another, moved either by attraction or aversion. Everything is seen either as something to be avoided or as something to be craved. As a result, a person shaped by ignorance is always driven—driven either by aversion or by craving.

Body-Mind. A person's body and mind are depicted on the wheel as two passengers in a boat, totally dependent on each other. Just as in the example of the garden hose wrongly perceived as a snake, the body-mind of the person was conditioned by consciousness to flee (or to attack), so in ignorance of interdependent arising, the person (body-mind) is conditioned by consciousness so that he is always driven to grasp at (or to avoid) things.

Six Senses. The body-mind operates through and conditions the six senses (the functions of seeing, hearing, tasting, smelling, touching, and thinking). They are depicted on the rim as the six windows of a house, for they enable us to look out on the world outside. Because of the previous conditionings, the senses apprehend their objects as separate and enduring.

Contact. Contact of the senses with their objects is depicted on the rim of the wheel by lovers embracing, for having separated objects from the self, there is now a longing to unite with them. As with lovers who have quarreled and separated, there is a craving to reunite, and to avoid that which caused the separation.

Feeling. The result of sense contact is feeling, depicted on the rim by a man with an arrow in his eye. Feelings, either painful or pleasant, are conditioned by contact (which is conditioned by the previous factors). Conditioned by pleasant or unpleasant feelings, a person moves toward objects of pleasure and away from objects of pain.

Craving. Conditioned by contact, feelings give rise to craving and aversion. When contact produces a pleasant feeling, we crave the object that produced the pleasant feeling. When contact produces an unpleasant feeling, we crave to avoid the object that produces the unpleasant feeling. On the wheel, craving is depicted by a thirsty person reaching for something to drink. This symbolizes the craving for life experienced by a person who sees life as something separate that comes and goes, that has to be continuously poured into this body-mind to keep it alive.

Grasping. Craving, in turn, conditions grasping, depicted by a man picking fruit from a tree, and gathering it in a basket. This symbolizes the grasping at the illusory separate and permanent existence that characterizes life lived in ignorance of interdependent arising, the desperate attempt to collect pieces of life for the self. It represents clinging to past existence and grasping at future existence, unable to find peace in the present because of the illusion of permanence.

Becoming Forces. This grasping perpetuates itself, conditioning future existence as the becoming forces carry existence forward into the next moment. The becoming forces are depicted by a pregnant woman, symbolizing the power of generating new existence. Conditioned by ignorance, even as they condition the succeeding factors on the wheel, the becoming forces perpetuate the presently experienced *duhkha* into the next moment of existence, where it takes on a new existence.

Birth. Becoming forces give rise to the birth of new *duhkha,* depicted on the wheel by a woman giving birth. Birth here stands for the renewal of existence that, because of the ignorance of interdependent arising, is actually the renewal of *duhkha.*

Suffering. Each renewal of existence, however, when taken by ignorance to be separate and permanent, is inevitably subject to decline and perishing, leading inevitably to death. Thus, the next picture on the rim of the wheel is that of a corpse being carried to the cremation grounds. It symbolizes the old age and death that represent the totality of human suffering.

But death is not the end of the story, for what dies furnishes the basis for new life and the cycle continues on, with the potentials generated at each stage of the life process being realized in subsequent stages, perpetuating the karmic cycle. For someone who lives in ignorance of the truth of interdependent arising, who takes separateness and permanence to be real, death is the ultimate tragedy; death that is experienced over and over again in the unending cycle of existence is unbearable suffering.

Hub of the Wheel

The twelve pictures on the rim of the wheel represent the twelvefold formulation of interdependent arising. At the very center of the wheel, in the small circle constituting the hub, are pictured a pig, a cock, and a snake, each grasping the other in a symbolic representation of the interrelated forces that drive the whole wheel of becoming. The pig represents delusion, the blind urge of ignorance to embody itself in the objects of aversion and attachment. The cock represents craving and grasping, while the snake represents aversion and hatred. These three, ignorance, craving, and hatred, are interrelated, for they mutually give rise to and condition one another, as well as the twelve interrelated conditions shown on the rim of the wheel. That ignorance is considered to be the root condition does not mean that it is independent of the other conditions; it too arises in dependence on conditions.

Realms of Existence

Between the hub and the rim, divided into six regions by the spokes of the wheel, are the six realms of samsaric existence. These six realms constitute the main types of existence in which separate and enduring selfhood is sought. In each realm, the craving for separate and permanent selfhood is pursued either by desiring and grasping at whatever promises to maintain this illusory self-hood or by avoiding and hating whatever threatens to destroy it.

Deities. The topmost region is the heavenly realm of the deities who enjoy long lives of great freedom and beauty, devoting themselves to aesthetic enjoyment. They symbolize the tendency to get so absorbed in one's own happiness that the sufferings of others are shut out. Completely removed from the obstacles and suffering of life, they lose their creative urge and fail to renew their existence from moment to moment. Consequently, when the store of life-energy created previously is exhausted, they inevitably descend into lower levels of existence.

Hell. Opposite the realm of the deities is hell, a realm filled with intense suffering of every conceivable kind. The suffering the beings in this realm experience is simply the fruit of their own previous evil actions, and when this fruit is exhausted by the purifying fire of suffering, they will ascend to higher levels of existence. In this realm, the suffering in their own lives awakens beings to the suffering in the lives of others and arouses compassion and energy to help other suffering beings. This is the polar opposite of the beings in the heavenly realm, who are so wrapped up in their own pleasures that they shut themselves off from all suffering, losing the creativity engendered by the experience of suffering.

Demons. To the right of the heavenly realm is the realm of demons, who know only the power of violence and force. They are imprisoned by this very violence, deprived of the power of knowledge and love.

Animals. Opposite the demons is the realm of beings who live in constant fear of persecution and slaughter. The animals depicted here are held in bondage by instinctive fear and unconscious drives. They are the victims of power and violence, helpless until liberated by knowledge and understanding.

Humans. The human realm is shown to the left of the heavenly realm. Humans have the capacity to use the creative energies provided by knowledge and compassion to attain release from *duhkha*. Only a few persons use their capacity to develop knowledge and compassion, however. The vast majority waste their capacity for liberation by pursuing desires for separate selfhood, desires that cannot be satisfied.

Ghosts. Opposite the human realm is the realm of ghosts. Their thirst and hunger are insatiable; the food they try to eat sticks in their throats, and the water they attempt to drink turns into fire.

At one level of understanding, these six regions are the homes of different kinds of beings, ranging from gods to demons. But at a deeper level of understanding, these different kinds of existence can be seen in human beings. Some people are so self-satisfied that they cannot interact with others (the deities); some are so touched by suffering that they become sensitive to the suffering of others (those in hell); some are so demonic that they constantly try to get their way through force and violence (the demons); some are so gripped by unconscious fears that they cannot see how to avoid becoming victims of violence (the animals); some are so driven by selfishness that they are bloated by their own consumption (the ghosts); and finally, some people use their capacity for knowledge and compassion to end suffering (the humans). But most people combine all of these different tendencies. Sometimes we are animal-like, sometimes god-like, sometimes demon-like, and so on. The challenge is to transform these different tendencies into a full and complete human existence.

Release from the Wheel

The wheel of becoming has been explained in terms of the conditions that give rise to *duhkha*. But the wheel can also be seen as an explanation of release from suffering, for removal of the conditions that give rise to *duhkha* removes *duhkha*. If ignorance, grasping, and aversion are the driving forces at the hub of the wheel that bring about this whole mass of *duhkha,* then replacing them with wisdom, compassion, and love will transform the wheel from a symbol of the arising of *duhkha* to a symbol of the way of overcoming *duhkha*. If all of the other factors on the wheel are conditioned by wisdom rather than ignorance, then volitions and consciousnesses will be conditioned to live in accord with the truth of interdependent arising. This will give rise to the peace and joy of nirvana.

Implications of Interdependent Arising

Interdependent arising has some profound metaphysical implications that need to be noted. First, if whatever exists depends upon everything else, then nothing can be the effect of any one cause. There can be no independent being that is responsible for the existence of everything else. Rather, whatever creates is also created, and the processes of creating and being created go on simultaneously without beginning or end.

Second, as a consequence of the mutual dependence of all beings, it follows that no beings are solely "other-created," but that all are mutually self-creating. The ongoing processes that make up the universe are co-dependent and mutually creative. Each aspect of the process shares in the creation and the continuation of the other aspects of the process.

Third, space and time as absolute containers or measures of existence are ruled out by the Buddhist theory of interdependent arising. Ordinary notions of space and time are derived from comparisons of the location and duration of independent beings. Spatial characteristics are derived from the comparison of the location of one being relative to another, whereas temporal characteristics are derived by comparing the duration of one being to another. But according to the theory of interdependent arising, there are no beings that exist independently of one another; there are only ongoing processes of mutually dependent factors. Reality is of the nature of process; *things* are merely abstractions. Ordinary notions of space and time, because they assume that things ultimately exist independently of one another, take space and time to be absolute containers of things. When it is seen that things are merely abstractions from the processes that constitute reality, then space and time are also seen to be merely abstractions.

Fourth, conceptual descriptions or definitions are constructions useful for organizing thinking, but they do not actually correspond to, or mirror, reality. If existence were constituted by separate, permanent, self-existing things, it might be possible for concepts to mirror or directly correspond to existence. But if, in accord with the insight of interdependent arising, existence is constituted by interrelated processes, then concepts cannot directly correspond to existence. The reason is twofold: first, concepts necessarily differentiate their objects by separating them from other objects and from the subject. This conceptual separation distorts the actual interrelatedness of existence. Second, concepts have no temporal extension; they are static, rather than dynamic, as existence itself is. A process, for example, a growing child, is continuously changing. A concept of this growing child, however, is like a still photo, incapable of capturing the dynamism constituting the process.

MINDFULNESS

Just as the understanding of interdependent arising is the foundation of all Buddhist thought, so the *experience* of interdependent arising is the foundation of all Buddhist practice. As a way of life, Buddhism goes beyond mere understanding to actual transformation; its aim is to stop the arising of *duhkha* by transforming life in accord with the insight of interdependent arising. In terms of the wheel of becoming, practice aims at transforming the driving forces of ignorance, grasping, and hatred at the center of the wheel into wisdom, compassion, and love. The previous chapter explained the Noble Eightfold Path that the Buddha established as the basic practice for achieving this transformation. The heart of this Noble Eightfold Path, the very core of Buddhist practice, is mindful living, living with full mindfulness and fully in accord with the truth of interdependent arising.

Shortly after his enlightenment, the Buddha explained to his followers the way of self-transformation that he discovered, saying:

> There is a most wonderful way to help living beings realize purification, overcome directly grief and sorrow, end pain and anxiety, travel the right path and realize *nirvana*. This way is the fourfold establishment of mindfulness.[3]

Contained in a text called the *Establishment of Mindfulness,* this is one of the most important teachings of the Buddha. It has been accepted by all Buddhist traditions for twenty-five hundred years as the basis of meditation practice.[4]

When the Buddha was deeply engaged in mindfulness, he saw deeply into his experience, seeing that it was the grasping for selfhood and things that had put him at odds with his own experience. This grasping covered over his own experience of interdependent arising with the falsehood of a separate and permanent cognizer and cognizable things. The reflective insight of his mindfulness revealed this ignorance to be at the heart of human suffering, for it fragments experience into a separate subject and object, creating the basis for selfish grasping and hatred.

To understand the establishment of mindfulness we have to answer two fundamental questions. First, of what must a person be mindful? Second, how does a person practice mindfulness? The general answer to the first question is that a person must be mindful of interdependent arising in every aspect of life. The general answer to the second question is that mindfulness is practiced by calming the mind and seeing directly into reality. But the text on establishing mindfulness gives specific answers to both of these questions.

The Fourfold Establishment of Mindfulness

According to the *Establishment of Mindfulness,* mindfulness, which is a deep and undivided awareness, should be established in (1) the observation of the body, (2) the observation of the feelings, (3) the observation of the mind, and (4) the observation of the objects of the mind.

Practicing the "letting go" that characterizes mindfulness, the practitioner neither rejects nor clings to any of the mental states observed. He just illumines the mental state that has arisen, seeing its full interdependent and dynamic nature, recognizing that at this moment he *is* this mental state. For example, becoming mindful of anger, the practitioner may see this anger arising out of fear and see it giving rise to hatred. Aware that this anger is his present being, the practitioner sees himself being born out of fear and reborn as hatred. This awareness of the conditions that gave rise to his fear and anger enables him to accept the anger that he is, in this moment, without either rejection or clinging. This acceptance, in turn, enables him to let the anger go, transforming its energy into constructive action that brings joy and peace.

Mindfulness in Observing the Body

The six aspects of the body on which awareness is to be focused are (1) breathing, (2) bodily processes, (3) activities of the body, (4) parts of the body, (5) elemental components of the body, and (6) decomposing of the body.

Mindfulness of Breathing. To focus awareness on breathing the text recommends three practices. The first practice consists in becoming fully aware of breathing in and breathing out.

The second practice consists in becoming mindful of *how* one is breathing. In this practice of following the breath, the mind becomes one with the entire breath.

The third breathing practice, which, like the first two, produces a great calming effect, focuses awareness of the breath in the whole body. The text says to practice like this: "Breathing in, I am aware of my whole body. Breathing out, I am aware of my whole body. Breathing in, I calm the activities of my body. Breathing out, I calm the activities of my body."

Mindfulness of Bodily Positions. The establishment of mindfulness of the body through awareness of different positions of the body makes clear that mindfulness can and should be practiced not only in sitting meditation, but in every bodily position. The *Establishment of Mindfulness* says

> When a practitioner walks, he is aware, "I am walking." When he is standing, he is aware, "I am standing." When he is sitting, he is aware, "I am sitting." When he is lying down, he is aware, "I am lying down." In whatever position his body happens to be, he is aware of the position of his body.

Mindfulness of Activities of the Body. In mindfulness of bodily activities, a person becomes fully aware of whatever he or she is doing in the present moment. As the text says, "in going forward or backward, when looking in front or behind, when bending down or standing up, when wearing the *sanghati* robe or carrying the alms bowl, when eating or drinking, . . . he applies full awareness to this."

The positive, joyful nature of mindfulness of the body is brought out clearly in the Sarvastivada version of the *Establishment of Mindfulness,* which was widely used in China. According to this version, "A practitioner is aware of body as body, when, thanks to having put aside the Five Desires, a feeling of bliss arises during his concentration and . . . envelops the whole of his body with a clear, calm mind, filled with understanding."[5]

Mindfulness in Observing Feelings

Establishing mindfulness of the feelings means becoming deeply aware of feelings, an awareness that sees if they are pleasant, unpleasant, or neutral, and that sees how these feelings arise, how they transform, and how they depend on one another and on the body and the mind. According to the text, a practitioner "remains established in the observation of the process of coming-to-be in the feelings or the process of dissolution in the feelings or both in the process of coming-to-be and the process of dissolution."

Deep insight into feelings is important because feelings profoundly influence all thoughts and bodily processes. To be mindful is to see how a feeling arises in dependence on bodily processes, perceptions, habits, and thoughts and to see how it gives rise to other feelings, bodily processes, perceptions, habits, and thoughts.

Mindfulness of feelings is neither rejection of them nor clinging to them. Rejection of and clinging to feelings are both forms of grasping. But to practice mindfulness, one must let go of all grasping. Mindfulness of feelings is simply the awareness of them in their full interdependent and dynamic nature.

Mindfulness in Observing Mind

In answer to the question, How does a practioner remain established in the observations of the mind in the mind? the *Establishment of Mindfulness* says, "When his mind is desiring, the practitioner is aware, 'My mind is desiring.' When his mind is not desiring, he is aware, 'My mind is not desiring.' "

The text then goes on to identify sixteen more states of mind of which the practitioner should be aware in this same manner. These states of mind are hating and not hating, ignorant and not ignorant, tense and not tense, distracted and not distracted, having a wide scope and having a narrow scope, capable of reaching a higher state and not capable of reaching a higher state, composed and not composed, and free and not free.

For each of these eighteen states of mind, practitioners are told to observe the processes of their arising, of their ceasing, and of both their arising and their ceasing, thereby becoming aware of their dependence on one another and on bodily processes, feelings, perceptions, and habits.

Mindfulness in Observing Objects of the Mind

The objects of the mind are all the things of which the mind can be aware. This includes the objects within the fields with which the first three establishments of mindfulness are concerned, namely the fields of feelings, the body, and the mind itself. The field in which the fourth mindfulness is established adds thirty-three objects of awareness, grouped in the following five categories: (1) the five hindrances to practice (desire, anger, dullness, remorse, and doubt); (2) the five attachment groups (body, feelings, perceptions, dispositions, and consciousness); (3) the six senses and their objects (eye/form, ear/sound, nose/smell, tongue/taste, body/touch, and mind/object-of-mind); (4) the seven factors of awakening (mindfulness, investigation of phenomena, energy, joy, ease, concentration, and letting go); and (5) the Noble Fourfold Truth (*duhkha*, its arising, its ceasing, and the way that leads to its cessation). As the categories themselves make clear, the objects of mind selected for this establishment of mindfulness are directly involved in the practice of eliminating *duhkha*.

In establishing mindfulness in each of these objects of the mind, the practitioner is advised to observe them in their presence, in their arising, in their ceasing, and in their interdependence with other factors. As in the other establishments of mindfulness, because of letting go of grasping (which here, as one of the seven factors of awakening, is specifically listed as an object of mindful awareness), there is neither rejection of, nor clinging to, any of these objects of the mind. There is simply the illumination through the deep awareness in which the practitioner realizes her identity with the object of the mind, an illumination that reveals the truth of interdependent arising in this very object.

Ultimately, the practice of mindfulness awakens a person to the truth of interdependent arising. And this awakening removes the ignorance that, through the various conditions depicted by the wheel of becoming, gives rise to *duhkha.*

How to Practice Mindfulness

To establish oneself in observation of the body, feelings, mind, and objects of the mind, the *Establishment of Mindfulness* says that a person's practice should be "diligent, with clear understanding, mindful, having abandoned every craving and every distaste for this life."

The establishment of mindfulness requires that the practitioner has to abandon every craving and every distaste for this life, because the mind must be calm and peaceful in order to see its objects clearly and deeply. A person whose mind is moved by craving or hatred sees things only in terms of self-interest; this person cannot see things as they truly are. It was only after the Buddha had abandoned the cravings of his youth and the self-hatred of ascetic practice that he acquired true insight.

Diligence is required because becoming established in mindfulness is not easy. The mind is accustomed to moving from object to object. To calm and focus the mind requires a strong resolve and a concerted effort. The Buddha, having decided to follow the Middle Way, free from every craving and distaste for life, resolved to remain seated under the Bodhi tree until he achieved insight into *duhkha* and the way to eliminate *duhkha.* According to tradition, even the Buddha was tempted by both fearful and attractive objects to abandon his resolve to continue his practice of mindfulness. By the diligence of his effort, he overcame these temptations and achieved insight.

Clear understanding means that there is no confusion or doubt. This understanding comes not from theories or dogmas, but directly from experience. This clear understanding of experiential knowledge was proclaimed by the Buddha in concluding his first teaching when he said,

> This suffering has been fully understood, this origin of suffering has been abandoned, this cessation of suffering has been realized, and this Path leading to the cessation of suffering has been followed: such was the vision, the knowledge, the wisdom, the science, the light, that arose in me with regard to things not heard before.[6]

It is this profound awareness achieved through deep, experiential insight that all Buddhist meditation seeks through the practice of establishing mindfulness.

To be mindful is to be focused, not distracted. When one is fully mindful, objects are seen in their arising, in their interactions, and in their ceasing. It was when established in mindfulness that the Buddha saw that interdependent arising is the true nature of existence and that *duhkha* arises when, in ignorance of this truth, a person grasps for separateness and permanence.

Perhaps the most important requirement of the practice of establishing mindfulness is that the practitioner become aware of the object of awareness *in that very object.* The text says, with respect to each of the four fields of mindfulness, namely, body, feelings, mind, and objects of mind, that one should remain established in the observation of the body *in* the body; ... of the feelings *in* the feelings; ... of the mind *in* the mind; and ... of the objects of the mind *in* the objects of the mind.

The point of saying that the awareness of the body is *in* the body, that the awareness of the feelings is *in* the feelings, and so forth is that the deep insight of mindfulness penetrates its object and becomes one with it. Ordinary knowledge of an object is indirect or secondhand, where the subject remains separate from the object, but has a perception or a concept of the object. Mindfulness penetrates the object directly, rather than indirectly through perceptions and concepts, thereby going beyond the duality of subject and object.

REVIEW QUESTIONS

1. How does the wheel of becoming illustrate the basic principle of the conditionedness of existence?
2. How, according to the wheel of becoming, does ignorance give rise to *duhkha?* Beginning with ignorance, explain how each of the twelve factors on the rim of the wheel condition and are conditioned by the others.
3. How is mindfulness established? Identify the characteristics of mindful practice that each establishment emphasizes.
4. How does the practice of mindfulness work to eliminate *duhkha?* Give an example from each of the four establishments.
5. How would you argue for (or against) the truth of the claim that ignorance is the root condition of *duhkha?*

FURTHER READING

Moment by Moment: The Art and Practice of Mindfulness, by Jerry Braza (Rutland, VT: Charles Tuttle: 1997), offers clear and simple instructions. It includes a foreword by Zen Master Thich Nhat Hanh.

Transformation and Healing: The Sutra on the Four Establishments of Mindfulness, by Thich Nhat Hanh (Berkeley, CA: Parallax Press, 1990), is an extremely helpful commentary on the *Satipatthana Sutta.* This highly respected Vietnamese Zen monk provides excellent explanations of concepts and techniques of mindfulness and makes good suggestions for practitioners.

Breathe! You Are Alive: The Sutra on the Full Awareness of Breathing, rev. ed., by Thich Nhat Hanh (Berkeley, CA: Parallax Press, 1995), is an excellent guide to meditation on breathing, the foundation for all practice of mindfulness.

Causality: The Central Philosophy of Buddhism, by David J. Kalupahana (Honolulu: University Press of Hawaii, 1975), is one of the best booklength explanations of the Buddhist principle of conditionality. It includes insightful comparisons with Western theories of causality. Pages 141ff describe the twelvefold causal formula employed by the wheel of becoming.

Early Buddhist Theory of Knowledge, by K.N. Jayatilleke (London: Allen and Unwin, 1963), is a classic study of Buddhist epistemology.

A Philosophical Analysis of Buddhist Notions: The Buddha and Wittgenstein, by A.D.P. Kalansuriya (Delhi: Satguru Publications, 1987), is a thoughtful analysis of key Buddhist ideas in comparison with key ideas in Wittgenstein's philosophy.

Selfless Persons: Imagery and Thought in Theravada Buddhism, by Steven Collins (Cambridge: Cambridge University Press, 1982), is a thorough analysis of selflessness from a Theravada perspective. It also contains a useful analysis of Indian thought at the time of the Buddha.

Foundations of Tibetan Mysticism, by Lama Anagarika Govinda (New York: Samuel Weiser [originally: Rider, 1960]), contains a good explanation of the principle of conditionality in terms of the wheel of becoming. See especially pp. 234–47. Another book by Lama Anagarika Govinda, *A Living Buddhism for the West,* translated by Maurice Walsh (Boston: Shambala Press, 1990), has an excellent summary of Buddhism in its three main forms, Hinayana, Mahayana, and Vajrayana.

Theravada Meditation: The Buddhist Transformation of Yoga, by Winston L. King (University Park: Pennsylvania State University Press, 1980), is an analysis of *The Path of Purification,* the classic Theravada guide to meditation, and an explanation of how Theravada meditation is practiced, including a description of contemporary forms of meditation in Burma.

NOTES

1. See John M. Koller and Patricia Koller, *Sourcebook in Asian Philosophy* (New York: Macmillan, 1991), pp. 333–34.
2. Ibid., p. 337.
3. *Satipatthana Sutta, Majjhima Nikaya,* 10, trans. by Thich Nhat Hanh and Annabel Laity, in *Transformation and Healing: The Sutra on the Four Establishments of Mindfulness* (Berkeley, CA: Parallax Press, 1990). Thich Nhat Hanh provides an extremely helpful commentary on this important text.
4. See Koller and Koller, *Sourcebook in Asian Philosophy,* pp. 205–12, for Walpola Rahula's translation of this text.
5. See Chapter 12.
6. *Madhya Agama,* in Hanh, *Transformation and Healing,* pp. 154–56.

CHAPTER 14

Sarvastivada

The practices of mindfulness examined in the previous chapter provide a way of experiencing interdependent arising, the central insight of Buddhism. Important as such experiential understanding is to Buddhist practice, philosophical understanding of interdependent arising is also very important. The attempts to understand and explain interdependent arising philosophically gave rise to the Sarvastivada, Madhyamaka, and Yogacara philosophical traditions within Buddhism.

SARVASTIVADA TEACHINGS

The Sarvastivadins were a strong philosophical force in northwest India from the first to the ninth centuries, excelling in their development of Abhidharma philosophy, a rigorous metaphysical analysis of the phenomena of experience.[1] Disagreements, particularly over the comparative importance of the *sutras* (P: *suttas*), the core teachings regarded as containing the Buddha's own words, and *abhidharma* analysis, and over how past and future exist in the present moment, resulted in the emergence of the Sautrantika and the Vaibhasika as the two main branches of Sarvastivada thought. Sarvastivada thought has had no significant development during the past thousand years; today there are no Sautrantikas or Vaibhasikas. The Sarvastivada philosophies are important primarily because the Madhyamaka and Yogacara developed their views, analyses, and arguments in the process of refuting the Sarvastivada claims.

The basic Sarvastivada claim is that unless the ultimate constituents of existence that make up interdependent arising are real, then nothing else could possibly exist. According to the Sarvastivadins, analysis of experience shows that there are two kinds of things that exist, ordinary things, which are constructed, and ultimate things, the basic constituents out of which ordinary things are constructed. They argue that unless the fundamental constituents of existence, to which ordinary kinds of existence can be reduced, are ultimately real in and of themselves, not reducible to anything else, then it would be impossible for things such as tables, trees, and persons to exist.

This argument leads the Sarvastivadins to define the ultimate existents *(dharmas)* out of which ordinary things are constructed as being self-existent *(svabhava)* and having their own essence *(svalaksana)*. That they are self-existent means that these ultimate things are not dependent on anything else for their existence. Having their own essence means that each ultimate thing has its own inherent and unique defining characteristic. Thus, according to the Sarvastivadins, the ultimate constituents of existence have their own separate and independent existence.

Because the Sarvastivadins accept interdependent arising, they view the ultimate constituents of existence as impermanent, arising and ceasing in dependence on other constituents. In order to account for the continuity of persons and things, however, they also claim that the ultimate constituents of existence endure through time, even if only for an instant. This insistence on endurance through time leads the Sarvastivadins to claim self-existence for the ultimate constituents of existence. But claiming self-existence for these ultimate constituents, despite their interpretation of them as momentary, appears to put the Sarvastivadins at odds with the Buddhist insight that existence is selfless because it is of the nature of interdependent arising.[2]

The relation between the fundamental constituents of existence *(dharmas)* and the things of ordinary experience is comparable to the relation in modern scientific theory between the atomistic components of things and the things of ordinary perception. Our common-sense view is that tables and chairs are solid and enduring things. But the scientist informs us that what is called a table and thought to be a solid and permanent thing is really mostly empty space, in which are found a variety of forces and elements in constant motion. Similarly, the Sarvastivadins tell us that the things of common sense are really no more than collections of the momentary existents that are their ultimate constituents. For the Sarvastivadin, as for the scientist, this way of looking at things does not deny their existence. Rather, it is a way of explaining *how* they exist. The things of ordinary experience really do exist; it is just that their reality is constituted in a different way than it is usually thought.

FOUNDATIONS OF ABHIDHARMA

The Sarvastivada view of the ultimate constituents of existence may have its roots in the Abhidharma analysis that grew out of the meditative experience of Buddhist practice. In the practice of mindfulness, practioners learn to see that what at first appeared to be a single separate, enduring reality, such as one's own body or one's own mind, is actually the functioning of interdependent groups of processes.

The earliest systematic reflections on the processes that constitute the objects of mindfulness are contained in the *Abhidharma*. The main concern of the Abhidharma writers was to classify these objects *(dharmas)* of experience and to establish their interrelations, thereby providing a map of the mind that would be useful in guiding mindfulness practice.

A second concern, which was very important to the Sarvastivada tradition (though not to the Theravada tradition), was to give a philosophical explanation of the objects of experience and of their ultimate constituents *(dharmas).*[3] Three questions had to be addressed: (1) What is the nature of these ultimate constituents of existence? (2) How do they provide continuity to things and persons? (3) How are the things constituted by these ultimate constituents of existence known?

In order to provide these explanations, the Sarvastivadins went beyond the data of experience to postulate the existence of ultimate constituents of experience, which they described as being ultimate and self-existent. These ultimate constituents of objects were to be contrasted with the objects of ordinary experience, with the latter viewed as constructions out of the ultimate constituents. It should be noted that the experience of mindfulness does not reveal that its objects are ultimate; it simply reveals their presence. It is only in trying to explain what they are and how they constitute ordinary things that the Sarvastivadins construed them as ultimate, momentary, and self-existent.

Theravada Abhidharma

The Theravada Abhidharma, whose main concern is to classify the objects *(dharmas)* of experience and to establish their interrelations, begins by classifying the groups of processes that constitute a person. This is a systemization of the basic Buddhist insight, realized in the practice of mindfulness, that a person is not a permanent and unchanging substance, that a person is not a self who possesses a body and a mind. Mindful observation reveals that a person consists in five interrelated groups or streams of continuously flowing processes. These five streams are (1) the bodily processes, (2) the processes of feeling, (3) the processes of perception, (4) the processes of action, and (5) the processes of consciousness. These interrelated streams of processes give rise to the appearance of a separate and permanent self. But this appearance is illusory, for the individual is never anything more than these interrelated streams of processes.

In a similar way, when each of these five streams of processes are investigated, they are seen to consist in even more streams of processes, which the Abhidharma proceeds to group into categories according to the type of object experienced in mindfulness. For example, bodily processes include seeing, which involves the eyes and colored objects; hearing, which involves the ears and sounds; and the other senses. Mental processes (feeling, perception, impulses to action and consciousness) include four groups of categories:

1. The *constituents of mental activity present in consciousness:* feeling, perception, will, immediate sensation, desire, understanding, memory, attention, inclination, and concentration.
2. The *constituents of virtue:* faith, courage, equanimity, modesty, disgust at objectionable things, nongreed, nonhatred, compassion, and mindfulness.
3. The *constituents of vice:* dullness, doubt, sloth, carelessness, immodesty, anger, hypocrisy, envy, jealousy, deceit, trickery, hatred, and pride.
4. The *constituents of consciousness:* pure, impure, and indeterminate (capable of being either pure or impure).

In this way, all the objects of experience are identified and classified into categories. Finally, in order to show their interdependence, the Abhidharma compares these categories, showing the interrelations among them. Not postulating any metaphysical ultimate entities as the real constituents of existence, the authors of the *Theravada Abhidharma* were satisfied that mindfulness of the objects of experience and reflection on their interrelationships provided an adequate understanding of the processes constituting existence.

Sarvastivada Abhidharma

The *Sarvastivada Abhidharma,* because of its reduction of experienced objects to their ultimate constituitive moments, has an additional objective. It is concerned not only to classify and compare the objects of experience, but also to give a philosophical explanation of the ultimate, momentary constituents of the objects of experience. According to the Sarvastivadins, only these momentary constituents are ultimately real.

If the reality of experienced things is reduced to the reality of their ultimate constituents, then the reality of these ultimate constituents must be explained in order to explain how the ordinary things that they constitute are real. The identity and the continuity of the ultimate constituents must also be explained in order to explain the identity and continuity of the things that they constitute. Because a world in which things have no identity, continuity, or reality is unintelligible, these explanations are crucial to the Sarvastivada.

Establishing Reality. According to the Sarvastivadins, a person's reality is derived from the reality of the interdependent groups of processes that constitute the person. The reality of these groups, however, is derived from the reality of their ultimate constituents. Only if the ultimate constituents are real in themselves can the groups that they constitute be real. But if the groups that constitute a person have no reality, then the person that they constitute is also completely unreal. But if persons are not real, then there is no Buddha, no teachings of the Buddha, no one to hear the teachings, no one who suffers, and no one who is released from suffering. Because such a conclusion is unacceptable, the Sarvastivadins do not claim that persons are unreal. Rather, they claim that because their reality is derived from their ultimate constituents, therefore the ultimate constituents of existence must be self-existent *(svabhava),* real in and of themselves.

Identity. The argument for a thing's identity is similar to the argument for its reality. That a thing has identity means that it is what it is, and is not something else. For example, a tree is what it is, and not a person. Without identity, there could not be something that is the Buddha; nor could there be something called a person practicing the Noble Eightfold Path. Since each thing that exists has its own identity, and since each thing's existence is derived from its ultimate constituents, so is its identity. Therefore, the Sarvastivadins argue, each thing's ultimate constituents must contain their own identity *(svalaksana).*

Continuity. The Sarvastivadins also had to argue that the ultimate constituents endure through time, at least long enough to establish continuity between successive moments of existence. Without continuity between the successive moments of their constituents, persons and things would not be continuous. Unless the same person who practices the path is the same person who eliminates *duhkha,* however, there is no point to practicing the path. By claiming that the ultimate constituents endured through time, the Sarvastivadins could explain how the effects of a person's actions at one time could affect that same person at a later time, an explanation crucial to the meaningfulness of Buddhist practice.

Knowability. The question of the knowability of things comes down to the question, How is it possible to recognize the reality of anything? If everything is continuously changing, then there never is an "it" that can be known. The Sarvastivadins, relying on the momentary endurance of ultimate constituents through time, said that there is at least one moment of time in which an object is what it is (that is, it is unchanging), a moment in which it can be recognized as a unique object.

Kinds of Ultimate Constituents in the Sarvastivada Abhidharma. Because of the need to explain how reality, identity, continuity, and knowability are derived from the ultimate constituents of existence, the *Sarvastivada Abhidharma* lists some kinds of constituents not found in the *Theravada Abhidharma.* For example, the Sarvastivada category called "unmanifest physical form" is intended to account for karmic transfer in which the unmanifest effects of actions become manifest at a later time. The fourteen kinds of things that are neither physical nor mental are postulated in order to solve conceptual problems in trying to explain the ultimate constituents of existence.[4]

ARGUMENTS AGAINST SUBSTANCE

We turn now to the Sarvastivada arguments against interpretations of existence as substance. Because it was seen as a wrong view that gives rise to *duhkha,* all the Buddhist philosophers, including the Sarvastivadins, argued against the essentialist view of existence based on the concept of substance. The essentialist view claims that existence is constituted by substances, each with its own enduring essence that separates it from other substances. Although various characteristics of a substance, its size, color, shape, and so forth, change, the underlying substance, which is the essence of the thing to which these characteristics belong, does not change. On this view, the essential substance of a person is the unchanging self, which is different and separate from every other self and thing.

The essentialist view of existence based on the conception of substance, a view of existence brought to its fullest development in the Hindu philosophical traditions of Nyaya and Vaishesika,[5] is exactly the opposite of the Buddhist view of existence as interdependent arising. Examining the Sarvastivada arguments against substance will help us see more clearly what Buddhists mean when they say that in accord with interdependent arising, selflessness and impermanence are the very nature of existence. It will also help us see whether or not the Sarvastivadins, despite their arguments against the essentialism of Hindu philosophies of substance, implicitly accepted a subtle form of essentialism themselves.

Substance

The essentialist view of existence that the Buddhists rejected had four basic features. First, existence consists of substances, unchanging or *permanent* at their core. Second, the essence of a substance is *universal,* the same everywhere and at all times. Third, substances remain *identical* with themselves over time despite their ever-changing characteristics. Fourth, the various components of a thing are *unified* by their inherence in the substance.

In rejecting essentialism, the Buddhists argued against these claims that existence is of the nature of (1) permanence, (2) universality, (3) identity, and (4) unity. Because the essentialists attribute the permanence, unity, identity, and universality of things to an inner, unperceived substance in which the perceivable characteristics of things are claimed to inhere, the Buddhists direct their arguments against this inner substance.

The overall argument is disjunctive in structure: either the essentialist view of existence based on substance is true or else its opposite, the view of existence as interdependent arising, is true.[6] Consequently, the major philosophical effort is directed toward showing the substance view to be untenable.

Arguments Against Permanence

The substance view takes permanence—the unchanging, rather than the changing, features of reality—as fundamental. Changelessness is the criterion of what is ultimately real. According to the essentialist view of the self set forth in the Upanishads, a view opposed by the Buddhist view of the selflessness of existence, a person's body and mind are claimed to be ultimately unreal because they change. Only the unchanging self, to whom body and mind belong as changing characteristics, is ultimately real.

The first Sarvastivada argument against permanence challenges the claim that changelessness is the criterion of the real. If the real is unchanging, then it cannot produce any effects, for the production of effects requires change. But if the real does not produce any effects, then it cannot be known, for causes are known only by the effects they produce. Therefore, to claim that the real is changeless is to claim that it is unknowable, which is absurd.

The second argument against defining the real as the changeless proceeds from the analysis of knowledge. Coming to know something represents a change in the knower. Therefore, if the self is unchanging, then it could never come to know anything. But to claim to know that the self cannot have knowledge is absurd.

The third argument is from causality. Change is a fact of our experience and must be caused by something. But how can an unchanging real cause change? Causation must either be temporally extended, occurring over time, or else it must be instantaneous. The action of causation cannot be instantaneous, for then all the effects would be produced at once, and reality would, except for that moment, be unchanging. This would force us to deny our experience of change.

The fourth argument is also aimed at instantaneous causality. If the causal action of the real were instantaneous, then either the real would cease to exist as a cause after the first instant of change or else it would continue to exist as a cause after the first instant of change. Both alternatives are absurd. If it continues to exist, then it should give rise to the same effects as it did in the first instant, and the same in each succeeding instant. This is absurd, because if it makes any sense at all it would mean that the real causes an infinity of complete universes. If the real ceases to exist, however, then it has undergone change, which contradicts the claim that the real is unchanging.

The fifth argument considers the alternative to instantaneous causality, namely, temporally extended causality. The claim that the real produces its effects over time is also untenable. If the unchanging real produced first x, then y, and then z, and so forth, then either (1) y or z could have been produced while x was being produced, or (2) the cause could not produce effects $y, z,$ at any given time, say when x was being produced. Alternative (1) is absurd because it means that all the effects were producible at once, making this alternative indistinguishable from instantaneous causality. Alternative (2) is absurd because if the real were incapable of producing an effect at a given time, it would be impossible for it to produce an effect at any later time, for what is not capable of producing a given effect at a given time cannot produce that effect at any other time, except by assuming other causal activity.

An objection might be made to the above argument on the grounds that while time itself does not produce a capability in the cause, nevertheless time may allow for certain modifications to take place so that causation is possible. For example, sometimes a seed does not cause a plant, sometimes it does. The reason is that time allows certain modifications in the conditions that enable the seed to cause a plant at one time, though not at another. But this objection begs the whole question of causation. If it is admitted that time itself does not cause things, then it cannot be admitted that time brings about modifications, for modifications are nothing other than effects that have been caused. Thus, some cause other than time would be required, and the same questions would arise concerning this cause.

Even if it were admitted that certain modifications in the cause are required, the Buddhist argument is still successful, for this would be an admission that the cause had changed. But if the cause changes, it cannot also be claimed to be permanent or unchanging.

Arguments Against Identity

Identity refers to the continuing sameness of things despite apparent changes in them. For example, advocates of identity would say that although a puppy grows into a dog and becomes old, and though in the process every cell is replaced, nevertheless, it is still the same individual animal. Despite the various changes, the old dog is said to be identical to the little puppy, except for age.

The Sarvastivada argument against identity proceeds by trying to show that its main underlying assumption is false. Advocates of a substance view of reality maintain that a thing remains identical with itself over a period of time by assuming that a thing naturally continues to exist unless destroyed or altered by outside and violent forces. The argument against this assumption claims that unless a thing were naturally subject to change and cessation, nothing could possibly bring about change and cessation with respect to that thing. For example, when forces such as a blow from a stick act upon a jar, the jar is destroyed. But one cannot conclude from this that the nature of a jar is to exist identical with itself, without change, unless acted upon by an outside force. Only if arising and ceasing belonged to the jar as part of its nature, could anything either produce or destroy it. If destruction was not inherent in the jar, then blows from sticks could not destroy it; the jar would continue to exist. But experience shows that the nature of a jar is such that blows from sticks provide the occasion for its cessation.

Arguments Against Unity

Unity means that although something is made up of many parts, it is still one whole, unified thing. The Sarvastivada argument against unity is based on the impossibility of knowledge of a *whole*. According to the substance view, an object such as a table, although consisting of many parts, is said to be one whole. The argument against this view claims that it is not possible to know the whole. For example, it is not possible to see the whole table. Only a small part of one surface of the table is seen. And only a small part of a surface can be touched, and so forth. Ordinarily this is not regarded as an obstacle to knowing the whole table because it is assumed that it is *one part of the whole table* that is seen or touched, and that by moving around to various other parts, one can consecutively come to see the whole table. But this explanation is unsatisfactory, for even at best, all that would be seen or touched would be the various *surfaces* of the table. It would not be possible to see or touch anything more than merely the surface of the table, even though the table is assumed to consist of more than mere surfaces. Even if more than surfaces could be seen or touched, the explanation would still be unsatisfactory, for the different visual and tactile perceptions attained from different perspectives do not of themselves also carry with them the perception that they are *of the same whole*. It is entirely possible that each different perception is the perception of a different thing. Nothing in the perception itself guarantees that it belongs to the same object as other perceptions. Therefore, there is no perceptual basis for claiming that there are wholes that are made up of different parts. All that can be claimed to be known are the perceptions themselves, and since there is no perception that connects these perceptions together into a whole, the supposed unity of things cannot be known.

From a Sarvastivada perspective, unity is not something that a thing has in virtue of being a substance. Rather, it is a construction of the mind that is imposed on experience as a way of organizing our experience in useful ways. From a Sarvastivada perspective, just as a movie is really no more than rapidly succeeding consecutive still pictures, so reality is no more than rapidly succeeding momentary elements. And just as the consecutive passage of still pictures gives rise to the appearance of one continuous whole moving picture, so the momentary rise and fall of elements gives rise to the appearance of the unity of whole things. In reality, however, the moments of existence are no more than "point-instants" of force, rising and falling in dependence upon one another.

Arguments Against Universality

When the differences between things are seen as less fundamental than their similarities, it is tempting to view particular things as the embodiment of universal essences. For example, a variety of different animals are lumped together into the category *dog* on the assumption that despite the differences between, say, a poodle and a St. Bernard, dogs are essentially the same. This sameness is their essence, their "dogness," which is taken to be the same everywhere, at all times, for all animals, within a certain category. This essence is regarded as a universal because it is independent of space and time. For example, because it is viewed as what really makes something a dog, this universal essence is considered the essential reality that resides in all dogs.

The argument against universals rests on the unknowability of a universal entity. The identity of one thing with another, such as the sameness of two tables, by virtue of their being tables, depends upon the supposition that a universal essence, "tableness," exists within them. How is it possible that the same universal entity could exist in many different things widely separated in space and time? And if it did, how could it be totally unaffected by what happens to all of the different things in which it existed? Furthermore, if such universals exist, how can they be known? Even supporters of the essentialist view admit that perception is always of particulars. To explain the perception of universals, they assume a kind of double perception. First, one perceives the particular concrete thing. Then, supposedly, one perceives the universal essence that inheres in the particular things as a sort of timeless, spaceless duplicate of the particular. The Sarvastivadins argue that there is no evidence for this kind of duplicative perception. But without a basis in perception, there can be no knowledge of anything. Therefore, the essentialist claim that the true reality of things is their universal essence must be rejected. The Sarvastivada position is that the universals attributed to reality are simply logical constructions placed on a reality that is in every respect particular.

REVIEW QUESTIONS

1. Why do the Sarvastivadins claim that there are ultimate, self-existing constituents of things? Are they right?
2. What are the Sarvastivada arguments against the substance view of existence? Examine each argument and evaluate its soundness.
3. On what bases do the Theravada and Sarvastivada categorize the objects of experience?

FURTHER READING

Zen Therapy: Transcending the Sorrows of the Human Mind, by David Brazier (New York: John Wiley & Sons, 1995), has an entire section on Buddhist psychology drawn from the Abhidharma (Part 2, pp. 77–188).

Studies in Abhidharma Literature and the Origins of Buddhist Philosophical Systems, by Erich Frauwallner, translated from the German by Sophie Francis Kidd, under the supervision of Ernst Steinkeller (Albany: State University of New York Press, 1995), is the best work on the relation between the development of Abhidharma thought and rise of Sarvastivada and other Buddhist philosophies.

Sarvastivada Literature, by Anukul C. Banerjee (Calcutta: University Press, 1957), is a reliable survey and provides some helpful interpretation.

On Being Mindless: Buddhist Meditation and the Mind-body Problem, by Paul J. Griffiths (LaSalle, IL: Open Court, 1986), has a good summary of Sarvastivada in chap. 2, "The Attainment of Cessation in the Vaibhasika Tradition," pp. 42–75.

A History of Buddhist Philosophy, by David J. Kalupahana (Honolulu: University of Hawaii Press, 1992), contains a critique of Sarvastivada in chap. 12, "The Emergence of Absolutism," pp. 121–31.

A History of Indian Buddhism from Sakyamuni to Early Mahayana, by Akira Hirakawa (Honolulu: University of Hawaii Press, 1990), pp. 127–69, contains a good historical discussion of Abhidharma and Sarvastivada thought.

Buddhist Logic, by Th. Stcherbatsky (Leningrad: Academy of Sciences of the USSR, 1932), vol. 1, pp. 79ff, has a translation and interpretation of a key Sarvastivada text.

NOTES

1. The Sarvastivada teachings are found in its two main traditions, the Vaibhasika and the Sautrantika. The principal texts of Vaibhashika are the *Mahavibasa;* the *Abhidharmarta* by Ghosaka; *Abhidharmahrdaya* by Dharmasri; and the *Abhidharmakosa (Treasury of Metaphysics)* by Vasubandhu.

2. According to Theravada tradition, the controversies that were discussed at the Third Council are included in the *Kathavatthu*. Included are controversies over the nature of objects of experience, persons, and enlightened beings. Mogaliputta-tissa, the author, argues against Sarvastivada views on all three of these issues. See David J. Kalupahana, *A History of Buddhist Philosophy* (Honolulu: University of Hawaii Press, 1992), pp. 132–43, for an analysis of this section of the *Kathavatthu*.

3. It is noteworthy that the Sarvastivada Abhidharma differs from the Theravada in that it has fourteen *dharmas* that appear not to be objects of mindfulness, but things that are needed to solve conceptual problems in the explanation of the ultimate constituents of existence.

4. See Akira Hirakawa, *A History of Indian Buddhism from Sakyamuni to Early Mahayana* (Honolulu: University of Hawaii Press, 1990), pp. 139–69, for a discussion of the Sarvastivada Abhidharma.

5. See Wilhelm Halbfass, *On Being and What There Is: Classical Vaisesika and the History of Indian Ontology* (Albany: State University of New York Press, 1992), for an excellent analysis of the Vaisesika theory of substance.

6. The following arguments are formulated historically by the Sautrantika school of Sarvastivada, but they are essentially the same as the arguments used by the Vaibhasikas. For fuller treatment of these arguments, the reader might consult Th. Stcherbatsky, *Buddhist Logic* (Leningrad: Academy of Sciences of the USSR, 1932), vol. 1, pp. 79ff.

CHAPTER 15

Perfection of Wisdom

PERFECTION OF WISDOM TRADITION

The Madhyamaka and Yogacara philosophical traditions, which argued against the Sarvastivada view of existence as being made up of fundamental realities called *dharmas*, developed out of the earlier Perfection of Wisdom tradition. This tradition, beginning around 200 BCE, emphasized that the surpassing wisdom of enlightenment, called *prajnaparamita*, was not ordinary knowledge but a direct and immediate awareness of reality.

The Perfection of Wisdom *(prajnaparamita)* tradition is usually associated with the beginnings of Mahayana Buddhism because of its emphasis on the Bodhisattva ideal and its emphasis on emptiness as the full understanding of interdependent arising. The conception of emptiness and the understanding that the truth of direct experience in mindfulness awareness is higher than the truth of conceptual understanding are central themes in the Perfection of Wisdom texts.

Texts

There are a total of thirty-eight Perfection of Wisdom texts composed between 200 BCE and 600 CE. Two of these, the *Diamond Sutra* and the *Heart Sutra,* have been especially important in the development of Mahayana Buddhism. Although the present form of both of these texts may date from as late as the fourth century CE, the core of the *Diamond Sutra* is probably one of the earliest texts of this tradition, dating from the second or first century BCE. The

Heart Sutra, however, is clearly a later summary of a vast Perfection of Wisdom literature.

Most Western readers find their first attempts to read the Perfection of Wisdom texts extremely baffling because these texts appear to be full of self-negations and contradictions. The *Diamond Sutra,* for example, proclaims: "Although innumerable beings have been led to nirvana, in fact, no being at all has been led to nirvana."[1] It goes on to say: "The Tathagata's [Buddha's] perfection of patience is really a non-perfection." Another passage appears to deny the Buddha's enlightenment and the truth of his teaching, for when the disciple Subhuti is asked, "Is there any true teaching [*dharma*] which the Tathagata has fully known as the utmost, right, and perfect enlightenment, or is there any true teaching [*dharma*] which the Tathagata has demonstrated?" Subhuti replies, "No, not as I understand what the Noble One has said." Since no Buddhist would deny that the Buddha was enlightened, it is impossible that the perfection of wisdom denies the Buddha's enlightenment and his teachings. So what do these apparent negations of central teachings mean?

The *Heart Sutra,* which, like the *Diamond Sutra,* presents itself as teaching how one should practice the Bodhisattva way that leads to enlightenment, begins by proclaiming that "form is emptiness, and emptiness is form."[2] This statement appears to negate itself, for how can what exists as form at the same time be empty of form? A couple of verses later we read, "There is no *duhkha,* no origination of *duhkha*, no cessation of *duhkha*, no way that leads to the cessation of *duhkha*." This appears to make nonsense of all Buddhist practice. And in the next paragraph we read, "Because of his nonattainment, a Bodhisattva ... is assured of attaining nirvana." How can nonattainment assure attainment? Furthermore, the previous sentence declares that there is no way to nirvana, and now we are told that the nonattainment of nirvana is the way to attain nirvana! To say that there is no nirvana and that it is attained by nonattainment certainly sounds like nonsense.

Reading the Texts

It is not likely, however, that these *prajnaparamita* texts, the foundational texts of all of Mahayana Buddhism, are actually filled with nonsense and self-contradiction. The challenge is to learn how to read these texts in a way that enables us to discover their deeper meaning, a way of reading the *Heart* and *Diamond Sutras* that reveals the fundamental Buddhist insight that the tradition has found in these texts.

The first clue is to be found in the meaning of the word *prajnaparamita,* the word that names the Perfection of Wisdom texts. The word *prajnaparamita,* is composed of three parts, *pra, jna,* and *paramita.* The root word is *jna,* which means ordinary understanding or knowledge. The first word, *pra,* which means "primary," combines with *jna* to form the word *prajna,* which means primary or deep understanding, called wisdom. The last component, *paramita,* means "surpassing," in the sense of that which goes beyond or is perfected, giving the word *prajnaparamita* the meaning "perfect wisdom."

Thus, perfect wisdom is to be distinguished not only from ordinary knowledge, but also from deep knowledge or wisdom. In ordinary knowledge, we are not fully present to (or fully mindful of) our experience; instead, we are aware of it through the constructions that cognition imposes on experience. These constructions, our percepts and concepts, separate the objects we experience from other objects, abstract them from their continuous stream of change, and separate these objects from ourselves as subjects having the experience, thereby creating a duality of subject and object. Wisdom *(prajna)* is distinguished from ordinary knowledge because it results from deep, penetrating insight and careful reflection. Despite this difference, ordinary knowledge and wisdom are both rooted in conceptual activity.

Perfect wisdom goes beyond the constructions of conceptual knowledge. As perfect *(paramita),* this wisdom goes beyond the secondhand, indirect awareness achieved through concepts and theories to an immediate, direct realization of the fullness of experience.[3] It is this perfect wisdom that constitutes the enlightenment of the Bodhisattva; the Perfection of Wisdom texts explain how one should practice this way of perfect wisdom.

But because no human thought or practice, not even practice of the Bodhisattva way, can proceed without relying on conceptual knowledge, the authors of these texts faced a double challenge. On one hand, they had to find ways of using conceptual knowledge to point beyond itself to reality itself. On the other hand, they had to present the understanding reached through direct realization in conceptual terms so that it could be understood and used to guide practice. In terms of the tradition's distinction between ultimate truth and conventional truth, the Perfection of Wisdom authors had to find a way of using conventional truths found in the constructions of ordinary knowledge to talk about ultimate truth.

One way of doing this, as utilized by the authors of the *prajnaparamita* texts, was to first state a truth conventionally, stating it in the way that an ordinary person, who regards every statement as referring to some independently existing reality, would state it. But then, in order to point out the constructed nature of conventional truth, the authors of these texts proceeded to negate the reference to an independent reality. So what at first appears to be a self-contradiction is actually a process of deconstructing ordinary knowledge by taking away its presupposition of an independent, external referent. Then, in the third stage of the process, these authors reconstructed the original statement without reference to any independent reality. This reconstruction is based on ultimate truth, achieved through direct insight into interdependent arising, but it is expressed in conventional, conceptual terms.

This three-stage technique of construction, deconstruction, and reconstruction is illustrated in the following passage from the *Diamond Sutra:* "What was taught by the Tathagata as heap of merit, as no heap of merit, that has been taught by the Tathagata. Therefore, the Tathagata teaches, 'heap of merit,' 'no heap of merit.' "[4] "Heap of merit" used the first time is a conventional statement that would ordinarily be taken to mean that there is some independently existing reality, a real heap of merit, accumulated as a result of practicing the way. "No heap of merit" deconstructs the conventional statement by declaring that it does not refer to anything because it has no referent. That is, there is no independently existing real heap of merit to which "heap of merit" could refer.

The third, reconstructive stage is indicated by putting the Tathagata's teaching in special quotes, " 'heap of merit,' " " 'no heap of merit,' " so the text can be read as saying that although merit is not some independently existing reality, nonetheless, practicing the way is meritorious. In other words, to say that one gains merit is not to say that there is something called merit that a person accumulates; it is merely to say that one's actions are meritorious. Neither a separate person nor a separate attainment by a person are implied in saying that a person's actions are meritorious.

By recognizing that the Perfection of Wisdom texts contain progressively deeper levels of meaning through this three-stage process of conventional statement, by deconstruction of the statement's ontological assumptions, and finally by a pragmatic reconstruction of the statement without assuming or implying any independently existing entities, we can read these texts without becoming confused. Indeed, read in this way, these texts show how the fundamental teachings of the Buddha are to be understood in accord with the fundamental insight of interdependent arising even on the level of constructed knowledge and conventional truth.

DIAMOND SUTRA

The *Diamond Sutra* advocates the Bodhisattva way and the practice of mindfulness as the way of perfect wisdom. Although it clearly opposes the interpretation of existence in terms of absolutes, rejecting self-existence, essential being, and the ultimacy of conceptual thought, it does not actually use the term "emptiness." The Sanskrit name of this sutra, *Vajracchedika,* means "the diamond that cuts through illusion." The illusion that it cuts through is the illusion that the conceptual is the real. When Subhuti, the disciple to whom the Buddha taught the *Diamond Sutra,* asked, "What should this *sutra* be called and how should we act regarding its teachings?" the Buddha replied, "This sutra should be called the *Diamond That Cuts Through Illusion,* because it has the capacity to cut through all illusions and afflictions and bring us to the shore of liberation."

Over and over again, this text reminds us that concepts are incapable of capturing reality; they only function as signs that point to reality. Things as conceived, therefore, should never be mistaken for things themselves. Near the beginning of the *sutra*, in answer to Subhuti's question about how a person wanting to become enlightened should practice, the Buddha explains how a Bodhisattva thinks: "However many species of living beings there are . . . , we must lead all these beings to the ultimate *nirvana* so that they can be liberated." "And when," the text continues, "this infinite number of beings has become liberated, we do not, in truth, think that a single being has been liberated."

Why, if all these beings have been liberated, would a Bodhisattva think that not even one being had been liberated? The text anticipates this question and gives the Buddha's answer: "If, Subhuti, a bodhisattva holds on to the idea that a self, a person, a living being, or a life span exists, that person is not an authentic bodhisattva." The reason is that a Bodhisattva is an enlightened being, and enlightened beings do not see existence in terms of separate, independent entities; enlightened beings see everything in terms of interdependent arising. To hold onto the idea that something—a self, person, living being, life span, or anything else—has a separate, independent existence means that one is not enlightened. Because a Bodhisattva would not see the self as a separate self or person and would not see others as separate beings, he or she would not think, "I, myself, am the liberator, liberating those other helpless beings."

In Chapter 7 of the *Diamond Sutra,* Subhuti shows that he understands that nothing, not even the Buddha or his teaching, has separate, independent existence. The Buddha asks Subhuti, "Has the Tathagata arrived at the highest, most fulfilled, awakened mind? Does the Tathagata give any teaching?" By definition, the Tathagata (meaning "one gone thus to enlightenment") has experienced the highest, fullest awakening. Furthermore, all of Buddhism, including the *Diamond Sutra,* is the teaching given by the Buddha. In fact, without the context, which is the dialectic of the Perfection of Wisdom and which aims to reinterpret ordinary understanding based on the idea of self-existence in terms of interdependent arising, the Buddha's question as well as Subhuti's answer would be very strange.

Subhuti answers: "As far as I have understood the Lord Buddha's teachings, there is no independently existing object of mind called the highest, most fulfilled, awakened mind, nor is there any independently existing teaching that the Tathagata gives." This answer makes clear that what Subhuti is denying is not the Buddha's enlightenment or his teaching, but only that neither this enlightenment nor this teaching exists as a separate, independent thing. Subhuti makes this explicit: "The teachings that the Tathagata has realized and spoken of cannot be conceived of as separate, independent existences and therefore cannot be described." By saying that they cannot be described, Subhuti means that their descriptions are only conceptual constructions. As conceptual constructions, they can point to the Buddha's enlightenment and teachings, but they cannot capture the full reality of that enlightenment and those teachings. Thus, in his reply and his explanation of it, Subhuti shows that he understands the distinction between conventional and perfect understanding as well as the importance of not mistaking the conventional for the perfected.

Having made sure that Subhuti realized that the Buddha's own enlightenment and teaching should not be understood in terms of separate, independent existence, the Buddha next turns to how an Arhat's realization should be understood. The ultimate goal of practice in early Buddhism was to become an Arhat. An *Arhat* ("noble one") is a Buddhist practitioner who has been ennobled by the enlightenment achieved through his practice. It is the highest attainment possible. Because only if the fruits of his practice bring him to arhatship can one become an Arhat, we would expect Subhuti to answer affirmatively when the Buddha asks him, "Does an Arhat think like this, 'I have attained the fruits of Arhatship'?" But Subhuti replies, "No, World-Honored One."

Again, Subhuti goes on to explain that to think "I have attained the fruits of Arhatship" is to think in terms of separate, independent existences, but an Arhat thinks in terms of interdependent arising. He says, "There is no separately existing thing that can be called Arhat. If an Arhat gives rise to the thought that he has attained the fruit of Arhatship, then he is still caught up in the idea of a self, a person, a living being, and a life span." And of course, a person still caught up in the idea of self-existence cannot be an Arhat, for an Arhat has overcome the idea of self, both in the self and in others.

These examples illustrate the central teaching of the *Diamond Sutra* that the understanding of things in terms of separate, independent existence is limited and imperfect. To mistake this wrong conception of things for the way that they actually exist is the ignorance that separates us from others, leading to the grasping and hatred that give rise to all the various forms of *duhkha*. To understand things as they really are, one must first see that ordinary conceptions of them in terms of self-existence are actually a misunderstanding.

By understanding things in terms of interdependent arising, we can see how ordinary conceptual understanding of something is actually a misunderstanding. For example, take our ordinary conception of a kernel of wheat. We view it as something that exists by itself, separate from other things. It came into existence at a certain time, and it will cease to exist at a certain time. Because it is a kernel of wheat, it cannot be something else. For example, it cannot be water or earth or sunshine.

Now contrast this ordinary understanding with understanding in terms of interdependent arising. If we see the kernel of wheat in terms of interdependent arising, then we see that it is not just wheat, existing by itself. We see that in its arising, it absorbed the warmth and light of the sun, the nutrients of the earth, the moisture of water, and so forth. And the soil, energy from the sun, and water that make up this kernel have been recycling through existence for billions of years. We see also that before it was a kernel of wheat, it was a pollinated plant, which itself was made up of the earth's nutrients, water, and sun, and which had earlier been a kernel of wheat.

It is precisely because a kernel of wheat is not just a kernel of wheat, existing by itself, that it can be planted in the soil and become a plant, a process that requires the soil's nutrients, the sun's warmth, and the sky's moisture to become part of it. Only if the kernel is not separate can water, soil, and sun be part of its existence; and only then can it become a plant.

Viewed as a self-existent entity, we could say simply that a thing, such as a kernel of wheat, exists. It is what it is in itself, nothing more and nothing less. Viewed as an interdependent process, however, we cannot say simply that something exists; now we have to say that it *interexists* with everything else. To be a kernel of wheat the kernel cannot be just itself; it must be sun, water, and soil in order to be wheat.

So the full meaning of the dialectic of the *Diamond Sutra* is that for something to be what it is, it cannot be just what it is by itself; to be what it is, it must interexist with everything else. Only when a kernel of wheat is understood to not be just a kernel of wheat is it really understood to be a kernel of wheat.

HEART SUTRA

The *Heart Sutra,* a one-page summary of the voluminous Perfection of Wisdom texts, is the single most important Mahayana text on emptiness. "Emptiness" is a new word introduced into Buddhist vocabulary by the Perfection of Wisdom texts, but it is not a totally new idea. It is actually a new interpretation of interdependent arising, the central insight of Buddhism. It appears to be directed primarily against interpretations of interdependent arising in terms of ultimate constituents that are inherently self-existent, the kind of interpretation most fully and clearly developed by the Sarvastivada tradition.

According to the introduction to the *Heart Sutra,* the great Bodhisattva Avalokita achieved enlightenment and realized the cessation of *duhkha* by practicing the Perfection of Wisdom, which enabled him to see that persons and things are empty. To understand what this means, we must first ask, Of what are persons and things empty? The answer is that they are empty of inherent self-existence; no permanence or separateness is to be found in persons or things.

So why not just say that persons and things lack permanent and separate existence? To say that they are empty sounds like saying that they do not exist, whereas to say that their existence is not permanent and separate sounds like saying that they *do* exist, but not as separate and permanent beings. Why does the *Heart Sutra* use the strong language of emptiness, which can easily be interpreted as denying the existence of things, when it is only claiming that nothing exists as a permanent or separate being? It would seem that the text could have simply said that Avalokita realized the cessation of *duhkha* upon realizing that interdependent arising is the way persons and things exist.

Perhaps such a statement would have been adequate if the Sarvastivadins and others had not interpreted interdependent arising in terms of the separate and enduring self-existence of the constituents of existence *(dharmas).* But the fact that many Buddhists accepted the Sarvastivada view, which implicitly denied that the ultimate constituents were selfless and impermanent, meant that strong language was needed to counteract such a wrong interpretation. Furthermore, by looking at interdependent arising in terms of persons and things lacking permanent and separate existence, it was tempting to think that first things exist, and then later become dynamic and enter into relationships with other things. After all, how can anything change unless it first exists? And how can anything enter into relationships with others unless it (and the other thing to which it is related) already exists? But to interpret interdependent arising this way is to claim that inherent self-existence is basic and that interdependent arising is secondary, merely a way in which self-existent entities function. Such an interpretation is actually a rejection of the Buddha's insight that interdependent arising is the way that everything exists fundamentally. If interdependent arising is the way things actually exist, then there can be no self-existence at any level. Therefore the *Heart Sutra* makes the strong claim that all the constituents of persons and things are empty of self-existence.

The teaching of emptiness is designed to make clear that interdependent arising is primary, that it is the way that everything actually exists. Only when interdependence and change are seen as the very nature of existence, and only when separate, independent, enduring things and persons are seen, from the perspective of emptiness, as mere conventions, abstracted from the reality of interdependent arising, is interdependent arising fully understood.

Because the teaching of emptiness does not deny their existence, but only claims that persons and things are empty of permanence and self-existence, it also teaches something positive about their existence. Declaring that persons and things are empty of separateness and permanence points to the fullness and richness of existence when experienced as interdependent processes.

After the introductory verse describing how Avalokita realized the emptiness of the five groups, the *Heart Sutra* goes on to declare: "Form is emptiness, emptiness is form, form does not differ from emptiness, emptiness does not differ from form. The same is true with feelings, perceptions, mental formations and consciousness." Form refers to the group of processes that constitute feelings, perceptions, mental formations, and consciousness. Because a person is simply these five interdependent groups of processes, the text is saying that a person is empty of a self to whom the groups belong. Furthermore, that very lack of self-existence is what constitutes a person's existence, for it is emptiness that makes interbeing possible. Thus, personal existence is not different from emptiness, and emptiness is not different from personal existence.

In the next verse, the *Heart Sutra* proceeds to the level of existence where the five groups are viewed in terms of their constituents *(dharmas)*. Here it declares that "all dharmas are marked with emptiness; they are neither produced nor destroyed, neither defiled nor immaculate, neither increasing nor decreasing." The Sarvastivadins were convinced that unless the ultimate constituents *(dharmas)* of the groups constituting a person were independently real, then they would be forced to accept the nihilistic conclusion that neither the groups nor persons are real. The *Heart Sutra*'s claim that the *dharmas* are marked by emptiness rejects the Sarvastivada view that they have self-existence. If *dharmas* interexist, rather than self-exist, then their arising and ceasing is neither production (of something totally new) nor destruction, but rather transformation that depends on other transformations.

Because the *dharmas* interexist in every respect, they cannot be either totally pure (immaculate) or totally impure (defiled); their purity and impurity are co-present. For example, a cow eats the green grass that we think is pure and produces the manure that we think is impure. But the manure becomes part of the soil and produces the pure green grass. So the impure manure is already present in the pure green grass, and the pure green grass is already present in the impure manure.

Drawing out the implications of emptiness for the understanding and practice of Buddhism, the *Heart Sutra* goes on to teach that *duhkha,* nirvana, and the path from *duhkha* to nirvana should also be understood in terms of interdependent arising. They, too, have no separate, independent existence; one should not cling to them any more than one should cling to the view of self. Avalokita says, "therefore in emptiness there is . . . no suffering, no origination of suffering, no extinction of suffering, no path; no understanding, no attainment." This means that clinging to the view that there is some self-existent thing called *duhkha,* or some self-existent thing called the attainment of nirvana, or some self-existing thing called the path would prevent a person from understanding these as processes that arise interdependently. And without understanding the Noble Fourfold Truth in terms of interdependent arising, enlightenment would be impossible.

The *Heart Sutra* goes on to say, therefore, that "because there is no attainment, the bodhisattvas, supported by the Perfection of Wisdom, find no obstacles for their minds. Having no obstacles, they overcome fear, liberating themselves forever from illusion and realizing nirvana." This means that enlightened beings understand, through practicing the Perfection of Wisdom, that there is no self-existence in anything, including nirvana. Because they understand the emptiness of nirvana, realizing that it is not a separate, permanent state that can be attained, these Bodhisattvas realize nirvana.

REVIEW QUESTIONS

1. What is the conception of emptiness taught in the *Heart Sutra*?
2. How, in the *Diamond Sutra,* is the method of construction, deconstruction, and reconstruction used to explain how things exist in emptiness?
3. Why did the Perfection of Wisdom tradition emphasize that enlightenment awareness is *prajnaparamita* (surpassing wisdom)?

FURTHER READING

The Perfection of Wisdom, Illustrated with Ancient Sanskrit Manuscripts, edited by R.C. Jamieson, with an introduction by the Dalai Lama (New York: Viking Press, 2000), is a careful, readable translation, with beautiful illustrations, that enables ordinary readers to understand the messages of these ancient texts. It is probably the best place to begin one's reading in the Perfection of Wisdom literature.

The Heart of Understanding: Commentaries on the Prajnaparamita Heart Sutra, by Thich Nhat Hanh, edited by Peter Levitt (Berkeley, CA: Parallax Press, 1988), is an excellent translation and the easiest and most helpful commentary available.

The Diamond That Cuts Through Illusion: Commentaries on the Prajnaparamita Diamond Sutra, by Thich Nhat Hanh (Berkeley, CA: Parallax Press, 1992), is an excellent translation and commentary.

The Heart Sutra Explained: Indian and Tibetan Commentaries, by Donald S. Lopez Jr. (Albany: State University of New York Press, 1988), provides good translations of the classical Indian and Tibetan commentaries on the *Heart Sutra* and very helpful introductions.

Echoes of Voidness, by Geshe Rabten (London: Wisdom, 1983), is a very good introduction to the philosophy of emptiness. It contains a very clear commentary on the *Heart Sutra.*

NOTES

1. In Thich Nhat Hanh, *The Diamond That Cuts Through Illusion: Commentaries on the Prajnaparamita Diamond Sutra* (Berkeley, CA: Parallax Press, 1992), p. 11. Unless noted otherwise, all translations of the *Diamond Sutra* are from this source.

2. Thich Nhat Hanh, *The Heart of Understanding: Commentaries on the Prajna-paramita Heart Sutra,* edited by Peter Levitt (Berkeley, CA: Parallax Press, 1988). All quotations from the *Heart Sutra* are from this source.

3. The *Sutra on the Establishment of Mindfulness* calls this direct awareness "awareness of the body in the body," "awareness of objects of the mind in the objects of the mind," and so on. See chap. 3 in *Sutra on the Establishment of Mindfulness.*

4. Translation and analysis follows David Kalupahana, *A History of Buddhist Philosophy* (Honolulu: University of Hawaii Press, 1992), pp. 156–57.

CHAPTER 16

Madhyamaka: The Middle Way Tradition

OVERVIEW OF MADHYAMAKA

The Madhyamaka (Middle Way) tradition that Nagarjuna founded in India in the second century BCE grew out of a need to explain and defend the core insights of the Perfection of Wisdom tradition. Nagarjuna believed it necessary to defend interdependent arising, understood as the emptiness of self-existence, as the truth about how things exist against not only the Sarvastivadins, but also against the prevailing substantialist interpretations of existence by Jain and Hindu philosophers. Nagarjuna's success made Madhyamaka a major influence on the development of Buddhist thought and practice throughout Asia. Even today, it is central to Tibetan Buddhism and remains one of the foundations of Zen thought and practice.

The centerpiece of Madhyamaka thought is its analysis of and arguments for the teaching of "emptiness" *(shunyata)*. As in the Perfection of Wisdom tradition, emptiness means that existence is empty of self-existence and permanence, that everything is connected to everything else and is constantly changing. One of the implications of seeing existence as empty of permanence and separateness is that because conceptual thought represents things as separate and nondynamic, it cannot be the highest truth. The highest truth, as emphasized in the Perfection of Wisdom texts, is realized directly in the experience of mindfulness.

Madhyamaka is called the Middle Way philosophy because it is *midway* between the two extreme views of existence. It rejects the extreme view that existence is permanent, consisting of self-existing things with their own essences.

It also rejects the view that nothing really exists, that the appearance of things is merely an illusion. In positive terms, the Madhyamaka view is that things exist as processes, continuously arising and ceasing in dependence on one another. This vision, taught by the Buddha as interdependent arising, and taught by the Madhyamakas as emptiness, is the heart of the Middle Way tradition. As Nagarjuna says, "Emptiness is interdependent arising; indeed, it is the middle path."[1]

The Madhyamakas interpreted interdependent arising as emptiness in order to overcome the tendency to interpret it in terms of separate, permanent entities. Because there is a strong human tendency to seek absolute certainty in understanding existence and because it appears to most people that this quest for certainty can be satisfied only when understanding is grounded in absolute entities, the Buddha's teaching of interdependent arising was hard to understand and often misinterpreted. Within Buddhism, such wrong interpretation gave rise to the substantialist and essentialist views of the Sarvastivadins. To counteract the tendency to try to understand interdependent arising in terms of self-existence and essences, the philosophical absolutes of the Sarvastivadins and like-minded thinkers, the Middle Way tradition argued vigorously that absolutes do not exist in reality, that they are merely conceptual constructions. Being merely conceptual constructions, the absolutes postulated to explain existence are themselves empty of actual existence.

This teaching of the emptiness of essences and self-existence is one of the two pillars of Middle Way thought. The second pillar is the reconciliation of the higher truth of direct experience with the lower truth of conceptual understanding. This is accomplished by first showing the absurdity of explanations based on absolutes and then explaining existence in terms of interdependent arising, without recourse to any absolutes. Because it is the Middle Way, emptiness not only declares the absence of permanence and self-existence in things, but also indicates the fullness of existence as experienced directly in mindfulness.

The philosophical aspect of Madhyamaka thought, however, represents only one side of the development of the Middle Way tradition. Not only is emptiness to be understood, but it is also to be practiced. By eliminating the inclination to understand things as separate, permanent existences, it is possible to overcome the grasping that gives rise to *duhkha*. On the other side is found the customary Buddhist emphasis on the practice of discipline, meditation, and direct realization. Through the meditative practices, one can go beyond the emptiness of concepts and theories to the direct experience of reality. Understanding the relation between truth found in conceptual understanding and truth found in the direct experience of mindfulness allows the Middle Way tradition to combine both kinds of understanding in the practice of Buddhism.

MIDDLE WAY PHILOSOPHY OF NAGARJUNA

With an understanding of the meaning of emptiness in mind, we can examine the Madhyamaka analysis and the defense of this central Mahayana teaching. Throughout its history, the Madhyamaka tradition has been studied in terms of

Nagarjuna's *Fundamental Verses on the Middle Way,* which consists of twenty-seven chapters, each examining an important topic of Buddhist teaching. The Noble Fourfold Truth, nirvana, *duhkha,* the Buddha, self, action, causality, motion, perception, and views are among the topics examined. In his examination of these topics, Nagarjuna does two things. First, he methodically shows that explanations of the topics in terms of absolutes are self-refuting. Second, he offers an explanation of the topic that is not dependent on any absolutes, an explanation consistent with interdependent arising.

Method

The method used to clear away mistaken, absolutist interpretations of the key Buddhist teachings examined in the *Fundamental Verses on the Middle Way* is one of showing their absurdity by revealing internal inconsistencies. This method neither constitutes nor rests on Nagarjuna's own view of reality; it simply uses the opponents' own claims and arguments to show that their views were self-contradictory. For each topic that Nagarjuna examined, he showed that the absolutist view of it contains within itself the seeds of its own contradiction. In effect, the argument against the opponent is the opponent's own argument, presented in a way that reveals its own absurdity. Thus, the method itself was not something new; it simply rigorously applied the canons of logic and reasoning that were accepted by the opponents to their own claims.

The point of eliminating absolutist interpretations of important teachings is to show that concepts do not refer to some independently existing reality. The logic of this method is the logic of *reductio ad absurdum.* The general form of the argument is disjunctive: either S self-exists or else S does not self-exist, where S is the subject being examined, causality, perception, self, motion, and so forth. Since Nagarjuna wants to establish that things do not self-exist, that they are empty of self-existence, he undertakes to show that it cannot be the case that S self-exists. This he does by showing that if self-existence is assumed to be true, then absurd consequences follow. If "S self-exists" leads to absurdity, it cannot be true. But if it is false that S self-exists, then it must be true that S does not self-exist.

After clearing away the mistaken, absolutist explanation, Nagarjuna proceeds to explain the topic without invoking any absolutes. His own explanation, based on emptiness, is put forth as being fully in accord with the teaching of interdependent arising. But since emptiness, and the explanation based on it, also lacks separate, independent existence, Nagarjuna advises that one should not grasp at it as though it were something absolute.

Causality

Nagarjuna's method can be seen in his examination of causality in the first chapter of the *Fundamental Verses on the Middle Way.* Causality is an especially important topic because it plays such a crucial role in knowledge and action. We think that we understand something when we know its causes, and we think that we can achieve something when we know what causes will bring about the intended state of affairs. Buddhism emphasizes the importance of understanding what gives rise to *duhkha* in order to know how to eliminate it. But because Buddhism also emphasizes the complete interdependence of everything, it cannot explain the arising or ceasing of *duhkha* in terms of separate causes that have as their effect *duhkha* or nirvana. This is why the first part of the examination focuses on showing the impossibility of causality when it is interpreted as something called a cause, having the power to produce another thing called the effect. It is also why the second part of the examination shows how it is possible to understand the arising and ceasing of things by coming to know the conditions of arising and ceasing, conditions that have no inherent self-existence and which contain no essential causal power.

Nagarjuna begins his examination of causality by setting out the four possible ways that effects can be produced by causes: (1) an effect produces itself; (2) an effect is produced by something other than itself; (3) an effect both produces itself and is produced by something other than itself; (4) an effect is produced without a cause. In the following verses, Nagarjuna shows that none of these alternatives are possible if causality is viewed as the production of an effect by a causal power that inheres in a self-existent cause.

Suppose that the first view of causality, that an effect produces itself, is true. That means that the cause that produces the effect is identical with the effect. To claim that cause and effect are identical is to claim that there is only one thing. Because causality is a relationship between two things, one of which has the power to produce the other, if there is only one thing, then no causal relation is possible. And if no causal relation is possible, then it is absurd to claim that an effect causes itself.

Now suppose that the second view of causality, that an effect is produced by something other than itself, is true. This means that the cause that produces the effect is essentially different from the effect. But if they are essentially different, how can one be the effect of the other? For example, when a bean sprouts, we would say that the bean sprout is the effect of the seed (or that the seed caused the sprout) because the seed was transformed into the sprout. But the seed can transform into a sprout precisely because it is *not* essentially different. If two separate, independently existing things are essentially different, as, for example, a stone and a sprout, then one cannot transform into the other, and we could not say that the stone caused the sprout. The examples show that only when things are *not* inherently or essentially different can a causal relationship exist between them. But if a causal relationship cannot obtain between two things that are essentially different, then it is absurd to claim that an effect is produced by something other than itself.

Consider also that if the effect is essentially different from the cause that produces it, then, as effect, it was nonexistent before it was produced. But when it was nonexistent, no other thing could have been in causal relation with it. And without a causal relation, nothing can be either an effect or a cause. It is not possible, therefore, that an effect could be caused by something essentially different from itself.

Turning now to the third view of causality, that an effect both produces itself and is produced by something other than itself, we see that it is simply the conjunction of the first two views. Since both conjuncts have already been shown to be false, the third view has also been shown to be false, for if any of its conjuncts are false, then the whole conjunctive statement is false.

The fourth view of causality, that an effect is produced without a cause, is really a claim that there are no causes; it is to abandon the whole idea of causal relations. Since our sense of the order of things as well as our ability to explain that order depends on understanding causal relationships, why would anyone reject causality completely? Probably only because they felt that there was no other alternative. For example, if the only explanations of causality are the three views just examined and all three are seen to be absurd, the only reasonable alternative would be to reject the whole idea of causality.

Causal Conditions

Nagarjuna, who clearly did reject all four views examined as absurd, did not reject causal connectedness completely. Rather, he proceeded to offer an alternative view of relationships that are responsible for order and knowledge. This alternative is the view that things arise, exist, and cease in dependence on conditions, but that none of these conditions are self-existent causes. In the second verse, Nagarjuna specifies the four kinds of conditions on which change, that is, the arising and ceasing of things, depends: (1) efficient conditions, (2) percept-object conditions, (3) immediate conditions, and (4) dominant conditions.

The first kind of conditions, efficient conditions, account for change by identifying appropriate prior changes. For example, the efficient condition of the arising of words on the computer screen is the striking of certain keys. An efficient condition of striking keys is movement of the fingers.

The second kind of conditions, percept-object conditions, account for the arising of perceptions in terms of the objects perceived. For example, the presence of the computer in front of me is the percept-object condition of my perceiving a computer. Similarly, the presence of the idea of conditions in my mind is the percept-object condition of my thinking about conditions.

The third kind of conditions, immediate conditions, account for change in terms of activities triggered by efficient conditions. For example, the immediate conditions of moving one's fingers to strike the keys of the computer include skeletal and muscular changes in the hands and arms, movement of nerve impulses, firing of neurons in the brain, and so forth.

The fourth kind of conditions, dominant conditions, account for change in terms of ends or goals. For example, the dominant conditions of striking these computer keys include the goals of wanting to help students understand Buddhism, of wanting to improve one's understanding of Nagarjuna, of wanting to share research with other teachers, and so forth.

It is important to note that no essences or causal powers are invoked in explaining change in terms of any of these conditions. In the remaining twelve verses of the chapter on causality, Nagarjuna argues that any attempt to view the conditions of change as self-existent causes with inherent causal powers is self-defeating. In effect, it reduces explanation in terms of conditions to explanations in terms of causes, which on Nagarjuna's analysis makes change completely unintelligible. Only if causes are seen as empty of self-existence and causal power can they produce effects. But this very emptiness means that they are not causes in the usual sense, but simply conditions of change. And it is this position, that things arise and cease interdependently due to conditions without independent, self-existing entities, that Nagarjuna defends because it is fully in accord with the teaching of interdependent arising.

Motion

Nagarjuna's first chapter, on causality, explains the first part of interdependent arising, namely the *interdependence* of conditions in the absence of essences or self-existent entities that could function as causes. The second chapter, on motion (or change), explains the second part of interdependent arising, namely, the *arising* of things in the absence of essences or self-existent entities.

It would be natural for Nagarjuna's opponents to respond to his claim that there are no causes (in the sense of self-existent entities that have in them the power to produce effects) by saying that if there are no real causes, then there can be no effects. But in that case, there is no change, because change is simply the arising and ceasing of effects. Nagarjuna argues against this response by showing that if change is viewed in terms of self-existent entities, it is impossible.

If motion is an entity, as Nagarjuna argues in verses 18–20, then it must either be identical to the mover or different from it. If the motion is identical to the mover, then the mover would be a different thing every time it moved. For example, a person walking would be a different person than the same person running, who, in turn, would be a different person than the same person standing still. But this is absurd. If the motion is different from the mover, however, the two would be separate from each other. But if they are separate from each other, it would be possible for there to be motion without a mover and for there to be a mover without any motion. This is also absurd.

The absurdity that results from trying to understand change as an entity that another entity, the substance or agent of change, undergoes, does not imply that there is no change. Rather, it suggests that instead of viewing change as a succession of entities or properties of entities, it needs to be understood differently, in terms of relations between stages of continuous processes. Viewing change relationally does not force one to separate motion from the mover; it allows change to be explained as a continuous process, dependent upon conditions.

Self

In chapter 18, Nagarjuna argues against the essentialist view of the self. The argument is straightforward. The self (as a self-existent, enduring entity) must be either identical with its components or different from them. If it is identical with its components (which in Buddhist analysis are the five groups of processes), then any change in the components is a change in the self. If, however, the components are constantly changing, different from moment to moment, then so is the self that is identical with the components. Because a self-existent, enduring self cannot be different from itself from moment to moment, it is absurd to claim that it is identical with its components.

The other alternative, that the self is essentially different from its components, is also absurd, for then no changes in its constituitive components can have any effect on the self. For example, becoming virtuous or wise, which are changes in the consciousness and disposition components, would not affect the self in any way. Furthermore, because knowledge takes place in consciousness, a separate self would be unknowable. And most importantly, from a Buddhist perspective, no amount of practice could ever free such a self from ignorance, grasping, and hatred.

The Buddha

It is important for Nagarjuna to show not only that our views of ordinary things are conceptual constructions, but that even the Buddhist views of the Buddha, the Noble Fourfold Truth, and nirvana are conceptual constructs. All conceptions, whether of ordinary or ultimate things, are empty of ultimate reality, even though, as valid mental constructions, they constitute signs that point to reality. If the Buddha is thought to have permanent, independent existence, there would be a basis for the tendency to grasp at the Buddha as ultimately real while rejecting the world as merely illusory. Therefore, in chapter 22, Nagarjuna shows that even the Buddha is empty of self-existence.

He begins by examining how the self of the Buddha could be related to the five groups of processes that constitute every person's existence. The four possible relationships are (1) the self is identical with the groups; (2) the self is different from the groups; (3) the groups exist in the self as its properties; or (4) the self is not in the groups. The first alternative, that the self is identical with the groups, is not possible because the self is one thing, but the groups are five things. Furthermore, the groups are constantly changing, but the self is something enduring. The second alternative, that the self is completely different from the groups, is also impossible, for then it would be unaffected by any changes in the groups. Not only is this contrary to experience, but it would make enlightenment impossible because enlightenment arises through a transformation of the groups. The third alternative, that the groups exist in the self, would mean that the self exists independently of the groups as the entity in which they inhere. Not only has Nagarjuna already shown that nothing exists independently, but when the groups are analyzed, no underlying entity is found. For the same reasons, the fourth alternative is absurd, for analysis does not reveal any self inhering in the groups any more than it reveals groups inhering in a self.

If the Buddha is empty of self-existence, is the real Buddha unknowable? Indeed, is it the implication of the emptiness of everything that nothing is knowable? If this were the case, it would seem that Nagarjuna's whole project would be absurd, for then he could not possibly know how ultimate truth differs from conventional truth and could not make the crucial distinction between the two levels of truth on which his entire analysis rests. It is important, therefore, for Nagarjuna to explain emptiness in a way that avoids this implication.

In verse eleven he says:

"Empty" should not be asserted.
"Non-empty" should not be asserted.
Neither both nor neither should be asserted.
They are only used nominally.[2]

This means that because it is a conceptual construction, emptiness itself has only conventional existence. It applies only to reality as known conventionally, through concepts; it does not apply to ultimate reality, which is not known through concepts, but directly, through mindfulness. But because the conceptually known reality is not in itself (but only in the way it is known) different from the ultimate reality, conceptual knowledge points to the ultimate; and although conceptual knowledge is limited, it does reveal something of that reality. Thus, it is possible to have conventional knowledge of the distinction between the conventional and the ultimate.

Because our ordinary understanding of the Buddha is conceptual, the Buddha's existence, as we know it, is empty of independent, permanent existence. To think that this conceptual understanding reveals a real, independent Buddha is simply to construct another conceptual view. Grasping at the conceptual construct of the Buddha will not reveal the reality of the Buddha. As Nagarjuna says in verse 15, "Because the Buddha is beyond all conceptual constructions, those who seek the Buddha in conceptual constructions fail to see the Buddha."[3]

The Noble Fourfold Truth

Chapter 24 applies the analyses of the previous chapters to the core teachings of Buddhism, the Noble Fourfold Truth, showing that only when this truth and the existence to which it applies is understood in terms of emptiness can it be effective in achieving freedom from suffering. In the process, Nagarjuna explains the theory of two truths and the relationship between conventional truth, emptiness, and interdependent arising.

The first six verses present an objection to the teaching of emptiness as the way things exist, claiming that if things are empty of reality, then no truth is possible and therefore even the Noble Fourfold Truth is implicitly denied. Nagarjuna replies to this objection by pointing out that its underlying nihilistic interpretation of emptiness is a misunderstanding that stems from the opponent's mistaken view that emptiness is a self-existent property that applies to everything. According to Nagarjuna (verse 8), "the Buddha's teaching is based on two truths: a truth of worldly convention and an ultimate truth."[4] As a result of not distinguishing between ultimate and conventional truth, the opponent mistakenly assumes that not only things, but emptiness as well, are ultimately true. This leads the opponent to think that emptiness is an ultimate truth that denies the existence of ordinary things. Nagarjuna removes the objection by pointing out that emptiness is a conventional truth, operating on the same level as the conventional reality to which it refers. In other words, emptiness is also empty; it is simply a view about what views are, and not a denial that there are things of which we have views. Indeed, without understanding that views about things (including ultimate things such as the Buddha, the Noble Fourfold Truth, or nirvana) are only views, not to be mistaken for reality itself, the significance of the ultimate cannot be understood.

In verse 18, Nagarjuna explains that because emptiness means that nothing exists by itself, independently of others, its positive meaning is that everything exists as interdependently arisen. In other words, emptiness is actually interdependent arising. Furthermore, he says, because emptiness is conventionally true, it is a middle path between nonexistence and eternal existence, the two extreme views that the Buddha avoided in proclaiming the Middle Path of interdependent arising. Thus, emptiness, interdependent arising, and the Middle Path are all equivalent. By showing that nothing has separate, independent existence, Nagarjuna has defended the Buddha's insight into interdependent arising as the Middle Path by disproving its wrong interpretations. That is why, in concluding this key chapter, Nagarjuna says, "Whoever sees interdependent arising also sees duhkha, its arising, its cessation, and also the path."

Nirvana

In his analysis of nirvana in chapter 25, Nagarjuna applies the same logic that he used in his analysis of the Buddha and the Noble Fourfold Truth, and he arrives at a similar conclusion: there is no independently real entity or state called nirvana. Nirvana is just ordinary existence in this ordinary world, but without the *duhkha* that arises from ignorance. But it is not the case that suffering is one kind of existence and nirvana another. The only difference between them is that the suffering person lives in this world in the mode of ignorance, grasping, and hatred, while in nirvana the person is free from ignorance, grasping, and hatred. As Nagarjuna says in verse 19, "There is not the slightest difference between samsara and nirvana." If *samsara* and nirvana were completely different kinds of existence, then the Buddha's attainment of nirvana would have meant that he could not have continued to live in this world, teaching the Middle Way for forty years.

A DIALOGUE ON THE TEACHING AND PRACTICE OF EMPTINESS

The following imaginary dialogue between a student and Madhya, a Middle Way Buddhist, summarizes the teaching of emptiness in terms of challenges encountered in trying to understand this rather difficult teaching. It is based on actual conversations with students.

Understanding Emptiness

Student: I'm confused. Just when I thought I was beginning to understand that Buddhism is the quest for nirvana through the realization of the Four Noble Truths and the practice of the eightfold path, I encountered the *Heart*

Sutra. This text proclaims that everything is empty of reality—even a person, when viewed as simply the five groups of processes, namely forms, feelings, perceptions, formative impulses, and consciousness, is empty. But if everything is empty of reality, including oneself, how can one practice the Path? There would be no one to practice and nothing to be practiced. And since nirvana is also empty, there is nothing to be realized. This sounds like nihilism, the complete denial of all reality and meaning. Either the teaching of emptiness contradicts the teachings of the Buddha or else my understanding of emptiness is faulty.

Madhya: I assure you, emptiness does not contradict the Buddha's teachings. But let me try to explain emptiness, for we understand this to be the deeper understanding of the Buddha's teaching of interdependent arising, the teaching that underlies the Four Noble Truths and the Noble Eightfold Path.

Student: Good! Please explain how emptiness can be equivalent to interdependent arising. I think I understand interdependent arising, which affirms that things are really of the nature of process, ever-changing, and that these processes are all interconnected. It rules out permanence and separateness, but it does not deny the reality of the processes that are connected to one another. If their reality were denied, there would be nothing to be connected, and this would be nihilism.

Madhya: Very good! Your concern, to affirm the interconnectedness of things and to avoid nihilism, is precisely our concern. That is why we insist that all things are empty of inherent existence and that this emptiness is the nature of existence. You understand emptiness at the first level, that of the emptiness of things, but do not yet understand it at the second level, the emptiness of the constituents of things *(dharmas)*.

Student: I don't understand: if the constituents of processes are empty of reality, isn't this the complete denial of the processes themselves?

Madhya: On the contrary: if the constituents are affirmed to have inherent existence, then the problem of their interrelatedness will be exactly that of the problem of the interrelatedness of things when things are affirmed to have inherent existence. Constituents can be interrelated as constituitive elements of processes only if they lack separate, permanent, independent existence.

Student: You mean that unless constituents are empty of self-existence *(svabhava)*, it will be impossible to explain interdependent arising because neither change nor relatedness will be intelligible?

Madhya: Just so. Remember Nagarjuna's analysis of causality. He showed that if you assume that things have separate existence, then causality as an explanation of their interrelatedness and of their change becomes unintelligible.

Student: I remember that Nagarjuna said that things are not caused by themselves, nor by others, nor by themselves and others, nor by neither themselves or others. And I remember that Candrakirti explained that something cannot cause itself, for it already exists and therefore is not in need of a cause. Something cannot be caused by something other than itself, however, for causality is a relation between two things, and before the second thing exists, it cannot be in relation to anything. But after it exists, it does not require a cause. And I also understand that if neither self-causation nor other-causation are intelligible, then neither is their combination, nor the rejection of both.

Madhya: Your understanding is excellent indeed! But if you understand this, what is your problem?

Student: My problem is this: If you show that causality is unintelligible, how can you understand the interrelatedness of things? And this question is not only theoretical, but also practical, for unless practicing the Noble Eightfold Path is causally related to removing ignorance, grasping, and aversion, what reason can there be for practice?

Madhya: Now I see your confusion. First, you think that I deny causal interrelatedness. Second, you think that unless things have inherent existence at some level—if not at the level of things, then at the level of their constituents—their reality must be completely denied. Concerning the first point, Nagarjuna's argument is in hypothetical form: *If* things have inherent existence, *then* causality is unintelligible. Nagarjuna concludes that because causality cannot be rejected, the assumption that things have inherent existence must be rejected.

Student: You mean that Nagarjuna's argument against causality is really an argument against the metaphysical assumptions underlying a certain *view* of causality?

Madhya: Exactly. He is saying that if you assume that things have inherent existence as separate and permanent things, then you are forced to deny the possibility of explaining their interrelatedness and their change in terms of conditions and causes.

Student: And since the Buddha's teachings are teachings of the conditions and causes of *duhkha* and the elimination of these conditions and causes, to accept these teachings one must deny the inherent existence of things as separate and permanent entities?

Madhya: Quite right. This is why we insist that all things are empty of inherent existence. This explains your second confusion. You thought that unless the *dharmas* constituting things have inherent existence, one would be forced to deny the reality of things. But we think that only by recognizing the emptiness of inherent existence at every level can interdependent arising as the very nature of existence be affirmed.

Student: Okay, so not only are things empty of inherent existence, but so are the *dharmas* or processes that constitute things. But what about *duhkha* and nirvana—don't they have inherent existence? Or are they also empty of inherent existence?

Madhya: If *duhkha* existed in and of itself, as something separate and permanent, then it could never be eliminated. Likewise, if nirvana had inherent existence as something separate and permanent, then it could never be achieved, for it would be separate from any activities that could bring it about.

Student: Does this mean that *duhkha* and nirvana are not real?

Madhya: No, it means that their reality is interrelational, that the reality of *duhkha* is not to be found apart from the reality of nirvana and the reality of nirvana is not to be found apart from the reality of *duhkha*. Further, there is no *duhkha* or nirvana apart from lived experience. This is why we say that emptiness is the way things truly exist.

Student: So is emptiness simply a way of seeing that *duhkha* is the delusory experience of separateness and permanence, which is rooted in the false notion of inherent existence? And nirvana is simply the lived experience of interdependent arising?

Madhya: Precisely! I think you are already on the way to enlightenment!

Student: But what about emptiness itself—does it have inherent existence or is it also empty?

Madhya: Emptiness works to eliminate the grasping and aversion that follows upon taking inherent existence to be the nature of things only because it too is empty of self-existence. Otherwise it would be unrelated to insight and practice.

Student: So, if things are empty, *dharmas* are empty, nirvana is empty, and emptiness is empty, what is not empty? What is real?

Madhya: Interdependent arising is real, as is the insight that sees this reality.

Practicing Emptiness

Student: How can one achieve this insight? How can one realize the truth of interdependent arising in one's life?

Madhya: This is a very important question, for ultimately all Buddhist teachings are practical teachings, aimed at overcoming duhkha. From the perspective of practice, emptiness is really a process, the practice of emptying oneself of the wrong views that give rise to grasping and hatred.

Student: I don't understand. Nagarjuna explained emptiness as the way everything actually exists, that is, without inherent self-existence. But now you speak of emptiness as a practice. This sounds like something quite different.

Madhya: Not really. In terms of knowledge, emptiness is the lack of enduring, separate self-existence of things and persons. But in terms of practice, this emptiness must be realized in daily life as the fullness of interdependent arising. It is this realization that constitutes enlightenment.

Student: But I thought that in enlightenment one experiences the presence of the Buddha-nature in everything that appears, whether a grain of rice, a blade of grass, or a smile. This doesn't sound like an emptying process to me.

Madhya: But remember, only when grasping for self and other are abandoned can one encounter things in their true nature as interdependent arising, that is, in their Buddha nature. Abandoning grasping for self and other is the practical realization of emptiness. As long as you view yourself as a separate, inherently existing self, you cannot avoid imposing your constructions on experience, ignorantly mistaking these constructions for reality. In our sitting, work, and play, we practice emptying ourselves of wrong views in order to abandon grasping so that we might experience ourselves and things as they really are, empty of own-being. Emptying ourselves of the mental constructions that obscure the true nature of existence as interdependent arising, we see directly into the true nature of ourselves and things as interdependent arising, becoming enlightened.

Student: Is this what Buddhists mean when they say, "To practice the Way is to forget the self?"

Madhya: Precisely! Forgetting the self is simply emptying oneself of the false construction of inherent selfhood. And this makes possible authentic encounter with others, thereby authenticating one's own existence.

Student: What is the connection between forgetting the self and authentic existence?

Madhya: Just as emptiness reveals interdependent arising, so the practice of emptying oneself of the constructions of ignorance reveals the authentic existence of oneself and others in their true natures as interdependently arisen.

Student: So the presencing of the ultimate in the ordinary—experiencing the Buddha-nature in eating a grain of rice—is simply the practical realization of emptiness! But because emptiness is nothing but interdependent arising, its realization affirms the plurality of unique events and moments as manifestations of the ultimate.

Madhya: Yes, and that is why we say that each being is unique and precious in every moment of its existence. Experientially, each moment of existence is realized as each being's total fullness of being.

Student: Thank you very much. I think I understand emptiness much better now—even though my understanding is still merely intellectual. Indeed, I even think I am beginning to understand the distinction between two levels of truth. The conventional level affirms ordinary things and points beyond itself to the ultimate level, which affirms the true nature of things as emptiness or interdependent arising. But this ultimate truth can be realized only through the selves and things encountered on the conventional level.

Madhya: Yes, but only when the conventional is experienced as the ultimate through full mindfulness, that is, without the constructions of ignorance. That is why we emphasize the practice of mindfulness; mindfulness is the practice of experiencing things directly. It is the practice of being fully present to our nondual experience of existence as interdependent arising.

Student: Let's stop for now. Trying to keep the two truths distinct while seeing them relationally at the same time is giving me a headache! And from what you say about practice, I am not sure I will ever understand this fully until I realize the truth of interdependent arising experientially, through the practice of mindfulness.

REVIEW QUESTIONS

1. Why does Nagarjuna interpret interdependent arising as emptiness *(shunyata)*?
2. What is Nagarjuna's method in the *Fundamental Verses on the Middle Way*?
3. How does Nagarjuna argue against self-existent causes and effects?
4. Explain how emptiness, interdependent arising, and the Middle Way are related to one another.
5. How are *samsara* and nirvana different? How are they the same?

FURTHER READING

Nagarjuna and Philosophy of Openness, by Nancy McCagney (Lanham, MD: Rowman & Littlefield, 1997), offers a careful study of the early Buddhist and Mahayana background of the teaching of emptiness by Nagarjuna in his treatise on the Fundamentals of the Middle Way.

Introduction to the Philosophy of Nagarjuna, by Musashi Tachikawa (Columbia, MO: South Asia Books, 1997), provides an interesting account of Nagarjuna's philosophy.

Emptiness Appraised: A Critical Study of Nagarjuna's Philosophy, by David F. Burton (London: Curzon Press, 2000), a careful, critical appraisal of the philosophy of emptiness, is the most recent study of Nagarjuna's philosophy.

The Fundamental Wisdom of the Middle Way: Nagarjuna's Mulamadhymakakarika. A Translation and Commentary, by Jay L. Garfield (New York: Oxford University Press, 1995), is a good translation and an excellent verse-by-verse philosophical interpretation from a Tibetan perspective.

Emptiness: A Study in Religious Meaning, by Frederick J. Streng (Nashville, TN: Abingdon Press, 1967), is a classic study of the concept of emptiness in Nagarjuna's thought.

A History of Buddhist Philosophy, by David J. Kalupahana (Honolulu: University of Hawaii Press, 1992), has a helpful chapter on the *Diamond Sutra* (pp. 153–59) and another on Nagarjuna (pp. 160–69).

Nagarjuna: A Translation of his Mulamadhymakakarika with an Introductory Essay, by Kenneth Inada (Tokyo: Hokuseido Press, 1970), is an excellent translation. The introductory essay, though not easy, is a masterpiece.

To See the Buddha: A Philosopher's Quest for the Meaning of Emptiness, by Malcolm David Eckel (Princeton, NJ: Princeton University Press, 1995), shows, through an analysis of Bhavaviveka's thought, how the logical mind and the devotional heart function together in Madhyamaka.

NOTES

1. Mulamadhyamaka Karika, ch. 24. Author's translation.
2. Jay L. Garfield, *The Fundamental Wisdom of the Middle Way: Nagarjuna's Mulamadhymakakarika. A Translation and Commentary* (New York: Oxford University Press, 1995), p. 61.
3. Author's translation.
4. Ibid.

CHAPTER 17

Yogacara

OVERVIEW OF YOGACARA

Yogacara was founded in the late fourth century CE by Asanga (ca. 365–440) and his brother Vasubandhu (ca. 380–460) as the second of the two major Mahayana philosophical traditions. *Yoga,* meaning "discipline," and *cara,* meaning "practice," combine in *yogacara* to mean "the practice of discipline." Because Yogacara, like Madhyamaka, is grounded in the Mahayana tradition, which interprets the highest goal as a Bodhisattva's enlightenment, the fundamental question for Yogacara is, What is the discipline that one needs to practice in order to become a Bodhisattva? Thus, Yogacara philosophy is concerned primarily with examining how enlightenment arises and how the obstacles to its arising can be overcome.

The discipline that a Bodhisattva practices is basically that of the Noble Eightfold Path, which Mahayana interprets as the practice of the perfections *(paramitas)*—giving, patience, effort, moral conduct, meditation, and wisdom— that overcome the afflictions that give rise to *duhkha.* Because ignorance is the primary affliction, giving rise to the afflictions of grasping and hatred that underlie all suffering, Yogacara is especially interested in understanding what ignorance is and how it arises. And because enlightenment is the removal of ignorance, Yogacara is especially interested in what enlightenment is and how it arises. Furthermore, because ignorance and enlightenment pertain to cognition and because cognition occurs in consciousness, the Yogacara interest in understanding the arising of ignorance and enlightenment led naturally to an examination of the nature and function of consciousness. Thus, the two primary foci of Yogacara are the nature of knowledge and the processes of consciousness that produce ignorance and knowledge.

Yogacara accepts and develops the Mahayana emphasis on the emptiness of self-existence as the right understanding of interdependent arising. Furthermore, because Yogacara agrees with the Madhyamaka understanding of emptiness, it also claims that the only difference between nirvana and *samsara* is that a person's ignorance has been transformed into enlightenment. But Yogacara understands that this insight shifts the burden of explaining the practice of becoming a Bodhisattva from merely explaining how a Bodhisattva understands emptiness to explaining (1) what ignorance is and how it arises; (2) what enlightenment (perfect wisdom) is and how it arises; and (3) how ignorance and enlightenment are related. Thus, Yogacara focuses on the processes of consciousness that produce both ignorance and knowledge in order to explain how and why the Bodhisattva way should be practiced.

Furthermore, unless the enlightened person could be shown to be the same person who previously had been ignorant, the Bodhisattva practice (and all Buddhist practice) would be meaningless. It was crucial, therefore, to give an account of consciousness that establishes continuity between different states of consciousness. But of course, this continuity could not be based on a permanent consciousness or on identity between its various states because everything that exists is empty of permanence and self-existence. To explain how personal continuity is compatible with emptiness, Yogacara developed its theory of the store consciousness *(alaya vijnana),* a theory that transformed the Buddhist understanding of consciousness.

EXISTENCE AND CONSCIOUSNESS

Three Aspects of Things

To be able to maintain that persons and things are empty of self-existence without the risk of being seen as nihilists, denying that things actually exist, Yogacara thinkers developed a theory of knowledge that claimed that things can be known in three ways or under three aspects *(trisvabhava).* A thing can be known as (1) something conceptually constructed, (2) something conditioned by other things, or (3) something as it is in itself *(tathata),* free of conceptual construction.

That in ordinary cognition, a thing appears to a cognizing subject as a separate, self-existent object is its conceptually constructed aspect. But the conceptually constructed object is not the reality of the thing itself, but merely a mental construction that represents the thing. To mistake the conceptual construction, which is only a sign that points to the thing, for the reality that it represents is like mistaking the finger that points to the moon for the moon itself.

The conditioned aspect of the thing that appears as an object of knowledge is its interdependent nature. For example, conditions on which the existence of a shiny red apple depends include seeds, peel, stem, and so forth, all of which were conditioned by sun, water, soil, and other conditions. Furthermore, what is present in the cognizer's experience in coming to know an apple is a flow of mutually conditioning sensations, feelings, perceptions, and so on that arise in dependence upon the thing perceived. That the things we know appear to us as conditioned things means that the object is conceptually constructed out of the flow of interdependent mental phenomena that arise in the presence of the conditioned thing that is perceived.

The third aspect, the perfected aspect of the known thing, is realized in mindfulness when all conceptual construction is left aside. In full mindfulness, there is no subject and no object; here, the flow of experience is realized to be simply a flow, entirely empty of objects and subject. Here, one becomes aware of the body in the body, feelings in the feelings, and so forth, without construing this awareness dualistically into subject and objects. Direct insight is said to provide the perfected knowledge of things because while conceptual constructions can provide a mental representation of the thing that is known, only the insight of direct awareness can reveal it as it really is.

Traditionally, these three aspects are explained by the analogy of a mirage in which water is seen. Because it is a mirage, there is no real water. What is perceived as water is just the flow of perceptions, which is the dependent aspect. That this flow of perceptions is taken to be real water is the conceptually constructed aspect. The realization that there is no real water present in the flow of perceptions is the perfected aspect.

Nature and Function of Consciousness

Knowledge is a function of consciousness. How does consciousness function to produce knowledge of the three aspects of things? According to Yogacara, consciousness functions in two basically different ways. The first way is that of ordinary, dualistic consciousness, where cognition involves a subject and an object. This is usually referred to as discursive consciousness because it moves between its subject and its objects. Discursive consciousness knows a given thing by representing it as an object to the subject. Thus, although there is a given thing that is the basis of the perceived object, the object as perceived is not the given thing itself, but merely a mental representation of it. The knowing subject is also a mental representation of the self. Although there is an actual person who is the basis of the representation, the subject of consciousness that knows the object in ordinary cognition is not the actual person, but merely a representation of the actual person, just as the object is merely a representation of the actual thing.

The second way that consciousness functions is nondualistic, where knowledge is immediate and direct, not involving the representations of subject and object. Because ordinary knowledge is dualistic, when it attempts to understand this immediate and direct knowledge in terms of knowledge of an object by a subject, it inevitably sees it as something other than it is, mistaking it for an object of discursive consciousness. But in mindfulness, which is nondualistic, this second way that consciousness functions is experienced directly. To talk about it, however, is necessarily to talk about it as an object known by a subject, for words, like thoughts, are only signs of reality and not the reality itself. As Vasubandhu says in the conclusion of the *Twenty Verses,* the full understanding of things, even of discursive thought, is beyond merely discursive thought.[1]

Store Consciousness

To explain the relations between the different kinds of intentional consciousness and to account for their coherence and continuity, the Yogacarins refer to a fundamental consciousness called *store consciousness (alayavijnana)*.[2] Ordinary consciousness always has an object because it is always *of* something, and it always has a subject because it always is *for* someone. Because the object is *intended* by the subject, this kind of consciousness is sometimes called *intentional consciousness.* In Yogacara, it is usually called *discursive consciousness* because it moves back and forth between subject (called the "grasper") and object (called the "grasped"). By contrast, store consciousness is not discursive or intentional; it does not require the duality of subject and object in order to function.

In many respects, the nature and functions of the store consciousness are comparable to the nature and functions of the unconscious in Western psychology. Both are regarded as deeper, underlying kinds of consciousness, and both are used to explain the origins and continuity of ordinary consciousness. A major difference, of course, is that for Yogacara, nothing, not even the store consciousness, can have separate, permanent existence. Store consciousness, like everything else, is conditioned and always changing. Furthermore, unlike the Freudian unconscious, the store consciousness, even though it is a very deep consciousness of which we are usually unaware, is something of which we can become aware.

Eight Kinds of Consciousness

To get a better sense of what the store (or storehouse) consciousness is, it is useful to examine the various kinds of consciousness recognized by Yogacara. Eight different kinds of consciousness are distinguished by the Yogacarins, corresponding to the eight different ways consciousness functions. The first six are the kinds of consciousness that produce the awareness of the various objects of the senses and the mind, namely (1) sight, produced by eye consciousness; (2) sound, produced by ear consciousness; (3) smell, produced by nose consciousness; (4) taste, produced by tongue consciousness; (5) feel, produced by touch consciousness; and (6) thought, produced by mind consciousness. The seventh kind of consciousness recognizes the store consciousness but mistakes it for an object that it wrongly views as a permanent, independent self. Because it produces this mistaken and wrong view, the seventh kind of consciousness is called *defiled consciousness.* These first seven kinds of consciousness are all intentional, operating dualistically, in terms of subject and object.

The eighth kind of consciousness is the store consciousness that underlies the other kinds and functions of consciousness. When purified of graspings and ignorance, this fundamental consciousness becomes directly aware of itself, an awareness that constitutes enlightenment. This direct awareness is not to be confused with the objects experienced in the other seven functions of consciousness, for it is not differentiated into the subject and object of consciousness. As Vasubandhu says in verse 29 of the *Thirty Verses:* "The supermundane knowledge of enlightenment is beyond thought and realized without grasping."

The theory of store consciousness is one of the greatest Yogacara contributions to Mahayana thought, enabling it to explain the continuity of a person through the transformations of suffering into nirvana in the absence of an independently existing, enduring self. According to this theory, the store consciousness is an extremely subtle and pervasive consciousness that underlies ordinary consciousness. It collects and stores the effects or seeds of experience until they mature and give rise to new experiences. Just as a tiny seed contains a mighty tree in embryonic form, so do the seeds of consciousness contain all conscious experience embryonically. All experiences arise from these seeds and derive their unique characteristics from the codes contained in the seeds.

The seeds that the store consciousness collects as the fruits of past experiences and then reissues as the beginnings of new experiences provide the continuity between past, present, and future activities of consciousness, which are required to give coherence to the individual's mental activity. This explanation of the continuity of experience also provides an answer to the question of how the ignorant person practicing the Middle Way is related to the person who becomes enlightened, for the continuity of the seeds in the store consciousness provide a continuous consciousness in which the transformation of ignorance into enlightenment takes place.

Most important, from the perspective of true understanding (enlightenment), the distinction between store consciousness and the intentional consciousness of thought and perception helps to explain how ignorance and enlightenment arise. Ignorance arises because discursive consciousness mistakes the subject and the objects of knowledge for the reality they merely represent. This gives rise to the wrong view that objects exist independently of and external to consciousness, as well as to the wrong view that the subject is a self that exists separately and independently. In ignorance of the truth that both object-consciousness and self-consciousness are nothing other than manifestations of store consciousness, the self-consciousness distinguishes itself from object-consciousness and relates itself to object-consciousness as subject is related to object. This is manifested in the constant grasping for objects characterizing the lower levels of consciousness. This grasping, however, is without real basis, for as Vasubandhu points out in verse 17 of the *Thirty Verses:* "The various consciousnesses are but transformations. That which discriminates and that which is discriminated, are, because of this, both unreal."

The arising of enlightenment begins when the subject of knowledge is seen to be empty of the reality of the person and the objects of knowledge are seen to be empty of the reality of things. It is fully established when the true reality of person and things are known directly by the fundamental consciousness in mindfulness.

In mindfulness, duality is overcome as both the subject and the object of experience are dissolved in the immediacy of the experience itself. For example, in mindful breathing, one begins as a subject aware of the breath as an object. But as awareness deepens, one *becomes* the breathing, leaving behind breath as an object and oneself as the subject for whom breathing was an object.

Furthermore, the theory of store consciousness explains the continuity of the person who is ignorant with the person who becomes enlightened in terms of the defilement and the purification of seeds within the continuing store consciousness. Seeds containing the defilements of discursive thought and of confusion, grasping, and hatred can be purified through practice of the perfections. When purified, these seeds give rise to the bodhi mind of the bodhisattva.

The store consciousness also provides an explanation of *karma,* the retribution of effects of actions to the doer. Unless the results of a person's actions could be stored somewhere in some form, it is impossible to explain how they can affect that person in the future. But according to the theory of store consciousness, the effects of action are stored as seeds from which future experiences arise.

One traditional way of understanding what store consciousness is and how it relates to ordinary sensory and mental consciousness is to compare it with water and waves. The ocean is just water. What we notice about this water are its waves, which constantly arise and fall, each with its own shape and power. But the waves are only water; it is only water that arises with the shape and power of a wave, and it is only water that returns its shape and power to the ocean, from which it can arise again with a new shape and power. In a similar way, the particular intentional consciousnesses are only manifestations of the great ocean of store consciousness, out of which they arise and to which they return.

Neither Realism nor Idealism

Because they took the store consciousness to be the fundamental source of all knowledge, the Yogacarins were sometimes regarded as philosophical idealists. Later interpreters sometimes contrasted their idealism with the realism of the Sarvastivadins. The basic difference between realism and idealism is that realism takes the reality of external things to be ultimate, and everything else, including consciousness, is relative to external reality. Idealism, on the other hand, takes consciousness to be ultimate; everything else, including external reality, is real only relative to consciousness.

The Yogacara school takes consciousness to be the source of both objects and subjects. It denies the existence of objects or subjects separate from and independent of consciousness on the grounds that objects and subjects arise only in the process of knowledge and knowledge occurs only in consciousness. Because they are constructed by consciousness, there is nowhere else they could arise or exist except in consciousness. But because both Asanga and Vasubandhu recognize the reality of things out of which objects are constructed, as well as the reality of persons out of which subjects are constructed, they clearly are not idealists. They do not deny that objects have a basis in things or that subjects have a basis in persons. Indeed, the third aspect of things as known, the perfected aspect, explicitly recognizes that things and persons really exist and that in the direct, nondiscursive knowledge of mindfulness they can be known as they really are.

The theories of store consciousness and the three aspects come together in early Yogacara philosophy to provide a middle way between realism and idealism. In light of the perfected aspect of things, Yogacara can see their conditioned aspects, as known through discursive consciousness, to be merely the constructions of this consciousness. They thereby avoid the realist error of mistaking the subject and object of discursive knowledge for independent, real existences. At the same time, because they recognize that there is a basis for the constructions of object and subject and that this basis can be known directly, they avoid the idealist error of claiming that persons and things exist only as ideas in the mind.

Vasubandhu explains the middle way of Yogacara in verse 17 of his *Twenty Verses:* "Someone who has not yet awakened does not understand that the things he sees in a dream do not exist." What he means is that so long as a person is dreaming, whatever that person sees in the dream appears real. But when the person wakes, there is the realization that the dream objects were merely dream objects. Vasubandhu does not claim that the things seen in dreams do not exist as objects in the dream; to deny dream objects would be to deny dream experience. Rather, he is making the point that dream objects are merely dream objects and therefore do not exist outside of the dream experience. Because waking experience is taken to have greater cognitive validity than dreaming experience, Vasubandhu can say that the objects of dream experience do not really exist.

In his commentary on the above statement, Vasubandhu goes on to say that the objects experienced in ordinary waking consciousness are like objects experienced in dreams when compared with things experienced directly in full mindfulness. Dream objects are constructed out of elements of prior waking experiences and do not exist outside of the dream. Similarly, the objects of ordinary discursive consciousness are constructed out of various sensory and mental data and do not exist outside of the realm of discursive thought. Both dream objects and the objects of discursive thought have a basis in reality, but in both cases what consciousness constructs on that basis is different from the reality the construct represents. Furthermore, just as one cannot know that dream objects are unreal until one wakes up, even so one cannot know that the objects of discursive thought are unreal until one experiences things as they really are, in the direct, nondiscursive awareness of mindfulness.

The chief obstacle in the way of accepting this view of knowledge is the common tendency to suppose that consciousness is always consciousness *of* something. Unless there were objects outside of consciousness, there would be nothing for consciousness to be consciousness of, and then there could be no consciousness. Since this latter view is held by the realists, the Yogacarins directed many of their arguments against the realists.

ARGUMENTS AGAINST REALISM

In the first place, the Yogacarins argue, the realist view that there are objects external to consciousness can at best be regarded as a speculative theory designed to answer questions concerning the arising of consciousness and changes in consciousness. The existence of external objects cannot be regarded as a *fact,* for there is no direct evidence for them. It is not possible for anyone to experience an object outside of consciousness, for to experience something means to experience it in consciousness. Consequently, all the purported evidence and proofs for the existence of objects independent of consciousness must come from consciousness itself. No one denies that there are objects of consciousness, but as Yogacara points out, these objects of consciousness exist within consciousness itself. The existence of objects within consciousness, however, does not prove that objects exist outside of consciousness.

How, ask the Yogacarins, could there be direct evidence, independent of consciousness, for the existence of objects external to consciousness? To be known, this evidence would have to exist within consciousness. Realists argue that when we see a blue flower, for example, a distinction must be made between the awareness of the color blue and the color blue itself, for the perception of a blue object could occur only if there was a blue thing to be perceived. According to the Yogacarins, however, this distinction is without basis, for the color blue is never perceived except in awareness of something blue. And since they are never perceived independently or separately, there is no evidence that the awareness of the color blue and the color blue itself are separate from each other. But if they cannot be separated, the distinction between them disappears. And when this happens, the basis for claiming an extra-conscious reality disappears.

Another Yogacara argument against realism is based on the relationship of the part to the whole. If objects exist independently of consciousness, either they must be simple wholes, without any parts, or else they must be wholes composed of parts. Knowledge of the independent existence of a simple whole is ruled out by the nature of knowledge claimed by the realist, who holds that to know something is to know how it is related to other things. Since there are no relations unless there are parts to be related, there could be no knowledge of simple wholes.

Even if the realist replies that it is the simple wholes that are related to one another, the difficulty remains, for now all the wholes together are taken as composing a new whole, in which simple wholes (which are now parts of this new whole) inhere in their various relations. This is equivalent to the atomistic view of reality, according to which objects are composed of atoms or parts. And the problem with this view is that the atoms or parts in themselves are unknowable but are simply postulated to account for the objects of consciousness.

Do the Yogacarins go too far in their rejection of the existence of independent objects? The realists counterattack by arguing that because consciousness is always consciousness of something, any proof that there is no "something" is, by the same argument, proof that there is no consciousness. And just as the attempt to prove the nonexistence of consciousness by the exercise of consciousness is absurd, so also the attempt to disprove objects of consciousness is absurd.

The Yogacara reply is twofold. First, Yogacara admits that discursive consciousness is always of something, but it insists that the something is the object taken as a mental construction, merely a representation of this something. Second, consciousness cannot be denied because it is self-revealing. But this does not provide evidence for the existence of independent objects, for it is the nature of consciousness to be self-existent, but it is not the nature of external objects to be self-existent. That the object of consciousness does not have to be an independently existing thing is clear from the example of dreams, where the dream objects are recognized as not having independent existence, even though they exist in the dreamer's consciousness. If this is the case with some instances of consciousness, it disproves the realist claim that consciousness cannot function without independently existing objects. Granted the impossibility of proving that there are extra-conscious objects and granted the possibility of consciousness without extra-conscious objects, as evident from dreams, the Yogacarins maintain that it is more reasonable to hold that the various objects of consciousness are simply the creations and projections of consciousness. The purported difficulty of accounting for the variety of objects and modes of consciousness disappears upon recognition that consciousness is itself a dynamic unfolding of its own inherent tendencies.

KNOWLEDGE OF REALITY

For the Yogacara theory of knowledge we turn to Asanga, who provides the classical Yogacara analysis of cognition in his treatise *The Stages of Bodhisattva Practice.*[3] The chapter on knowledge opens with the question, "What is knowledge of reality?" Asanga's answer is that four kinds of knowledge should be distinguished, namely:

1. What is universally accepted by ordinary beings;
2. What is universally accepted by reason;
3. Cognition completely purified of the obscurations of defilements; and
4. Cognition completely purified of obscurations to the knowable.

The rest of the text is devoted to the analysis of these four kinds of knowlege. It is interesting that Asanga does not reject either the unreflective opinions of ordinary people or the carefully reasoned judgments of rational, scientific inquiry as knowledge. It is just that these kinds of knowledge are regarded as lower because they are less revealing of reality—because of obscurations arising from grasping. It is also interesting that higher knowledge requires self-purification and training in the methods of insight. From a different perspective, what is striking is that the aim of knowledge is neither knowledge for its own sake nor for the sake of transforming the environment (that is, the technological application of scientific knowledge), but for the sake of transforming oneself in order to help others.

Ordinary Knowledge

Asanga refers to *ordinary knowledge* as "the shared opinion of people based on habitual association of names and things." Ordinary knowledge is rooted in the assumption that names or verbal descriptions correspond to the things they name or describe. This kind of knowledge assumes that we know what a thing is when we know its name. For example, we think that we know what snow is when we know that it is called "snow." But knowing that the English word for snow is "snow" does not tell us what snow is. Neither does knowing that the

Japanese word for snow is *yuki* tell us what snow is. Clearly, knowing the name of something and knowing what that something is are two different things.

The fact that names and verbal descriptions are different from what they name or describe is not regarded by Asanga as a reason to reject such knowledge of names and descriptions as providing no knowledge whatever. It is just that names and verbal descriptions provide very limited knowledge. What Asanga does reject is the claim that because nothing but names and descriptions exist, names and descriptions provide no knowledge of reality whatever. This claim is rooted in the view that only names exist, with everything that can be named or described being only a mental construction. Asanga's view is that names and named arise together and are useful in many ways.

Scientific Knowledge

The second kind of knowledge is described as "well-analyzed knowledge wherein the thing being investigated is established and proven by demonstration and proof." Asanga goes on to say, "This is the knowledge of people governed by reason, skilled in logic, highly intelligent, who are skillful investigators with great reasoning power." This is probably a good description of contemporary science and scientists. But why is scientific, rational knowledge, so highly regarded in our culture, regarded as inferior within the Buddhist view of cognition? The answer, in a word, is because this knowledge is based on discursive thought, which cuts the seamless flow of reality into little separate pieces, called concepts, which are then spliced together, with the aid of abstract concepts, into a theory about reality. With such thinking, the things themselves, as they really are, are never encountered. This is why Asanga regards cognition based on discursive thought, no matter how rigorous, as inferior to cognition based on direct insight into things as they really are, into what he calls their "suchness."

Asanga accepts that in themselves, in their "suchness," things totally interpenetrate with other things. Everything is present in any given thing, and any given thing is present in everything else. Not only is this what interdependent arising means, but in mindfulness this interpenetration is actually experienced. Thus, in his analysis of rigorous discursive knowledge, in answer to why discursive thought arises, he says, "Precisely because suchness is not known, the eight kinds of discursive thought arise for immature beings." "Immature beings" here means those who have not yet achieved the enlightenment mind.

The eight kinds of discursive thought are grouped according to the ways they obscure reality. They include discursive thought concerning

1. Essential nature
2. Particularity
3. Grasping wholes
4. "I"
5. "Mine"
6. The aggreeable
7. The disagreeable
8. What is contrary to both aggreeable and disagreeable

The first three, discursive thought about essential natures, particularity, and grasping wholes, produce the sense of an external thing, self-existing and separate both from other things and from the knowing subject. Having produced the sense of external objects, discursive thought then proliferates itself in the process of establishing relations among them and between them and the self.

Discursive thought about "I" and "mine" produces the sense of self as a permanent, separate, self-existing inner being, the counterpart of self-existent external things. Having produced this sense of self, discursive thought then proliferates itself in the process of relating self to the processes and functions that constitute personal existence and to external things.

Discursive thought about the agreeable, disagreeable, and the neither agreeable nor disagreeable, in relation to the discursively produced self and things, generates grasping, hatred, and delusion, respectively. Grasping, hatred, and delusion are, of course, the defilements that obscure reality and hinder self-transformation and acting to help others.

Both kinds of discursive knowledge, ordinary and scientific, are described by Asanga as "inferior" for three reasons: first, this kind of knowledge gives rise to the defilements; second, it cannot provide a basis for successful practice; and third, it is incapable of penetrating reality as it really is.

Knowledge Free of Personal Defilements

The third kind of knowledge, one of the two higher kinds of knowledge, is described as being free of personal defilements. The personal defilements are ignorance, grasping, and hatred. By defiling a person's consciousness and volitions, they give rise to all of the attitudes and action that give rise to *duhkha.* Ignorance, grasping, and hatred are considered defilements because they contaminate the ways in which a person acts and thinks. For example, thinking that one is a separate, permanent self, a person becomes obsessed with self-interest, acting only in terms of protecting the self. One sees other persons and things only in terms of whether they promote or destroy self-interest.

Ignorance is taken as the root of defilement because a person dominated by the mistaken view that everything exists separately and independently cannot see things as they really are, of the nature of interdependent arising. Because the defilements obscure the true nature of reality, the third kind of knowledge is defined as knowledge that is free of defilement.

Asanga goes on to answer the question, "And what reality does knowledge free of defilements know?" by saying that such knowledge provides understanding that there is no separate self either apart from or within the five groups of processes that constitute personal existence. Further, this knowledge provides deep understanding of *duhkha,* its origins, its cessation, and the way to its cessation in terms of interdependent arising.

Knowledge Free from Discursive Thought

The highest kind of knowledge, free of all obscurations to the knowable, is the knowledge that Buddhas and Bodhisattvas have of reality. They know, through the use of rigorous discursive thought, that both self and the constituents of things are selfless and that discursive thought itself is merely conceptual construction. Furthermore, Buddhas and Bodhisattvas know, through direct insight, the great means of enlightenment, the actual reality of the things that are merely represented by the conceptual constructions of discursive thought. This highest kind of knowledge reveals that the ways things really are is neither existent nor nonexistent, but midway between existence and nonexistence. And this middle way between existence and nonexistence, according to Asanga, is the incomparable Middle Path that was taught by the Buddha as the way that avoids the extremes.

Although this highest kind of knowledge cannot be adequately explained by discursive thought, it is accepted by all Buddhists. For those in whom the enlightened mind has been awakened, its existence is established experientially. For those who have not achieved such a direct realization, there is still the evidence provided by the practice of mindfulness that the objects of consciousness are merely constructions. For those without even the experience of mindfulness, there remains the faith in the reports of the enlightened who have experienced ultimate reality. For others, there are the various arguments against realism, as well as the various explanations of the nature of consciousness, to lend plausibility to the existence of this highest kind of knowledge. But for Asanga and Vasubandhu, as for all Mahayana Buddhists, the important thing is the actual practice of awakening the enlightened mind. That is why, despite its philosophical importance, the chapter on knowledge is only a tiny portion of Asanga's text, which primarily focuses on the stages of practice that lead to becoming a Bodhisattva.

REVIEW QUESTIONS

1. What are the three aspects of things, and why did Yogacara think it important to distinguish between them?

2. What is the store consciousness, and how is it related to the other kinds of consciousness? How would you argue for (or against) the existence and function of store consciousness?

3. According to Asanga, what are the main characteristics of ordinary and scientific knowledge? How do these two kinds of knowledge differ? How are they similar?

4. What are the main characteristics of knowledge free from defilements and knowledge free from discursive thought, according to Asanga? How do these two kinds of knowledge differ? How are they similar?

5. How, according to Yogacara, does *duhkha* arise? How does enlightenment arise?

FURTHER READING

Cultivating the Mind of Love: The Practice of Looking Deeply in the Mahayana Buddhist Tradition, by Thich Nhat Hanh (Berkeley, CA: Parallax Press, 1996), is a profound analysis of key Mahayana ideas in simple language.

Mahayana Buddhism: The Doctrinal Foundations, by Paul Williams (London and New York: Routledge & Kegan Paul, 1989), is probably the single best book on Mahayana Buddhism. Chapter 4, "Cittamatra," pp. 77–95, is on Yogacara.

Seven Works of Vasubandhu: The Buddhist Psychological Doctor, by Stefan Anacker (Delhi: Motilal Banarsidass, 1984), is a useful study of the Yogacara tradition. It provides good translations and analyses of seven important writings of Vasubandhu.

On Knowing Reality: The Tattvartha Chapter of Asanga's Bodhisattvabhumi, by Janice Dean Willis (New York: Columbia University Press, 1979), is an excellent study and translation of this very important text.

"Early Yogacara and Its Relationship with the Madhyamaka School," by Richard King, in *Philosophy East and West*, 44, no. 4 (October 1994), pp. 659–83, explains why early Yogacara should be seen as a further development of Madhyamaka thought.

Madhyamika and Yogacara, by Gadjin M. Nagao (Albany: State University of New York Press, 1991), is a good analysis of the relations between these two traditions that argues for the view that Yogacara is a sympathetic development of Madhyamaka.

On Being Mindless: Buddhist Meditation and the Mind-Body Problem, by Paul J. Griffiths (LaSalle, IL: Open Court, 1986), pp. 76–106, contains a good summary and analysis of the ideas of store consciousness, the three aspects of cognized objects, and the eight arguments for the existence of the store consciousness.

NOTES

1. See John M. Koller and Patricia Koller, *Sourcebook in Asian Philosophy,* pp. 330–41, for a translation of Vasubandhu's *Twenty Verses.* See pp. 341–44 for a translation of his *Thirty Verses.*
2. Paul J. Griffiths provides an annotated translation of *Abhidharmasamuccayabhasya* 11.18–13.20, the portion of the text containing the eight proofs for the store consciousness, in *On Being Mindless: Buddhist Meditation and the Mind-body Problem* (LaSalle, IL: Open Court, 1986).
3. The "Tattvartha" chapter of *The Stages of Bodhisattva Practice* by Asanga contains his analysis of knowledge. It is translated and explained in Janice Dean Willis, *On Knowing Reality: The Tattvartha Chapter of Asanga's Bodhisattvabhumi* (New York: Columbia University Press, 1979).

CHAPTER 18

Buddhism in Japan: Zen

OVERVIEW

Buddhism entered Japan in the seventh century CE by way of Korea and China. Throughout its history, Japanese Buddhism has had significant interaction with the indigenous Shinto tradition. Initially, Buddhism was supported by a series of emperors who thought that it would benefit the nation. Of the earliest forms of Buddhism introduced to Japan, only the Hosso school, based on the Chinese Fa-hsiang tradition, had a lasting influence, continuing up to the present time.

In the eighth century, the Chinese tradition of Hua-yen was established as the Kegon school, which became influential, in part because of the identification of the Buddha Vairocana with the emperor. The colossal Buddha image of Vairocana at the Todaiji Temple in Nara dedicated in 752 continues to remind us of the influence of Kegon, even though it has only a small following today.

Early in the ninth century, Kukai (774–835), often called Kobo Daishi, established the Shingon school. A form of tantric Buddhism that emphasized gestures, sounds, colors, and rituals, Shingon had a lasting influence on the arts of Japan.

Also early in the ninth century, Saicho (767–822), better known as Dengyo Daishi, after a year's study of T'ien-t'ai in China, established the Tendai tradition at Mount Hiei, near the new capital of Kyoto. Tendai was an important catalyst for new thought and art in Japan in the succeeding centuries and gave rise to the Pure Land (Jodo) School founded by Honen (1133–1212) and the True Pure Land School founded by Shinran (1173–1262). The Nichiren sect, which emphasized the *Lotus Sutra,* was founded by Nichiren (1222–82) as a reform of Tendai.

Zen Buddhism in its Rinzai form was introduced to Japan in 1191 by Eisai (1141–1215), a Tendai monk who went to China to train in the Lin-chi method of meditation. Because of Eisai's ability to integrate politics, art, and religion, Rinzai quickly became an important influence on Japanese culture. Eisai himself is revered not only as the founder of Rinzai, but also as the father of Japanese tea culture.

The other major form of Zen Buddhism, Soto Zen, was established at Eihei-ji in 1227 by Dogen (1200–1253) after four years of study and practice of Ts'ao-tung Buddhism in China. Today, Soto Zen has nearly fifteen thousand temples and five million members.

Because Zen has had such great influence on the life and culture of Japan, and because Dogen is regarded as one of Japan's greatest and most influential thinkers, the rest of this chapter is devoted to Zen, particularly as understood and taught by Dogen. His major philosophical work is the *Shobogenzo* ("Treasury-Eye of the True Teaching"), written in Japanese. Prior to Dogen, the classical Chinese had been used for writing all important Buddhist texts. In the *Shobogenzo,* Dogen creatively transforms fundamental Buddhist teachings in accord with the experience of mindfulness in the practice of seated meditation *(zazen).*

For Dogen, practice of the Buddhist way is simply the meditational practice of realizing enlightenment. Through this practice, called *zazen,* the individual awakens to the fullness of reality that is present in all things, though as yet unrealized. Dogen uses the light of the moon that at one and the same time illumines the universe and is reflected in a dewdrop, as a symbol of enlightenment. In his verse, "On Zazen Practice," Dogen says:

> The moon
> abiding in the midst of
> serene mind;
> billows break
> into light.[1]

This verse makes two important points. First, enlightenment is realized in calm stillness of a mind that has let go of all grasping and aversion. Second, this enlightenment illumines the vast energy and richness of reality, just as the moonlight illumines the countless bits of light that divide and comingle as the waves break into millions of tiny droplets as they crash against the rocks.

Dogen's emphasis on finding enlightenment in the directly experienced fullness of the present moment of experience is clearly expressed in the *Shobogenzo* chapter entitled "Birth and Death." Here, rejecting the mistaken view that enlightenment (which he calls "the life of the Buddha") takes one beyond the samsaric world of birth and death, he says:

> This birth and death is the life of the Buddha. If we try to reject or get rid of this, we would lose the life of the Buddha. If we linger in this and cling to birth and death, this too is losing the life of the Buddha, it is stopping the Buddha's manner of being. When we have no aversion or longing, only then do we reach the heart of the Buddha.[2]

Immediately after this statement, Dogen cautions the reader that although enlightenment is simply living the present life without attachment or aversion, one should not get caught up in this view of enlightenment, thereby substituting a view, which is merely a mental construction, for the actual experience of enlightenment:

> However, don't figure it in your mind, don't say it in words. Just letting go of and forgetting body and mind, casting them into the house of Buddha, being activated by the Buddha—when we go along in accord with this, then without applying effort or expending the mind we part from birth and death and become Buddhas. Who would linger in the mind?[3]

These two statements summarize the heart of Japanese Zen. First, to overcome suffering and birth and death, one should not try to get rid of death. Nor should one cling to life. Second, enlightenment occurs when aversion and clinging are abandoned. Third, to abandon aversion and clinging, one must let go of all mental constructions, especially the mental constructions of body and mind that constitute one's view of the self. Fourth, enlightenment is not a goal to be attained; it is effortlessly realized as the way things naturally are when aversion and clinging are abandoned.

INDIAN AND CHINESE FOUNDATIONS

The Zen Buddhism that Eisai and Dogen brought to Japan had developed in China seven hundred years earlier. It originated with Bodhidharma, an Indian Buddhist said to have come to China in the fifth century to transmit the practice of sitting meditation and the teaching of sudden enlightenment.

According to Dogen, the true teaching of Buddhism is the practice that leads to enlightenment, which is attained directly through meditative insight into reality, not by study of the teachings. This "wordless transmission" of the true teaching has its origins in an encounter between Shakyamuni (the historical Buddha) and his disciple, Maha Kashyapa. According to the *Mumonkoan* (a collection of *koans* [Zen sayings] with Master Mumon's commentary):

> Long ago when the World-Honored One [Shakyamuni Buddha] was at Mount Gridhrakuta to give a talk, he held up a flower before the assemblage. At this all remained silent. The Venerable Kasho [Maha Kashyapa] alone broke into a smile. The World-Honored One said, "I have the all-pervading True Dharma, incomparable Nirvana, exquisite teaching of formless form. It does not rely on letters and is transmitted outside scriptures. I now hand it to Maha Kasho [Maha Kashyapa]."[4]

Not only does this passage from the *Mumonkoan* connect Zen practice and enlightenment with the historical Buddha, but it also provides the reason why Zen regards the fundamental teachings as being transmitted outside of the scriptures, directly through experience. The Buddha himself announced that the teaching *(dharma)* is "of formless form." That is, it is beyond words and concepts: "It does not rely on letters and is transmitted outside scriptures." True to the spirit of this teaching, Zen has always maintained that the highest truth cannot be put into words. A profound silence, punctuated by a smile, may reveal the transformation wrought by the enlightenment experience, but no words can describe it.

Although little is known of the historical person, the legendary Bodhidharma is important in the Zen tradition. He symbolizes the emphasis on sitting meditation, sudden enlightenment, and the wisdom beyond words that give Zen its unique character. Bodhidharma is said to have spent nine years in sitting meditation or zazen, motionlessly gazing at a wall. The wall at which he gazed during his practice symbolizes the precipitousness of the enlightenment experience, in which all constructs placed on experience suddenly fall away, revealing the underlying experiential process in its own undivided nature. This experience, precisely because it goes beyond the dualities of thought constructs, cannot be grasped or communicated intellectually; only profound silence can express it.

Good works to gain merit and verbal formulations of truth are brushed aside in Zen's emphasis on direct, experiential knowing. Bodhidharma's attitude toward the institutional aspects of Buddhism is clearly revealed in a popular Zen account of a conversation with Emperor Wu-ti shortly after Bodhidharma's arrival in China. Wu-ti, a zealous Buddhist, very proud of his accomplishments in fostering the development of Buddhism during his reign, asked Bodhidharma what merit he (Wu-ti) had gained by building many temples, having many monks initiated, and having many scriptures copied. When Bodhidharma replied that all this had gained him no merit whatsoever, the emperor was dumbfounded. "How could all these wonderful works have gained no merit whatever?" he asked. "Because they are impure motives for merit," replied Bodhidharma. "Like a shadow following a person, they have no reality."

When the emperor asked, What does have true merit? What is real? Bodhidharma said, "It is pure knowing, wonderful and perfect, the essence of which is emptiness. Such merit cannot be gained by producing worldly things." Wondering how there could be such knowledge, the emperor asked for the foundation of this sacred truth, but Bodhidharma said simply, "Vast emptiness, nothing sacred." Now, thinking to test Bodhidharma, the emperor asked, "Who now stands before me?" But Bodhidharma would not be led into making some final affirmative statement: "I don't know," he replied.[5]

This conversation reveals the typical Zen attitude that efforts to promote religious institutions are not the same as the direct insight into the undivided nature of reality that Zen regards as a necessary condition of holistic living. So Bodhidharma tells the emperor that all of his efforts to support Buddhism have earned him no merit whatsoever. But when the emperor asks for the central truth or doctrine of the wonderful, pure, and perfect knowing at which Zen aims, Bodhidharma says there is no such doctrine, for he knows that this knowing is beyond all concepts and words. Indeed, he tells the emperor that this knowing should not even be called sacred, for this would introduce precisely the kind of dichotomy Zen wants to leave behind. The opposition between "sacred" and "ordinary" divides reality into two diametrically opposed objects. It is the same kind of thinking that divides everything into the opposites of "I" and "that" and the opposites of "is" and "is not." The discursive thinking that divides reality into opposing segments and distances these segments from ourselves as objects of knowledge is viewed as a defilement, contaminating our knowledge of reality. The concepts through which this kind of knowing attempts to grasp reality are seen as constructions that the subject imposes on a reality that in itself is undivided. Thus, when the emperor asked who stood before him, Bodhidharma refused to get caught in dualistic thought. Rather than say either that there is someone or that there is no one, he simply said, "I don't know."

The emphasis on direct seeing that goes beyond the constructs of experience to the ultimate, undivided reality that Zen associates with Bodhidharma reveals the influence of the Mahayana tradition. The Perfection of Wisdom scriptures constituting the core of the Mahayana teachings stress the emptiness of all the constructions we place on the undivided flow of reality. Not only are the things and the self that are constructed in conceptual knowledge said to be empty of reality, but even *samsara* and nirvana are declared empty. Mistaking these constructions for reality is the root of the incomplete, fragmented, and meaningless life characterized as *duhkha,* for it underlies all forms of grasping and hatred. The emptiness of the constructions imposed on the undivided process constituting reality can be seen conceptually, but the reality to which conceptual constructions can only point can be known as it is only when it is experienced directly, without the mediation of concepts. Only through the meditative experience of letting go of the constructs of the mind can the undivided wholeness of reality be experienced. This experience of the wholeness of reality, of the nonduality of self and the world, cannot be expressed in words; it cannot be taught. Thus, Bodhidharma's motionless sitting and insistence on wordless teaching are entirely consistent with earlier Mahayana teachings.

TAOIST INFLUENCES

These Mahayana teachings echoed the fundamental teachings of Taoism, a way of life rooted in the teachings of Lao Tzu, a Chinese sage who lived in the fifth century BCE. Lao Tzu emphasized that the ultimate Way *(Tao)* is beyond all words, itself undivided. It is the source of all things, giving rise to the many distinct things that make up the world around us, and thus in some sense is present in all things. Yet in its undivided nature, it goes beyond the things which arise from it and through which it flows. Lao Tzu regards the *Tao* as the root of all things, nourishing them and giving them life. To live in accord with the *Tao,* he says, is to return to one's roots, to reunite with the Source. But words do not reach the Source; here, at the source of life, is vast and profound stillness.[6]

Taoism also emphasized meditative practices for calming the mind and allowing the spirit to reunite with its source. "Sitting in forgetfulness" was a recommended Taoist practice long before Buddhism appeared in China. In chapter 6 of the *Chuang Tzu,* a Taoist text composed in the fourth century BCE, Yen Hui is pictured in conversation with Confucius, explaining how he sits in forgetfulness: "I cast aside my limbs, detach from both body and mind, and become one with the Great *Tao.* This is called sitting down and forgetting everything."[7] This Taoist *yoga* is similar in spirit to the meditative practices Buddhism borrowed from the Indian *yoga* tradition. For all we know, Bodhidharma's motionless sitting in front of the wall may owe as much to the Taoist meditative tradition as to the Buddhist. Undoubtedly, the Taoist tradition reinforced key practices and teachings of Mahayana Buddhism, contributing significantly to the development of Zen.

AIMS OF ZEN

Does the Zen distrust of conceptual thought and words, and its insistence on direct seeing into the undivided nature of self and reality, mean that Zen itself cannot be described? Not at all. If we remember that descriptions of Zen are simply descriptions and not Zen itself, then there are many useful things that can be said to help us understand what Zen is. But this distinction is important, for no amount of intellectual understanding will provide the direct seeing into reality at which Zen practice aims.

Zen is a way of life that has certain aims, prescribes various practices, and rests upon an understanding of reality that distinguishes it from other ways of life. Even though we may not be able to fully understand Zen without practicing it, if we study its aims, practices, and teachings about reality, we will get a good sense of what it is about.

As a way of life, Zen is not so much a matter of beliefs, but of doing. The core of practice consists in training in the experience of seeing directly into one's complete self in the fullness of the experienced moment without the mediation of intellect. Somewhat paradoxically, this is not training in doing something, but training in *not* doing. Learning to let go of all the things we habitually grasp at, including self and objects, is the heart of Zen practice. Emphasizing that *zazen* is not thinking, but letting go of thinking, Dogen says, "As long as we only think about the buddha-dharma with our minds, the Way will never be grasped, even in a thousand lifetimes."[8]

Within the context of Zen experience, this attempt at definition suffers the inevitable inadequacies of every attempt to understand things in a merely intellectual way. The reason for this is that intellectual understanding is incapable of understanding things in their true nature as interdependent arising. Intellectual understanding only enables the subject to grasp the representations of things, not the things themselves. Zen emphasizes the integrity and completeness of the present experience wherein there is no distinction between subject and object. Here one sees directly into the interdependent flow of reality. This is why Dogen tells his students, "Put your whole mind into the practice of the Way. Remember that you are alive only today in this moment."[9]

What Zen does, rather than postponing life to some moment in the future, is to make the most of the present moment, finding therein the wholeness of self and the completeness of life. It is the quality of experience here and now that assumes paramount importance for the Zen Buddhist.

Dogen refers to the story of Zen Master Zhaozhou (Joshu) to explain the importance of the here and now. Zhaozhou asked a newly arrived monk:

> "Have you been here before?"
> The monk said, "Yes, I have been here."
> The master said, "Have some tea."
> Again, he asked another monk, "Have you been here before?"
> The monk said, "No, I haven't been here."

The master said, "Have some tea."

The temple director then asked the master, "Why do you say, 'Have some tea,' to someone who has been here, and 'Have some tea,' to someone who has not?"

The master said, "Director." When the director responded, the master said, "Have some tea."

Dogen explains the meaning of this dialog as follows:

Zhaozhou's word "here" does not mean the top of the head, the nostrils, or Zhaozhou. Since "here" leaps off "here," a monk said, "I have been here," and another said, "I have not been here." It means, "What is now?" I only say, "I have been here, I have not been here."

Therefore my late master said:

"In your picture of the wine shop
Who faces you, drinking Zhaozhou's tea?"

Thus, the everyday activity of buddha ancestors is nothing but having tea and rice.[10]

This Zen aim of discovering the fullness of life in each moment of experience reflects both the Taoist and Mahayana teachings that the ultimate is not separate from the everyday, that ordinary things, when rightly seen, are the supreme reality. Enlightenment does not take us beyond the ordinary things of life, but allows us to experience them in a new light, revealing their profundity.

Dogen tells two stories about his experience in China that brought home to him the fact that the real aim of Zen is to live ordinary life fully, rather than to transcend it. Both involve conversations with a *tenzo* monk (the senior monk in charge of cooking). The first story records a conversation Dogen had with the *tenzo* monk from Ayuwan monastery who had come to buy some Japanese mushrooms from the ship on which Dogen was staying during his first visit to China in April 1223. Eager to talk to this monk, Dogen hoped to persuade him to remain on ship for the rest of the day, saying,

"I am very glad to have this unexpected chance to meet and chat with you for a while here on board ship. Please allow me to serve you, Zen Master tenzo."

"I'm sorry, but without my supervision tomorrow's meals will not go well."

"In such a large monastery as Ayuwan-shan there must be enough other cooking monks to prepare the meals. They can surely get along without a single tenzo monk."

"Old as I am, I hold the office of tenzo. This is my training during my old age. How can I leave this duty to others? Moreover, I didn't get permission to stay out overnight when I left."

"Venerable sir! Why don't you do zazen or study the koan of ancient masters? What is the use of working so hard as a tenzo monk?"

On hearing my remarks, he broke into laughter and said, "Good foreigner! You seem to be ignorant of the true training and meaning of Buddhism."

In a moment, ashamed and surprised at his remark, I said to him, "What are they?"

"If you understand the true meaning of your question, you will have already realized the true meaning of Buddhism," he answered. At that time, however, I was unable to understand what he meant.[11]

What the *tenzo* monk is saying is that Zen is life; it is cooking, cleaning, studying, or whatever one is doing at the time. *Zazen* and *koan* practice are important training, but the real practice of Zen is the daily living of life. Buying mushrooms is *zazen* and talking to Dogen is *koan* practice for the *tenzo* monk. Walking back to the monastery and preparing the mushrooms is also Zen practice for him. Living life fully in his daily activities is the *tenzo*'s Zen practice; no one else can live his life for him.

Dogen's second story also involves a *tenzo* monk. After he left ship, Dogen went to the T'ien-t'ung monastery for further training under Master Wu-chi. One day, on his way to visit the Master, Dogen met a *tenzo* monk with a bamboo stick in his hand, earnestly drying some mushrooms in front of the Buddha hall. The sun's rays beat down upon him, causing him to perspire profusely. Still he continued to move here and there, drying the mushrooms. Moved by this sight, Dogen drew near him and asked,

> "What is your Buddhist age?"
> "Sixty-eight," the tenzo monk answered.
> "Why don't you make the other cooking monks under your supervision do it?"
> "They are not me."
> "You are really one with Buddhism, but I wonder why you work so hard in the burning sun."
> "When else can I do it but now?"[12]

This story, like the first, emphasizes that Zen and life are not two different things, but that Zen is simply living life in full awareness, in the fullest way possible. But the second story brings out the urgency of living each moment fully. There is no time other than the present moment to live life. The past is gone, retained only as memory. The future is present only as an anticipation. It is in the precious present that life is lived. Knowing that he can only live his life now, the monk asks, "When else can I do it but now?"

The Zen emphasis on the immediacy and completeness of present experience shows up in the underlying principles of Zen practice, in the quality of enlightened life, and in the teachings underlying Zen. Of these three basic features of Zen—practice, enlightenment, and teachings—it is practice that comes first. Enlightenment cannot be separated from practice, and teachings support and are determined by practice and enlightenment. It is fitting, therefore, that we should turn now to a description of the practice of Zen.

PRACTICE

Zazen

Zazen, the chief discipline of Zen, is practiced in order to see directly into reality. In the direct insight of mindfulness practice, one discovers in the purity of one's own mind the true nature of all existence. This discipline requires assuming complete control and regulation of the hands, feet, legs, arms, trunk, and head. Next, breathing must be regulated and the activities of the mind calmed.

Through a series of special forms of concentration, the activities of the mind are brought together, unified, and stilled. The emotions and volitions are also brought under control and harmonized with the mind. Having attained the foregoing, it remains to cultivate what is sometimes called a profound silence in the deepest recesses of one's being, letting go of all dualistic thought and all graspings.

Why engage in the discipline of *zazen?* There are many good reasons to practice *zazen.* For example, centuries ago, Japanese warriors practiced *zazen* to improve their fighting skills. Today, athletes around the world practice *zazen* to improve their performance. Many people practice *zazen* as a kind of therapy to relieve personal stress. Some Japanese companies send their managers for a week of *zazen* practice to learn self-discipline. But the traditional reason is that *zazen* is the practice of mindfulness that the Buddha taught as the way of overcoming suffering. The practice of *zazen* brings peace through the deep insight into reality that Buddhists recognize as enlightenment.

Zen presupposes that ordinarily a person is caught up in a confusion of ideas, theories, reflections, prejudices, feelings, and emotions that prevent one from experiencing things in their wholeness, as they really are. The discursive mind divides reality into segments, which it then arranges into objects, connected to one another and to the subject through a series of relationships created by the mind. Thus, ordinarily a person does not really experience reality, but only the mind's network of ideas and feelings about reality. These ideas and feelings always stand between the individual and reality, mediating the experience. The aim of *zazen* is to free us from this mediating network, allowing us to enter directly and fully into reality.

Three Aims of Zazen

Concentration. The first aim of *zazen* is to increase the powers of concentration by getting rid of all distracting factors and all dualities. Usually the energies of the mind are scattered in many directions, creating a flood of distractions that makes concentration almost impossible. By unifying the mind, these distractions can be overcome and the dynamic energy of the mind focused completely on things at hand. Cultivating this power of concentrated consciousness gives one a freedom and equanimity that creates a sense of well-being even as it prepares one for *satori.*

Satori. The second aim of *zazen* is *satori,* the awakening of enlightenment that sees directly into one's own existence and the existence of others. This direct insight reveals the true nature of things in their dynamic interdependence. The enlightenment of *satori* may come like a flash, but it presupposes intensive training for most people. The *koans,* or problems, that are commonly used in the group sessions in the monasteries and the questions and answers used in the private sessions between master and disciple are famous as devices for triggering enlightenment. For example, Dogen, who had been doing *zazen* for many years, had heard his master say on numerous occasions that in order to realize enlightenment, body and mind must "fall off." But finally one day when he heard this, his mind and body actually fell off. That is, he had now reached the level of awareness that allowed him to let go of the *conceptions* of mind and body and to experience body-mind directly.

Because the enlightenment experience goes beyond the dualities of conceptual thought, it cannot be completely described with words. But Zen masters frequently test their students by asking them about their experiences. In the case of Hui-neng, the sixth Chinese patriarch, the verse testifying to the depth of his enlightenment has become a Zen classic. Hung-jen, the fifth patriarch, asked his disciples to compose a poem revealing the extent of their enlightenment. Shen-hsiu, a very bright and learned monk, foremost of all Hung-jen's disciples, wrote the following verse on the temple wall that night:

> The body is the Bodhi tree [enlightenment],
> The mind is like a clear mirror standing.
> Take care to wipe it all the time,
> Allow no grain of dust to cling.

Hui-neng, an uneducated young man who had been relegated to the rice pounding shed because he could neither read nor write, had Shen-hsiu's verse read to him. Seeing at once that it showed little sign of enlightenment, Hui-neng composed his own verse, asking a temple boy to write it on the wall:

> The Bodhi is not like a tree,
> The clear mirror is nowhere standing
> Fundamentally not one thing exists;
> Where, then, is a grain of dust to cling?[13]

The fifth patriarch, realizing from his verse that it was Hui-neng, not Shen-hsiu, who was enlightened, entrusted him with the line of succession, making him the sixth Chinese patriarch. Shen-hsiu's verse is regarded as inferior because it is still dualistic and because it fails to recognize the dynamic character of one's true mind. He takes the true mind to be passive; Zen practice for him is simply a matter of not allowing its purity to be sullied. The grains of dust represent the pollution caused by wrong thoughts, feelings, and desires. Meditation aims to prevent this pollution from arising.

Hui-neng's verse is much deeper. The mirror-like mind and the tree-like enlightenment are both repudiated as Hui-neng goes beyond all categories and constructions, declaring that "fundamentally, not one thing exists." The dualistic thinking expressed in Shen-hsiu's verse is left behind here, as Hui-neng intimates that the fullness of reality cannot be caught in the conceptual net. To the enlightened mind, reality is dynamic and whole, not passive and divided. The enlightened mind sees that the conception of dust as well as the conception of self to which dust might cling are both merely the constructions of dualistic thinking.

Living Enlightenment.   The third aim of *zazen* is to incorporate one's enlightenment into all of one's daily activities. Enlightenment is not just a momentary experience. It is to be lived; every action and every moment should be an action and a moment lived in enlightenment. We have already referred to Dogen's conversations with the two *tenzo* monks, which brings out the identity of Zen practice and daily activities of even the most routine kind. The depth of enlightenment can be gauged by the extent to which it bathes all of life in its radiance. As Dogen says,

> To study the Way is to study the self.
> To study the self is to forget the self.
> To forget the self is to be enlightened by all things.
> To be enlightened by all things is to remove
> The barriers between one's self and others.[14]

The meaning of this verse is that Zen practice is the practice of self-realization. But self-realization requires letting go of all ideas of self. When all ideas of self, the components of the ego, are relinquished, then the barriers between oneself and others disappear. When these barriers disappear, things and self are experienced as they really are, not separate from each other. In this nonseparation, self is experienced as present in all things, and all things are experienced as present in oneself. This is "to be enlightened by all things."

Dogen explains the enlightenment experience of the nonseparation of self and things with the analogy of the moon reflected in water:

> Enlightenment is like the moon reflected on the water. The moon does not get wet, nor is the water broken. Although its light is wide and great, the moon is reflected even in a puddle an inch wide. The whole moon and the entire sky are reflected in dewdrops on the grass, or even in one drop of water.
>
> Enlightenment does not divide you, just as the moon does not break the water. You cannot hinder enlightenment, just as a drop of water does not hinder the moon in the sky.
>
> The depth of the drop is the height of the moon. Each reflection, however long or short its duration, manifests the vastness of the dewdrop, and realizes the limitlessness of the moonlight in the sky.[15]

Koan Practice

In addition to zazen, *koans* are frequently used in Zen practice, though the way in which they are used and the emphasis placed on them varies according to school and master. *Koans* are statements by Zen masters, often in response to questions about the teachings. In Rinzai, they are used as objects of meditation by novice monks, helping them overcome dualistic thinking. The Soto school also uses *koans,* but here they are usually studied only in reference to one's own life and practice and not as manifestations of the truth of underlying teachings. This is because Soto, after Dogen, came to emphasize the identity of daily life and Zen practice. Thus, life itself is the *koan* with which one must deal; one's ordinary life must be the manifestation of the supreme truth.

Koans serve both to teach and to test the aspirant. As teaching devices, *koans* are used to lead a person beyond intellectual constructions to the direct and immediate participation in the living, whole, and complete reality. Used as a test, they reveal whether or not the *zazen* efforts have succeeded in reaching a given level of concentration and enlightenment.

One of the most famous *koans* is known, by way of the answer, as the *mu-koan*. A monk, in all seriousness, once asked master Joshu (Zhaozhou), "Has a dog a Buddha-nature?" Joshu replied, immediately, "Mu!" "Mu" literally means "nothing" but is used here as a nonsense word, indicating that because the question is inappropriate, there is no appropriate answer.

What is ordinarily meant by Buddha-nature is that the nature of everything is such that it can become enlightened. This is a common Mahayana teaching, found in many texts. But Joshu refused to say, "Yes, like everything else, a dog has Buddha-nature." No doubt he would have been right in refusing to answer affirmatively if he had suspected that the monk was thinking that there was something called the Buddha-nature, hidden somewhere within beings. Joshu's refusal to answer either yes or no was more radical. He saw that the question not only presupposed the conceptions of Buddha-nature and dog, but worse, in asking if a dog has a Buddha-nature, it presupposes the ultimacy of the dichotomy between is and is not—between being and non-being. This shows that the question is merely conceptual, that the questioner has not gotten outside the confines of his dualistic mind. Since it is the aim of Zen to go beyond the limitations of merely conceptual understanding, Joshu says "Mu!" That is, he said nothing (but said it immediately!). This is one of the main points about *koans*—they have no intellectual answers. They appear to be problems only upon the assumption of dualistic conceptions. When one lets go of the underlying dualistic assumptions, the problem disappears.

Emphasizing that it is the rationally constructed view of things that distorts reality and causes suffering, Dogen says: "Students of the Way, the reason you do not attain enlightenment is because you hold onto your old views. . . . You think that 'mind' is the function of your brain—thought and discrimination." Then, pointing out that these views are not the result of either careful examination or direct experience, he goes on to say, "The views you cling to are . . . the result of having listened for a long time to what people have said."[16]

Once a monk asked the master, "What happens to our thought systems when being and non-being are not distinguished?" In reply, the master laughed heartily and drank tea. And of course, this nonanswer was the only answer! No conceptual answer to the question would have sufficed, for it would have required accepting the distinctions making possible the question, in this case the very distinction between being and non-being that the monk assumed.

The enlightenment at which Zen aims requires going beyond all distinctions, including the distinction between is and is not, upon which all thought systems rest. Consequently, all definitions of enlightenment are inadequate. Even negative descriptions, which point out what it is not, presuppose the dichotomy between is and is not. Without experiencing at least a degree of enlightenment, perhaps the only way to get a sense of the experience is to talk with people who have achieved *satori* or to read their biographies. Although such accounts are rare because there is little point in trying to describe such experience, they are usually impressive in their almost unanimous reference to the overcoming of distinctions, and to the beauty and perfection of things just as they are—without any distinctions. For example, Yaeko Iwasaki, a disciple of Harada-roshi, wrote to him, "You can appreciate how enormously satisfying it is for me to discover at last, through full realization, that just as I am I lack nothing."[17]

TEACHINGS

Turning to the teachings of Zen, it must be pointed out that the actual teachings of Zen are primarily teachings connected with the practice of *zazen, koan,* and question-and-answer sessions. That is, they are practical teachings, directed to fostering the way of life that Zen is. Nevertheless, these practices have certain philosophical presuppositions. These presuppositions can be seen most clearly in the Yogacara and Madhyamaka philosophies of Mahayana Buddhism.

As the Yogacara philosophy developed, it came to regard the things known in ordinary, dualistic consciousness as merely mental constructions because all that was known were the objects of consciousness. But a reality beyond this, on which mental constructions were based and to which they pointed, was presupposed. This reality was, of course, beyond the grasp of ordinary knowledge. But through the practice of mindfulness, it could be known by direct insight. And this deep insight removes the ignorance that gives rise to suffering, thereby bringing the peace of nirvana.

Although it is beyond all names and descriptions, the reality of things, as they really are, in their fully dynamic and interdependent existence, is provisionally referred to variously as the "pure mind," "undivided being," and "Buddha-nature." Seeing true reality as Buddha-nature, or as the pure mind, underlies the Mahayana aim of becoming one with the all-illumining Buddha-consciousness. Mahayana emphasizes that to achieve enlightenment is to go beyond seeing everything merely in terms of mental phenomenon, or of the nature of consciousness, to seeing reality as a whole, undivided and totally interconnected.

This teaching is important for Zen, but the texts containing the teachings about this point are often confusing, because the expression "mind" is used in different ways. One sense of mind found in Mahayana is the ordinary view of mind as consciousness engaged in differentiating things. The other notion of mind, as we have seen, is called variously Buddha-nature, the enlightened mind, emptiness, no-mind, mind-only, and suchness. These expressions all refer to the same reality, which is the true reality of interdependent arising experienced by the enlightened person. Ordinary, dualistic consciousness is merely one function of consciousness. Feelings, emotions, and volitions are other functions of consciousness. But these various functions of consciousness are enumerated in terms of objects created by mind in its dualistic functioning.

As long as it is recognized that the objects of dualistic consciousness are merely mental representations of things, there is no problem. The problem occurs when this dualistic consciousness is taken as the ultimate judge of truth. The result is that the objects of mental consciousness are mistaken for the reality of things and self. Then the distinction between subject and object is mistaken for an absolute separation of self and things. The result is that we set ourselves apart from the reality that is our real existence, limiting ourselves to a life of grasping at mentally constructed objects and self in the delusory hope of thereby making ourselves whole.

Chinese Buddhism, both T'ien t'ai and Hua-yen, emphasized the importance of experiencing the true reality that was beyond the duality of words and concepts, an emphasis that led directly to the development of Ch'an (Zen). In Ch'an Buddhism, the practice of direct realization of things is considered the way of the Buddhas. According to Dogen, who practiced Zen with Master Ju-ching in China, it is this direct realization that constitutes the enlightenment experience. Dogen emphasizes that because this experience is realized only in unique and creative expression, it cannot be described in ordinary ways. This is why symbolic expressions, such as the ox-herding pictures and accompanying verses, assumed such great importance in Zen.

OX-HERDING: STAGES OF PRACTICE

Although the enlightenment at which Zen aims comes of itself, suddenly breaking through the veils of construction that hide the true self and reality, disciplined practice is required to clear the way. The ten ox-herding pictures (on pages 246–50) with the accompanying commentaries depict the stages of practice leading to enlightenment. They dramatize the fact that enlightenment reveals the true self, showing it to be the ordinary self doing ordinary things in the most extraordinary way.

The story of the ox and oxherd, separate at first, but united in the realization of the inner unity of all existence, is an old Taoist story, updated and modified by a twelfth-century Chinese Zen master to explain the path to enlightenment. The ox (sometimes called a bull) symbolizes the ultimate, undivided reality, the Buddha-nature, which is the ground of all existence. The oxherd is the self, who initially identifies with the individuated ego, separate from the ox, but who, with progressive enlightenment, comes to realize the fundamental identity with the ultimate reality that transcends all distinctions. When this happens, the oxherd realizes the ultimacy of all existence; there is nothing that is not the Buddha-nature. He now understands the preciousness and profundity of the most ordinary things of life, illuminating ordinary living with his enlightenment.

The first picture shows the oxherd desperately looking everywhere for his lost ox. He is dissatisfied with his life, unable to find the true happiness that he seeks. His efforts to secure wealth, friends, fame, and pleasure have not brought him the fulfillment he is seeking. Like many of us, he is seeking something, though he is not sure exactly what it is, that will make life meaningful and bring him lasting happiness.

The second picture shows that he has now caught sight of the tracks of the ox, bringing hope that his ox is not lost forever. This could be interpreted to mean that he has recognized his distress and has begun to seek a solution in the teachings of Buddhism or in other teachings. But he is still at the stage of thinking and talking about his problems and various possible solutions. He has not yet found a path to follow and has not yet started to practice.

In the third picture, he actually catches sight of the ox. Now, having started to practice, he glimpses the hidden powers to heal his suffering. But he does not yet understand the source of these powers and how to apply them in his search for peace and contentment. The verse, in saying that "I hear the song of the nightingale. The sun is warm, the wind is mild," suggests that the reality the oxherd glimpses is not something separate from the ordinary things that he experiences, even though he does not yet know this.

The fourth picture shows that he has now caught hold of the ox, using the bridle of discipline to control it. This symbolizes the rigorous discipline required of the Zen practitioner. Although he now realizes that the power to transform his life lies within himself, in his Buddha-nature, all of his previous conditionings are pulling and pushing him in different directions. Holding the rope tightly means that he must work hard to overcome his bad habits of the past that developed through the ignorance, hatred, and craving that gave rise to all of his afflictions.

The fifth picture shows that disciplined practice can overcome the bad habits of previous conditioning and bring one into accord with the true nature of reality. Although discipline is still needed because the old habits of mind still have power, living in greater awareness of the true reality gives one the energy and direction to live a wholesome life. Now the ox willingly follows the oxherd home, meaning that the separation between oneself and true reality is being overcome.

The sixth picture suggests the tranquility and joy that reunion with the source of existence brings; now the oxherd rides on the back of the ox, joyously playing his flute. "Slowly I return homeward" suggests that he has been freed from old fears and anxieties. So freed, the seeker says, "I direct the endless rhythm," meaning that he can now express his creative energies in celebration of life.

In the seventh picture, the oxherd has realized his identity with the ox; the ox can be forgotten, for it is none other than his experience of everyday things. This can be interpreted to mean that the separation of practice and realization has been overcome, as has the separation of ordinary reality and ultimate reality. Until now he has been practicing *zazen* as a means of achieving enlightenment. But with realization of the nonduality of existence comes awareness of the identity of means and ends; practice itself is realization.

The eighth picture tells us that when the duality of self and reality has been overcome, not only is reality (the ox) forgotten, but so is the self (the oxherd); the circle symbolizes the all-encompassing emptiness that constitutes the ground of all things. Now, in the awareness of unceasing transformation and total interconnectedness in every experience, one is freed from all craving and hatred for the other. In this freedom, there is a sense of the wholeness and perfection of ordinary things.

As the ninth picture shows, when self and reality (as constructs) are left behind, then things are revealed to be just what they are in themselves; streams meander on of themselves and red flowers naturally bloom red. In the ordinary events of life are found the most profound truths. Only by seeking the ox as a separate ultimate reality could the oxherd discover that there is no separate reality—that the ultimate is to be found in the ordinary. But how extraordinary the ordinary is when experienced in its wholeness!

Finally, the tenth picture shows the enlightened oxherd entering the town marketplace, doing all of the ordinary things that everyone else does. But because of his deep awareness, everything he does is quite extraordinary. He does not retreat from the world, but shares his enlightened existence with everyone around him. Not only does he lead fishmongers and innkeepers in the way of the Buddha, but, because of his creative energy and the radiance of his life, even withered trees come alive.

1. The Search for the Bull

In the pasture of the world,
I endlessly push aside the tall
grasses in search of the bull.
Following unnamed rivers,
lost upon the interpenet-
rating
paths of distant mountains,
My strength failing and my
vitality
exhausted, I cannot find the
bull.
I only hear the locusts
chirping
through the forest at night.

2. Discovering the Footprints

Along the riverbank under
the trees,
I discover footprints.
Even under the fragrant
grass,
I see his prints.
Deep in remote mountains
they are found.
These traces can no more be
hidden
than one's nose, looking
heavenward.

The oxherding pictures by Master Jikihara and the accompanying verses are used with the kind permission of the Zen Mountain Monastery, Mt. Tremper, New York.

246

3. Perceiving the Bull

I hear the song of the
  nightingale.
The sun is warm, the wind is
  mild,
willows are green along the
  shore—
Here no bull can hide!
What artist can draw that
  massive head,
those majestic horns?

4. Catching the Bull

I seize him with a terrific
  stuggle.
His great will and power
are inexhaustible.
He charges to the high
  plateau
far above the cloud-mists,
Or in an impenetrable
  ravine he stands.

247

5. Taming the Bull

The whip and rope are
  necessary,
Else he might stray off down
some dusty road.
Being well-trained, he
  becomes
naturally gentle.
Then, unfettered, he obeys
  his master.

6. Riding the Bull Home

Mounting the bull, slowly
I return homeward.
The voice of my flute
  intones
through the evening.
Measuring with hand-beats
the pulsating harmony,
I direct the enless rhythm.
Whoever hears this melody
will join me.

248

7. *The Bull Transcended*

Astride the bull, I reach home.
I am serene. The bull too can rest.
The dawn has come. In blissful repose,
Within my thatched dwelling
I have abandoned the whip and ropes.

8. *Both Bull and Self Transcended*

Whip, rope, person, and bull—
all merge in No Thing.
This heaven is so vast,
no message can stain it.
How may a snowflake exist
in a raging fire.
Here are the footprints of
the Ancestors.

249

9. Reaching the Source

Too many steps have been taken
returning to the root and the source.
Better to have been blind and deaf
from the beginning!
Dwelling in one's true abode,
unconcerned with and without—
The river flows tranquilly on
and the flowers are red.

10. In the World

Barefooted and naked of breast,
I mingle with the people
of the world.
My clothes are ragged and dust-laden,
and I am ever blissful.
I use no magic to extend my life;
Now, before me, the dead trees
become alive.

250

REVIEW QUESTIONS

1. What is Zen practice? Discuss the relationship between daily life, *zazen*, and enlightenment, according to Dogen.
2. What are the basic aims of Zen?
3. What are the important differences between Hui-neng and Shen-hsiu as evidenced in their verses?
4. What philosophical teachings underlie Zen?
5. Explain, picture by picture, how the ox-herding pictures (and commentaries) illustrate the Zen way of enlightenment.

FURTHER READING

Enlightenment Unfolds: The Essential Teachings of Zen Master Dogen, translated and edited by Kazuaki Tanahashi (Boston and London: Shambala, 1999), is a collection of Dogen's writings on practice and enlightenment. The introductory essay traces Dogen's own enlightenment practice.

Zen's Chinese Heritage: The Masters and Their Teachings, by Andrew Ferguson (Boston: Wisdom Publications, 2000), is a translation of famous sayings of twenty-five generations of Ch'an masters, from Bodhidharma to Wumen Huikai.

Zen Keys: A Guide to Zen Practice, by Thich Nhat Hanh (Berkeley, CA: Parallax Press, 1995), is an excellent introduction to Zen by one of greatest living teachers of Zen practice. As Philip Kapleau remarks, *"Zen Keys* conveys the authentic 'feel' and flavor of Zen."

Zen Mind, Beginners Mind, by Shunryu Suzuki (New York: John Weatherhill, 1970), conveys the spirit of Zen practice and teaching in a very simple and direct way. Suzuki was a Soto Zen master, in the tradition of Dogen, who emphasized that the important thing about Zen is practice.

The Three Pillars of Zen, compiled and edited by Philip Kapleau (New York: Harper & Row, 1969), provides a many-faceted look at Zen. Instructions for practice and autobiographical statements describing the achievements of Zen practitioners accompany the explanations of principles underlying Zen.

Zen Enlightenment: Origins and Meanings, by Heinrich Dumoulin (New York: John Weatherhill, 1979), is an outstanding account of the understanding of enlightenment in the history of Zen.

Zen Comments on the Mumonkan, by Zenki Shibayama (New York: New American Library, Mentor Books, 1975), is a thirteenth-century collection of the sayings of Zen masters, with the commentary of Master Mumon on each saying, or *koan.* A widely used manual of Zen training over the centuries, it has been made more accessible to modern readers by the commentary and fine introduction by Shibayama Roshi.

Zen Action, Zen Person, by Thomas P. Kasulis (Honolulu: University of Hawaii Press, 1981), is a study of the philosophical significance of Zen. Kasulis uses traditional Japanese concepts to explore the meaning of action and personhood in Zen thought, providing many helpful insights into Japanese culture.

Zen Buddhism: Selected Writings of D.T. Suzuki, edited by William Barret (Garden City, NY: Doubleday, 1956), traces the development of Zen, exploring its central concepts. Illuminating comparisons with the West help make this work one of the best bridges to Eastern ways of thinking.

Moon in a Dewdrop: Writings of Zen Master Dogen, edited by Kazuaki Tanahashi (San Francisco: North Point Press, 1985), is an excellent introduction to Dogen's thought. It contains translations of some of his most important writings.

Zen, by Eugen Herrigel, including *Zen in the Art of Archery* and *The Method of Zen* (New York: McGraw-Hill, 1964), is a fascinating look at Zen through the way of archery.

Zen Flesh, Zen Bones: A Collection of Zen and Pre-Zen Writings, compiled by Paul Reps and Nyogen Senzaki (Boston: Shambala Publications, 1994), is a classic collection of Zen stories that generations of students have enjoyed.

NOTES

1. As trans. in *Moon in a Dewdrop: Writings of Zen Master Dogen,* ed. by Kazuaki Tanahashi (San Francisco: North Point Press, 1985), p. 13.
2. As trans. by Thomas Cleary in John M. Koller and Patricia Koller, *Sourcebook in Asian Philosophy* (New York: Macmillan, 1991), p. 361.
3. Ibid.
4. Zenkei Shibayama, *Zen Comments on the Mumonkan,* English translation by Sumiko Kudo (New York: New American Library, Mentor edition, 1975), p. 53.
5. Adapted from H. DuMoulin, *Zen Enlightenment* (New York: John Weatherhill, 1976), p. 40.
6. See *Tao Te Ching,* chaps. 1–4, in Wing-tsit Chan, *The Way of Lao Tzu* (Indianapolis, IN: Bobbs-Merrill, 1963), pp. 97–106.
7. See Wing-tsit Chan, *Source Book in Chinese Philosophy* (Princeton, NJ: Princeton University Press, 1963), p. 201.
8. *Zuimonki,* as trans. by Okumura Shohaku in *World Philosophy: A Text with Readings,* ed. by Robert C. Solomon and Kathleen Higgins (New York: McGraw-Hill, 1995), p. 12.
9. Ibid., p. 11.
10. Dogen, *Kajo,* as trans. in *Moon in a Dewdrop: Writings of Zen Master Dogen,*. ed by Kazuaki Tanahashi (San Francisco: North Point Press, 1985), p. 128.
11. Taken from Yuho Yokoi, *Zen Master Dogen* (New York: John Weatherhill, 1981), p. 29.
12. Ibid, p. 30.
13. DuMoulin, *Zen Enlightenment,* p. 44.
14. Quoted in the frontispiece of Yokoi, *Zen Master Dogen.*

15. Dogen, *Genjo Koan,* as trans. in *Moon in a Dewdrop: Writings of Zen Master Dogen,* ed. by Kazuaki Tanahashi (San Francisco: North Point Press, 1985), p. 71.

16. *Shobogenzo-Zuimonki,* as trans. by Okumura Shohaku in *World Philosophy: A Text with Readings,* ed. by Robert C. Solomon and Kathleen Higgins (New York: McGraw-Hill, 1995), p. 11.

17. Quoted in Philip Kapleau, *The Three Pillars of Zen* (New York: Harper & Row, 1969), p. 288.

PART III

CHINESE PHILOSOPHIES

Yin-yang symbol.

CHINESE CHRONOLOGY

BCE	Events and Thinkers
2183–1752	Hsia dynasty
1751–1027	Shang dynasty
1027–249	Chou dynasty; the Five Classics
600–400	Yin-Yang school (seventh century?); Confucius (551–479); Lao Tzu (sixth century); Mo Tzu (fl. 479–438?)
400–200	The Four Books; Hsun Tzu (fl. 298–238?); Mencius (371–289?); Chuang Tzu (fourth century); Han Fei (d. 233); School of Names (Hui Shih and Kung–sun Lung, fourth century)
200–0	Tung Chung-shu (179–104?); Ch'in dynasty (221–206); Han dynasty (206 BCE–220 CE); Huai-nan Tzu (d. 122 BCE)

CE	
0–200	Yang Hsiung (53 BCE–18CE); Buddhism introduced to China (67 CE)
200–400	Translations of Buddhist texts; development of Taoist religion
400–600	Kumarajiva translates *Lotus Sutra*; Pure Land Buddhism flourishes; Bodhidharma
600–800	Hua-yen Buddhism develops under Fa-tsang (643–712); Ch'an Buddhism develops under Hui-neng (638–713), Sixth Chinese Zen patriach
800–1000	Beginnings of Neo-Confucianism; Yan Yu (768–824); Li Ao (ninth century)
1000–1400	Neo-Confucian School of Principal; Chou Tun-i (1017–73); Ch'eng Hao (1032–85); Ch'eng I (1033–1107); Chu Hsi (1130–1200)
1400–1600	Wang Yang-ming (1472–1529)
1600–1800	Tai Chen (1723–77)
1800–2000	Opium War (1840–42); Chinese Republic (1912); People's Republic (1949); K'ang Yu-wei (1858–1927); Chang Tung-sun (1886–1962); Hsiung Shi-li (1885–1968); Fung Yu-lan (1895–1900); Mao Tse-tung (1894–1976); Post-Mao revival of Confucian thought (1976–present)

CHAPTER 19

Historical Perspectives

Chinese civilization and culture rest upon a philosophical basis shaped primarily by Confucianism, Taoism, and Buddhism. Stressing the importance of human life, preserving, cultivating, and making it great, Chinese philosophy has been closely connected with politics and morality and has assumed most of the functions of religion. Consequently, the study of Chinese philosophy is valuable not only because of its intrinsic merit, but also because of the insights into the Chinese mind and Chinese culture that it makes possible.

As a critical investigation of human nature and the way of right living, Chinese philosophy has its beginnings in the teachings of Confucius and Lao Tzu in the sixth century BCE. Prior Chinese thought tended to be prephilosophical in the sense that it was, for the most part, not self-critical. But this precritical thought of earlier times is important to the understanding of the thought of Confucius and Lao Tzu, who were both reacting to earlier theories and practices. Thus, it is imperative to have a picture of prephilosophical China in mind in order to give Confucianism and Taoism the context required for their understanding.

PRE-CONFUCIAN CHINA

Although there is evidence of advanced civilization in China in very ancient times, actual recorded history begins with the Shang dynasty, in the fourteenth century BCE. Available evidence indicates that this was an advanced civilization. For example, art from this period is quite sophisticated, even according to modern standards. This dynasty ended with the invasion by the more primitive Chou people, who, according to tradition, established the Chou dynasty in 1122 BCE.

Although more primitive artistically and culturally, the Chou were a powerful and determined people. They conquered huge portions of China by sheer force and might. Not having the means to administer all of the conquered territory as one central state, the Chou delegated administrative power to friendly chiefs and nobles, providing parcels of land in exchange for the friendship and cooperation of these newly endowed landholders. Apparently this feudal system worked quite well during the early Chou period, as each vassal had considerable freedom and power within his own territory, and these privileges seemed well worth the taxes and military conscription owed the king in return. Although there is nothing to indicate that the first half of the Chou period was nearly as advanced as the earlier Shang period, it was a time of relative peace and security within the structure of the new feudal system. And because of this peace, it came to be regarded later on as a "golden period" in China's early history.

This peace was relatively short-lived, however. It was only the might of the Chou kings that prevented the vassals and the oppressed serfs from rebelling. As time went on, it was recognized that the kings did not really have the strength to control all of the conquered land, even through the device of feudalism. There came to be greater and greater unrest in the country. Feudal lord turned against feudal lord, and serfs rebelled when they thought the lords sufficiently weak and ineffectual. As neighboring states became weakened by war and strife, they were attacked by larger and more remote lords.

By 770 BCE, things had degenerated to the point where a coalition of feudal lords was able to launch a successful attack on the Chou capital in the west. They killed the king and usurped his power. From this date on, the Chou kings were puppets controlled by the coalition of feudal lords who happened to be in power at the time. Power was constantly shifting hands, and war and strife were the order of the day during the two centuries immediately prior to Confucius' birth. Violence and intrigue characterized the political scene, and expediency took the place of morality. These intrigues and the resulting wars caused great poverty, suffering, and death.

CONFUCIANISM

It is in the context of this severe crisis crippling China in the centuries immediately preceding the birth of Confucius and Lao Tzu that their thought must be viewed. This crisis explains their emphasis on social reform and personal transformation. For Confucius, born in 551 BCE, it seemed obvious that the problems of the people stemmed from sovereign power exerted without moral principle and solely for the benefit of sovereign luxury. That is why he advocated the personal development of moral virtue and urged social reforms that would allow government to be administered for the benefit of all the people. This could be done, he urged, if the members of the government were of the highest personal integrity, understood the needs of the people, and cared as much for the welfare and happiness of the people as they did for themselves.

"Do unto others as you would have them do unto you," represents a brilliant and daring principle of reform in the context of the pre-Confucian China just outlined. This principle resulted from reflections on the conditions required for an ideal society. The attitude underlying these reflections regards knowing humanity as more important than knowing nature and moral development as more fundamental than political policies. If people cannot know and regulate themselves, how can they hope to know and control all of nature? Confucius did not look for the basis of human goodness and morality outside of human beings. Within humanity itself is to be found the source of human goodness and happiness and the way to its full development. It is this attitude that makes Confucianism a humanistic philosophy.

Confucius lived from 551 to 479 BCE, but some of the ideas of Confucianism are derived from earlier times, while other ideas were not developed until later. According to tradition, Confucius drew inspiration from the Five Classics, and the expression of his thought, including its development by later Confucians, is contained in the Four Books. The Five Classics are (1) *Book of Poetry (Shih Ching)*, a collection of verses from the Chou period; (2) *Book of History (Shu Ching)*, a collection of records, speeches, and state documents from 2000 to 700 BCE; (3) *Book of Changes (I-Ching)*, a set of formulae for explaining nature, widely used for purposes of divination (this work is traditionally attributed to Wen Wang, 1100 BCE); (4) *Book of Rites (Li Chi)*, a collection of rules regulating social behavior, compiled long after Confucius, but probably representing rules and customs from much earlier times; and (5) *Spring and Autumn Annals (Ch'un Ch'iu)*, a chronicle of events from 722 to 464 BCE.

The Four Books are (1) *Analects (Lun Yu)*, the sayings of Confucius to his disciples, collected and edited by them; (2) *The Great Learning (Ta Hsueh)*, the teachings of Confucius containing his suggestions for ordering life and society. This text may reflect Hsun Tzu's (a later Confucian thinker) development of Confucius's thought; (3) *Doctrine of the Mean (Chung Yung)*, Confucian teachings about harmony and balance in life; and (4) *Book of Mencius (Meng Tzu)*, an elaboration of some Confucian principles by Mencius, an early commentator on Confucius.

The essence of the Confucian teachings contained in this literature is that by developing human nature *(jen)* through a process of moral self-cultivation, a person's life and conduct can be perfected and social order achieved. When everyone does this, society will be transformed; goodness and peace will abound, and the people will be happy.

In addition to the development of Confucianism by Mencius (ca. 371–283 BCE), further elaborations on the teachings of Confucius are found in the *Hsun Tzu*, attributed to Hsun Tzu (ca. 320–238 BCE). Hsun Tzu emphasized the need for the Confucian virtues by pointing to the evil inherent in human nature. Thus, whereas Mencius emphasized the need to practice the virtues of humanity, righteousness, and filial piety in order to preserve human goodness, Hsun Tzu claimed that they must be practiced to root out the evil inherent in human beings and to replace it with goodness.

TAOISM

The desperate conditions of the times also provide an explanatory context for the rise of Taoism, which emphasized the need to look beyond the promises and treaties of human beings for a source of peace and contentment. Lao Tzu, born late in the sixth century BCE, urged a simple and harmonious life, a life in which the profit motive is abandoned, cleverness discarded, selfishness eliminated, and desires reduced. In the context of a China in which greed and desire were bringing about nearly unimaginable hardship and suffering, a philosophy emphasizing the need to return to nature's way would understandably find a ready following. Lao Tzu believed that so long as human actions were motivated by greed, social position, and desire for power, there was no hope for harmony and peace. Consequently, he advocated the principle that only those actions that were in accord with nature should be undertaken.

Taoism, the philosophy of the natural and the simple way initiated by Lao Tzu, was given an epistemological and metaphysical foundation by Chuang Tzu (fourth century BCE). Chuang Tzu also sharpened the emphasis on the natural way as opposed to the artificial and contrived way of persons. In fact, it was a revival of Chuang Tzu's metaphysical doctrines of naturalism that provided the common meeting ground for Taoism and the Buddhism that developed in China during the fourth and fifth centuries CE.

MOHISM

Although Confucianism and Taoism were to become the most influential of the early philosophies of China, they were not the only philosophies of the day. Mohism, which received its main direction from Mo Tzu (468–376 BCE), shared the Confucian interest in advocating the increased welfare of the people. Like Confucius, he claimed that the measure of human welfare was people rather than nature or the spirits. But Mo Tzu believed that the Confucian emphasis on cultivating humanity was too vague for actually improving the human condition. He argued that the way to improve the human condition was to tend to the immediate welfare of the people. The slogan of the Mohists was "promote general welfare and remove evil." The criterion advocated for measuring how good anything is was its usefulness in achieving human happiness. Ultimately, according to Mohism, value was to be measured in terms of benefits to the people. Benefits, in turn, could be measured in terms of increased wealth, population, and contentment.

Although Mo Tzu saw himself in opposition to Confucius, probably thinking of himself as a practical reformer and Confucius as an idealistic dreamer, the long-run effect of his philosophy was to strengthen Confucianism by adding utilitarian incentives and criteria to the moral principles and criteria advocated by Confucius. The result was a humanism with a utilitarian flavor and a greater practical emphasis.

SCHOOL OF NAMES

The School of Names had its early development in the work of the logicians Hui Shih (380–305? BCE) and Kung-sun Lung (b. ca. 380 BCE). The main interest of this school was in the relationship between language and reality. These philosophers were motivated primarily by theoretical issues, and they were interested in knowledge for its own sake rather than for its utility. Their focus on logical issues made the School of Names unique, sometimes even making it the target of ridicule because of its impracticality. But despite the opposition between these logicians and the other philosophers and schools of China at this time, the investigation of the relations between words and things and the concern with knowledge for its own sake served as an important antidote to the excessive practicalness of the other philosophers. It served to keep alive an interest in theory, and the studies in the relations between words and things became useful later in both Taoism and Confucianism, as they sought a metaphysical basis for their social philosophies.

YIN-YANG

The Yin-Yang school, concerned with cosmogony and cosmology, was also influential in the time of early Confucianism and Taoism. Since no individual philosophers connected with this school are known, it is not possible to provide specific dates for its activities. But most likely this school, as a general philosophy of change, goes back to late Shang or early Chou times in its beginnings, and it continues to be important until long after Confucius.

The beginnings of *yin-yang* speculation are contained in a natural curiosity about the workings of nature. For an agrarian people living very close to nature and feeling the rhythms of its workings, it is natural to speculate about the principles, or "inner workings," of nature's functions. Two questions were implicit in this early curiosity about nature. The first question was about the structure of the world: By what principles do the processes and things that make up the world function? The second question was about the origin of things: Where did the universe come from, and how did it originate?

Five Agencies

The theory of the five agencies is essentially an answer to the *yin-yang* question about the structure, rather than the origin, of the universe. According to early versions of the five agencies theory, the five powers of the universe that control the functioning of nature are symbolically represented by wood, fire, metal, water, and earth. The combinations of these powers determine the workings of the universe. For example, when the power represented by wood is dominant, it is spring. When the power of fire dominates, it is summer. Autumn represents the ascendancy of metal, and winter results when water is dominant. In late summer, earth is dominant. The important thing about the five agencies theory is that it was an attempt to explain the functions of nature by appeal to inner principles or powers. All of the characteristics and tendencies of nature are the results of various combinations of the five agencies.

Yin-Yang

The *yin-yang* theory is essentially an answer to the question of the origin of the universe. According to the *yin-yang* theory, the universe came to be as a result of the interactions between the two opposing universal forces of *yin* and *yang*. The existence of the universe is seen to reside in the tensions resulting from the universal force of non-being, or *yin,* and the universal force of being, or *yang.* Because things are experienced as changing, coming into being and passing out of being, it is obvious that things both have being and lack being. But this is just to say that existence is constituted by the forces of *yin* and *yang.* The world of changing things that constitutes nature can exist only when there is both being and non-being. Without being, nothing can come into existence. Without non-being, nothing can pass out of existence. Hence both *yin,* the negative force of non-being, and *yang,* the positive force of being, are required as a source of nature.

Both the five agencies theory and the *yin-yang* theory were influential in the rise of Neo-Confucianism in the ninth century CE. In the formulations of various later thinkers, these theories underwent metaphysical interpretation and found their place in a general theory of existence.

LEGALISM

The other early school of considerable importance is that of Legalism. The most important philosopher of this school is Han Fei Tzu (d. 233 BCE), though the tradition predates him by several hundred years. The basic presupposition of this school is that people are naturally inclined to wrongdoing, and therefore the authority of laws and the state are required for human welfare. This school is opposed to Confucianism in that, especially after Mencius, Confucianism emphasized the inherent goodness of human nature. Because they assumed that people are naturally inclined toward goodness, the Confucians advocated moral persuasion rather than laws and punishment as a means for promoting human happiness and social well-being. Despite these fundamental differences, the long-term effect of the Legalist emphasis on laws and punishment was to strengthen Confucianism by making legal institutions a vehicle for Confucian morality.

EARLY MEDIEVAL DEVELOPMENTS

In early medieval times, Hui-nan Tzu (d. 122 CE), a relatively late Taoist, developed a cosmology according to which the unfolding of *Tao* produced successively, space, the world, the material forces, *yin* and *yang,* and all the things. According to this theory, *yin* and *yang* become the principles of production and change among all the things in the world. Tung Chung-shu (176–104 BCE), a late Confucianist, also referred to the *yin* and *yang* as the principles of things. According to him, all activities are due to the forces of *yin* and *yang,* which manifest themselves through the five agencies.

That the Taoist Hui-nan and the Confucianist Tung Chung-shu should both make use of the *yin-yang* and five agencies theories shows that Confucianism and Taoism were coming closer together at this time, finding a common ground of explanation. The revitalization of both of these philosophies as a result of their meeting, and the resulting cross-fertilization, had to wait for many centuries, however, until the catalyst of Buddhism had been introduced.

In fact, it was not until around 900 CE that the meeting of Confucianism and Taoism prepared by Hui-nan Tzu and Tung Chung-shu bore fruit in the form of the vigorous new philosophy of Neo-Confucianism.

Part of the reason for the long delay of this development is that Tung Chung-shu was successful in getting Confucianism adopted as the state ideology. This of course meant that Taoism was out of official favor, removing most of the critical challenges required for a vigorous and healthy philosophy. For nearly one thousand years after being adopted as the state ideology, the philosophy of Confucianism was to see relatively little development, as most of the emphasis was upon putting the philosophy that had already been developed into practice, rather than on developing further the philosophy itself.

CHINESE BUDDHISM

Although Buddhism was introduced into China from India prior to the end of the first century CE, it remained almost entirely without influence until the fourth century. All of the different Buddhist schools of philosophy were introduced into China, but only those that could be reconciled with the principles of either Taoism or Confucianism became forces in shaping the Chinese mind. The realistic philosophies of the Vaibhashikas and the Sautrantikas failed to take hold in China because of their insistence on the momentary and fleeting character of reality. The idealism of the Yogacara philosophy did not suit the practical emphasis of the Chinese temperament, but, thanks to a thousand-year tradition of Taoist *yoga*, the Yogacara emphasis on meditative practice was well received. Similarly, though the Madhyamaka skepticism of ordinary knowledge was too radical for the Chinese, they welcomed its emphasis on the undivided nature of reality, an emphasis that reinforced the traditional vision of the unity of all things.

Hua-yen and T'ien-t'ai

The Madhyamaka and Yogacara traditions were transformed into the Hua-yen and T'ien-t'ai schools of Chinese Buddhism. But in both Hua-yen and T'ien-t'ai, the Indian emphasis on the mentally constructed nature of knowledge and on emptiness as the nature of existence received strongly positive reinterpretations. Interdependent arising was interpreted as universal or total causation, according to which all the elements of reality are perfectly real and completely reflect one another. The totality of reality was seen as a grand harmony of conscious and unconscious, pure and impure, simple and complex. The Indian disjunction, "either real or unreal," had become the Chinese conjunction, "both real and unreal." The Grand Harmony, the harmony of all opposites in the universe, is possible because each of the ultimate elements of which the universe is composed contains within itself all of the other elements, thereby embracing all the differing aspects and tendencies in the world.

Pure Land and Ch'an

The other two schools of Chinese Buddhism that flourished during the T'ang dynasty are the Pure Land school, which is mainly religious, and the Ch'an (Zen) school. Both of these traditions were also heavily influenced by Madhyamaka and Yogacara. The Ch'an school is really a method of meditation rather than a philosophy, but it is underwritten by the philosophical attitude that through the negation of opposites, reality is affirmed in its true nature. The meditation involves seeing things directly, through the practice of mindfulness, without cognitive constructions. This direct seeing has the effect of negating both production and extinction, arising and ceasing, annihilation and permanence, and unity and plurality, for these pairs of opposites are merely conceptual constructions. Thus, their negation is simply an aspect of affirming the presence of the true nature of all things through direct realization. The enlightenment marked by coming to see all things in their true nature is the aim of Ch'an meditation.

NEO-CONFUCIANISM

The strong influence of Chinese Buddhism, along with a revival of Taoist thought, contributed to a powerful renewal of Confucianism during the Sung period, a renewal usually referred to as Neo-Confucianism. The tendency to synthesize opposing features of metaphysical views, so clearly evident in Chinese Buddhism, was a very significant factor in the rise of Neo-Confucianism. Indeed, it provided a basis for criticism of Buddhism. Confucian philosophers had tended to be highly critical of Buddhist philosophies ever since their introduction to China. They objected to the emphasis on overcoming suffering and death, which to them seemed little more than selfish escapism. The monastic aspect of Buddhism, which involved the renunciation of the family and society, seemed wrong-headed, because it was clearly impossible that human beings could ever escape society. They were also critical of the Buddhist emphasis on emptiness, because this appeared to negate the reality and value of everything. To regard all things—including food and clothes—as unreal and yet to depend on them was contradictory, they said. But perhaps the deepest difference between the Chinese philosophers and the Buddhist schools was the Chinese emphasis on social and moral reality as fundamental, as opposed to the Buddhist emphasis on metaphysical reality and knowledge.

Granted these differences, and the accompanying critical attitude of Chinese philosophers toward Buddhism, the rise of Neo-Confucianism is not hard to understand. It represents the attempt to counteract Buddhism with a more comprehensive and superior Chinese philosophy. Because of its synthetic tendency, it was possible for the new philosophy to incorporate features of Buddhism along with features of Taoism into Confucianism. Given the preoccupation with social and moral reality that characterized earlier Chinese philosophy, it was natural for Confucianism to have the primary role in this reconstruction.

Although the beginnings of Neo-Confucianism can be traced to Han Yu (768–824), it was not until Sung times (960–1279) that a comprehensive and definitive formulation was achieved. It was during the Sung period that the

School of Principle of the Ch'eng brothers (Ch'eng Hao, 1032–85, and Ch'eng Yi, 1033–1108) arose and the great synthesis of Chu Hsi (1130–1200) was achieved. The School of Mind, which leaned in the direction of idealism, also originated during this period. Its most illustrious philosophers are Lu Chiu-yuan (1139–93) and Wang Yang-ming (1472–1529). The third phase of the development of Neo-Confucianism is represented by the Empirical School of the Ching period (1644–1911). These three developments within Neo-Confucian thought are discussed in Chapter 20.

In summing up the historical development of philosophy in China, it could be said that philosophy, as everything else, has its *yin* and *yang,* and it finds its perfection in the grand harmony of these two opposing principles. Confucianism represents the *yang* of Chinese philosophy in that it emphasizes strong, purposeful human effort to transform self and society. Taoism represents the *yin* of Chinese philosophy in that it emphasizes letting go of human striving so that transformation will occur naturally and spontaneously in accord with the *Tao.* Neo-Confucianism, in seeking the harmony of all principles, and in combining the strengths of Buddhism, Confucianism, and Taoism, represents the harmonious integration of *yin* and *yang.*

BASIC CHARACTERISTICS OF CHINESE PHILOSOPHY

This brief historical overview of Chinese philosophy reveals certain basic and enduring characteristics of Chinese thought. Most importantly, perhaps, it shows that the primary purpose of Chinese philosophy has been that of self-transformation aimed at realizing the potential perfection of human beings. Chinese thinkers were convinced that through the realization of their human potential, people could find harmony and fulfillment in their relations with one another and with nature.

Although the various Chinese philosophies agreed that realizing human perfection should be the primary aim, we have seen that they disagreed considerably on the way this perfection was to be realized. The Taoist insight was that perfection can be realized by following the inner Way *(Tao)* of nature. The Confucian insight was that perfection can be realized by cultivating human nature *(jen)* and the social virtues. The Buddhist insight was that perfection can be realized through meditative insight into the mind. Neo-Confucianism, inspired to some extent by Chinese Buddhism, combines the insights of both Taoism and Confucianism.

Human perfection has a double aspect in Chinese thought. First of all, it involves an inner perfection that is reflected in the peace and contentment of the individual and in the harmony in his or her relationships with others and with nature. Second, it involves excellence in the external conduct of life, the ability to live well practically, dignifying the social context of one's ordinary day-to-day existence. This ideal of inner and outer perfection is called "sageliness within and kingliness without."

Both Confucianism and Taoism, which provide the foundations and inspiration for the later Neo-Confucian philosophy, share this ideal of inner and outer perfection. Lao Tzu says that unless one knows and lives according to the inner laws of the universe, which he calls the "normal," he ends up in disaster. But by following the norm of the universe, all things can be achieved. According to this mystic sage who established the foundations of Taoism:

> Not to know the normal is to be without basis.
> To innovate without basis bodes ill.
> To know the normal is to be tolerant.
> Tolerance leads to impartiality,
> Impartiality to kingliness,
> Kingliness to heaven,
> Heaven to the way,
> The way to perpetuity,
> And to the end of one's days one will meet with no danger.[1]

For Confucius, the most basic goal was to cultivate one's humanness and to regulate all activities in accord with this developed humanness. According to *The Great Learning,* one of the chief texts of Confucianism,

> The ancients who wished to manifest their clear character to the world would first bring order to their states. Those who wished to bring order to their states would first regulate their families. Those who wished to regulate their families would first cultivate their personal lives.[2]

This pervasive aim of realizing inner perfection and manifesting this perfection externally has tended to make Chinese philosophy inclusive of all aspects of human activity. Philosophy was not separated from life, and practice was considered inseparable from theory. Nearly all of China's great philosophers held administrative positions in government or were artists. The assessment of philosophers in China has always depended, in the last analysis, upon their moral character. It is not conceivable that a bad person could be a good philosopher. In China, the real test of a philosophy has always been its ability to transform its advocates into better persons.

Since human perfection is the basic concern, considerations for people come first in China. The human world is primary; the world of things is of secondary importance. In Confucianism, this characteristic is manifested in the emphasis on moral development and on social humanism. In Taoism, it is evident in the emphasis on transforming the self and society through patterning human life in accord with the way of nature.

Emphasis on human perfection leads naturally to emphasis on the cultivation of virtue and concern for the family and community. This is a very obvious characteristic of Confucianism, which emphasizes the cultivation of virtue as a fundamental feature of personal development, and as a key to harmony and peace in the family and the community. But it is also a characteristic of Taoism, which stresses the importance of personal transformation through attaining the virtue that comes from following the natural way (*Tao*).

Practicing perfection led naturally to emphasis on the familial virtues, especially the concept of filial love, that provides the very cornerstone of Chinese morality. The immediate environment of children is a social structure constituted by the family. Here the child's moral and spiritual character is shaped and molded. Here, through parents' exemplification of love and respect, the beginnings of perfection are established.

Turning to methodology, the Chinese emphasis on inclusiveness of views illustrated so well by the correlative thinking that led to the *yin-yang* philosophy has been a primary consideration in Chinese thought. Rather than seek truth by excluding various alternative views as false, Chinese thought has tended to look for truth in the combination of partially true views. This leads to a spirit of synthesis and harmony resulting in tolerance and sympathy. Persons, practices, and views that are different are to be tolerated and considered sympathetically in order to appreciate their value.

This emphasis on complementariness is reflected in a synthetic attitude, which sees harmony in apparently conflicting theories and modes of life and fuses them together into a new whole in the same way that *yin* and *yang*, though opposites, come together to constitute the whole. For example, there are basic differences between Taoism and Confucianism, and Buddhism does not appear to have a great deal in common with either of these philosophies. Yet Buddhism found a welcome home in China, and more than a thousand years ago, these three philosophies contributed the ideas and methods required to create the imposing edifice of Neo-Confucianism. In addition, this synthetic attitude leads to tolerance for the thoughts and actions of others, and it promotes sympathy and appreciation for what is different.

This summary of the basic characteristics of Chinese philosophy indicates a rich heritage. The emphasis on attaining human perfection and the preference for methodological inclusiveness suggest that the Western reader should attempt to consider this tradition in its own context and in terms of its own merit. It does not fit neatly into Western intellectual categories, which have resulted from an emphasis on knowledge of the external world and a preference for methodological exclusiveness. Indeed, one of the main challenges to understanding Chinese thought is to see where it is like and where it is unlike Western thought.

REVIEW QUESTIONS

1. How did conditions in pre-Confucian China influence the development of Confucian and Taoist thought?

2. Compare and contrast the Confucian and Taoist philosophies. What are the main differences? How are they similar?

3. What are the theories of the five agencies and *yin-yang* about? What do they have in common? How do they differ?

4. What is Neo-Confucianism? How did it incorporate features of earlier thought?

5. What has been the fundamental aim of Chinese philosophy? Explain this aim in terms of "sageliness within and kingliness without."

6. What are the main characteristics of Chinese thought?

FURTHER READING

Disputers of the Tao: Philosophical Argument in Ancient China, by A.C. Graham (La Salle, IL: Open Court, 1989), is a brilliant account of the early development of Chinese philosophy that gives a good sense of the interplay between the early philosophical schools.

East Asian Civilizations: A Dialogue in Five Stages, by William Theodore de Bary (Cambridge, MA: Harvard University Press, 1988), is a good overall account of the development and influence of Chinese thought in China, Korea, and Japan.

The World of Thought in Ancient China, by Benjamin I. Schwartz (Cambridge, MA: Harvard University Press, 1985), is a reflective and sophisticated analysis of the interactions between the main ways of thought in ancient China.

The Tao Encounters the West: Explorations in Comparative Philosophy, by Chenyang Li (Albany: State University of New York Press, 1999), is an illuminating comparison of concepts and ways of thinking in Chinese and Western philosophy.

A Chinese Mirror: Moral Reflections on Political Economy and Society, by Henry Rosemont Jr. (LaSalle, IL: Open Court, 1991), is an insightful comparison of Chinese and Western conceptions of person and society.

Understanding the Chinese Mind: The Philosophical Roots, edited by Robert E. Allinson (Oxford: Oxford University Press, 1989), is a very good collection of essays exploring the philosophical roots of Chinese culture.

A Short History of Chinese Philosophy, by Fung Yu-lan (New York: Macmillan, 1960), is an excellent scholarly account of the development of Chinese philosophy, written by one of China's outstanding recent philosophers. *Short History* is a shorter version of the two-volume work by Fung entitled *A History of Chinese Philosophy* (Princeton, NJ: Princeton University Press, 1959–60), which is generally acknowledged to be the most comprehensive and authoritative survey of Chinese philosophy available.

A Sourcebook in Chinese Philosophy, translated and compiled by Wing-tsit Chan (Princeton, NJ: Princeton University Press, 1963), contains nearly eight hundred pages of the most important Chinese philosophical texts arranged in chronological order. The readability of the translations, the choice of materials, and the explanations of difficult passages provided by the late Professor Chan combine to make this an exceedingly useful aid for the study of Chinese philosophy.

Sources of Chinese Tradition, 2 vols., compiled by William Theodore de Bary, Wing-tsit Chan, and Burton Watson (New York: Columbia University Press, 1964), contains literary, historical, political, and philosophical texts, making it a good source for a broader study of Chinese civilization. The introductions are extremely useful and the translations reliable.

Guide to Chinese Philosophy, by Charles Wei-hsun Fu and Wing-tsit Chan (Boston: G.K. Hall, 1978), though now somewhat dated, was the standard bibliography for Chinese philosophy. The annotations are especially helpful for the nonexpert, and the table of contents provides a useful survey of the main schools and topics.

Journal of Chinese Philosophy, edited by Chung-ying Cheng (Cambridge, MA: Blackwell), perhaps the leading journal in the field, has an updated bibliography of Chinese philosophy in its combined March and June 2001 issue.

The Chinese Mind: Essentials of Chinese Philosophy and Culture, edited by Charles A. Moore (Honolulu: University of Hawaii Press, 1967), consists of papers given at four major East-West philosophers' conferences. The introduction, "The Humanistic Chinese Mind," by Moore, and the chapter "Chinese Theory and Practice with Special Reference to 'Humanism,' " by Chan, are especially relevant.

Chinese Thought from Confucius to Mao Tse-tung, by H.G. Creel (copyright 1953 by H.G. Creel; New York: New American Library, Mentor edition, n.d.), is a lucid account of the main trends in Chinese philosophy intended for the nonspecialist.

Three Ways of Thought in Ancient China, by Arthur Waley (first published in 1939; Garden City, NY: Doubleday, Anchor edition, n.d.), contains excerpts from Mencius, Chuang Tzu, and Han Fei-tzu, arranged and introduced by Waley in a way that gives the reader a sense of taking part in a lively discussion.

NOTES

1. *Tao Te Ching*, chap. 16, trans. by D.C. Lau, in John M. Koller and Patricia Koller, *A Sourcebook in Asian Philosophy* (New York: Macmillan, 1991), p. 447.
2. *The Great Learning (Ta-Hsueh)*, in *A Sourcebook in Chinese Philosophy*, trans. and compiled by Wing-tsit Chan (Princeton, NJ: Princeton University Press, 1963), pp. 86–87.

CHAPTER 20

Confucianism

The fundamental question underlying Confucianism is that of how to become good. And the heart of the Confucian answer to this question, although there are important differences among Confucian thinkers, is that human goodness is achieved through the cultivation of moral virtue, a process of moral development through which a person learns to be really human. The conviction that it is possible to transform oneself and all of society through the cultivation of virtue, and that this transformation is necessary if society and the individual are to flourish, is shared by all Confucians, despite disagreements among them concerning exactly what virtue is and how it should be cultivated. This chapter explores what moral virtue is and how it is cultivated through an examination of the teachings of Confucius and the two most important Confucians of the early period, Mencius and Hsun Tzu.

CONFUCIUS

The times in which Confucius lived help explain his search for a way of cultivating virtue in order to establish a basis for badly needed social reforms. As already noted, Confucius lived in an age marked by political and social disintegration and a widespread breakdown of morality. As he was growing up, he personally experienced the poverty, political abuse, and hardship that affected the lives of ordinary people. Through his studies, he became acquainted with the noble ideals, including the ideal of virtue, that had inspired rulers in the past. Given the deplorable conditions that Confucius had personally experienced and his conviction that the ideals of the previous dynasties could provide the guidelines for restoring the order of society and the well-being of the people, it was natural that he should turn his attention to the study of the ideals of the previous "golden age," as he worked to reform society.

As a young man Confucius accepted a position in the government of his native state of Lu. There he could not only observe the inadequate administration of the kingdom of Lu, but also, in a small way, do something about this administration by properly carrying out his own duties. This experience in practical politics was probably a factor in his decision to turn his attention to social reform.

Recognizing the need for social reform, how could Confucius bring it about? What principles would guide this reform and how would they be implemented? Confucius's answer is contained in his philosophy, a humanistic social philosophy. What does this mean? First, it means that Confucius's philosophy is about human beings and their society rather than about nature or knowledge of nature. Second, it means that he regarded the human community as the source of human and social values. It is because of this conviction that Confucius's philosophy is usually thought of as a kind of social humanism.

The most significant feature of humanism is the conviction that human beings are the ultimate source of values. To see what this means, it is helpful to contrast humanism with naturalism and supernaturalism. According to naturalism, nature—the nonhuman world—is taken as the ultimate source of values. Here the principles for human action and life are taken from nature. Discovering how human beings should act is a matter of discovering how nature acts so that human actions can be in accord with those of nature.

According to supernaturalism, a force or power other than humans or nature is taken to be the ultimate source of values. A supernatural force is seen as regulating both nature and humans, making them subordinate to this supernatural and superhuman power. The supernatural may be regarded as creating both nature and humanity, as well as determining their behavior. According to this view, discovering how humans should act is a matter of discovering how this supernatural power intended them to act.

Humanism becomes possible when humanity rather than nature or supernature is taken as the ultimate source of values. Here people look neither to nature nor to the supernatural for norms of life and action; rather, they look to the best of their own human practices to find the principles that provide for goodness and happiness. Thus, to call Confucianism a humanism is to say that it is a philosophy that answers the question, "How can goodness and happiness be achieved?" by pointing to the principles of action found within humanity itself.

HUMANITY (*JEN*)

According to Confucius, what makes human beings uniquely human is *jen*. This is why the Confucian way is essentially the way of *jen*. What is *jen*? The word *jen* has been translated in many different ways: "virtue," "humanity," "benevolence," "true manhood," "moral character," "love," "human goodness," and "human-heartedness," to name only a few. The English word "human-heartedness" seems to capture the most important meanings of *jen,* for it suggests that *jen* is what makes us human, that it is a matter of feeling as well as thinking, and that it is the foundation for all human relationships. Translating *jen* as "human-heartedness" also reveals the Chinese emphasis on the heart, rather than the head, as the central feature of human nature.

In his *Sayings (Lun-yu),* Confucius neither gives nor defends a definition of *jen.* This may reflect his understanding that the way of humanity is highly personal, that it lies within each human being and must be realized in one's personal life and one's personal relationships. To make it an objective characteristic or feature of the world would be a distortion of *jen.* Although Confucius did not define *jen,* he often talked about it with his students, trying to help them to realize its meaning in their own lives. For example, when Fan Ch'ih asked what *jen* is, Confucius replied, "It is to love men" (12:22), suggesting that the human ability to love constitutes the core of human nature.[1]

The human ability to love others has important moral implications, however, requiring that *jen* also be thought of in moral terms. Thus, Confucius says,

> Wealth and honor are what every man desires. But if they have been obtained in violation of moral principles, they must not be kept. Poverty and humble stations are what every man dislikes. But if they can be avoided only in violation of moral principles, they must not be avoided. If a superior person departs from humanity *(jen)* how can he fulfill that name? A superior man never abandons humanity *(jen)* even for the lapse of a single meal. In moments of haste, he acts according to it. In times of difficulty or confusion, he acts according to it. (4.5)

This statement indicates clearly that *jen* is the ultimate principle of human action. A true human being never departs from the way of *jen;* one who departs from the way of *jen* is not expressing the fullness of humanity. The word translated as "moral principles" in this passage is *tao* or "way," implying that the right way of human action is not that of satisfying likes and avoiding dislikes, but that of acting in accord with a deeper principle, that of *jen.*

So important is *jen* that life without it is not worth living. According to Confucius, "A resolute scholar and a man of humanity *(jen)* would never seek to live at the expense of injuring humanity *(jen).* He would rather sacrifice his life in order to realize humanity *(jen)*" (15.8).

Precisely because *jen* is what makes us truly human, to abandon it is to give up a fully human life. *Jen* is worth sacrificing one's life for; it is the basis of all human value and worth. It is *jen,* ultimately, that makes life worth living.

What does it mean to live according to the way of *jen?* Confucius's followers understood that to live according to *jen* required the development of one's own human-heartedness and the extension of that developed human-heartedness to others. Thus, Tzeng Tzu reminded other followers of Confucius that "The Way of our Master is none other than conscientiousness *(chung)* and altruism *(shu)*" (4.15). Conscientiousness or *chung* consists in the careful development and manifestation of one's own humanity, while altruism *(shu)* consists in extending *jen* to others. The way of *chung* and *shu* incorporates the principle of reciprocity that underlies the famous Golden Rule of Confucius; namely, treat others as you wish to be treated or, "Do not do to others what you do not want them to do to you" (12.2).

PROPRIETY *(LI)*

Although *jen* is the basis of humanity and, therefore, the ultimate guide to human action, Confucius recognized that more immediate and concrete guides to action are needed in everyday life. These concrete guides he found in the rules of propriety *(li)* governing customs, ceremonies, and relationships established by human practice over the ages. Thus, *li* refers to the ceremonial or ritual means by which the potential of humanity *(jen)* is realized. The best of these practices reflect the concrete embodiment and expression of *jen* in the past and therefore serve as a guide to its realization in the present. This is why when Yen Yuan asked about *jen,* Confucius said, "To master oneself and return to propriety *(li)* is humanity *(jen)*" (12.1).

Self-mastery in this quotation refers to the self-development that overcomes selfishness and cultivates the inner qualities of humanity that include sincerity and personal rectitude. That Confucius regards it as the basis of *li* seems clear, for he immediately adds, "If a man (the ruler) can for one day master himself and return to propriety, all under heaven will return to humanity *(jen).* To practice humanity depends on oneself." This suggests that *jen* is the ground of *li,* that what makes *li* a standard of conduct is the fact that it is in accord with *jen.* Customs and regulations not in accord with *jen* are not really *li,* according to Confucius. But the true *li,* those rules of proper action that genuinely embody *jen,* become the means whereby the individual's own humanity can be evoked and developed. They are emphasized by Confucius (who uses the word *li* seventy-five times in the *Sayings*) as the means by which we tame our unruly impulses, transforming them into civilized expressions of human nature.

Ceremonial activities, as embodiments of *li,* were very dear to Confucius's heart. It is recorded that one day, after a ceremony, Confucius heaved a great sigh. Upon being asked why he was sighing, he replied, "Oh, I was thinking of the Golden Age and regretting that I was not able to have been born in it and to associate with the wise rulers and ministers of the three Dynasties."[2] Confucius went on to explain that this golden age came about because of the emphasis on *jen* and *li,* noting that the founders of the Great Dynasties

> were deeply concerned over the principle of li, through which justice was maintained, general confidence was tested, and errors of malpractice were exposed. An ideal of true manhood, Jen, was set up and good manners or courtesy was cultivated, as solid principles for the common people to follow.[3]

The importance Confucius attached to *li* is also seen by his remark that *"li* is the principle by which the ancient kings embodied the laws of heaven and regulated the expression of human nature. Therefore he who has attained *li* lives, and he who has lost it, dies."[4]

To understand the importance Confucius attributed to *li,* we must examine the meanings this concept had for him and his predecessors. The word *li* means many things. It means religion; it means the general principle of the social order; it means the entire body of social, moral, and religious practices taught and rationalized by Confucius. It also means ritual and ceremony. It means a system of well-defined social relationships with definite attitudes toward one another, love in the parents, filial piety in the children, respect in the younger brothers, friendliness in the elder brothers, loyalty among friends, respect for authority among subjects, and benevolence in rulers. It means moral discipline in personal conduct. It means propriety in everything.

Because *li* is of such importance in Confucian philosophy, it is appropriate that the concept be explored both from the point of view of its history and from the point of view of its content. The earliest notion of *li* is religious, where it is concerned with rites for the religious activities performed by the emperor to secure the blessings of Heaven and support of the spirits for his reign. It soon came to denote all of the emperor's duties as well as a wide range of other rituals, such as marriage, and military and government festivals. This sense of *li* coincides with a more or less elaborate set of rules and conventions, requiring strict observation, for public activities.

The second notion of *li* refers to a customary code of social behavior. In this sense, *li* is the customary law or common morality. *Li,* in this sense, takes the place of written law, although it differs from written law in that it is positive rather than negative ("do this," rather than "don't do this"), it does not bring with it automatic punishment, and it generally was assumed to refer to the behavior of the aristocracy rather than that of ordinary persons.

The third, and extended, meaning of *li* is anything that is proper in the sense that it conforms to the norms of humanity *(jen)*. This third sense of *li* is most important for understanding Confucius, although Confucius uses the term *li* in all of its meanings. This is not surprising, because the meanings of *li* are related. They all refer to acts that are public and ceremonial, acts constituting the important rituals of life. The rituals may be as simple as the exchange of greeting between two people when they meet, or as complex as the mourning rites for a deceased relative. Regardless of complexity, however, ritual acts have a ceremonial dimension that emphasizes the social and public character of human action. Ceremony is public in the sense that it involves at least two people in relationship with each other. Furthermore, ceremonial action, because it is out in the open, not private or secret, emphasizes the openness of the participants to each other. It is precisely this open, shared participation in life with other persons who are fundamentally alike in their common human nature that evokes and fosters the development of *jen*. If we think of *jen* as the seed of humanity present in all human beings, we can regard *li* as that which provides the conditions and support needed for this seed to grow and flower.

FILIAL PIETY *(HSIAO)*

Because the family constitutes the immediate social environment of the child, Confucius emphasized its importance in developing *jen*. In the family, the child learns to respect and love others, first parents, brothers and sisters, and relatives, then, by gradual extension, all humankind. Yu Tzu, a favorite student of Confucius, said, "filial piety *(hsiao)* and brotherly respect are the root of humanity" (1.2).

Hsiao, or filial piety, is the virtue of reverence and respect for family. First of all, parents are revered because life itself is generated from them. In showing reverence for parents, it is important to protect the body from harm, because the body is from the parents. Therefore, to protect the body is to honor the parents. But even more, reverence should be shown for parents by doing well and making their name known and respected. If it is not possible to bring honor to the name of one's parents, at least they should not be disgraced. Thus, *hsiao* does not consist merely in giving one's parents physical care, but also in bringing them emotional and spiritual richness. And equally important, after parents are dead, their unfulfilled aims and purposes should be the aims and purposes of the children. This is even more important than offering sacrifices to the departed spirits of deceased parents.

But *hsiao* is not merely a family virtue. Originating in the family, this virtue influences actions outside the family circle. It becomes, by extension, a moral and social virtue. When children learn respect and reverence for their parents, they can have respect and love for their brothers and sisters. And when they have accomplished this, they can respect and love all humankind. And when all actions are directed by love of humankind, they are acting according to their humanity, or *jen.* Thus the beginnings of *jen* are found in *hsiao.*

RIGHTEOUSNESS *(YI)*

The other virtue stressed by Confucius as necessary for developing *jen* is *yi,* usually translated as "righteousness." Confucius said, "The superior man regards righteousness *(yi)* as the substance of everything. He practices it according to the principle of propriety *(li).* He brings it forth in modesty. And he carries it to its conclusion in faithfulness. He is indeed a superior man!" (15.17).

Yi informs us of the right way of acting in specific situations so that we will be in accord with *jen.* It is thus both a moral disposition to do what is right and an ability to recognize what is right, an ability that functions like a kind of moral sense or intuition. Confucius sometimes talks of this ability in terms of a person's character or uprightness. A person of strong moral character who sees an opportunity for personal gain thinks first about whether it would be morally right *(yi)* to do so. Such a person is ready to sacrifice his or her own life for someone in danger (14.13).

What is according to *yi* is unconditional and absolute. Some actions must be performed for the sole reason that they are right. A person ought to respect and obey his or her parents because it is morally right and obligatory to do so, and for no other reason. Other actions may be performed for the sake of something valuable they bring about, for the sake of profit. These are to be contrasted with actions performed according to *yi,* which are performed only because they are right, and not because of what they produce. A person who acts for the sake of *yi,* because that action is the right thing to do, is not far from *jen.* To practice *jen* is to act out of a love and respect for humanity for no other reason than that it is the right, or human, way to act.

Li, hsiao, and *yi* are the characteristics of the superior person whose humanity is developed and who is morally cultivated and aware. This superior person is the opposite of the person who is morally uncultivated.

It is the conviction of Confucius that the cultivation of *jen* through *li, hsiao,* and *yi* will lead to a personal embodiment of virtue, resulting in a well-ordered society. No sharp distinction is made here between ethics and politics. If people are true to themselves, having good faith or sincerity, then they will embody the various virtues. And if every person does this, good government and a harmonious social order will be assured.

RECTIFICATION OF NAMES (CHENG-MING)

One of the keys to cultivating the basic human virtues that Confucius stressed was that of the right use of words *(cheng-ming),* usually referred to as the "rectification of names." *Right use* means that the word should correspond to the reality it names. Although right use of words can be applied to all uses of language, in Confucianism it applies primarily to human actions and relationships. Thus, when Duke Ching asked Confucius about government, Confucius replied, "Let the ruler be a ruler, the subject a subject, the father a father, the son a son."[5] This means that the ruler should truly rule; that is, his actions should conform to the ideals of action that constitute the meaning of the word *ruler.* Similarly, to truly be a father, the father should relate to a son or daughter in the ideal ways that are part of the very meaning of the word *father.*

Rectifying names is thus not about choosing the right words to describe things, but about bringing one's character and actions into agreement with the normative ideals built into the names of fundamental human relationships. For a son to be truly a son, his relationship to his parents must fulfill the ideal of *hsiao.* For a friend to be truly a friend, the relationship must fulfill the ideal of loyalty. Thus, when names are rectified, all human relationships will be in accord with their ideals. This is why, according to Confucianism, when names are rectified, society will be harmonious and people will be happy.

GOVERNING BY VIRTUE

The Confucian idea that virtue, rather than law, should be the basis of government may seem excessively idealistic. But Confucius was convinced that the well-being of society depended on the cultivation and exemplification of *jen* by the rulers. The most comprehensive statement of the Confucian philosophy of government by virtue is contained in the *Great Learning,* which begins by observing: "The way of greater learning lies in keeping one's inborn luminous Virtue unobscured, in renewing the people, and in coming to rest in perfect goodness."[6] The text continues as follows:

> The ancients who wished to preserve the fresh or clear character of the people of the world would first set about ordering their national life. Those who wished to order their national life, would first set about regulating their family life. Those who

wished to regulate their family life would set about cultivating their personal life. Those who wished to cultivate their personal lives would first set about setting their hearts right. Those who wished to set their hearts right would first set about making their wills sincere. Those who wished to make their wills sincere would first set about achieving true knowledge. The achieving of true knowledge depends upon the investigation of things. When things are investigated, then true knowledge is achieved; when true knowledge is achieved then the will becomes sincere; when the will is sincere, then the heart is set right; when the heart is set right, then the personal life is cultivated; when the personal life is cultivated, then the family life is regulated; when the family life is regulated, then the national life is orderly, and when the national life is orderly, then there is peace in this world.[7]

The last statement in this quotation—"When the national life is orderly, then there is peace in the world"—is an expression of what the Confucians expected government to achieve, namely, an orderly, peaceful society. They understood that peace within a particular nation and peace among neighboring nations depends upon a great many factors, such as enough to eat, a place to sleep, security against disease, self-expression, and so on, all of which may be reduced to the factors of material and spiritual sufficiency. But sufficient material wealth and ample means and opportunity for spiritual development and expression (through art, education, religion, and so forth), while viewed as necessary conditions of peace and order, were not seen as sufficient conditions. The Confucians insisted that ultimately the well-being of society depends on the cultivation of *jen.* And because it is the business of government to ensure social well-being, they thought that the most important function of government was to promote the cultivation of *jen* and the practice of virtue throughout the society.

Unlike the modern conception of government as political statecraft, the Confucian concept of government was that of a moral community. When all relations between people are based on virtue *(jen),* and when actions are carried out in accord with *li,* society will be well-ordered and the people happy. This is why the *Great Learning* could say that to achieve world peace, it is necessary and sufficient to set right one's heart, cultivate one's personal life, and regulate family life properly. When these three things are done, *jen* will be developed, virtue practiced, and community well-being achieved.

Learning

The way to world peace outlined in the *Great Learning* reflects the idea that education (the investigation of things) is a basic element of Confucian social philosophy. Confucianism emphasizes a certain philosophy of education, which stresses that the most important goal is to come to know humanity. It is necessary to know both what humanity is and what things are so that life may be ordered in a way conducive to human welfare, making the best use of things in the world. Confucius says, "The principles of the higher education consist in preserving man's clear character, in giving new life to the people and in dwelling (or resting) in perfection, or the ultimate good."[8] Only through education will people come to know themselves and the world. Without this knowledge, it is very difficult to order life so that it will be in harmony with things of the world; only when life is in harmony with the world is there peace and happiness.

According to Confucius, "true knowledge" ensues when the root, or basis, of things is known. An example of what it is to have true knowledge is offered by Confucius when he says, "In presiding over lawsuits I am as good as anyone. The thing is we should make it our aim that there not be any lawsuits at all."[9] In other words, one should remove the evil by removing the causes of the evil. Knowing the basic causes is primary in the rectification of malfunctions. So if one has true knowledge, that is, knowledge of the basic causes of crime, then it may be possible to do away with crime itself, thereby eliminating lawsuits.

The most important knowledge, however, is self-knowledge rather than knowledge about external things, such as social conditions and institutions. "Having knowledge" is above all knowing who and what one is, which means knowing how to relate to others and knowing the principles upon which one acts. Accordingly, true knowledge is obtained only when there is self-knowledge, for in Confucianism, it is always the moral and social self that is taken as ultimate.

When it is said that the will becomes sincere when there is knowledge, the reference is to self-knowledge. The point is that one who has self-knowledge will not deceive himself or herself about the motives and principles of one's actions. Thus it is said, "What is meant by making the will sincere is that one should not deceive himself."[10] People should not deceive themselves by thinking that if they do something in private no one will know. The wrong action will be known to the one who commits it immediately, and soon the effects will be known to others as well. Corruptness of private character does not remain purely private — a person does not live in isolation — but affects, and is affected by, the whole community of human beings.

When a person is upset by worries and cares, or overcome with passion, then the heart is disturbed. Such a person is hardly in a position to make fair and just decisions concerning any matters, personal or public. Thus the *Great Learning* recommends that when "the heart is set right," one can avoid the excesses and defects that affect one's ability to make good decisions. That is why the text says, "The cultivation of the personal life depends on setting one's heart right." With the proper attitude toward life, a person will remain calm even in joy and sorrow.

Familial Relationships

Psychologists report that the first five years of human life are the most important for establishing basic attitudes and behavior patterns. This being so, what better way of ensuring respect for law, government, and people than by good education of the child in these early years? Because ordinarily these first five years are spent in the home, basic education must take place in the home. Education will take place, based mainly on imitation of a model, and the question is whether the education will be good or bad. This, in turn, becomes a question of whether the parents provide proper models for their children.

The Confucian conviction is that if parents have cultivated their personal lives, they can have a family in which the proper relationships exist. By the example of their own lives, parents can demonstrate the way of *jen* to their children. When the family follows the way of *jen*, there will be harmony in the home. And if there is harmony in every home, then there will be harmony in the whole country.

This emphasis on proper familial relationships is one of the most important ideas of Confucius. Suppose children are born into a family where love and goodness abound. These children will grow up seeing parents who love and respect each other and will have a model on which to develop their own sense of respect and love. Here the children see their parents respecting other adults, the various offices and officials of government, morality, and law. Not only is it possible for the parents to govern properly in this home, but respect and obedience are natural to the children.

In the Confucian view, nothing is more important for good government and peace than proper family relationships. *Hsiao,* familial love, is the basis of the kind of familial relationships that enable children to grow up with respect and love for other people and a sense of propriety in human relationships. A nation is essentially a family, in which the good of the individual is inseparably linked to the good of the whole community. By the same token, the good of the community is the good of many individuals. Therefore government ought to be concerned primarily with human beings and their relationships to one another. This is precisely what Confucius emphasized, focusing on the most fundamental human relationships, those between members of a family. A person begins life in a family. If education is the key to a good society, education must begin in that family structure.

With the individual and the family viewed in this way, it is easy to understand why Confucius stressed the virtue of *hsiao* and regarded it as basic to all the virtues. Nothing can be more important than developing a child's proper attitudes to the rest of the family. By developing respect and love for parents and siblings, and learning respect for other people from them, the child develops both self-respect and respect for others.

Human Nature

Is Confucius's analysis of the role of virtue in social development and government relevant to our own times? Government based on virtue may appear an impossible ideal for most people today, but this is what Confucius recommended, and what Mencius, a follower of Confucius, taught even more clearly. It is not so much that Confucius had a different view of the nature of human beings than is commonly held today, but rather that Confucius had quite a different idea concerning the aims of education and government. While Confucius nowhere explicitly affirms that human nature is basically good, he clearly assumes that humans possess the potential for goodness and regards the development of this potential through moral self-cultivation to be a central concern of government. Indeed, the development of moral virtue is the fundamental task of society.

Many people today also hold that human beings are basically good and need only develop this goodness. Others hold a Hobbesian view, believing people to be basically selfish and demanding, using other people to serve their own ends. But regardless of which of these views is held, most people today would probably think that power, rather than virtue, must be the basis for government. The need to develop laws and to punish infractions is thought to be basic to government, and these functions require governmental power. If people are good, it may be easier to enforce the laws, but it will never make law unnecessary; this is the modern attitude as well as the opinion of the Legalists in ancient China.

An important reason exists for this attitude in our times. Today, in the Western world, whether people are regarded as basically good or basically evil, the purpose of education is the mastery of a skill or trade to enable the acquisition of sufficient material goods. Young people are urged to go to college so that they can get a good job; once enrolled, they are advised how best to prepare themselves for the professional labor market. This points to a fundamental difference between our contemporary philosophy of education and the Confucian view of education as the development of moral character. Confucius tells us that "the only way for the superior man to civilize the people and establish good social customs is through education. A piece of jade cannot become an object of art without chiseling, and a man cannot come to know the moral law without education."[11]

If, without enforced positive law (in the relevant sense), there is to be peace and well-being, it is necessary that everyone act appropriately, or practice the virtue of *li*. To act appropriately, one must respect and care for others, or practice the virtue of *jen,* and this respect is learned early through respect for the parents, by practicing the virtue of *hsiao*. Through this cultivation of the basic virtues, the realization of one's true nature *(jen)* is possible. When one's true human nature is realized, one is in harmony with others and with all things. Then there will be peace and fulfillment, according to the Confucian vision.

In explaining how the development of *jen* permeates society, a modern scholar summarizes Confucius's conviction that

> to be kept stable, society must have leaders who can be trusted; that the only leaders to be trusted are men of character; that character is to be developed through education acquired both from others and through self-discipline; that no man is a safe leader who goes to extremes; that the right cultivation of his own character must be the chief concern of every leader; that no parent, teacher, or public officer has the right to take lightly his responsibilities for guiding, through precept, rules and example, the conduct of those who are under him.[12]

The Confucian philosophy outlined so far probably represents primarily the thought of Confucius, though it is extremely difficult to keep separate the various streams of thought contributing to Confucianism. The realism of Hsun Tzu and the idealism of Mencius were undoubtedly influential in the development of Confucius's thought into Confucianism. While Confucius emphasized *jen* and regarded *li, yi,* and *hsiao* as necessary for a well-developed person and for a well-ordered society, he did not discuss the question of *why* one should practice these virtues in terms of the natural endowments of human nature. He simply saw that to achieve harmonious human relationships, a stable, well-ordered society, and personal happiness, it is necessary to practice moral self-cultivation. Mencius and Hsun Tzu, however, were very much concerned with the question of why one should live in accord with *jen,* practicing *yi* and *hsiao.* Mencius held that it was in order to develop the original goodness of human nature that one should practice the virtues stressed by Confucius. Hsun Tzu, in contrast, took the view that because of the original evil inherent in human nature, one should practice these virtues in order to remove these innate evil tendencies and replace them with moral virtue.

MENCIUS

Mencius agreed with Confucius that *jen* is basic, that it is the source and foundation of all goodness and virtue. And he also agreed with Confucius that *li,* or rules for proper behavior, were required for the development and manifestation of *jen.* In addition, *hsiao* was recognized to be the beginning point for goodness. But Mencius gave a more important role to *yi* than did Confucius. It is *yi,* or righteousness, that above all else contains the key to the development and cultivation of *jen,* according to Mencius.

The reason for the emphasis on *yi* is the recognition by Mencius of the distinction between goodness and rightness. *Jen* refers to the goodness that is basic to human nature. But *yi* refers to the rightness of human actions. The need for the distinction comes from the fact that although all people possess *jen,* not all people act in the right way.

For Mencius, who claimed that *jen* was an actual beginning of goodness present in each person, the problem was to explain the presence of evil in the world. If evil is due to wrong actions, it becomes necessary to distinguish between the rightness of actions and the goodness of human nature. Despite the presence of goodness, it is possible for human beings to act in a wrong way and thus bring about evil in the world. Because this is so, it is necessary to emphasize *yi,* the correctness of action, in order to rid the world of evil. Of course, Mencius did not hold that *yi* and *jen* are totally different and do not meet. Rather, he held that if *jen* is completely developed, *yi* will naturally follow. And if all actions are in accord with *yi, jen* will be developed. But because it is easier and more successful to begin the development of human nature with the correction of a person's actions, Mencius emphasizes *yi.*

The two most significant differences between Confucius and Mencius are found in their views about human nature and about the relation between goodness and rightness. Whereas Confucius claimed that people have a potential for goodness, Mencius claimed that they possess an actual goodness as part of their nature. Furthermore, Confucius did not distinguish between goodness and rightness, whereas for Mencius the distinction was important.

Arguments for the Goodness of Human Beings

Mencius did not simply state that people possess an innate goodness; he presented arguments for this view. The first argument runs as follows: (1) all human beings are alike by nature; (2) the sage, who is good by nature, is a person; (3) therefore, all human beings are good by nature.

According to the second argument, the goodness of human beings is evident in the virtues of *jen, yi, li,* and *chih* (moral wisdom). All human beings possess the beginnings of these virtues as can be seen by the universality of the basic feelings that constitute their beginnings. Mencius's argument proceeds by identifying the feelings that constitute the beginnings in each of these virtues, illustrating them with examples.

Compassion is the beginning of *jen.* Any person would have compassion for a child about to fall into a well and would attempt to save the child.

Shamefulness is the root of *yi.* Any person who robs another person or causes the death of that person will feel shame and try to make restitution.

Reverence is the beginning of *li.* The universality of this beginning can be seen in the fact that all children have a natural reverence for their parents, and in the presence of superiors, all people feel their own shortcomings and are modest and reverent. Mencius says that if one were to simply throw the body of a parent in a ditch instead of burying it, and later were to come and see the birds and beasts preying on it, a natural reverence would cause one to hurry and bury the body.

The knowledge of right and wrong is the root of the virtue *chih.* Since every person draws his or her ideas about the rightness and wrongness of actions from reflections in his or her own mind, it follows that these innate ideas of right and wrong must be found in every person.

The conclusion of these arguments is that human beings are innately moral. Because of this innate goodness, they know right and wrong; have compassion, reverence, and modesty; and know shame. This means that because they possess the basis of moral judgment, they can distinguish between right and wrong and it is possible to perfect their human nature.

Sources of Evil

But if this innate goodness of human beings is granted, how is one to account for the presence of evil in the world? According to Mencius, evil in the world has three sources. First, evil is due to external circumstances. Although people are by nature good, still their nature is distorted by the externals of life. Because competition in society encourages greed and selfishness, society itself is partially responsible for the presence of wrong actions and evil in the world despite the presence of goodness in human nature. Second, evil is due to the abandonment of self: people abandon their innate goodness. Rather than allowing their nature to manifest itself in goodness, they forsake this goodness and become evil. Third, evil is due to a failure to nourish the feelings and the senses. That is, though the intentions are good, one is incapable of doing the right things because of a lack of knowledge with which to make the correct decision.

If one accepts Mencius's arguments for the innate goodness of human nature and agrees with his explanation of the source of evil in the world, it follows that people should live according to *jen, yi,* and *li* because acting correctly develops one's humanity, leading to harmonious social relationships and an orderly society. Furthermore, to regulate one's actions by *li* is to live according to the innate goodness that is basic to human nature. In brief, one should practice the Confucian way because it is the way of fulfilling human nature.

HSUN TZU

The views of Hsun Tzu on this point are diametrically opposed to those of Mencius. According to Hsun Tzu, human nature is originally evil. Through education and participation in social institutions and culture, people become good. Human beings not only lack the beginnings of the four virtues claimed by Mencius, but actually possess the beginnings of evil in their inherent desire for profit and pleasure. Yet it is possible for every person to become a sage, because every person possesses intelligence, and through the employment of intelligence, goodness can be brought about, according to Hsun Tzu.

Sources of Goodness

The problem for Hsun Tzu is to show how it is that if human beings are born evil, they can become good. He argues that goodness follows from social organization and culture, which are the results of the drive to live better and the need to overcome other creatures. The arguments are that people cannot provide the goods needed to live, let alone to live well, except through the cooperation of other persons, and people cannot make themselves secure from the various creatures and forces of nature without mutual cooperation.

Since it is clear, for these two reasons, that people require social organization, the question is this: How does social organization bring about goodness? Hsun Tzu's answer is that social organization requires rules of conduct, and following these rules brings about goodness. His theory is that people are born with desires, some of which are ordinarily unsatisfied. When desires remain unsatisfied, people strive for their satisfaction. And when many persons are striving for the satisfaction of their conflicting desires without rules or limits, there is contention and strife, which bring about disorder and are harmful to everyone. Accordingly, the early kings established rules of conduct regulating the activities involved in attempting to satisfy desires, leading to the various rules for social living. By this line of reasoning, moral goodness is brought about as a result of the regulation of human conduct required for social living.

Hsun Tzu also argues for the creation of goodness through the use of human intelligence. He observes that it is not the absence of fur or feathers on this two-legged creature that distinguishes humans from other animals; rather, it is their ability to make distinctions. Human intelligence is displayed in the making of social distinctions. Since it is the making of social distinctions and the resulting social relationships regulated by *li* that distinguish human beings from the birds and the beasts, people ought to act according to *li* in order to overcome their evil inclinations and acquire virtue.

Both lines of argument given by Hsun Tzu emphasize that goodness is the result of human creation, either through the employment of intelligence or through the making of distinctions in the social sphere. Unlike Mencius, who stressed the importance of developing the beginnings of goodness already present in human beings, Hsun Tzu stressed the importance of overcoming the inborn human tendencies to evil through processes of education and socialization that would give people a virtuous nature. Hsun Tzu differs from Confucius primarily in distinguishing between goodness and intelligence and in stressing the actual evil present in nature. But all three agreed that cultivation of moral virtue was the key to individual and social well-being.

Through their attempts to support the social philosophy of Confucius by answering the questions, Why regulate life by *li*? and Why develop *jen* by practicing *yi*? Hsun Tzu and Mencius strengthened the Confucian philosophy considerably. What happened historically was that neither of these philosophers was rejected in favor of the other; rather, both the idealism of Mencius and the realism of Hsun Tzu were added to the philosophy of Confucius, thus rounding out Confucianism. From Mencius was taken the emphasis on determining the correctness of action as a means to the development of humanity. From Hsun Tzu was taken the emphasis on following rules of behavior for developing human nature. By adopting both views, Confucianism endorsed respect both for internal sanctions, using the internal feelings as guides to behavior, and for external sanctions, using social rules as guides to behavior. This is roughly equivalent to employing both the internal criterion of conscience and the external criterion of law to determine how one should live. Of course, conscience tended to have priority in the Confucian way because only those social rules that conformed to *jen* were part of the moral way.

Even though Confucianism, as a result of the influence of various other schools and the contributions of Mencius and Hsun Tzu, had various external criteria available for determining the correctness of actions, it continued to stress that each person possesses the basis for determining right action, because everyone possesses *jen,* or humanity. All that is required is that the principle of reciprocity, the Golden Rule, be applied: if you would not like something done to you, then do not do it to anyone else. It is probably the emphasis on moral cultivation based on this humanistic measure of goodness that constitutes the timeless essence of Confucianism.

REVIEW QUESTIONS

1. Confucianism has been described as a "social humanism." What does this mean? How does humanism differ from naturalism or supernaturalism?
2. What is *jen?* What is the importance of *jen* in Confucianism?
3. Distinguish between *li, hsiao,* and *yi.* How are these virtues related to the way of *jen?*
4. Confucius has been described as advocating government by virtue, rather than government by laws and punishments. Do you agree with this description? How would you argue for this claim?
5. How does Mencius argue for his view that human beings are inherently good?
6. According to Hsun Tzu, how does goodness come about?

FURTHER READING

An Introduction to Confucianism, by Xinzhong Yao (Cambridge: Cambridge University Press, 2000), is an accessible, but comprehensive, introduction to Confucianism that concludes with discussions of contemporary Confucian thought.

Confucian Moral Self Cultivation, 2d ed., by Philip J. Ivanhoe (Indianapolis: Hackett Publishing, 2000), is probably the best introduction to the subject of Confucian moral self-cultivation.

Confucius and the Analects: New Essays, edited by Bryan W. Van Norden (New York: Oxford University Press, 2000), is the single best collection of essays representing the latest scholarship on the teachings of Confucius. It is not always easy reading.

The Ways of Confucianism: Investigations in Chinese Philosophy, edited by Bryan W. Van Norden (LaSalle, IL: Open Court, 1996), is a collection of outstanding essays, many of them recent, on Confucianism.

Confucius and the Chinese Way, by H.G. Creel (New York: Harper & Row, 1960, originally published in 1949), is quite accessible to students and is still one of the better studies of Confucius.

Thinking Through Confucius, by David L. Hall and Roger T. Ames (Albany: State University of New York Press, 1987), may be the most helpful analysis of the thought of Confucius for contemporary Western readers. The most philosophical passages of the *Analects (Sayings)* are translated and commented on carefully, providing a coherent Confucian vision.

The Ways of Confucianism, by David S. Nivison (La Salle, IL: Open Court, 1997), is a careful and sophisticated study of Confucian philosophy by one of the outstanding Confucian scholars of our time.

Confucius — The Secular as Sacred, by Herbert Fingarette (New York: Harper & Row, 1972), a modern classic of Confucian interpretation, is a very rich philosophical interpretation of ceremony and ritual *(li)* in the thought of Confucius.

Confucius: The Analects, by D.C. Lau (Harmondsworth: Penguin Books, 1979), is an excellent translation of the whole text, with a good introduction and helpful notes.

Centrality and Commonality, by Wei-ming Tu (Albany: State University of New York Press, 1989), is the single best study of the *Chung-yung.* Not only is Tu's interpretation brilliant, but it is presented so clearly that it is accessible to most readers.

NOTES

1. Although the translations use "man" and "men," these terms should be understood in a gender-neutral way, as referring to human beings. Unless otherwise indi-

cated, translations are taken from Wing-tsit Chan, *A Sourcebook in Chinese Philosophy* (Princeton, NJ: Princeton University Press, 1963). Quotations from the *Sayings (Analects)* give the chapter and section of the quotation in the *Sayings.*

2. *Li Chi,* chap. 9, trans. by Lin Yutang, in *The Wisdom of Confucius* (New York: Modern Library, copyright 1938), p. 227.

3. *Li Chi,* p. 225.

4. Ibid.

5. *Sayings,* 12.11, *A Sourcebook in Asian Philosophy,* p. 416.

6. *A Sourcebook in Asian Philosophy,* p. 424.

7. *The Great Learning (Ta Hsueh),* trans. by Lin Yutang, in *The Wisdom of Confucius,* p. 139.

8. Ibid.

9. Ibid., p. 143.

10. Ibid., p. 144.

11. *Book of Rites (Li Chi),* trans. by Lin Yutang, in *The Wisdom of Confucius,* p. 241.

12. D. Willard Lyons, as quoted by Clarence Burton Day, *The Philosophers of China* (New York: Citadel Press, 1962), p. 43.

CHAPTER 21

Taoism: The Natural Way of Freedom

Taoism, in contrast to Confucianism, finds the guidelines for human life in nature rather than in human moral practices aimed at developing virtue. Consequently, instead of emphasizing the cultivation of virtue and the development of human relationships, Taoism emphasizes the freedom attained by following the way of nature.

The story of Taoism can be told in two installments. The first part of the story deals with the philosophy developed in the classical work known as *The Treatise on the Way and Its Power (Tao Te Ching)*. This is traditionally regarded as the philosophy of Lao Tzu. The second part of the story is concerned with the vision of Chuang Tzu, who drew out the epistemological and mystical implications of Taoism.

LAO TZU

Taoism, just as Confucianism, had its beginnings in a response to the deteriorating social conditions of the times. Lao Tzu, probably a contemporary of Confucius, charges that poverty and starvation were caused by bad rulers, that greed and avarice caused wars and killings, and that desires for wealth, power, and glory were bringing about the destruction of society. Although both Lao Tzu and Confucius were concerned with the deterioration of society and the quality of human life, their philosophies developed in quite different and even opposing ways. Whereas Confucianism stressed the moral goodness of human beings as the key to happiness, the Taoists stressed the harmony and perfection of nature.

287

The Taoist attitude is that the contrivances and artifacts of human beings lead to evil and unhappiness. To find peace and contentment, people must follow the Way, or *Tao,* of nature, becoming one with this *Tao.*

In Confucianism the complex and well-developed life is taken to be the ideal. Lao Tzu, however, considered the ideal life to be simple and harmonious. He described the simple life as one that is plain, wherein profit is ignored, cleverness abandoned, selfishness minimized, and desires reduced. This last feature of the simple life serves well to contrast Lao Tzu and Confucius. Confucius advocated rites and music so that the desires and emotions might be developed and regulated, for therein lay the development of *jen,* or humanity. To Lao Tzu, efforts to develop and regulate the desires and emotions seemed artificial, tending to interfere with the harmony of nature. Rather than organize and regulate things to achieve perfection, Lao Tzu advocated letting things work to their perfection naturally. This means supporting all things in their natural state, allowing them to transform spontaneously. In this way no action is needed, no regulations required, and yet everything is done and all things are regulated. It is not the case that the contrast between Confucius and Lao Tzu is that between action and inaction, or doing and nondoing. Rather, the fundamental contrast is between holding that human beings are the measure and source of all things, and holding that nature is the measure and source of all things.

In Confucianism, human beings and nature are differentiated, and goodness and well-being are considered to proceed from what belongs to humanity rather than nature. Taoism sees humanity and nature as a unity and does not differentiate between the two. According to Taoism, the basis of humanity is not of our own making but is contained in the being and the function of the totality of the universe. Consequently, in its critical and negative aspects, Taoism analyzes the deficiencies and evils confronting human society and concludes that they stem primarily from a wrong view of humanity and the universe.

Constructively, Taoism offers a view of the universe and man as a unity. Human knowledge transcends the limits of percepts and concepts. It is direct and immediate, not dependent upon a false duality between the knowing subject and the known object. The principles that should guide life and regulate the actions of human beings are the principles that regulate nature. Life is lived well only when people are completely in tune with the whole universe and their actions are the action of the *Tao* flowing through them. The institutions of society are regulated by allowing them to be what they are naturally; society, too, must be in tune with the universe.

The purpose of knowledge is to lead a person to a unity with the universe by illuminating its *Tao,* or Way. The word *Tao* refers to a path or a way, and in Taoism it means the source and principle of the functioning of whatever exists. When the *Tao* of humanity and the *Tao* of the universe are one, then, according to Lao Tzu, human beings will realize their infinite nature. Then peace and harmony will reign.

Lao Tzu's teachings represent a constructive attempt to preserve and make great human life. To preserve life is to protect it from threats to its very existence. Making life great assumes the preservation of life and consists in improving its quality. For Lao Tzu, this means following the natural way of things. Only by conforming to the *Tao* can one live a completely satisfying and fulfilled life. Lao

Tzu's teachings concerning the *Tao* of human life in society can be summed up in the following nine principles found in various places in the *Tao Te Ching:*

1. People generally act to fulfill their desires.
2. The result of many individuals attempting to satisfy their desires is competition and conflict.
3. In order to provide peace and harmony among individuals competing to satisfy their desires, standards of human rightness and morality are devised.
4. But the presence of moral standards does not solve the problem, for competition and conflict remain. Rules to enforce standards are broken, and new rules devised to protect the old rules are also broken. In this way, old conflicts remain, desires remain unsatisfied, and new wrongdoing and evil are fostered.
5. Since instituting moral standards and rules does not solve the problem, why not abandon them?
6. Moral standards can be abandoned, however, only when desires as sources of action are given up.
7. Actions arising out of desires can be given up only when people adopt the natural way of things.
8. Following the natural way presupposes being in tune with the universe and acting in accord with the universal *Tao.*
9. Therefore, regulation of society by the ruler should be according to the *Tao* of the universe.

The concluding principle is the advice that Lao Tzu offered the rulers of his society to rectify its deplorable conditions. In attempting to rectify the evils present in his society, Lao Tzu recognized the necessity of understanding the basic causes of these evils. For this it is important to know the sources and guides of human actions. As he turned his attention to these matters, it appeared obvious to Lao Tzu that the choices and actions of most people proceed from their desires and are guided by the satisfaction of these desires. Accordingly, the most basic regulatory principle of action is the fulfillment of desires.

If, however, people act in order to fulfill their desires, and if different persons desire the same things, then when there aren't enough goods to go around, there will be competing and conflicting actions. It appears to be the case that people are never able to satisfy all of their desires, and that they often desire the same things. Consequently, they compete with one another and conflicts arise. When competition is unregulated and conflicts are settled through the use of power and force, the whole fabric of society is threatened. Therefore, to regulate competition and reduce conflicts, moral rules are introduced as guides to human behavior.

The primary function of moral rules and social institutions is to regulate the actions of the people in order to provide for a maximum satisfaction of everyone's desires. Lao Tzu has no quarrel with the aims of morality; rather, he questions whether it is possible to achieve this aim through the regulation of competition and conflict. Observing that when the great *Tao* prevailed, there was no strife and competition, he remarks, "When the Great *Tao* declined, the doctrines of humanity and righteousness arose."[1] The doctrines of humanity *(jen)* and righteousness *(yi)* are the basis of the Confucian morality and have as their object the satisfactory ordering of all human actions and social institutions. Lao Tzu's remark, however, reveals that he considers morality an inadequate solution, for it comes about only as a result of the decline of the great Way of nature.

Undoubtedly, Lao Tzu saw the failure of Confucian morality to achieve ideal social conditions as a sign of the inadequacy of the moral approach. Morality does not attack the problem at its root. By allowing desires to function as legitimate sources of human action, morality could not remove competition and strife. The best it could do was to regulate the competition and reduce the strife. But this simply complicates the matter of satisfying desires in accord with the moral rules, and leads to rule breaking, thereby bringing about immorality. It does not remove the competition and does not provide for the complete satisfaction of desires. Hence Lao Tzu said, "Therefore when *Tao* is lost, only then does the doctrine of virtue arise. When virtue is lost, only then does the doctrine of humanity arise" (*Tao Te Ching,* chap. 38).

Because, according to Lao Tzu, morality is incapable of providing for peace and happiness, it should be regarded as an unsuccessful solution to the problem of achieving the ideal society and abandoned in favor of a different solution. But morality cannot be abandoned without changing the conditions that inevitably lead to the regulation of action by moral rules. These conditions, a world of competition and strife where the powerful subdue the weak at their pleasure, are the result of acting for the sake of satisfying desires. Because acting to satisfy desires brings about the conditions requiring morality, morality cannot be abandoned until desires as a source of actions are abandoned. The reason why acting out of desires leads to evil is that it is contrary to the Way, for the great *Tao* is always without desires. The good is accomplished not by action driven by desire, but by inaction inspired by the simplicity of *Tao,* according to Lao Tzu. Nonaction *(wu-wei)* is an important Taoist concept. It means doing nothing except what proceeds freely and spontaneously from one's own nature. Snakes should not attempt to walk or fly; their *wu-wei* is to crawl. A bird's *wu-wei* is to fly; attempting to crawl would be forced action for a bird. For people to act to fulfill their desires is the way of greed and corruption; to live simply, without desires, is nonaction in accord with their nature. As Lao Tzu says, "Simplicity, which has no name, is free of desires. Being free of desires it is tranquil. And the world will be at peace of its own accord" (chap. 37).

If people give up desires as a basis for action, why will they act at all? Lao Tzu answers this important question by recommending that people should adopt the way of *Tao,* not inflicting their desires upon nature, but following nature's principles. With regard to society, he advocates a government of the people that is in accord with the easy and natural way of *Tao,* and that fosters the natural way in the lives of the people.

THE *TAO* AND ITS MANIFESTATIONS

To understand this answer of Lao Tzu, it is necessary to turn to his conception of *Tao* and its function *(te).* Prior to Lao Tzu, the principles of *yin* and *yang* were known. They were regarded as opposites, and all of the things in the world were considered to be the production of their interaction. But *yin* and *yang,* seen in such opposites as dark and light, cold and warm, non-being and being, and so on, because they are opposites, could not of their own nature either produce themselves or interact with each other. A third something providing a basis and a context for the interaction of *yin* and *yang* was required. The great contribution of Lao Tzu was his recognition of *Tao* as the source of both non-being and being—of *yin* and *yang*—and the function of *Tao* as the basis for the interaction of *yin* and *yang.*

As the absolute first principle of existence, *Tao* is completely without characteristics, being the very source and condition of all characteristics. In this sense it is non-being. But it is not simply nothing, for it is the source of everything. Although it is prior to all existing things, it gives them life and function, and it constitutes the oneness underlying all the diversity and multiplicity of the world. Lao Tzu says, "The *Tao* that can be told of is not the eternal *Tao;* the name that can be named is not the eternal name. The Nameless is the origin of Heaven and Earth; the named is the mother of all things" (chap. 1).

The reason *Tao* cannot be named is that it is without divisions, distinctions, or characteristics. According to Lao Tzu, it is unified, like an uncarved block, changeless in itself, though the source of all change. But if *Tao* cannot be named or grasped, what is named by the word *Tao*? Lao Tzu's point in saying that the *Tao* is beyond all names is that the fundamental source and principle cannot be named, for it is the very source of names and descriptions. Consequently, *Tao* is a nonname; it does not name anything. Rather, it points to that which enables things to be what they are; it is that which gives them existence and allows them to pass into nonexistence. When it is said that *Tao* is the source of all being and non-being, the word *Tao* functions very much like the word "that" when it is said "the 'that' from which being and non-being proceed."

This nameless *Tao* is the source of the various particular things that exist in the world; it is that which gives unity to all the existing things; and it determines the function of everything. What that nameless *Tao* is cannot, of course, be said, for whatever can be talked about is limited and determined. But the ultimate source cannot be limited and determined, for it is the very condition of limits and determinations.

Although what *Tao* is cannot be said, but can only be pointed to, a sense of what *Tao* is can be achieved by considering the functioning of *Tao*. Strictly speaking, the function *(te)* of *Tao* cannot be stated, but because *Tao* supports all things in their natural state, its function can be seen, at least partially, by looking to nature. The *Tao* is manifested in the workings of nature, for what individual things possess of *Tao* is the *te,* or function, of *Tao. Tao,* as a source, provides for the very existence of things, but the function of *Tao* provides for their distinctness.

Examining the workings of things in their natural conditions, Lao Tzu observes that nonaction *(wu-wei)* is what they inherit from *Tao* as their function. He says, *"Tao* invariably takes no action, and yet there is nothing left undone" (chap. 37). What he means by "no action" is not straining and contriving to accomplish, but letting things be accomplished in a natural and spontaneous way. Thus, immediately after the remark quoted above, he says, "If kings and barons can keep it [the *Tao*], all things will transform spontaneously" (chap.

37). If the ruler will keep to the way of *Tao,* government will proceed in a natural and spontaneous way. There will be no need for harsh laws, conscriptions, punishment, and wars.

Lao Tzu's advice to the rulers is that they should govern as little as possible, keeping to the natural way, letting people go their own way. What the ruler should keep in mind is that "ruling a big country is like cooking a small fish." In cooking a small fish, one must take care not to handle it too roughly, for too much handling will spoil it. In ruling a country, care must be taken not to push the people around, forcing them to rebel. When the people are satisfied, there will be no rebellion or wars. Therefore, the easy way of governing is to give the people what they want and make government conform to the will of the people rather than trying to force the people to conform to the will of the government.

A ruler who knows the *Tao* and its *te* knows how to stay out of the way of the people and serve them without intruding. Thus, Lao Tzu says that the people "are difficult to rule because the ruler does too many things" (chap. 25). In accord with the function of *Tao,* Lao Tzu says, "Administer the empire by engaging in no activity." Supporting this advice, he notes that "the more taboos and prohibitions there are in the world, the poorer the people will be," and "the more laws and orders are made prominent, the more thieves and robbers there will be" (chap. 57).

When Lao Tzu suggests that the ruler should know the mystic *Tao* and in his ruling emulate the function of *Tao,* he has in mind that the perfection of all things lies in expressing the *Tao* they possess. The job of the ruler is to let the *Tao* operate freely, rather than trying to resist and change its function. What *Tao* is, and how it functions, is revealed in the fourth chapter of the *Tao Te Ching*:

> Tao is empty (like a bowl).
> It may be used but its capacity is never exhausted.
> It is bottomless, perhaps the ancestor of all things.
> It blunts its sharpness.
> It unties its tangles.
> It softens its light.
> It becomes one with the dusty world.
> Deep and still, it appears to exist forever.

To say *Tao* is empty is to note that it is without characteristics; it is empty of all particularity, for it is the possibility and source of all particularity. Even though it is empty of particular things, it is the most useful of all things. Just as the most useful thing about a house is its emptiness—its space—so the most useful thing about *Tao* is its emptiness of characteristics, for this means it has infinite capacity. Thus, the emptiness of *Tao* is synonymous with its being the infinite source of all things.

The functioning of *Tao* is eternal and recurrent, producing all things and directing their activities. Comparing the functioning of *Tao* to blunting sharpness, untying tangles, and softening light draws attention to reversal as the movement of the *Tao.* The lesson the Taoists drew from nature is that when a thing reaches one extreme, it reverses and returns to the other extreme. When it gets very cold, reversal sets in and it begins to get warm. When it gets very warm, reversal again sets in and it begins to get cold. This is the way of nature as seen in the passing of the seasons. In similar fashion, when a person becomes extremely proud and conceited, disgrace and humility will follow. To know the reversals that constitute the functioning of Tao and to adapt oneself to these movements is the way to peace and contentment. Just as one does not dress lightly in winter and suffer in the cold, and does not dress warmly in the summer and suffer in the heat, but dresses warmly in the winter and enjoys the cold, and dresses lightly in the summer and enjoys the warm weather, so one should not resist the natural way, but should act in accord with the Way of the great *Tao* in all things.

To recognize that *Tao* becomes one with the dusty world is to understand that *Tao* is not transcendental, but immanent. That is, *Tao* does not remain aloof from the world, directing it from afar, but functions through the world, and it is indistinguishable from the functioning of the world. Tao is not to be found aside from life, but within life in the world.

Thus, Lao Tzu's advice is to give up desires and let oneself merge with the *Tao.* Thereby one can rise above the distinctions of good and evil. When all activity proceeds from *Tao,* the very source of existence, then humanity will be one with the world.

CHUANG TZU

Although the foundations of Taoism are beyond the limits of rational analysis, there are good reasons for seriously considering this way of life, as Chuang Tzu points out. Chuang Tzu (ca. 369–286 BCE) developed a philosophy that is similar in many respects to Lao Tzu's. A basic difference, however, is that Chuang Tzu does not attempt to provide advice to rulers. Because he thinks that rulership is part of the problem, he suggests that to follow the *Tao,* people need to withdraw from society.

Chuang Tzu also developed the concepts of the total spontaneity of nature, the incessant activity of things, and the underlying unity of all existence. He emphasized that ultimate freedom is achieved through identifying with the *Tao,* not by fulfilling social roles and functions. In addition, Chuang Tzu provided arguments for rejecting other ways of life and accepting the Taoist Way.

The philosophy of Chuang Tzu is based on the conviction that true happiness is dependent upon transcending the world of ordinary experience and cognition and identifying oneself with the infinity of the universe. This conviction appears quite clearly in his description of the person who has achieved complete happiness. Of the happy person, the true sage, Chuang Tzu says,

> Suppose there is one who chariots upon the normality of the universe, rides upon the transformation of the six elements, and thus makes excursions into the unlimited, what has he to depend upon? Therefore it is said that the Perfect Man has no self; the Spiritual Man has no achievement; the Sage has no name.[2]

This remark is intended to suggest that the ordinary cognitive scheme wherein one distinguishes between self and other, between doing and not doing, and between names (words) and realities (things) is inadequate. It is claimed to be inadequate because it is extremely limited. Consequently, the *Book of Chuang Tzu* suggests that this limited point of view, which is dependent upon ordinary perception and conceptual distinctions, should be exchanged for an unlimited point of view. Attaining this unlimited point of view is regarded as becoming one with *Tao,* the fundamental Way of the universe.

Not infrequently, the aspects of his philosophy just referred to are regarded as evidence that Chuang Tzu was a mystic whose views were beyond the reach of reason. Being so labeled, he could be dismissed from further philosophical consideration. But such dismissal is unfortunate, for Chuang Tzu does not merely suggest that the limited point of view should be exchanged for the unlimited. He argues, quite ingeniously, for the acceptance of the unlimited point of view by trying to show that the limited point of view (the ordinary cognitive scheme) is inadequate.

The arguments against accepting the ordinary cognitive scheme, which constitute Chuang Tzu's arguments for an unlimited point of view, can be classified as (1) the argument from the relativity of distinctions, (2) the argument from the complementariness of opposites, (3) the argument from perspectives, and (4) the argument from general skepticism.

Relativity of Distinctions

The first argument, from the relativity of distinctions, claims that judgments about values and matters of taste are subjective and therefore relative. A particular sauce may be sour to A's taste, but sweet to B's taste. Thinking about the relativity of distinctions may be good for X, and bad for Y. This relativity is taken to hold for all distinctions. Chuang Tzu gives a number of examples of the relativity of distinctions: "Let us take, for instance, a large beam and a small beam, or an ugly woman and Hsi-shih [a famous beauty of ancient China], or generosity, strangeness, deceit, and abnormality. The *Tao* identifies them all as one."[3] By saying that the *Tao* identifies all these differences as one, Chuang Tzu is claiming that these kinds of distinctions are relative to a certain perspective. From another perspective, that of the *Tao,* there are no differences between these things.

Chuang Tzu gives other examples of the relativity of distinctions: "There is nothing in the world greater than the tip of a hair that grows in autumn, while Mount T'ai is small. No one lives a longer life than a child who dies in infancy, but P'eng-tsu (who lived many hundred years) died prematurely. The universe and I exist together, and all things and I are one."[4] Here again, Chuang Tzu is claiming that distinctions are valid only from a certain perspective; from another perspective, that of the *Tao,* these same distinctions make no sense.

The basic reason for regarding all distinctions as relative is that the characteristics attributed to things or events in the making of distinctions are generated by the mind, which is regarded as independent of the so-called characteristics of things generated by it. Chuang Tzu says, "A road becomes so when people walk on it, and things become so-and-so [to people] because people call them so-and-so. How have they become so? They have become so because people say they are so. How have they become not so? They have become not so because [people] say they are not so."[5] The argument from the relativity of distinctions is intended to prove the relativity of knowledge. If the concepts of good, big, and sweet are relative, then knowledge of what is good, or big, or sweet, because it is based on relative concepts, is merely relative.

This argument is directed primarily against the Confucians and Mohists, both of whom claimed they had genuine knowledge of right and wrong, but who disagreed with each other on nearly every point. Chuang Tzu says, "There have arisen the controversies between the Confucians and the Mohists, each school regarding as right what the other regards as wrong."[6] The Mohists were pragmatists, accepting practice as the criterion of knowledge. Their view was that knowledge is possible, for in the main, people live in such a way as to avoid a lot of unpleasantness. Now, because on pragmatic or utilitarian grounds the rightness and wrongness of actions is determined by the amounts of pleasantness and unpleasantness, respectively, right and wrong can be known simply by looking to the pleasantness and unpleasantness brought about by actions. The Confucians, in contrast, maintained that knowledge of right and wrong proceeded immediately and intuitively from an internal moral sense.

Chuang Tzu uses the argument from relativity to show that pleasantness and unpleasantness are relative concepts, and though people appear to get on well in this life, this may be a mere appearance and not the case at all. Furthermore, it is not clear how practice can serve as a criterion of knowledge, and it may be possible that there is no way of knowing whether or not practice is an adequate criterion of knowledge, for a practice that is successful one time may fail at another time. In the chapter entitled "Autumn Floods," Chuang Tzu compares two different ways of securing a position, in this case the position of emperor, either fighting for it or waiting for it to be given to one. Comparing the practices of previous emperors, Chuang Tzu says,

> In former times, Shun took the throne yielded by Yao and became Emperor, Chieh took the throne yielded by K'uai and was ruined. T'ang and Wu fought for a throne and reigned, Po-kung fought for a throne and perished. Judging by these cases, the propriety of contending or deferring, the conduct of a Yao or a Chieh, will be noble at one time and base at another, and is not to be taken as a constant.[7]

If what is right is determined by successful practice and what is wrong is determined by unsuccessful practice, then the examples Chuang Tzu uses show that fighting for the throne and waiting for it to be given to one are both right sometimes, but sometimes both are wrong. But a standard that does not distinguish between right and wrong is not a standard at all; hence Chuang Tzu says it "is not to be taken as a constant."

For the Confucian, the problem lies in showing that the moral sense, which is supposed to provide knowledge of right and wrong, is any less relative than any of the other senses. Chuang Tzu presents a dialogue between Gaptooth, who may represent the Confucian position, and Wang Ni, who is probably expressing Chuang Tzu's own view:

> Gaptooth put a question to Wang Ni.
> "Would you know something of which all things agreed 'That's it'?"
> "How would I know that?"
> "Would you know what you did not know?"
> "How would I know that?"
> "Then does no thing know anything?"
> "How would I know that? However, let me try to say it—'How do I know that what I call knowing is not ignorance? How do I know that what I call ignorance is not knowing?' ... In my judgment the principles of Goodwill and Duty, the paths of 'That's it, that's not,' are inextricably confused; how could I know how to discriminate between them?"[8]

Here Chuang Tzu appears to be using the relativity of knowledge to support the skeptical position that it is not possible to know that what is claimed as knowledge really is knowledge. The Confucians, in particular Mencius, whom Chuang Tzu probably has in mind, claim that goodwill and duty can be known by moral intuition. Chuang Tzu casts doubt on this claim, suggesting that there is no way to know that the knowledge claimed is really knowledge. And therefore the claims "that's right" and "that's wrong" ("the paths of 'That's it, that's not' ") cannot be shown to be true.

Of course, it might be argued against Chuang Tzu that if all knowledge is purely relative, then so is this knowledge, namely, the knowledge that all knowledge is relative. But Chuang's suggestion is that because of the relativity of knowledge, you could never really know that that knowledge is relative. It is not possible to turn this argument against Chuang Tzu by claiming that he can never really know whether that knowledge, or any other knowledge, either is or is not relative, because the point of his argument from skepticism is precisely this: to maintain the impossibility of certain, indubitable knowledge.

Chuang Tzu's position is clear. If it is certitude of knowledge that is doubted, indubitable knowledge is impossible without committing the logical fallacy of "begging the question." And there seems no way, other than by knowing, of ascertaining that there is indubitable knowledge. Thus, Chuang Tzu's argument, on these grounds at least, is unanswerable.

Complementariness of Opposites

The second argument, from the complementariness of opposites, suggests that any concept logically implies its negation, and that without its negation, or opposite, a concept could not exist. The argument is intended to show that affirmation and negation are simply different ways of looking at the same thing. If A is A, then A is not *not-A*. Or the negation of A is the affirmation of *not-A*. In a similar way, right and wrong are the same thing looked at differently. If A is right, then A is not wrong. If there were no right, there would be no wrong (and vice versa). For if A is right, then A is not wrong, implying a wrong that A is not.

It is because of the wrong that *A* is not that *A* is, or can be, right. In other words, *what is* involves *what is not,* and opposites, from this point of view, turn out to be complementary. Chuang Tzu says, "Nevertheless, when there is life there is death, and when there is death there is life. When there is possibility, there is impossibility, and when there is impossibility there is possibility. Because of the right, there is the wrong, and because of the wrong there is the right."[9] He also says, "There is nothing that is not the 'that' and there is nothing that is not the 'this.' Therefore I say that the 'that' is produced by the 'this' and the 'this' is also caused by the 'that.' "[10]

Chuang Tzu appears to be thinking in terms of pairs of correlative terms. For example, if there were no concept of up, there could be none of down, and the same holds true for left and right, right and wrong, self and other, and so on. For such pairs of concepts, the existence of one presupposes the other and the removal of one is the removal of the other. It might be objected that it is by no means clear that all concepts can function only as correlatives. In fact, if one avoids adjectival concepts and concentrates on substantive concepts, it is by no means clear that a concept is possible only if it is opposed by another concept. By what concept need the concept *horse* be opposed in order to function as a concept?

According to Chuang Tzu's argument, however, even a concept such as *horse* involves, at least implicitly, the concept of *not-horse,* for if there were no concept of *not-horse,* the concept of *horse* could not be used discriminately. That is, it would be impossible to decide what to call and what not to call a horse. And not being able to properly use a concept in a discriminatory fashion would be sufficient evidence for claiming that a person did not have the concept at all. But a necessary condition of using a concept properly is being able to discriminate between what the concept refers to and what it does not. Thus, in terms of the present example, having the concept *horse* involves knowing what is not a horse, or of having the concept of *not-horse.* But because *not-horse* refers to everything except *horse,* and *horse* refers only to one thing, horses, Chuang Tzu suggests that it is better to use the negation of particular concepts to understand the universe. He says, in a rather cryptic statement, "Rather than use a horse to show that 'A horse is not a horse,' use what is *not* a horse."[11]

The same line of reasoning can be used with any substantive concept, for having a concept of anything presupposes an ability to discriminate between that to which the concept refers and that to which it does not, and this involves knowing what the concept is not. In this way, it is seen that a concept of something is always relative to what that something is not. Thus, Chuang Tzu says,

> What is It is also Other, what is Other is also It. There they say "That's it, that's not" from one point of view, here we say "That's it, that's not" from another point of view. Are there really It and Other? Or really no It and Other? Where neither It nor Other finds its opposite is called the axis of the *Way.*[12]

The question could be asked, Which is the essential feature of knowledge, the *not-horse* or the *horse*? According to Chuang Tzu, the answer is neither, because both are necessary. Coupled with the argument from skepticism, this argument implies neither that there is no real knowledge nor that real knowledge is impossible, but that we can never know (that is, be certain) either what this or that knowledge really consists in, or whether or not we really have knowledge.

Argument from Perspectives

The third argument, the argument from perspectives, presupposes the previous two arguments. It is obvious that the same thing appears different to different people if their perspectives are different. Or the same thing appears different to the same person if he changes his perspective. And if someone had different senses, they would perceive things differently. The point is that the same thing has many appearances, depending upon the perceiver. Which of the appearances is the correct or true appearance?

Chuang Tzu's point is that these questions cannot be answered. Each thing is just what it is and not something else, and what it is, is independent of how it appears to anything or anyone. It is contained in itself, in its own perspective, and the only way to see it as it really is, is to transcend our own perspective and view the other as a totality, from its own perspective. The implicit claim about how things exist is that everything in the world is an independent, self-sufficient totality with its own unique perspective and function. To view it from a different perspective is to distort it. But this means that the claims of knowledge and morality, which are always made from a human perspective, always distort reality because they are always made relative to a particular perspective. If everything is looked at only from its own point of view, however, right and wrong disappear completely, as do true and false. Thus, the judgment that something is right or wrong, or that something is true or false, because it is made from a particular human perspective, is only relative to that perspective. This is why Chuang Tzu recommends that we should obtain the unlimited point of view from which everything is seen from its own perspective. Only then can the ease and freedom that comes from each thing naturally following its natural way be realized.

According to Chuang Tzu, "Things do not know that they are the 'that' of other things; they only know what they themselves know."[13] Chuang Tzu illustrates the point that all knowledge is relative to a particular perspective with the butterfly story:

> Last night Chuang Chou [Chuang Tzu] dreamed he was a butterfly, spirits soaring he was a butterfly (is it that in showing what he was he suited his own fancy?), and did not know about Chou. When all of a sudden he awoke, he was Chou with all his wits about him. He does not know whether he is Chou who dreams he is a butterfly or a butterfly who dreams he is Chou.[14]

The wise person, knowing that each thing is a totality with its own perspective, realizes that what all things have in common is that they all naturally follow their own way, given them by the *Tao*. Thus, Chuang Tzu says, "Only the intelligent knows how to identify all things as one."[15] But to see that the unique function of each thing is due to the *Tao* that they all share requires giving up one's particular perspective and adopting a universal perspective.

According to Chuang Tzu, to abandon the limited perspective is to abandon the strife that it engenders, and to adopt an unlimited perspective is to enjoy the peace and tranquillity of the infinite:

> We say this is right or wrong, and is so or is not so. If the right is really right, then the fact that it is different from the wrong leaves no room for argument. Forget the passage of time (life and death) and forget the distinction of right and wrong. Relax in the realm of the infinite and thus abide in the realm of the infinite.[16]

The point of the argument from perspectives is that we can never really know what a thing is in itself. To make this point, the argument assumes a transcendent point of view, for by its own premises, ordinary experience, because it is always from a particular perspective, can never reveal things as they are in themselves. Only by assuming a transcendent point of view can it be known that there are things in themselves, existing within their own perspectives and not accessible to ordinary means of knowledge. To *assume* a point of view is not the same thing as to argue for a point of view. The argument for a transcendent point of view depends on showing that the ordinary cognitive point of view leads to an unacceptable skepticism. That is why Chuang Tzu develops the argument from skepticism.

Argument from Skepticism

Chuang Tzu's fourth argument, the argument from skepticism, advances the claim that the question, Is that really so? can never be answered. Suppose, for example, it is claimed that X is red. The skeptic asks, "But how can X be known to be really red?" The difficulty in trying to prove that the claim "X is red" is true is that the claim cannot be compared with the supposed fact, namely, the redness of X. Presumably, the only thing that would convince the skeptic, who doubts that the original claim, "X is red" is really true, is to show that the claim "X is red" corresponds to the fact that X is red. But the supposed fact that X is red is precisely what is in doubt. Therefore comparing the claim "X is red" to the supposed fact of X's redness is simply to compare one dubious claim to another dubious claim.

What is needed is an independent standard to judge the correspondence of the first claim to the second, a second standard to judge the appropriateness of the first standard, a third standard to judge the appropriateness of the second standard, and so forth, ad infinitum. But it appears that choosing such standards is impossible, for if A and B have different views, a standard acceptable to A would be unacceptable to B, and a standard acceptable to B would be unacceptable to A. And if the standard is acceptable to no one, it is of no use. Therefore it seems impossible to refute the skeptic's claim that it is impossible to know that X is really red.

On one occasion, Chuang Tzu presented the skeptical argument in the form of the following question: "How can it be known that what I call knowing is not really not knowing and what I call not knowing is not really knowing?"[17] On another occasion, he presented the argument in the form of a different question: "For knowledge depends on something to be correct, but what it depends on is uncertain and changeable. How do we know that what I call nature is not really man and what I call man is not really nature?"[18]

This skepticism is pushed even further by Chuang Tzu in the following statement:

> Suppose we make a statement. We don't know whether it belongs to one category or another. Whether one or the other, if we put them in one, then one is not different from the other. However, let me explain. There was a beginning. There was a time before that beginning. And there was a time before the time which was before that beginning. There was being. There was non-being. There was a time that was before that non-being, and there was a time before the time that was before that non-being. Suddenly there is being and non-being, but I don't know which of being and non-being is really being or really non-being. I have just said something, but I don't know if what I have said really says something or says nothing.[19]

Chuang Tzu's argument from skepticism is grounded in the insight that there is no indubitable criterion to which one can appeal to prove that what is claimed to be true is really true. In the butterfly example, Chuang Tzu suggests that there is a problem in ascertaining whether he was dreaming or being dreamed. The problem is that there is no indubitable criteria that can be used to distinguish between being awake and dreaming. If both the butterfly and Chuang Tzu exist only in a dream, what is the indubitable criteria that distinguishes between Chuang Tzu existing in the butterfly's dream from the butterfly existing in Chuang Tzu's dream? Hence Chuang Tzu suggests that he cannot be sure that he does not exist merely as a character in a butterfly's dream.

The obvious answer to this kind of skepticism is that the doubts expressed make sense only within a cognitive scheme in which certain things can be assumed to be true. Unless Chuang Tzu assumes that butterflies and people are different and that these differences can be known, he cannot call into question the criteria by which the identities of butterflies and people and the differences between them are known. When Chuang Tzu goes on to use the same cognitive scheme in which the criteria for identifying differences between things are assumed to reject these criteria, he is rejecting the very conditions in terms of which it makes sense to question such criteria. In this way, he rejects the grounds that make possible the first doubt and which are needed to make sense of his skepticism. For unless Chuang Tzu could accept "Once I, Chuang Tzu, dreamed I was a butterfly" as true, he could not go on to doubt whether he dreamed or was dreamed.

Though this answer may be sufficient to refute skepticism generally, it will not refute Chuang Tzu's position. To see this, recall that Chuang Tzu is arguing for an unlimited point of view. His arguments are negative, in the sense that they are aimed at refuting a limited point of view. Suppose for a moment that Chuang Tzu's only argument is the skeptical one, and that the above argument adequately refutes the skeptical argument.

Has Chuang Tzu been refuted by the above argument? Not at all. In fact, his position has been strengthened. The reason for this is that Chuang Tzu is arguing that the ordinary cognitive framework is inadequate, and that a new cognitive framework, a universal cognitive framework, must be adopted in order to escape the limitations of the limited cognitive framework ordinarily employed. It is for this reason that, although thoroughgoing skepticism is self-contradictory in terms of a conceptual framework that is limited in the relevant ways (for example, a conceptual framework that is essentially spatial-temporal), this very self-contradictoriness of skepticism within a limited cognitive perspective becomes an argument for rejecting the limited cognitive framework.

Does recognition of the limitations of ordinary cognitive frameworks and adoption of a transcendent perspective mean rejecting the ordinary and mundane world? The answer is no, for to interpret Lao Tzu and Chuang Tzu in this way is to ignore their concern with social rectification, the concern inspiring their philosophies. Kuo Hsiang, a later commentator on Chuang Tzu, puts the matter as follows:

> To cry as people cry is a manifestation of the mundane world. To identify life and death, forget joy and sorrow, and be able to sing in the presence of the corpse is the perfection of the transcendental world.

He then goes on to point out that the true sage, the person who is fully able to transcend the mundane world, finds happiness in the mundane world. He says,

> There has never been a person who has roamed over the transcendental world to the utmost and yet was not silently in harmony with the mundane world, nor has there been anyone who was silently in harmony with the mundane world and yet did not roam over the transcendental world. Therefore the sage always roams in the transcendental world in order to enlarge the mundane world. By having no deliberate mind of his own, he is in accord with things.[20]

In the sage, the transcendental and the mundane meet, for here the *Tao* of human beings is identical with the *Tao* of the universe. Chuang Tzu puts it this way:

> With the sage, his life is the working of Heaven, his death the transformation of things. In stillness, he and the yin share a single Virtue; in motion, he and the yang share a single flow. He is not the bearer of good fortune, nor the initiator of bad fortune. Roused by something outside himself, only then does he respond; pressed, only then does he move; finding he has no choice, only then does he rise up. He discards knowledge and purpose and follows along with the reasonableness of Heaven. Therefore he incurs no disaster from Heaven, no entanglement from things, no opposition from man, no blame from the spirits.[21]

REVIEW QUESTIONS

1. Contrast the philosophies of Taoism and Confucianism. How are they similar? How are they different?

2. What does Lao Tzu mean when he says, "Therefore when *Tao* is lost, only then does the doctrine of virtue arise. When virtue is lost, only then does the doctrine of humanity arise"? Is this a criticism of the Confucian way? If so, on what grounds?

3. What is the *Tao* to which Lao Tzu refers? How does it function?

4. Chuang Tzu's philosophy is concerned primarily with freedom. What is the relation between human conventions and freedom, according to his philosophy?

5. How does Chuang Tzu argue against the ordinary or conventional cognitive framework? Explain each of his four arguments. Are they valid?

FURTHER READING

On Lao Tzu, by David Hong Cheng (Belmont, CA: Wadsworth, 1999), is a small book written to introduce students to Lao Tzu's thinking.

The Butterfly as Companion: Meditations on the First Three Chapters of the Chuang Tzu, by Kuang-ming Wu (Albany: State University of New York Press, 1990), contains insightful reflections that will enrich the reader's life in many ways. Students often recommend this book to one another.

Tao Te Ching: The Classic Book of Integrity and the Way, translated by Victor H. Mair (New York: Bantam Books, 1990), is an extremely readable translation of the Ma-Wang-Tui manuscript, now widely accepted as the earliest and most authentic edition of the *Tao Te Ching.* The notes and commentary (pp. 107–61) are very useful and, among other things, compare Taoist yoga to classical Indian yoga.

Tao: A New Way of Thinking. A Translation of the Tao Te Ching, with an Introduction and commentaries, by Chang Chung-yuan (New York: Harper & Row, 1975), is of special interest to students of comparative thought. Chang's comments relate Taoist thought to a whole range of Western and Eastern thinkers, with a special focus on Heidegger's philosophy. Chang's *Creativity and Taoism* (New York: Harper & Row, 1970), is also a rich study of comparative thought, focusing on aesthetic experience through a study of art and poetry, East and West.

Tao Te Ching, Part Two, translated by D.C. Lau, (Hong Kong: Chinese University Press, 1982), is an excellent translation of the Ma-Wang-Tui manuscript of *Lao-tzu,* the oldest authentic version of the text available. It is accompanied by an excellent introduction and useful comparisons with the Wang Pi text—which is translated in Part One.

The Complete Works of Chuang Tzu, translated by Burton Watson (New York: Columbia University Press, 1968), remains the standard English translation of the *Chuang Tzu.* Watson captures Chuang Tzu's skillful combination of playful humor and profundity.

Chuang-tzu: The Seven Inner Chapters and Other Writings from the Book Chuang-tzu, by A.C. Graham (London: Allen & Unwin, 1981), is the most philosophically astute translation of the *Chuang-tzu.* It contains a very helpful introduction and useful notes.

Chuang Tzu: World Philosopher at Play, by Kuang-ming Wu (New York: Crossroad, and Chico, CA: Scholars' Press, 1982), explores the relevance of Chuang Tzu's thought and style for today's world.

Chuang-Tzu for Spiritual Transformation: An Analysis of the Inner Chapters, by Robert E. Allinson (Albany: State University of New York Press, 1989), argues clearly and convincingly that the style of Chuang-Tzu is consistent with his commitment to the fundamental importance of achieving spiritual transformation.

NOTES

1. *Tao Te Ching,* chap. 18, trans. by Wing-tsit Chan, in *A Sourcebook in Chinese Philosophy* (Princeton, NJ: Princeton University Press, 1969), p. 148. Hereafter references to this work will be cited by chapter in the text.
2. As quoted in Fung Yu-Lan, *History of Chinese Philosophy,* trans. by Derek Bodde (Princeton, NJ: Princeton University Press, 1952), vol. 1, p. 243.
3. In Wing-tsit Chan, *A Sourcebook in Chinese Philosophy,* p. 184.
4. Ibid., p. 186.
5. Ibid., pp. 183–84 (brackets are Chan's).
6. Ibid., p. 182.
7. Trans. by A.C. Graham, in *Disputers of the Tao: Philosophical Argument in Ancient China* (La Salle, IL: Open Court, 1989), p. 207.
8. John M. Koller and Patricia Koller, *A Sourcebook in Asian Philosophy* (New York: Macmillan, 1991), p. 458.
9. Wing-tsit Chan, *A Sourcebook in Chinese Philosophy,* p. 183.
10. Ibid., p. 182.
11. Koller and Koller, *A Sourcebook in Asian Philosophy,* p. 455.
12. Ibid., p. 454.
13. Wing-tsit Chan, *A Sourcebook in Chinese Philosophy,* p. 182.
14. Koller and Koller, *A Sourcebook in Asian Philosophy,* p. 460.
15. Chan, *A Sourcebook in Chinese Philosophy,* p. 184.
16. Ibid., p. 190.
17. Ibid., p. 187.
18. Ibid., p. 191.
19. Ibid., pp. 185–86.
20. Ibid., p. 330.
21. *The Complete Works of Chuang Tzu,* trans. by Burton Watson (New York: Columbia University Press, 1968), p. 168.

CHAPTER 22

Neo-Confucianism: The Grand Harmony

Neo-Confucianism is a renewal of Confucian thought in response to philosophical challenges from Buddhism, Neo-Taoism, the School of Names, and the Yin-Yang tradition. Neo-Confucian thinkers reinterpreted Confucianism to include the principles of the other major schools of philosophy, thereby creating a comprehensive new philosophy that was Confucian at its core.

THE BUDDHIST CHALLENGE

Buddhism was introduced into China in the first century CE, and by 700 CE, it had become extremely influential. Although they were deeply influenced by Buddhist thought, all of the Neo-Confucian philosophers criticized the weaknesses of Buddhism in their attempts to decrease its influence and to increase the importance of Confucianism. Chinese Buddhism represented a systematic explanation of the world and human life in which practical living was defined by reference to theoretical principles, such as the nature of causality, the nature of Buddhahood, and the nature of the mind.

China's own philosophical traditions had not managed to combine systematic theoretical completeness with detailed prescriptions for living. In Taoism, the base was sufficiently broad, but the philosophy remained too abstract to be practical. In Confucianism, there was a wealth of detailed rules for the guidance of life but an insufficient theoretical foundation for these prescriptions. By contrast, therefore, Buddhism immediately appeared attractive and won sufficient attention from Chinese scholars to ensure translation not only into the Chinese language, but also into Chinese philosophical concepts and practice. It turned out that many of the Buddhist schools were too theoretical in their emphasis to catch on in China, and the Buddhist philosophies that did take hold underwent modifications that increased their concern with morality and politics, giving them a more practical bent.

But despite the extent to which schools such as the Hua-yen, Chen-yen, T'ien-t'ai, Ch'an, and Ching-t'u were modified by the Chinese scholars responsible for their development, and genuinely transformed into Chinese schools of Buddhism, they continued to be regarded as foreign and extraneous philosophies. Among the Confucian scholars, there was an increasing concern to replace these foreign philosophies with something having roots in China's ancient past. Since Confucianism was still officially the state philosophy, and the civil service and university systems were based on this philosophy, it was natural that it should be regarded as the basis from which a philosophy could be derived that might prove superior to the Buddhist philosophies. In this way, Buddhism proved to be the critical catalyst in the Confucian studies that produced Neo-Confucianism.

NEO-CONFUCIAN BEGINNINGS

Neo-Confucianism began with an attempt to find a metaphysical explanation of the universe that was as comprehensive as the Buddhist explanation. But the new metaphysics was completely affirmative, built upon the supremacy of individual persons and particular things. It emphasized the moral features of the universe, providing a way for achieving moral goodness. With this metaphysical accomplishment, the ethical and social philosophies of Confucianism were recast, putting them upon this new basis. In effect, this new basis allowed for a synthesis of Taoist, Buddhist, and Confucian philosophies. Buddhism was very influential in China from around 800 CE to 1200 CE. From about the beginning of the thirteenth century, however, when Neo-Confucianism was solidly established, Buddhism declined, and the next seven hundred years of Chinese philosophical history are clearly Neo-Confucianist.

Han Yu

Han Yu (768–824), who planted the seeds of Neo-Confucianism, was expressing a prevalent criticism of his day when he said, "But now the followers of Lao-tzu and the Buddha who talk about rectification of the mind ignore this world and their native land and reduce the normal duties required by heaven to nothingness. Following the ideas of Lao-tzu, a son does not have to consider his father as a father, nor does a man have to regard the king as a king. He does not even have to discharge his duties as a subject."[1]

Han Yu went beyond mere criticism, however, and urged a return to Confucius. As he saw it, this meant a return to an all-pervasive love as the common basis for all human activity. This universal love proceeds from basic human nature, for it represents what is basic to all people. In addition to love, human nature is constituted by propriety, sincerity, righteousness, and wisdom.

Three grades of persons can be distinguished on the basis of how these five virtues constituting human nature are practiced, according to Han Yu. If one of these, *jen,* is the ruling virtue and if the other four are also practiced, the person is superior. If no one of these is perfected and they are practiced only sometimes, and in impure form, the person belongs to the medium grade. When *jen* is rejected and actions are not in accord with the other four, the person is inferior. This system of three grades, usually acknowledged to be an original contribution of Han Yu, emphasizes the priority he gave to the moral principles of Confucianism.

Han Yu's objections to Buddhism and Taoism were primarily due to the excessive interest in metaphysical speculation in Taoism and Buddhism, at the expense of practical things. Therefore he argued that the *Tao* (Way) of life consists in loving the people and observing proper human relationships.

Li Ao

This concern for practical things and the belief that Confucianism was fully the equal of Buddhism and Taoism is also clearly evident in the teachings of Li Ao, a pupil of Han Yu. Li Ao says, "Everybody has joined the schools of Lao-tzu, the Buddha, Chuang-tzu, and Lieh-tzu. They all believe that the Confucianist scholars were not learned enough to know about nature and the heavenly order, but that they themselves are. Before those who raise this hue and cry I do my best to demonstrate the opposite."[3]

In his attempt to demonstrate the adequacy of Confucianism, Li Ao argued that human nature is originally good, but failure to control and quiet the feelings, or emotions, leads to corruption. The Confucian virtues are required to regulate the feelings. But apparently he did not distinguish clearly between the Confucian virtues and the Buddhist (Ch'an) way of overcoming desires and cravings, for when he was asked how man can return to the original goodness of his nature, he replied almost as a Buddhist might: "As long as there is no deliberating and no thinking, one's emotions are not in action. When emotions are checked, one has the right way of thinking. Right thinking means no deliberating and thinking. In the I-Ching it is said: 'Where evil thoughts are cleared, truth will be kept.' "[4]

Although Han Yu and Li Ao did manage to focus attention on Confucian teachings, they did not succeed in their attempts to revive Confucianism as a powerful rival of Buddhism. They did, however, pave the way for the first attempts to provide a new theoretical basis for Confucianism by Ou-yang Hsiu and Chou Tun-i, who were born at a time when the ascendancy of Buddhist philosophies in China was viewed by government officials as a threat to the social organization of the country. These officials misunderstood Buddhism, mistaking Buddhist practice of mindfulness as a kind of negativity toward life in the world. This misunderstanding was reenforced by the Buddhist practice of retreating from active social life into monasteries, a practice that officials claimed would undermine the traditional forms of Chinese social organization.

Ou-yang Hsiu

Ou-yang Hsiu (1007–1072 CE), was among the first Confucian thinkers who tried to transform this public concern with the threat of Buddhism to Chinese traditions into a program that would simultaneously destroy Buddhism and re-establish Confucianism as the dominant way of thought. He suggested that Buddhism be opposed by displaying the indigenous philosophies of China, showing them to be superior to Buddhist philosophies.

The difficulty of achieving what Ou-yang Hsiu proposed was due largely to the fact that the various Buddhist philosophies could boast a complete philosophy of life that grounded practical considerations in metaphysical principles. The Chinese philosophies, in contrast, were not so well grounded in metaphysics and epistemology. Chinese philosophers had tended to be concerned with things at hand, focusing their attention on practical matters, and had not concerned themselves with logical and metaphysical theories. Consequently, they were not in a good position to justify their practical philosophies by appeal to broader metaphysical principles.

Although it turned out that Ou-yang Hsiu was not able to develop the requisite metaphysical basis for a systematic philosophy of human nature and the external world that would support the Confucian emphasis on particular things and individual persons, his efforts helped prepare the way for Chou Tun-i's successful attempt at system-building.

Chou Tun-i

It was Chou Tun-i (1017–73 CE) who was directly responsible for laying the foundations of Neo-Confucianism. By bringing together and reinterpreting concepts from a variety of philosophies, Chou Tun-i managed to construct a metaphysical system broad enough to explain all existence. The notions of *yin* and *yang,* as negative and positive concepts of reality respectively, were familiar to Chou Tun-i. The idea that these two principles were not absolutely fundamental was also familiar to him, for the Taoists had argued that *Tao* was prior to all things and was the source of being and non-being, or *yin* and *yang.* The difficulty with the Taoist notion, however, was that *Tao* itself was regarded as non-being, and therefore the whole philosophy tended to have a negative character. But if the source of the principles of *yin* and *yang* were positive instead of negative, it could be a basis for a philosophical explanation that would emphasize the ultimacy of the particular, while at the same time having a principle for explaining the particular. This is precisely what Chou Tun-i achieved by regarding the Great Ultimate *(T'ai-chi)* as the source of all things, productive of *yin* and *yang.* In turn, the interactions between *yin* and *yang* produce the five agencies of water, fire, wood, metal, and earth. By further interaction, all of the rest of reality is produced.

Concept of the Great Ultimate. Describing the production of *yin* and *yang* from the Great Ultimate, Chou Tun-i says, "The Great Ultimate through movement generates *yang*. When its activity reaches its limit, it becomes tranquil. Through tranquillity the Great Ultimate generates *yin*."[5] His explanation of how the *yin* and the *yang* are produced from the Great Ultimate leans heavily on the Taoist notion of "reversal as the movement of the *Tao*." According to the Taoists, reality is the manifestation of the reversing of *Tao*, as it goes from one extreme back to the other. Thus, he goes on to say, "When tranquillity reaches its limit, activity begins. So movement and tranquillity alternate and become the root of each other, giving rise to the distinction of *yin* and *yang*, and the two modes are thus established" (p. 463).

Having thus provided a basis for the principles of *yin* and *yang* in the Great Ultimate, Chou Tun-i explains that through the interaction of these two principles and their resulting mutual transformation, the powers or principles of particular things came to be produced. He says, "By the transformation of *yang* and its union with *yin*, the five agencies of Water, Fire, Wood, Metal, and Earth arise" (p. 463). These five agencies are taken to be the material principles of things. For example, as principle of direction, wood is east; as principle of the seasons, wood is spring; as principle of the body, it is liver; and as principle of color, it is blue. Because these five agencies are not conceived of as things, but as principles, they can be considered to be the common basis of all things.

Given the Great Ultimate, the principles of *yin* and *yang*, and the principles of the material agencies of the universe, it remains to explain how these can act on the nonexistent to bring it into existence. Chou Tun-i explains this as follows:

> When the reality of the non-ultimate [nonexistent] and the essence of yin, yang, and the Five Agents come into mysterious union, integration ensues. *Ch'ien* (heaven) constitutes the male element, and *K'un* (earth) constitutes the female element. The interaction of these two material forces engenders and transforms the myriad things. The myriad things produce and reproduce, resulting in unending transformation. (p. 463)

The model for production is the symbolic male and the symbolic female, for male and female are readily understood as principles which by their union bring into existence what was previously nonexistent. The union between the nonexistent and the principles of *yin* and *yang* and the five agencies is said to be mysterious, for it is not clear how what exists can be related to what does not exist. Yet if some relation were not possible, how could the nonexistent be brought into existence? The particular things that are brought into existence through this mysterious union possess their own modes for reproduction, and consequently there is the ceaseless productive activity of things.

In this part of his explanation of the Great Ultimate, Chou Tun-i has managed to give a metaphysical picture of the origin of things, tracing them to the Great Ultimate. To complete his explanation, he needs to show how human beings fit into this picture. This he does in the following words:

> It is man alone who receives (the material forces) in their highest excellence, and therefore he is most intelligent. His physical form appears, and his spirit develops consciousness. The five moral principles of his nature (humanity or *jen*, righ-

teousness, propriety, wisdom and faithfulness) are aroused by, and react to, the external world and engage in activity; good and evil are distinguished; and human affairs take place. (p. 463)

The point of this description of the place of humanity in the total order of the universe is that the principle of the sage, or perfect person, is one with the principle of the Great Ultimate, and therefore human beings, in their perfection, form a harmony with the universe. The beginnings of sagehood are received from the Great Ultimate, just as are the beginnings of everything else that exists. In human beings, these beginnings are the moral principles of humanity *(jen)*, righteousness, propriety, wisdom, and faithfulness. To become a sage and be in harmony with the universe, one must be true to these moral principles. This is what Chou Tun-i means when he says that *ch'eng* is the foundation of the sage, for *ch'eng* (faithfulness or sincerity) means being true to one's nature.

In this way, the moral principles advocated by Confucius are put on a metaphysical foundation by Chou tun-i. The reason a person must act in accord with the fundamental moral principles is that these constitute one's fundamental nature as produced by the Great Ultimate.

CH'ENG HAO AND CH'ENG I

Neo-Confucianism was given its enduring structure by Ch'eng Hao (1032–85) and Ch'eng I (1033–1107), who made principle *(li)* its basis. Building upon the work of Chou Tun-i, who had been their teacher for one year, the Ch'eng brothers replaced the concept of the Great Ultimate—which impressed them as being too abstract and excessively Taoistic—with the concept of *li* (principle).

The main philosophical reason for the substitution was to put the perfection of human nature on a secure basis. Chou Tun-i was concerned primarily with establishing a metaphysics of reality, and he found in the concept of the Great Ultimate the key to the overarching unity of things. The Great Ultimate was too abstract, however, to provide a foundation for a practical philosophy of morality, the chief concern of Ch'eng Hao and Ch'eng I.

The Ch'eng brothers could concentrate almost exclusively upon the philosophy of human action because Chou Tun-i had already provided an explanation for the metaphysical unity of reality. Concentrating on explaining how human nature could be perfected so that every person could become a sage, and so that all persons could live harmoniously together, the Ch'eng brothers realized the need to have a first principle that is operative in every thing, person, and action. This principle must be more than simply a source from which everything proceeds. It must also function as the law of being inherent in everything that exists, giving it existence and directing its function.

Principle and Material Force

Because the principle from which all things originate is the same as the principle inherent in particular things (the difference being only one of manifestation or embodiment), all things form a unity with respect to principle. When principle is realized and exhibited in all actions, the perfect harmony will be achieved. Ch'eng I says, "That which is inherent in things is principle," and,

> Principle in the world is one. Although there are many roads in the world, the destination is the same, and although there are a hundred deliberations, the result is one. Although things involve many manifestations and events go through infinite variation, when they are united by the one, there cannot be any contradiction. (p. 571)

Ch'eng Hao, discussing principle as the unifying factor in reality, says, "The reason why it is said that all things form one body is that all have this principle, simply because they all have come from it" (p. 533). He also says, "There is only one principle in the world" (p. 534).

These remarks by the Ch'eng brothers reveal that they regarded principle both as a source of things and as the directive force within things. That is, although principle is regarded as one, the source of all, it is also regarded as many, for it is inherent in all of the many things that have proceeded from the source. How can principle be both one and many? To answer this question, it is necessary to understand the concept of principle that they used.

According to the Ch'eng brothers, for anything to be produced, it is necessary that there be both material force *(ch'i)* and principle *(li)*. Material force is the dynamic "stuff" of which things are composed, a kind of primordial matter-energy. Principle is the organization of material force that shapes it into specific things, giving them their unique form and function. It is obvious that different things are different; apples are not trees and trees are not people. To what is the difference due? The Ch'engs' answer is that it is due to form and function. Apples do not function or behave the way trees or people do. They do not have the same colors, odors, sounds, flavors, and so forth. The reason they appear different in color, odor, sound, taste, and shape is because of their different principles. If this is the case, it is clear that the general concept of principle is that of the reason why something is just what it is rather than something else. Since there are differences between things, and since these differences can be explained, it follows that there are reasons for the differences, and reasons are possible because things are distinguished according to their principles. That is, in the last analysis, the reasons for distinguishing between any two things consist in identifying the principles of those things; the reasons reveal the principles.

The Ch'eng brothers extended this notion of principle to the totality of what exists. Everything that exists—heaven and earth and "the ten thousand things"—exists due to principle. That is, there is a reason for the existence of things. Furthermore, this principle of the universe is not really different from the principle in any particular thing, for the particular thing exists only as a manifestation of the supreme principle. Things are distinguished according to the embodiment of principle, not according to principle as such. What makes a particular thing what it is, is the principle embodied and manifested in a certain way in material force.

It would appear, therefore, that *principle* in the philosophy of the Ch'eng brothers referred to the reason, or law, that operates within things, which gives the universe its order. The importance, therefore, of making principle the basis of their philosophy is that it provided them with an ordered universe. Thus, the order in society that issues from the ordering and rectification of the individual was held to have a foundation in the very structure of the universe. This concept gave to Neo-Confucianism the metaphysical basis for its social philosophy that it had been lacking.

With a general understanding of the concept of principle, and the function it served in the philosophy of the Ch'eng brothers, it is possible to turn to their writings for a more detailed analysis of principle and its application to practical human affairs.

Jen as Principle

Once someone asked Ch'eng I if, in investigating things in order to gain understanding that would allow one to become a sage, a person should be concerned with internal things, such as feelings and thoughts, or with external things, such as natural happenings. He replied, "It does not matter. All that is before our eyes is nothing but things, and all things have their principles. For example, from that by which fire is hot or water is cold to the relations between ruler and minister, and father and son, are all principle" (p. 568).

This makes clear that the principle of a thing is regarded as the source of that thing's essential activity, for the essential activity of fire is to produce heat, and that which makes fire hot is principle. But it is also clear that it is not the multiplicity of detail that is to be investigated, but only the principles operating through the detailed manifestations of things. Thus, in answer to the question, "If one investigates only one thing, does he understand only one thing or does he understand the various principles?" the answer is, "We must seek to understand all. However, even Yen Tzu [a wise man referred to in the *Analects* of Confucius] could only understand ten points when he heard one. When one finally understands principle, even millions of things can be understood" (pp. 568–69).

Obviously, millions of things in their details could not be understood, so the meaning is that millions of things could be understood in terms of their basic principle. For example, when the correct relation between father and son is understood, the relations between fathers and sons in millions of particular cases are understood. When the love one mother has for her newborn child is understood, then the love of millions of mothers for their newborn children is understood. The reason is that one knows the principle involved. This is why Ch'eng I says, "All things under heaven can be understood in the light of their principle. As there are things, there must be specific principles" (p. 563).

On another occasion he said, "A thing is an event. If the principles underlying the event are investigated to the utmost, then all principles will be understood" (p. 552). It would appear, therefore, that the principles of specific things, or specific kinds of things—qua principle—are the same, although with respect to their embodiment and manifestation in material force they differ. In comparing pieces of china, one might notice that cups differ from saucers. It might be thought that this is due to their different principles. But both cup and saucer are the same insofar as they are constituted by the kind of stuff called bone. It must be admitted that the bone embodied in the cup and the saucer is not different in the two cases. Likewise, it could be said that the great principle participating in the ten thousand things is not different in each case, though the embodiment is different.

The questions that arise from this analysis are (1) What is the nature of the principle that is responsible for the substance and the function of the universe? (2) How is the principle of the universe related to human beings? and (3) Is mind different from this principle, or one with it? The answers to these questions are revealed in the practical philosophy advocated by the Ch'engs.

According to Ch'eng Hao, "The student must first of all understand the nature of *jen*. The man of *jen* forms one body with all things without any differentiation. Rightness, propriety, wisdom, and faithfulness are all (expressions) of *jen*" (p. 523). The reason the student must first understand *jen* is that *jen* is principle. In other words, the nature of principle in humans is *jen*. But since principle is the same in nature as it is in humans, the cultivation of *jen* is at the same time the establishing of a unity with all things. As Ch'eng Hao points out, "There is no difference between Nature and man" (p. 538). Thus, to know *jen* is to know principle, and to know principle is to know (in a way) all things and to be in harmony ("form one body") with all things.

Ch'eng I points out that knowing *jen* is not a matter of having information about it, but of having experienced this principle. He explained this point as follows:

> True knowledge and ordinary knowledge are different. I once saw a farmer who had been wounded by a tiger. When someone said that the tiger was hurting people, everyone was startled. But in his facial expression the farmer reacted differently from the rest. Even a young boy knows that tigers can hurt people, but his is not true knowledge. It is true knowledge only when it is like the farmer's. Therefore when men know evil and still do it, this also is not true knowledge. If it were, they would surely not do it. (p. 551)

So when Ch'eng Hao says that the student must first of all understand *jen,* he is really saying that he must first of all cultivate his own humanity, living according to the principle of *jen*. This, of course, is the most important, and most difficult, of all tasks, for it is the task of becoming a sage.

Ch'eng I notes that in the school of Confucius there were three thousand pupils, but only one—Yen Tzu—was praised as loving to learn. The reason Yen Tzu was singled out is that he alone concentrated wholeheartedly on learning the way of becoming a sage. Becoming a sage is the highest goal, for the sage represents the perfect person, and in a philosophy where the reality of the person is regarded as the highest reality, the perfection of a person represents perfection of the ultimate reality.

But is it possible for a person to learn to become a sage? Ch'eng I answers this question in the affirmative:

> From the essence of life accumulated in Heaven and Earth, man receives the Five Agents (Water, Fire, Wood, Metal, and Earth) in their highest excellence. His original nature is pure and tranquil. Before it is aroused, the five moral principles of

his nature called humanity, righteousness, propriety, wisdom, and faithfulness, are complete. As his physical form appears, it comes into contact with external things and is aroused from within. As it is aroused from within, the seven feelings, called pleasure, anger, sorrow, joy, love, hate, and desire, ensue. As feeling becomes strong and increasingly reckless, his nature becomes damaged. (p. 548)

Having thus postulated the original goodness and purity of man and having attributed the evil in man to a disturbance of this original goodness due to uncontrolled feelings, it is possible to suggest that one can learn to become a sage by learning to control the feelings and thereby return to the original principle in its purity. Accordingly, Ch'eng I said, "The way to learn is none other than rectifying one's mind and nourishing one's nature. When one abides by the mean and correctness and becomes sincere, he is a Sage" (p. 548).

These statements reveal that for the Ch'eng brothers, principle is the inner law of a thing's nature, which is received from the inner law of the universe. Human beings also receive the law of their being from the inner law of the universe, and therefore they are in union with the universe with respect to principle. Because mind refers to the original essence of humanity, it turns out that mind is identical with principle. To be human is to be moral, and because morality issues from *jen,* it follows that human nature is *jen.* Because this is the original principle of our being, to realize perfection, we must be true to this principle (by practicing *ch'eng,* or sincerity) and cultivate it. For this, the virtues of propriety, wisdom, and righteousness are also needed.

CHU HSI

Chu Hsi (1130–1200 CE) is considered to be the third most important Confucian thinker, outranked only by Confucius and Mencius. His importance is due primarily to his ability to reinterpret and synthesize the thought of earlier Neo-Confucian thinkers, providing a solid theoretical basis for a practical philosophy that emphasized a way of recovering one's original pure and good nature through moral self-cultivation. In constructing a complete systematic philosophy, Chu Hsi was also able to reconcile the presence of evil with the basic goodness of human nature. This he was able to do along the lines suggested by Mencius by incorporating the metaphysical thought of earlier Neo-Confucian philosophers, enabling him to achieve a systematic completeness that Confucius and Mencius lacked, while providing a more detailed practical philosophy than his Neo-Confucian predecessors had managed.

For both Confucians and Neo-Confucians, the central concern of philosophy was the cultivation of *jen,* the rectification of the basic human relationships, and the development of the constant virtues. The five basic relations between persons are those between (1) ruler and subject, (2) father and son, (3) husband and wife, (4) elder and younger children, and (5) friends. The constant virtues are righteousness, propriety, sincerity, and wisdom. The three activities of learning or applied philosophy, namely, cultivation, rectification, and development, are all part of the same program of moral self-cultivation, for when human relations are rectified and the virtues developed, *jen* will be cultivated.

And when *jen* is cultivated, the virtues will be developed and human relations will be rectified. And when these three are accomplished, evil will be removed, society will be peaceful, and goodness will reign supreme in the world.

The Goodness of Human Nature

The chief difficulty Confucianism encountered was that of explaining the origins of good and evil and the relations between them. The difficulty was felt already prior to Mencius, on one hand, who attempted to resolve the problem by claiming that human nature is essentially good but is corrupted by society and culture. Hsun Tzu, on the other hand, had tried to resolve the problem by arguing that human nature is essentially evil, but through education and culture, this evil can be rooted out and replaced with goodness. Neither of these theories proved entirely satisfactory, however, for if human nature is essentially good, as Mencius claimed, then how can society and culture, which proceed from human beings, be evil and corrupting? But if human nature is essentially evil, as Hsun Tzu claimed, how can what proceeds from human nature—in the form of culture and education—be good?

During the centuries following the Mencius–Hsun Tzu controversy, it was generally agreed by Confucians that human nature is basically good, but no satisfactory theoretical support for this position was worked out. As we have seen, Han Yu, a pioneering figure in the Neo-Confucian movement, suggested that human nature was of three kinds: good, bad, and good and bad mixed. But there was no satisfactory explanation of how human nature could be all three simultaneously. Consequently, the need for a philosophical theory of the nature of good and evil that would explain their origin continued to be keenly felt by the Neo-Confucians, for without it their emphasis on the removal of evil by cultivation of *jen* would lack a theoretical base.

Chang Tsai (1020–77), another important Neo-Confucian thinker, had made a significant step forward when he distinguished between essential human nature and physical nature. But because he failed to establish a satisfactory relationship between the two, his theory was deficient. The Ch'eng brothers also made an important contribution to the problem with their theory that principle and human nature were identical. But it was left for Chu Hsi to show how basic human nature was identical with the supreme principle of the universe, and that it was therefore of the nature of pure goodness, while secondary human nature, created by the association of principle with material stuff *(ch'i)*, was impure and the source of evil. According to Chu Hsi's theory, the source of goodness is human nature itself. But this human nature is embodied in a person, giving rise to feelings. It is the feelings, originating in bodily passions, that give rise to evil, for they obscure the original goodness of human nature, which in itself is of the nature of *jen*.

Distinguishing between principle as it is in itself and principle as it is embodied in concrete persons and things, Chu Hsi says, "What exists before physical form is the one principle harmonious and undifferentiated, and is invariably good. What exists after physical form, however, is confused and mixed, and good and evil are thereby differentiated" (p. 597). This statement is the key to

Chu Hsi's solution to the problem of how the presence of evil can be reconciled with the inherent goodness of human nature. The distinction he makes is between the goodness of principle and the evil-producing material stuff of which particular things are composed. In humans, as in all things, principle combines with material stuff, and therefore goodness is mixed with evil. But human nature itself is identical with principle, which is of the nature of *jen;* the material stuff constitutes a secondary nature. Because *jen* is basic, the removal of evil depends upon the cultivation and development of *jen* over the secondary nature.

Principal and Material Stuff

This distinction between basic and secondary natures on the basis of the difference between principle and material stuff requires a general theory of the nature and source of things as an explanatory context. According to Chu Hsi, all things are the result of a combination of material stuff *(ch'i)* and principle *(li)*. He says, "Man and things are all endowed with the principle of the universe as their nature, and receive the material force of the universe as their physical form" (p. 620). That there is principle is obvious from the fact that things are what they are rather than something else.

Differences in things, however, are due not only to different principles but also to differences in matter. Whatever actually exists is a combination of both principle and material stuff. How the principle is manifested in actual things is regulated by the material stuff even while principle determines the material stuff. When Chu Hsi was asked for evidence that there is principle in material force, he replied, "For example, there is order in the complicated interfusion of the *yin* and *yang* and of the five agents. Principle is there. If material force does not consolidate and integrate, principle would have nothing to attach itself to" (p. 635).

In explanation of what principle and material stuff are, and how they are related, Chu Hsi said,

> Throughout the universe there are both principle and material force. Principle refers to the Way, which exists before physical form [and is without it] and is the course from which all things are produced. Material force refers to material objects, which exist after physical form [and is with it]; it is the instrument by which things are produced. Therefore in the production of man and things, they must be endowed with principle before they have their nature, and they must be endowed with material force before they have physical form. (p. 636)

It would appear from this explanation that principle is prior to material stuff in two senses. First, principle is the essential reason for the being of something. Second, principle is the knowable characteristic of a thing. But despite this priority of principle, it remains the case that nothing exists except through the combination of principle and material stuff.

For Chu Hsi's explanation to be complete, he must relate principle and material stuff—as the two determinants of things—to their source. This he accomplishes by integrating Chou Tun-i's concept of the Great Ultimate into his own system, claiming the Great Ultimate is the ultimate source. But he interprets the Great Ultimate in terms of principle, saying that "The Great Ultimate is nothing other than principle" (p. 638). This enables him to regard principle as the primary nature of things and material stuff as their secondary nature. In other words, principle itself is the ultimate source of all things, giving a unity to the manifoldness of reality. This unity integrates all of reality into a harmonious whole. In the teachings of Chu Hsi, the Great Ultimate is regarded as "the principle of heaven and earth and the myriad things":

> With respect to the myriad things, there is the Great Ultimate in each and every one of them. Before heaven and earth existed, there was assuredly this principle. It is the principle that "through movement generates the yang." It is also this principle that "through tranquillity generates the yin." (p. 638)

Here Chu Hsi adapts the older cosmologies based on *yin-yang* and the five agencies theories to his philosophy of principle. This enables him to explain the origin and structure of the world, for it was generally accepted that through the activity of *yin* and *yang,* the five agencies came to be and by their power produced the "ten thousand things" that make up the world.

Applying this explanation to the problem of evil in human nature, Chu Hsi said, "The Great Ultimate is simply the principle of the highest good. Each and every person has in him the Great Ultimate and each and every thing has in it the Great Ultimate" (p. 640). Because principle is more fundamental than material stuff, the goodness of human nature is basic, and the human inclination to evil is secondary.

Because humans possess the Great Ultimate as their principle, it follows that *jen* is the basic nature of humanity. Chu Hsi shows this by pointing to the two essential relationships involved. First, after identifying mind with the basic nature of man, he says, "The principle of the mind is the Great Ultimate" (p. 628). Second, he says, "*Jen* is man's mind" (p. 594). These two statements together mean that the Great Ultimate is identical to *jen.* Chu Hsi supports this view in his treatise on *jen:*

> In the production of man and things, they receive the mind of Heaven and Earth as their mind. Therefore, with reference to the character of the mind, although it embraces and penetrates all and leaves nothing to be desired, nevertheless, one word will cover all of it, namely, *jen* (humanity). (pp. 593–94)

Realizing *Jen*

Granted that *jen* is basic—"the principle originally inherent in man's mind" (p. 633)—the question of greatest importance is how to realize *jen.* According to Chu Hsi, there are two equally important practices essential to the realization of *jen.* On one hand, because *jen* is already present as the basic nature, one must concentrate on preserving one's true nature. On the other hand, because a person's nature is learned and realized through its functioning in daily life, one must carefully investigate the actual functioning of principle in daily life. Thus Chu Hsi says,

The mind embraces all principles and all principles are complete in this single entity, the mind. If one is not able to preserve the mind, he will be unable to investigate principle to the utmost. If he is unable to investigate principle to the utmost, he will be unable to exert his mind to the utmost. (p. 606)

The twin doctrines of preservation (of goodness) and investigation (of principle) rest upon the distinction between substance and function. Substance refers to what something is, and function refers to how something operates. The distinction itself goes back as far as Lao Tzu, who distinguished between *Tao* (the substance) and *te* (the function of *Tao*), but in Chu Hsi's teaching, the distinction is applied to principle. Thus basic human nature, or principle—the character of mind—as substance is *jen*. But according to Chu Hsi, the function of the human mind is love. In other words, the function of humanity is love. Love, as the function of *jen,* comprises the other virtues and is the basis for proper human relations. Chu Hsi puts the matter as follows:

The moral qualities of the mind of Heaven and Earth are four: origination, flourish, advantages, and firmness. . . . Therefore in the mind of man there are also four moral qualities—namely jen, righteousness, propriety, and wisdom—and jen embraces them all. In their emanation and function, they constitute the feelings of love, respect, being right, and discrimination between being right and wrong—and the feeling of commiseration pervades them all. (p. 594)

The nature of something provides for its function, and its function expresses its nature. Therefore *jen* provides for the function of humanity, namely, acting in accord with the moral qualities, and functioning in accord with the moral qualities is the expression of *jen*. According to Chu Hsi,

If we can truly practice love and preserve it, then we have in it the spring of all virtues and the root of all good deeds. This is why in the teachings of the Confucian school, the student is always urged to exert anxious and unceasing effort in the pursuit of *jen*. (p. 534)

This, then, is the foundation Chu Hsi provides for the practical philosophy of Neo-Confucianism, which can be summed up in his own words as follows: "To be sincere, empty of self, courteous, and calm is the foundation of the practice of love. . . . To love others as we love ourselves is to perfect love."[6]

WANG YANG-MING

The distinction between principle and material force enabled Chu Hsi to recognize both the reality of the mind and the reality of things external to the mind. In philosophical terminology, he was a rationalist to the extent that he emphasized principle, but an empiricist to the extent that he emphasized the investigation of things. He was an idealist to the extent that he emphasized the Great Ultimate as both the basic nature of all things and the essence of mind, but a materialist to the extent that he also insisted that without material force to embody principle, there could be nothing.

After Chu Hsi, however, developments in the School of Principle, through the work of Lu Hsiang-shan and his pupils, led to the identification of principle with mind. Wang Yang-ming (1472–1523), the most brilliant representative of Neo-Confucian idealism, said "there are neither principles nor things outside the mind" (p. 673). This philosophy is quite sharply opposed to Chu Hsi's, for only when a distinction is made between what belongs to mind and what is outside of mind can the investigation of things be emphasized as the key to the cultivation of *jen*. The empirical investigation of things is one of the two pillars upon which Chu Hsi's philosophy rests. The other pillar—preservation of the original mind—was perfectly acceptable to Wang Yang-ming, but it was not emphasized by Chu Hsi's followers.

Among the reasons for the ascendancy of Wang Yang-ming's idealism during the Ming dynasty (1368–1644), two stand out. First, from 1313 on, Chu Hsi's interpretation of the Confucian classics enjoyed the status of being the official state philosophy in China. In addition to discouraging other philosophies, this meant that the civil service examinations were based on his interpretations. Without the need to establish itself against other strong systems of thought, there came to be increasing attempts to consolidate and refine translations and definitions, and there was too little attention given to reexamining and rethinking basic principles and arguments. Since Chu Hsi's interpretation of Confucianism had, as Wing-tsit Chan, the foremost Chinese scholar in America, pointed out, "degenerated into trifling with what Wang [Yang-ming] called 'fragmentary and isolated details and broken pieces' " (p. 654), it did not provide an adequate basis for assisting the people in forming a satisfactory philosophy of life. Consequently, there was a ready reception for a fresh and vigorous philosophy such as Wang Yang-ming proposed.

Second, following his emphasis on investigating things, but slighting his emphasis on preserving the original mind of man, Chu Hsi's followers got further and further away from the moral emphasis that was the distinguishing characteristic of Confucian thought. When Wang Yang-ming turned his attention almost exclusively to moral matters, it was greeted as a welcome return to the central concern of philosophy.

The Unity of Knowledge and Action

Wang Yang-ming's philosophy is characterized by its preoccupation with moral values. It rests upon two principles: (1) the all-inclusive character of the mind and (2) the unity of knowledge and action. These two principles give rise to the doctrine of the extension of the innate knowledge of the good *(chih liang-chih)*. These features of his philosophy are reflected in the following statement:

> The learning of the great man consists entirely in getting rid of the obscuration of selfish desires in order by his own efforts to make manifest his clear character, so as to restore the condition of forming one body with Heaven, Earth, and the myriad things, a condition that is originally so, that is all. It is not that outside of the original substance something can be added. (p. 660)

Here Wang does not appeal to the investigation of things as an essential part of learning *jen*. Nor does he distinguish knowledge from action, for he regards true knowledge as action that proceeds from the love that constitutes the basis of humanity. In his own words: "Knowledge is the beginning of action and action is the completion of knowledge. Learning to be a Sage involves only one effort. Knowledge and action should not be separated" (p. 674).

The basis for the unification of knowledge and action is Wang Yang-ming's emphasis on the human capacity to choose rather than on the capacity to know. Intellectual knowledge of the kind characteristic of the sciences can, of course, be separated from choice and morality. But practical knowledge of the value of things has no significance apart from human choice and action. When doing is regarded as more fundamental than knowing, then the practical kind of knowledge required for making choices becomes more important than theoretical knowledge. Furthermore, a person's choices are rooted in knowledge and lead to actions that validate knowledge. This is why Wang Yang-ming can claim that the true learning of the sage consists simply in getting rid of selfishness and in manifesting good character. Translated into the language of classical Western philosophy, Wang's point is that action is more basic than knowledge and all knowledge is for the sake of action because the will is a higher human faculty than reason.

Wang Yang-ming's philosophy is most clearly revealed in his interpretation of the *Great Learning (Ta Hsueh),* the classical Confucian text that served as an inspiration to many of the Neo-Confucian philosophers. The text of the *Great Learning* consists in a statement and explanation of "three major chords" and "eight minor wires." The three major chords are (1) manifesting the clear character, (2) loving the people, and (3) abiding in the highest good. Asked about "manifesting the clear character," Wang Yang-ming replied, "The great man regards Heaven and Earth and the myriad things as one body. He regards the world as one family and the country as one person. As to those who make a cleavage between objects and distinguish between the self and others, they are small men" (p. 659).

The thinking behind this claim is that all things really form integral parts of one whole, just as the children and the mother and the father really are one family. In the family, the bond of familial love that proceeds from the *jen* of the individual person creates the unity of one family. In the world, the bond of great love proceeding from the *jen* of the universe creates a unity. In the "great man," the *jen* of the universe is realized to be the *jen* of the individual, providing unity of all things.

When he was asked why the learning of the sage consists in loving the people, Wang Yang-ming replied,

> Manifesting the clear character consists in loving the people, and loving the people is the way to manifest the clear character. Therefore, only when I love my father, the fathers of others, and the fathers of all men can my humanity really form one body with my father, the fathers of others, and the fathers of all men. (p. 660)

"Clear character" refers to the original purity and goodness of fundamental human nature. According to Wang Yang-ming, this original goodness consists in love—a pervasive and universal love that both forms and proceeds from the basic principles of all things. When things are in accord with this love, they are perfected. When people are in accord with this love, they too are perfected. This can be seen in the fact that when the clear character of love is manifested, the constant virtues are perfected, and then human relations are rectified. That is why Wang Yang-ming goes on to say:

> Everything from ruler, minister, husband, wife, and friends to mountains, rivers, spiritual beings, birds, animals, and plants should be truly loved in order to realize my humanity that forms one body with them, and then my clear character will be completely manifested, and I will really form one body with Heaven, Earth and the myriad things. (p. 661)

When he was asked about the third major chord, why the learning of the sage consists in abiding in the highest good, Wang Yang-ming replied:

> The highest good is the ultimate principle of manifesting character and loving people. The nature endowed in us by Heaven is pure and perfect. The fact that it is intelligent, clear, and not beclouded is evidence of the emanation and revelation of the highest good. It is the original substance of the clear character which is called innate knowledge of the good. (p. 661)

Wang Yang-ming agreed with the earlier tradition that all things are present in *jen,* which is the basis of human nature, and that to realize perfection, people must therefore cultivate this basic nature. His departure from this tradition lies in his insistence that nothing external is required for the realization of this perfection because basic human nature is pure and perfect of itself. To know the good is simply to do the good, and knowledge of the good is already contained in human basic nature as *jen.* Therefore, all that is required is the extension of this innate knowledge of the good into all spheres of action. As Wang Yang-ming says:

> This is what is meant by "manifesting the clear character throughout the empire." This is what is meant by "regulation of the family," "ordering the state," and "bringing peace to the world." This is what is meant by "full development of one's nature." (p. 661)

TAI CHEN

Neo-Confucian philosophers through Wang Yang-ming had emphasized the importance of principle over matter and had elevated the "fundamental mind" over the feelings. In the seventeenth and eighteenth centuries, there was a reaction against this rationalism and idealism, and the empirical came to be emphasized more and more, both in the studies of human nature and in the studies of empirical things. The empirical study of things, characterized by careful, detailed investigations, came to be regarded as the path to truth. At the same time, the feelings of persons exhibited in day-to-day living, rather than innate human nature, came to be regarded as the real source of human actions. According to Tai Chen (1723–77), generally accepted as the greatest of the empiricist Neo-Confucian philosophers,

> A thing is an affair or event. When we talk about an event, we do not go beyond daily affairs such as drinking and eating. To neglect these and talk about principle is not what the ancient sages and worthies meant by principle. (p. 713)

This remark clearly indicates the empiricist's impatience with metaphysical speculation and idealistic introspection. Tai Chen was concerned with the principles that could be discovered empirically in things, feelings, and actions; abstract principles were useless. It is not the case that Tai Chen rejected the concepts and principles of earlier philosophers of the Sung period, but rather that he reinterpreted them in such a way that the concrete and particular were not overlooked. This, of course, gave a balance to Neo-Confucianism, bringing the metaphysics down to an empirically verifiable level. This was, by the same token, a paving of the way for the empirical sciences of physics and psychology that were to come later. In fact, much of Tai Chen's work is often regarded as scientific rather than philosophical because of his minute investigation of particular things.

The emphasis during this later period of Neo-Confucianism continued to be on human nature, however, which continued to be regarded as the source of morality. Consequently, the primary objects of investigation continued to be the actions of human beings, and the categories used in this investigation were primarily moral. This means that instead of classifying and investigating the relations between the components of external things, human actions and relations between persons were classified and investigated. When external things are investigated, it is important, for example, to know what neutrons, protons, and electrons are, and how they are related to one another. But when morality is being investigated, the virtues of humanity, righteousness, sincerity, propriety, and wisdom must be known, and the relations among these virtues in terms of the principal relations among persons must be investigated.

Throughout the earlier Confucian tradition, human beings as moral agents and society as a moral institution were regarded as the primary objects to be known. In the Neo-Confucian tradition, there was an attempt to provide metaphysical support for this view that held morality to be the subject of ultimate concern. To Tai Chen, it appeared that some of the Neo-Confucians had allowed the metaphysics of morality, rather than morality itself, to become the subject of primary importance. This he was concerned to rectify, for he regarded moral relations between persons and the moral virtues as primary concerns and the metaphysics of morality as secondary. As was the case for all Confucians, Tai Chen's foremost concern was the moral question of how one *becomes* good, not the metaphysical question of what goodness is.

Review Questions

1. How did Chinese Buddhism and Taoism influence the development of Neo-Confucianism?

2. How did Chou Tun-i's concept of the Great Ultimate *(Tai-chi)* provide a basis for Neo-Confucianism? In your answer, explain how this concept incorporated features of Taoist, *yin-yang*, and the theory of the five agencies thinking, and how it furthered the Confucian interest in morality.

3. What is the Ch'eng brothers' concept of principle? How does it differ from Chou Tun-i's concept of the Great Ultimate? What does it mean to say, "The man of *jen* forms one body with all things without any differentiation"?

4. What is Chu Hsi's solution to the problem of the relation between good and evil? Is his theory of the priority of principle *(li)* over material stuff *(ch'i)* sound? Does it support his distinction between basic and secondary human nature?

5. How does Wang Yang-ming explain "manifesting the clear character," "loving the people," and "abiding in the highest good"?

FURTHER READING

Confucian Moral Self Cultivation, 2d ed., by Philip J. Ivanhoe (Indianapolis: Hackett Publishing Company, 2000), has separate chapters on Chu Hsi, Wang Yang-ming, and Tai Chen.

The Ways of Confucianism: Investigations in Chinese Philosophy, edited by Bryan W. Van Norden (LaSalle, IL: Open Court, 1996), is a collection of outstanding essays, many of them recent, on Confucianism.

Learning to be a Sage, by Daniel K. Gardner (Berkeley, CA: University of California Press, 1990), is an excellent study of Chu Hsi's thought.

New Dimensions of Confucian and Neo-Confucian Philosophy, by Chung-ying Cheng (Albany: State University of New York Press, 1991), is a philosophically sophisticated interpretation of Confucian and Neo-Confucian philosophies in their historical context by one of today's leading Chinese philosophers.

Chu Hsi and Neo-Confucianism, by Wing-tsit Chan (Honolulu: University of Hawaii Press, 1986), explores Chu's thought in relation to other Neo-Confucian thinkers.

Ethics in the Confucian Tradition: The Thought of Mencius and Wang Yang-ming, by Philip J. Ivanhoe (Atlanta, GA: Scholars Press, 1990), shows the continuity of Confucian thought over the centuries through explorations of the affinities between these two great Confucian thinkers.

Neo-Confucian Orthodoxy and the Learning of Mind-and-Heart, by William Theodore de Bary (New York: Columbia University Press, 1981), is an excellent source for an in-depth study of Neo-Confucianism. The historical period emphasized is thirteenth and fourteenth century China, the formative period of Neo-Confucianism.

The Development of Neo-Confucian Thought, by Carsun Chang (New Haven, CT: College and University Press, 1963), has long been the standard survey of Neo-Confucian philosophy. Although partially superseded by more recent works, including de Bary's

Neo-Confucian Orthodoxy and the Learning of Mind-and-Heart, Chang's book remains a valuable source. It reveals the great influence of Buddhism on Confucian thought and shows the vitality and creative development of China's dominant philosophy over the past twenty-five hundred years.

Two Chinese Philosophers: The Metaphysics of the Brothers Ch'eng, by A.C. Graham (La Salle, IL: Open Court, 1992), although weak on Buddhist contributions to their thought, is the best available work on Ch'eng I and Ch'eng Hao. It contains many excerpts from their writings with careful analysis.

Instructions for Practical Living and Other Neo-Confucian Writings, by Wang Yang-ming, translated, with notes, by Wing-tsit Chan (New York: Columbia University Press, 1963), contains Wang's major writings. The introduction and notes are extremely useful.

The Liberal Tradition in China, by William Theodore de Bary (New York: Columbia University Press, 1983), focuses on the lasting significance of Neo-Confucian thought, emphasizing its contemporary relevance, thereby providing a historical perspective from which to evaluate Chinese thought and practice during the last five decades of the twentieth century.

NOTES

1. Carsun Chang, *The Development of Neo-Confucian Thought* (New Haven, CT: College and University Press, 1963), p. 36.
2. The point here is not that the Buddhist philosophies are life-negating and unconcerned with practical social matters, but that they were so regarded by the Chinese officials in question.
3. Chang, *The Development of Neo-Confucian Thought,* p. 109.
4. Ibid., p. 110.
5. As translated by Wing-tsit Chan, in *A Sourcebook in Chinese Philosophy* (Princeton, NJ: Princeton University Press, 1963), p. 463. Hereafter references to this work will be cited in the text, by page number.
6. As quoted by Clarence Burton Day, in *The Philosophers of China* (New York: Citadel Press, 1962), p. 209.

CHAPTER 23

Recent Chinese Philosophical Thought

During the past century and a half, Chinese philosophical thought has been concerned with establishing an appropriate basis for modernization. The Opium War (1840–42), in which the British decisively defeated China, marks a watershed in the history of Chinese thought. Invasion and conquest by Western countries during the early nineteenth century forced Chinese philosophers to reevaluate the very basis of their civilization and culture. What is wrong with our traditions, the philosophers asked, that they allow these foreign powers to conquer and rule China with such ease? The answer was not at all clear. Some thought it was because the ancient traditions had become corrupt and needed to be restored. Others argued that the attitude of looking to the past for solutions to contemporary problems was itself the root of the problem. Some of these thinkers urged turning to the West, borrowing the modes of thought and practice that had enabled the West to achieve world ascendancy. For these thinkers, the crucial question was whether the science and technology of the West could be borrowed and grafted to traditional Chinese culture, retaining the substance of Chinese culture but enabling it to function in the modern world on par with the West; or whether a much broader program of westernization would be required to make China a modern nation.

The debate over whether China's modernization should be based on its own traditions or whether it should be based on Western traditions stimulated a critical reassessment of traditional thought and opened the door to Western studies. This chapter examines the thought of representative thinkers who carried on this debate and influenced the shape and direction of China's twentieth-century development.

K'ANG YU-WEI

K'ang Yu-wei (1858–1927) is probably best known as leader of the Hundred Days' Reform of 1898. In 1895, after Japan defeated China in the first Sino-Japanese War, K'ang organized young intellectuals from eighteen provinces to protest the peace treaty with Japan. Urging the emperor to engage in reform rather than agree to Japanese demands, K'ang met with initial success, persuading the emperor to issue a series of edicts calling for far-reaching reforms in 1898. Opposition to the reforms by the empress dowager led to their abandonment after some three months, however, and K'ang had to flee the country. When he returned in 1912, he found himself playing the role of a political conservative, opposing the democratic policies of Sun Yat-sen. In 1918, K'ang advocated adopting Confucianism as the state religion, and three years later took part in an unsuccessful attempt to restore the deposed Hsuan-t'ung emperor. Although his whole life was spent trying to put Confucian principles into action, he began as a revolutionary thinker, but eventually ended up trying to restore the old ways.

The basis for K'ang's reform efforts was provided by a philosophy of historical progress and a vision of humanity as bound together by a universal love, a philosophy shaped by his education in both traditional Chinese and Western thought. His early education focused on Confucianism, Buddhism, and Taoism. At about the age of twenty-two, however, he began reading Western authors, becoming interested in the ideas of progress, reform, and ideal societies, ideas that fueled his ambition to reform Chinese society and that led him to search for parallels in traditional Chinese thought. When the parallels could not be found, he invented them, as when he reinterpreted Tung Chung-shu's cyclical theory of the Three Ages as a progressive theory of social evolution, or when he presented Confucius as an evolutionary thinker interested only in transforming the past.

K'ang's theory of historical progress is presented in his commentary on Confucius, in which he claims not only that Confucius actually wrote the Spring and Autumn Annals, but that he did so in order to advance his own progressive or evolutionary view of history. Chinese scholars have traditionally regarded the Annals as the work of earlier historians. K'ang even goes so far as to suggest that Confucius made up the historical reforms attributed to the legendary sages Yao and Shun of the third millennium so that he would have precedents for his own reforms. Because Confucius lived in the First Age, the Age of Disorder, it was necessary for him to invent the precedents of the legendary reforms of the ancient sages to persuade the people to change. Only then could they enter on the way to the Second Age, the Age of Rising Peace, and eventually reach the Third Age, the Age of Great Peace. K'ang says,

> Confucius was born in the Age of Disorder. Now that communications have extended throughout the great earth and important changes have taken place in Europe and America, the world has entered upon the Age of Rising Peace. Later, when all groups through the great earth, far and near, big and small, are like one, when nations will cease to exist, when racial distinctions are no longer made, and when customs are unified, all will be one and the Age of Great Peace will have come. Confucius knew all this in advance.[1]

K'ang's view of Confucius as a reformer provided him with a model for his own ambition to reform Chinese society. His progressive view of history, attributed, as we have seen, to Confucius, inspired confidence in the eventual success of reform efforts. In addition, K'ang needed a philosophical view of human nature and society as a basis for reform. This he also found in Confucianism, particularly in the Confucian view expressed by Mencius, that true humanity cannot bear the sufferings of others and therefore acts to alleviate their suffering. Furthermore, the human sharing that constitutes the essence of love begins between parents and children, but because it is a universal feature of human nature, with careful nurture it can be extended to all people. Indeed, in the Age of Great Unity, this love will be extended to all creatures as a benevolent kindness.

Building on the principle that "the mind that cannot bear to see the suffering of others is humanity *(jen),*" K'ang goes on to say that "the word *jen* consists of one part meaning man and another part meaning many. It means that the way of men is to live together. It connotes attraction. It is the power of love. It is really electrical energy."[2] Seeking support for his vision of progressive humanization through reform and nurture, K'ang invokes the authority of Confucius, saying,

> Confucius instituted the scheme of Three Ages. In the Age of Disorder, humanity cannot be extended far and therefore people are merely affectionate to their parents. In the Age of Rising Peace, humanity is extended to one's kind and therefore people are humane to all people. In the Age of Great Peace, all creatures form a unity and therefore people feel love for all creatures as well.[3]

The Age of Great Peace is the inspiration for K'ang's vision of a utopian world, a world he calls the Age of Great Unity. Here divisions between classes of people, between nations, between races, and between the sexes will be overcome so that all human beings may experience the unity of a single family. Drawing upon Buddhist, Taoist, and Western, as well as Confucian, thought, K'ang articulated the fullest utopian vision ever produced by a Chinese author. It was regarded as so radical that it was not published until 1936, eight years after K'ang's death. Even Mao Tse-tung found this vision of democratic communism attractive, although he criticized K'ang for failing to see the kind of revolutionary struggle needed to actually achieve such a society.[4]

CHANG TUNG-SUN

In the last decade of the nineteenth century and the first three decades of the twentieth, Western philosophy became very popular in China. Famous philosophers such as John Dewey and Bertrand Russell were invited to lecture. Others, such as Bergson and Whitehead, became the focus of special journals and clubs. Most of the classical and modern philosophers' works were translated into Chinese, becoming the subjects of intensive study. In the 1920s and 1930s, it appeared that the philosophy departments in Chinese universities were likely to become branch offices of the large philosophy departments in Europe and America.

Although this never happened—primarily because of the simultaneous revival of traditional thought in various reflective and self-critical forms on the one hand, and the influence of Marxist thought on the other—this surge of interest in the West has had a lasting impact on the development of modern China.

Chang Tung-sun (1886–1962), a largely self-educated philosopher, was one of the most influential interpreters of Western thought. Wing-tsit Chan says of him, "the one who has assimilated the most of Western thought, established the most comprehensive and well-coordinated system, and has exerted the greatest influence among the Western-oriented Chinese philosophers, however, is indisputably Chang Tung-sun."[5]

Chang's influence was due partially to his wide reading and deep understanding of Western philosophers. He translated many Western texts into Chinese, including works of Plato, Kant, and Bergson. His theory of knowledge, though based largely on Kant, reflects also the influence of Russell, Dewey, and C.I. Lewis. More important, his philosophy goes beyond the dualisms of modern Western thought, insisting on the unity of knowledge and action and the unity of substance and function. This enabled him to overcome the Kantian problems arising from the opposition between knowing and willing and between the unknowable structure of things in themselves and the imposed structure of cognitive process. His many books work out the details of his unique synthesis of modern and traditional insights into the nature of the human mind and social processes, which he combined with his understanding of modern logic and epistemology.

Although Chang's early interest was primarily in metaphysics and the theory of knowledge, as he matured he became more interested in society and culture. The combination of these interests led him to develop a theory of knowledge that stressed the role of social interests and feelings in the knowing process. This, in turn, brought him closer to Marxist philosophy—to which he had been strongly opposed in the mid-1930s. Indeed, his emphasis on concepts as products of social processes led him to see the necessity of a thoroughgoing social revolution in China. This, in turn, led him to move further to the left, as he joined first the Progressive Party, then the State Socialist Party, and, after the war, the Democratic League. In 1949, he became a member of the Central Committee of the People's Government.

According to Chang, people claim the truth of an idea when it meets their fundamental social needs. He suggests that people accepted the truth of God's existence for centuries because doing so gave them a sense of social unity, overcoming the forces of fragmentation inherent in their concrete social relations. He says in his 1946 book *Knowledge and Culture,* "For when society needs a centripetal force stronger than the centrifugal force, some theory or idea must arise to hold the people together so that they feel in their own minds that it is the truth."[6]

When people feel a need for change or revolution greater than their need for unity or cohesiveness, however, they will emphasize the truth of freedom or individuality or the class nature of society, ideas that inherently reflect social conflict. Thus, according to Chang, the most profound truths accepted by a people do not reflect the physical or metaphysical nature of reality, but only their own most strongly felt social needs. As he says,

What we have been talking about does not concern society as such but to show how social conditions are reflected in ideas so readers may realize that while ideas seem on the surface to be independent and represent laws of logic or the structure of the universe that we talk about, actually they are secretly controlled by social needs.[7]

HSIUNG SHIH-LI

Hsiung Shih-li (1885–1968) reflects the Chinese effort to find a basis for modernization in traditional thought. His philosophy may be broadly characterized as Neo-Confucian—a creative interpretation of the idealist wing of Neo-Confucian thought, very much in the spirit of Wang Yang-ming. But it also draws heavily upon the *Book of Changes* and the Buddhist Yogacara school. Modern scholars tend to regard him as the most original Neo-Confucian philosopher of his time, and his work has had considerable influence on contemporary studies in traditional thought.

Hsiung, like most young intellectuals in China at the turn of the century, began his studies with a strong interest in Western science and politics, seeking a way to modernize China as quickly as possible. For a number of reasons, including his conviction that the new China must be based on traditional culture if it was to endure, he soon turned his attention to more traditional studies. Initially he studied the Buddhist philosophy of Yogacara, tracing it back to its Indian roots. Eventually he found the dualisms inherent in the Indian Buddhist schools uncongenial to his sense of the unity of humanity and nature. He then turned to the study of the *Book of Changes (I-Ching)*, which emphasized not only the deep unity of existence, but also the process nature of reality.

Subsequently, when he turned his attention to the philosophy of humanity *(jen)* in Wang Yang-ming, he found that Wang's concept of "Original Mind" and the Buddhist concept of the "Buddha-nature of all things" combined to provide a solid metaphysical basis for the universal human nature stressed by Wang. The emphasis on eternal and constant transformation stressed in the *Book of Changes* enabled him to see human nature in terms of process rather than substance, providing a basis for a dialectic of change leading to greater and greater perfection and harmony. In this way, Hsiung was able to develop a philosophical basis for a modern and progressive China based on traditional thought, which he was then able to present as an alternative to the Marxist-Leninist thought stressed by Mao Tse-tung.

It was as a professor of philosophy at Peking University that Hsiung first worked out the philosophical ideas circulated privately in 1932, and published in 1944, as *The New Doctrine of Consciousness-Only.* In this work, he developed three central and interrelated ideas. First, the very nature of existence, which Hsiung calls "original substance," is that of constant change; unceasing production and reproduction characterizes reality at its very core. Second, the dynamic of change is provided by what he calls the "opening" and "closing" of the perpetually changing primordial reality. "Opening" is the tendency of reality to maintain and preserve itself. This tendency is observable in people's efforts to be their own masters, free of external domination. "Closing" is the tendency toward integration and manifestation found in specific things. Third, the primordial reality and its manifestations, substance and function, are not actually separate. Ultimately, they are simply different aspects of the same process, with "opening" and "closing" seen as simply different phases of the same process.

Concerning the first idea, that change is the very nature of existence, Hsiung says, "Thus if we say that original substance is that which can transform, or call it perpetual transformation, we must realize that perpetual transformation is formless and is subtle in its movement. This movement is continuous without cease."[8] He is concerned here to make clear that ultimate reality or original substance is not a particular thing, but the inner dynamic inherent in all things that enables them to be continuously changing. He emphasizes this again when he says, "We must realize that original substance has neither physical form nor character, is not physically obstructed by anything, is absolute, whole, pure, strong, and vigorous."[9]

In explaining the concept of "closing," the tendency of change to direct itself toward the production of something new, to consolidate beginnings into an integrated act of being, Hsiung continues,

> However, in the functioning of the original substance to become many manifestations, it is inevitable that there is what we called closing. This closing possesses a tendency to become physical forms and concrete stuff. In other words, through the processes of closing individual concrete things obtain their physical form. As perpetual transformation manifests itself as a tendency to close, it almost has to be completely materialized as if it were not going to preserve its own nature.[10]

Closing, however, is simply one aspect of the larger process of transformation. When this whole process is analytically broken down, the closing force can be seen more clearly. But this analysis also reveals an opposing kind of force, which works to open reality to its own primordial nature. Thus, Hsiung goes on to say,

> However, as the tendency to close arises, there is another tendency arising simultaneously. It rises with perpetual transformation as the basis. It is firm, self-sufficient, and would not change itself to a process of closing. That is to say, this tendency operates in the midst of closing but is its own master, thus showing its absolute firmness, and causes the process of closing to follow its own operations. This tendency— strong, vigorous and not materialized—is called opening.[11]

Opening and closing, like *yin* and *yang* in traditional thought, represent the dynamic function of reality, the active polarities of ceaseless transformation. These tendencies account for the simultaneous coming into existence and passing out of existence that characterize the life of everything that exists. When life is harmonized with the transforming activity of opening and closing, it is whole and strong; otherwise, it is fragmented and weak. Thus, to find the way of human and social progress, it is necessary to understand the processes of opening and closing that control the functioning of all existence.

After the war, with the establishment of the People's Republic, Hsiung retired to Shanghai, where he continued to think and write for almost two decades. Here he produced his most clearly Neo-Confucian work, published in 1956 as *An Inquiry into Confucianism,* and also the *Development of the Philosophy of Change,* published in 1961, a work he regarded as superseding *The New Doctrine of Consciousness-Only.*

In his *Inquiry into Confucianism,* Hsiung stresses the unity of substance and function. Explaining that substance means what is there originally, the ultimate reality, and that function means the universal operation of this ultimate reality, Hsiung goes on to explain how they are identical, yet different. He offers the analogy of the water and waves making up the ocean, pointing out that the water is one, but the waves are many. The waves, comparable to the function of the water, are distinguishable from one another and from the deeper stillness of the ocean. Yet all are just water, the original substance. Applying the analogy, he says,

> Therefore we say that the universal operation of the original substance is its great functioning. By functioning is meant putting substance into functioning, and by substance is meant the true character of function. Therefore substance and function are basically one. However, although they are one, yet in the final analysis they cannot but be different, for in universal operation there are physical forms which are fathomable, whereas the original substance of the universal operation has no physical form, is most hidden and subtle, and is difficult to know.[12]

In Part II of this work, Hsiung constructs a dialogue to clarify his position on the unity of substance and function. The questioner, agreeing that the central teaching of the *Book of Changes* is that substance is at the same time function, and function is at the same time substance, goes on to ask, Does this mean that the "ten thousand things" (all the concrete existences) are simply the functioning of original substance, or does it mean they are the products of this functioning? Hsiung answers that "The ten thousand things and the great functioning cannot be separated." He goes on to say that if production means something new and different coming into existence, then the ten thousand things cannot be thought of as products, for they are not separate from the great functioning of the original substance. Insisting that things and function are not ultimately different, he continues, "Put differently, the concrete self-nature of the ten thousand things consists in the great functioning which operates unceasingly and in a very lively and dynamic manner. Can they and the great functioning be said to be two?"[13]

Now the questioner objects, claiming that by this doctrine Hsiung has ruled out the distinctness of concrete things; ultimately everything is the same, the great functioning of the original substance. The questioner says, "If the ten thousand things and the great functioning are one, then the ten thousand things will lose their own selves. Why is this the case? The reason is that if the ten thousand things are merely traces of transformations, how can they possess evidently independent selves?"[14]

Hsiung replies strongly, insisting that the continuously changing processes we call the ten thousand things are not outside of or separate from the great function of the original substance, but are constituitive of the universal functioning of substance. That is, the great functioning is not something in addition

to the functioning of concrete things. Coming back
waves and water, Hsiung says,

> The many waves are also traces and forms. Do you think
> the waves? Or take, for example, a torrent bursting viole
> thousands of white drops lashing up and down. These whi
> and forms. Do you think that they are outside the torrent? Pl
> ten thousand things manifest themselves and seem to be in
> really their self-nature consists in the great functioning operat

Applying this theory of change, which insists on the identi
and function, to concrete human and social affairs, Hsiung adv
munally organized society. He argues that the implication of th
emphasis on developing "sageliness within and kingliness without
come the self-centeredness that sets individuals and groups at odd
another, and to establish the practice of treating all equally, using c
developed humanity as a guide. The Confucian principle, "Treat all fa
one's own father and treat all sons as one's own son," if put into practice
eliminate ruling and servile classes, replacing them with a humanitarian-
communalism.

Because of Hsiung's insistence on principle *(li)*, however, the diale
underlying this communalism is different from the Marxist materialistic dial
tic. Hsiung's social philosophy, like that of Confucius and Wang Yang-ming,
solidly rooted in humanity *(jen)*. The ultimate key to social progress and human
development is not economic transformation, but moral development. Only with
the development of one's inner humanity and its outer expression can effective
economic and political transformation take place, according to Hsiung.

FUNG YU-LAN

Fung Yu-lan (1895–1990) is well known in the West for his classic two-volume
History of Chinese Philosophy and *The Spirit of Chinese Philosophy*. He was an
international figure who graduated from Peking and Columbia Universities,
and taught at the Universities of Hawaii and Pennsylvania as well as in China.
After the establishment of the People's Republic, Fung, a professor at Peking
University, participated enthusiastically in Maoist efforts at political and ideological reform, engaging in self-criticism to root out his own bourgeois ideas
and to set a good example for other Chinese intellectuals. Eventually he became
an ardent supporter of Mao Tse-tung thought and China's leading critic of Confucius during the anti-Confucian campaign of the early 1970s. At this time, he
was an intellectual consultant to Mao's wife, Chiang Ch'ing, and her friends,
the group that later came to be called the "gang of four." Shortly after Mao's
death in 1976, Chiang and her group fell from power and were publicly disgraced, a disgrace in which Fung shared, bringing to a humiliating close a brilliant philosophical career.

Fung's philosophical development can be traced through a series of stages,
marking his journey from traditional thought to radical Maoist thought. During

stage, which ended with his return to China after getting his Ph.D. from
ɔia in 1923, Fung was sympathetic to the traditional Confucian philoso-
.d engaged in serious studies of pragmatism in an effort to find a modern
ɔphical formulation of the insights and wisdom of the Confucian tradition.
The fruition of this first stage is found in his early writings, which mark
ɩeginning of the second stage. Here he attempted to mediate the contro-
y between those who wanted to reject the tradition in favor of modern sci-
ɜ and those who argued that a traditional metaphysical basis was required
the adoption of Western science and technology. Fung's approach was to
ɔly the pragmatic philosophy he had studied at Columbia to this issue, argu-
ɡ that both scientific truth and human morality are derived from, and tested
y, action. His book *Philosophy of Life* is the expression of this second stage
f his development, where he was developing a comparative East-West per-
ɩpective on philosophy.

In his third stage, Fung turned to a global study of Chinese philosophy, producing the widely acclaimed two-volume *History of Chinese Philosophy*. While
this work is a mainly traditionalist interpretation of Chinese philosophy, it is
modern insofar as it attempts to locate the social influences on the development of metaphysical ideas. Although Fung was later to reject this work because
it did not adequately reflect the influence of material conditions on traditional
thought, it is a work of solid scholarship that continues to be influential.

The fourth stage of Fung's development is represented by a highly original
philosophical system set out in a series of six books, of which *The New Rational
Philosophy (Hsin li-hsueh)* is central. This system is the most original and most discussed philosophical work of this century, according to Professor Wing-tsit Chan.[16]

Taking the philosophy of the Ch'eng brothers and Chu Hsi as his basis,
Fung reconstructed Neo-Confucian philosophy in a fundamental and sweep-
ing way. Distinguishing sharply between philosophy and science, he construed
philosophical concepts as purely logical or formal, having no specific content or
material existence. Science, in contrast, deals with actual existence, studying the
structures embodied in matter. Because there are things, there are both principles or formal structures and matter or specific contents. Philosophy is concerned with principles or the logical nature of things, and science is concerned
with matter or the actual material existence of things. In this way, philosophy
provides the basis for science, but science is required to provide knowledge of
the actual world.

To explain the movement by which principle and material force interact,
Fung brought in the concept of *Tao*. As the dynamic way of all things, *Tao* is the
very process by which principle is embodied in actual things through its interaction with material force. Fung used this concept to explain the universe as
process, as incessant change and continuous renewal. Inspired by the *Book of
Changes* and modern Western process philosophy, emphasizing change as the
essential feature of reality, Fung saw becoming, rather than being, as the fundamental nature of reality.

But Fung did not ignore being. Recognizing that the unceasing movement
of the *Tao* is responsible for the continuous production and reproduction of
things, he employed the concept of the Great Whole to refer to the totality of
things. But this totality is neither static nor a mere plurality. It is a dynamic inter-

penetration of things wherein all things are identical. Here Fung incorporated the Buddhist insight that because of the mutual interdependency of all things, the whole universe is present in each particular thing, and no particular thing exists except in relation to everything else. To explain the relation between *Tao* and the Great Whole, Fung considered the question, "Why have Tao in addition to the Great Whole or the universe? Our answer is that when we talk about the Great Whole or the universe, we speak from the aspect of tranquillity of all things, whereas when we talk about Tao, we speak from the aspect of activity of all things."[17]

The interpenetration of principle and material force and the ultimate identity of *Tao* and the Great Whole provide a basis for the highest ideal of life, the realization of "sageliness within and kingliness without," that Fung championed in *The Spirit of Chinese Philosophy*. Here he stressed that precisely because the absolute (Great Whole) is present in the concrete things and actual processes of everyday living, the aim of life must be to achieve perfection within everyday practice. Perfection cannot be achieved through detachment from or abandonment of the actual world of experience. Rather, this world and this self must be transformed through regular practice of the highest ideal within the ordinary affairs of life.

With the establishment of the People's Republic in 1948, Fung entered into a fifth stage of his philosophical development. Turning to serious study of Marxism-Leninism and the thought of Mao Tse-tung, he searched for a way to apply philosophy to the task of transforming Chinese society. His goal now was to go beyond the idealism and abstract ideas of his earlier work in order to improve the lives of the people. In making this transition, Fung distinguished between the abstract and the concrete meaning of philosophical ideas, emphasizing the importance of the concrete for improving the lives of the people, but insisting also that without considering the abstract meaning, one could not see the whole picture.

In a major Chinese conference on philosophy in 1957, Fung said,

> In the past I have paid attention almost entirely to the abstract meaning of some of these [philosophical] premises. This, of course, is wrong. Only in the last several years have we paid attention to their concrete meaning. . . . But their abstract meaning should also be taken into consideration. To neglect it would be to miss the total picture.[18]

Later, in the spirit of mutual self-criticism that dominated the conference, Fung added,

> What we have to continue is essentially the materialistic thought in the history of Chinese philosophy, the type of thought that is for the people, scientific, and progressive. I did not particularly mention this because I thought it was a matter of course. That shows that I believed in continuing anything abstract whether it was idealistic or materialistic.[19]

This clearly shows Fung attempting to revise his own thought, trying to overcome what he perceived to be the idealistic errors of his earlier thought.

Through mutual self-criticism, he was able to see that earlier categories and habits of thought were still dominant. This led him to append still another "confessional" statement to his earlier remarks: "What I said in my article is incomplete and my presentation of the problem is also incorrect."[20]

In his practice of self-criticism, Fung now began to rewrite his *History of Chinese Philosophy*. But when the Cultural Revolution began in 1966, he decided that the first two volumes of his *New History of Chinese Philosophy* were still written from a largely idealistic and abstract perspective. Thoroughly committed now to Marxist and Maoist thought, Fung decided to rewrite the entire history from a Maoist-Marxist perspective, using the ideology of the Cultural Revolution as a guideline, a project on which he worked until his death in 1990. Between 1982 and 1992, the new version of the *History of Chinese Philosophy* was published in seven volumes.[21] But now, at the beginning of the twenty-first century, there is not a great deal of philosophical interest in Fung's work, although some historians are intrigued by the latter portions of his life.

MAO TSE-TUNG

The thought of Mao Tse-tung (1894–1976) dominated philosophy in contemporary China until 1978 and continues to be important to this day. Mao was influenced greatly by Marx and Lenin, but his philosophy is frequently in tune with the principles and attitudes of traditional Chinese philosophies. After his death, Mao, although still hailed as the "great Liberator" of China, was widely criticized for causing the violence, suffering, and death that affected tens of millions of Chinese by his ruthless revolutionary methods. Also, as China adopted a more conciliatory posture toward both the West and traditional thought, Mao's philosophy has undergone extensive criticism. But despite the criticisms, Maoist thought continues to be used as the leading guide to a creative interpretation of experience harmonizing Marxist and traditional thought.

Mao's most important philosophical work is probably his lecture delivered in 1937 entitled "On Practice." In this lecture, he explained the relation between theory and practice, showing how theory originates in practice and returns to practice for its justification and fulfillment. This approach to the relation between theory and practice grew out of Mao's practice in reconciling the differences among the people as leader of the revolutionary forces. It is not a theory worked out for its own sake, but for the practical purpose of establishing the Great Harmony—the age-old Chinese utopia.

To see the practical aims presupposed by Mao's theory of the relation between practice and theory, it is helpful to consider his address commemorating the twenty-eighth anniversary of the Communist Party of China. In that address, Mao outlined the aims of Communist practices in China as follows: "When classes disappear, all instruments of class struggle—parties and the state machinery—will lose their function, cease to be necessary, therefore will gradually wither away and end their historical mission; and human society will move to a higher stage."[22] The concluding phrase—"human society will move to a higher stage"—reveals Mao's concern for the human condition. Of course, improving the human condition has always been the foremost consideration among Chinese thinkers. It was the hope of the Confucians and Neo-Confucians that when *jen* was made to prevail, the Great Harmony would be achieved. That Mao saw the aim of Communist practice to be the achievement of the Great Harmony is clear from his remark that the Party's function is that of "working hard to create the conditions in which classes, state power, and political parties will die out very naturally and mankind will enter the realm of the Great Harmony."[23]

To achieve the Great Harmony, Mao considered it necessary to understand the conditions that regulate the growth and development of humanity and the world so that the natural processes of growth and development can be assisted in arriving at their final goal. Probably the most important principle to be understood in this connection is that "all processes have a beginning and an end; all processes transform themselves into their opposites. The stability of all processes is relative, but the mutuality manifested in the transformation of one process into another is absolute."[24] No doubt, this principle is the central feature of the dialectic of Marxism, but it also restates the Taoist principles that "reversal is the way of *Tao*" and that "all things have their opposites." It is also a restatement of the Neo-Confucian explanation of the source and structure of all things that has its initial expression in Chou Tun-i's concept of the Great Ultimate, which generates all things through the interaction of the opposites *yin* and *yang*. Mao is quite aware that he is here well within the mainstream of traditional Chinese thought, for he remarks in the same paragraph, "We Chinese often say, 'Things opposed to each other complement each other.' "[25]

According to the dialectical relation between knowing and doing that Mao presented in his lecture "On Practice," knowing begins with practice, moves to the stage of theory, and is completed in doing. Theory represents the halfway house of knowing. Taking seriously the principle that the great dialectic of nature is the "reversal of opposites," and holding that the dialectic of any particular thing is also according to this principle, Mao was concerned with the opposites of theory and practice. His concern, of course, was with the successful democratic socialization of the People's Republic. This process, like any other process, proceeds according to its inner dialectic, and for the sake of successful practice, Mao was concerned to understand the dialectical relation between practice and theory, for these are the two primary opposites in the Communist program.

This problem—the relation between knowing and doing—has nearly always been of central concern to Chinese philosophers. Mao's solution to the problem was in agreement with traditional solutions, for he held that knowing and doing form a unity. His theory of knowledge maintained that "human knowledge cannot be separated the least bit from practice, and repudiates all incorrect theories which deny the importance of practice or separate knowledge from practice."[26] Verification of knowledge is had only when the anticipated results are achieved in the process of social practice. The principle is that "if man wants to achieve success in his work, that is, to achieve the anticipated results, he must make his thoughts correspond to the laws of the objective world surrounding him; if they do not correspond, he will fail in practice."[27]

In attempting to show the plausibility of the claim that social practice is the only criterion of truth, Mao argued that all knowledge has its beginnings in practice, in the activity of changing the world. "If you want to know the taste of a pear you must change the pear by eating it yourself."[28] This is the first stage in acquiring knowledge, the stage of perception. The next step consists in "making a rearrangement or a reconstruction; this belongs to the stage of conception, judgment, and inference."[29] Conception, judgment, and inference constitute rational, as opposed to merely perceptual knowledge, and as such provide for theories about the things perceived. But the acquisition of knowledge does not stop here. Just as perceptual knowledge leads to rational knowledge and is incomplete without it, so rational knowledge remains incomplete until it is applied in practice. As Mao pointed out, "What Marxist philosophy regards as the most important problem does not lie in understanding the laws of the objective world, thereby becoming capable of explaining it, but in actively changing the world by applying the knowledge of its objective laws."[30]

What Mao means is that knowledge is nothing but meaningless words and empty ideas until it gets embodied in experience. Only in the changing of the person and the changing of the reality encountered in practical activity does knowledge become real. From practice comes theory, and from theory practice proceeds. But theory and practice are not two different things. They are simply the dialectical opposites of one process—living in the world. The advance of knowledge is dialectically coupled to the advance of practice. According to Mao, the development of democratic socialism in China must combine both theory and practice. He urged that "the development of things should be regarded as their internal and necessary self-movement, that a thing in its movement and the things around it should be regarded as interconnected and interacting upon each other. The basic cause of development of things does not lie outside but inside them, in their internal contradictions."[31]

This is remarkably similar to the Neo-Confucian theory that individual things develop and grow through the interaction of the opposites *li* (principle) and *ch'i* (material force), because the universe is a cosmic dynamic structure of *li* and *ch'i*. The universe as a whole—as the Great Ultimate—is a unity of all things, in which human beings participate, that functions through the opposing movements of *yin* and *yang,* according to Neo-Confucianism. Thus, the whole, the Great Ultimate, is known through its concrete processes, and concrete processes are known by understanding their place in the patterns of the whole. Mao's conception of how things are known is similar. He says, "In the absolute, total process of the development of the universe, the development of each concrete process is relative; hence in the great stream of absolute truth, man's knowledge of the concrete process at any given stage of development is only relatively true. The sum total of innumerable relative truths is the absolute truth."[32]

It would appear, therefore, that despite his use of Marxist terminology, Mao carried forward the traditional Chinese attitude that sees the unity of the whole in particular things and that regards knowledge as an open-ended, ongoing process, inseparable from practice. This is why his philosophy also emphasizes the unification of society through practical improvements in daily life.

POST-MAO THOUGHT

The post-Mao period of philosophy began in 1978, two years after the death of Mao Tse-tung. Marking the end of three decades of domination by Marxist-Maoist thought, this new era began with a flood of intellectual activity aimed at establishing a new basis for social order and human values. This torrent of thought penetrated almost all of the Chinese intellectual landscape, affecting economic, social, political, and cultural developments. This intellectual revolution was essentially a revolution in philosophical thought, for, as noted in a recent survey of contemporary philosophy in China, "Philosophers have been and still are the intellectual leaders of society."[33]

The question at the heart of this revolution was, How can self and culture be modernized? Motivation to address these two interrelated issues came from the sense of urgency in modernizing Chinese society—motivation that was fueled by the excitement and energy generated by the newly found freedom from the thought control and economic determinism dictated by the Communist government since 1948. The underlying philosophical questions, What is it to be human *(jen)?* and How is one's full humanity to be realized? are questions that have always been central to Chinese philosophical thought.

In the post-Mao era, these questions generated lively debate on a number of more specific questions, including (1) What is truth and how is truth verified? (2) How are self, society, and culture interrelated? (3) What constitutes alienation? (4) How is Confucianism relevant to modernization? (5) How can science and humanism reinforce each other? and (6) What is the best way to modernize Chinese culture?

Nature and Criteria of Truth

The post-Mao philosophical revolution began with discussions on the nature and criteria of truth. For three decades, the principal criterion of truth had been, What did the Communist Party's leadership say? The implication was that whatever the party said was true. When this criterion was challenged within the party itself by the late Deng Xiaoping (1904–97), who advocated the criterion "practice is the principle criterion of truth" in order to weaken the position of his Maoist political opponents and gain acceptance of his pragmatic economic reforms, it opened the door to a wide-ranging debate on the nature and criteria of truth.

Hu Jiwei, former editor of *The People's Daily,* in his article "Listen to Chairman Mao's Words" *(ting Mao zhuxi de hua),* criticized the principle that truth was determined by what party leadership said. He expressed the excitement felt by many intellectuals in this sudden awakening to the realization that alternative criteria of truth were genuine options. In his article "Listen to Party Leadership or Not?" Hu said, "As one who had been used to listening to the words of the Party's leadership . . . it was not until the discussions on the criteria of truth that I was really awakened and began to question the truth of this principle."[34]

The immediate results of the debate over the criteria of truth were the weakening of the party's hold over the thought of Chinese intellectuals and newly found support for pragmatic criteria of truth. More significant, this debate served to reestablish the importance of rational discourse in all discussions of the major issues confronting Chinese society. It is unlikely that the other questions constituting the core of this philosophical revolution could have been raised and discussed openly in a rational way had the debates on the criteria of truth not occurred in 1978.

Interrelatedness of Self, Society, and Culture

By 1980, a number of thinkers began discussing what it is to be a human being. In these discussions, the question of whether one's class nature or one's human nature was more important to the individual was debated. At stake was whether the stronghold of three decades of thinking of persons as mere members of the faceless mass of society could be broken, allowing the individual self to be seen in terms of his or her human nature. Li Zehou, one of the most important thinkers in post-Mao China, argued that the self should be seen as an autonomous subject, acting together with other autonomous subjects to create a civil society and a human culture. This means that class membership, which regards the individual merely as an object, is less important than the individual's human nature, which gives him or her the potential to create values and culture as an autonomous human subject interacting with other autonomous human subjects.

Alienation

Discussions of the self in relation to class, culture, and human nature led quickly to debate on the issue of whether or not even Mao's vision of utopian communism and Deng's vision of pragmatic modernization constituted forms of human alienation. If the individual person was to be thought of as an autonomous subject, then any attempt to place the needs and values of mass society ahead of the self-fulfillment of the human subject would be a form of alienation. The issue was set forth by Wang Ruoshui, a leading humanist spokesman, in the form of a question that arose out of the debate on the criteria of truth: "If the criterion of truth is practice, then what is the criterion of successful practice?"[35]

The answer, setting forth the humanist agenda, was provided by Gao Ertai, another humanist thinker:

> Human beings *(jen)* engage themselves in practice not for the purpose of realizing certain objective laws, but for their own happiness.... Human beings, of course, will pursue material interests, but the highest value they embrace is humanity itself, its self-fulfillment, its freedom and full development.[36]

Relevance of Confucianism to Modernization

As discussions of self, society, and culture began to focus more on human nature *(jen)* and less on membership in mass society, traditional philosophical thought began to take on a new relevance. Confucian thought, in particular, had been ridiculed and marginalized for three decades. With the rediscovery of the central importance of *jen* (human nature) to China's modernization, the door was opened to the influence of the "New Confucians" *(xinrujia)*. In his 1978 article "A reevaluation of Confucius," Li Zehou prepared the ground for a new appreciation of Confucian thought. Other New Confucians, including Chinese philosophers Tu Wei-ming, Cheng Chung-ying, and Charles Fu from the United States, helped bring the Confucian tradition into the mainstream of the new debate on the importance of self and human nature *(jen)* in China's modernization. In the late 1990s, even Chinese Marxist thinkers such as Zhang Dainian and Xiao Jeifu draw on the Confucian tradition to develop their own original theories of modernization. Mou Zongsan, an important Confucian scholar, has developed a new moral metaphysics rooted in Sung dynasty Neo-Confucian thought as a foundation for modernization of Chinese culture. Another major Confucian thinker, Zheng Jiadong, has written an important new book, *An Introduction to Modern New Confucianism.*[37]

Mutual Reinforcement of Science and Humanism

Whereas the Maoist era was dominated by its emphasis on scientific studies of social phenomena, the philosophical debates of the 1980s created room for the humanistic study of culture and society as well. Perhaps the most significant result of the rise of humanistic studies was a growing recognition of the scientific and humanistic approaches as complementary, reinforcing each other. Jin Guantao, for example, a leading figure in the scientific study of society, adopted the humanistic principles of Wang Roushui and welcomed Li Zehou's emphasis on the human subject. In his 1988 book, which even has a humanistic title, *Philosophy of Humanity,* Jin says: "Today we have to wake up from the dream of an objectivity that is irrelevant to humanity *(jen)* and find before us a world with human being as its center."[38]

The Best Way to Modernize Chinese Culture

By 1984, the various issues being debated as part of the post-Mao philosophical revolution converged in the debate on how to best modernize Chinese culture. Western, Marxist, and traditional Chinese views on how to creatively transform culture and society competed with one another in these discussions, with significant creative borrowing and adapting occurring between them. This important debate, which may well create a new synergistic vision to guide China's development, has produced thousands of articles, hundreds of books, and dozens of centers for cultural study. It is significant that the central issues of this debate were joined not only by intellectuals, but by officials in political circles and by the public as well.

The post-Mao philosophical revolution was dealt a serious setback by official repressions following the Tiananmen Square incident. Although discussion of central issues has continued on the Chinese mainland, many of the participants in the earlier debates have been forced to continue their discussion in exile.[39] But with the new economic freedoms and increased information made available through the World Wide Web, there has been a resurgence of interest in issues concerning democracy, modernization, and human rights in which the New Confucians are playing a significant role.

REVIEW QUESTIONS

1. What are the main issues in the debates over China's modernization, and how did they influence recent Chinese philosophy?
2. What is the basis for K'ang Yu-wei's reform efforts? What is your assessment of its adequacy?
3. Explain what Chang Tung-sun means when he says "ideas . . . are secretly controlled by social needs." Is he right?
4. What are the three central ideas worked out in Hsiung Shih-li's *New Doctrine of Consciousness-Only?*
5. How does Fung Yu-lan view the relation between science and metaphysics in his *New Rational Philosophy?* Compare his view of the relation between substance and function with that of Hsiung Shih-li.
6. According to Mao Tse-tung, what is the relationship between knowledge and practice? Is this a Marxist view or a traditional view?

FURTHER READING

The Living Tree: The Changing Meaning of Being Chinese Today, edited by Wei-ming Tu (Stanford: Stanford University Press, 1994), is a collection of essays that focuses on the values and attitudes that constitute the core of Chinese identity at the end of the twentieth century.

The Democracy of the Dead: Dewey, Confucius, and the Hope for Democracy in China, by David L. Hall and Roger T. Ames (Lasalle, IL: Open Court, 1999), is a philosophical exploration of contemporary culture in China and the West, in search of a common basis for democracy.

The Tao Encounters the West: Explorations in Comparative Philosophy, by Chenyang Li (Albany: State University of New York Press, 1999), is a clear and thoughtful exploration of the relation between democracy and Confucianism that illumines differences and similarities between fundamental Chinese and Western ways of thinking. The author argues for the compatibility and mutual reinforcement of Confucian and democratic value systems as a basis for China's continuing modernization.

Confucianism and Modernization: Industrialization and Democratization of the Confucian Regions, by Wei Bin Zhang (New York: St. Martin's Press, 1999), is a study of the relevance of Confucianism to industrialization and democracy by an economist with Confucian leanings.

Mao Tse-tung's Theory of Dialectic, by Francis Y.K. Soo (Dordrecht, Netherlands: D. Reidel, 1981), is a careful examination of Mao's understanding of the dialectical nature of reality. Using cross-cultural analysis, Soo argues that Mao's understanding is as much Chinese as it is Marxist.

A Sourcebook in Chinese Philosophy, translated and compiled by Wing-tsit Chan (Princeton, NJ: Princeton University Press, 1963), has separate chapters on some of the thinkers covered in this chapter. The concluding chapter, "Chinese Philosophy in Communist China," includes reports from the 1957 Conference on Philosophy.

Sources of Chinese Tradition, vol. 2, compiled by William Theodore de Bary et al. (New York: Columbia University Press, 1964), is devoted entirely to modern China. Beginning with the opening of China to the West, successive chapters trace the dialectic of China's modernization up to 1960.

Sowing the Seeds of Democracy in China: Political Reform in the Deng Xiaoping Era, by Merle Goldman (Cambridge: Harvard University Press, 1994), is a study of Chinese intellectual trends in the 1980s through analysis of the works of leading intellectuals.

NOTES

1. As translated by Wing-tsit Chan, in *A Sourcebook in Chinese Philosophy* (Princeton, NJ: Princeton University Press, 1963), p. 726.
2. Ibid., p. 735.
3. Ibid., pp. 734–35.
4. See *Selected Works of Mao Tse-tung,* vol. 5 (Peking: Foreign Language Press, 1977), pp. 329–32.
5. Wing-tsit Chan, *A Sourcebook in Chinese Philosophy,* p. 744.
6. Ibid., pp. 749–50.
7. Ibid., p. 750.
8. Ibid., p. 765.
9. Ibid., p. 766.
10. Ibid.
11. Ibid.
12. Ibid., p. 769.
13. Ibid., p. 771.
14. Ibid.
15. Ibid., p. 772.
16. Ibid., p. 751.
17. Ibid., p. 759.
18. Ibid., p. 778.
19. Ibid., p. 779.
20. Ibid.
21. For a recent review of Fung's work, see Nicolas Standaert, "The Discovery of the Center Through the Periphery: A Preliminary Study of Fung Youlan's *History of Chinese Philosophy* (new version)" in *Philosophy East and West,* vol. 45, no. 4 (October 1995), pp. 569–89.
22. Ann Freemantle, ed., with an introduction, *Mao Tse-tung: An Anthology of His Writings* (New York: New American Library, 1962), p. 184.

23. Ibid., p. 185.
24. Ibid., p. 237.
25. Ibid., p. 238.
26. Ibid., p. 203.
27. Ibid., pp. 201–2
28. Ibid., p. 205.
29. Ibid., p. 207.
30. Ibid., p. 209.
31. Ibid., p. 216.
32. Ibid., p. 212.
33. Lin Tongqi, Henry Rosemont Jr., and Roger T. Ames, "Chinese Philosophy: A Philosophical Essay on the 'State-of-the-Art,' " *Journal of Asian Studies,* vol. 54, no. 3 (August 1995), p. 727. I have relied heavily on this excellent essay for the discussion of post-Maoist philosophy.
34. Ibid., p. 731. It is significant that the title Hu chose for the book containing this and other articles germane to the post-Mao philosophical revolution was *The Moment of Sudden Awakening.*
35. Ibid., p. 732.
36. Ibid.
37. Ibid., pp. 734–37.
38. Ibid., p. 738.
39. Ibid., pp. 743–44.

Glossary

Abhidharma Buddhist system of classifying reality based on meditational experience.

Advaita Nondual view of reality.

Agni God of fire.

Ahiṁsā Nonhurting.

Ālaya Vijñāna The underlying store consciousness.

Anātman (P: Anatta) No-self; the Buddhist denial of a permanent self.

Anekānta Nonabsolutism; Jaina view of the many-sidedness of reality.

Anitya (P: Anicca) Impermanence; Buddhist denial of permanence.

Aparigraha Nongrasping.

Āraṇyaka Vedic texts that explain rituals.

Arhat One who is made noble by a pure mind and virtuous conduct.

Artha Success; one of the four aims of life.

Āsana Posture.

Asatkāryavāda Theory that a causal effect is something new, not previously existent.

Ashrama (Āśrama) Stage; any of the four stages of life.

Ātman The inner self that is unborn and undying.

Avidyā Ignorance.

Bhagavad Gītā Important Hindu scripture, "Song of the Lord," that sets out three paths to salvation through nonattachment in knowledge, action, and devotion.

Bhakti Devotion.

Bodhisattva Buddhist ideal of an enlightened, compassionate being dedicated to helping others overcome suffering.

Brahman The unchanging ultimate reality that is the ground of all existence.

Brāhmaṇa (1) Vedic texts dealing with ritual, (2) member of the priestly class.

Buddhi Awareness. In Samkhya, the principle of consciousness.

Cārvāka The materialist Indian tradition.

Ch'eng Sincerity.

Cheng-ming Rectification of names.

Ch'i Material energy.

Chih Knowledge of right and wrong.

Chih Liang-chih Innate knowledge of the good.

Ch'ung yung Central harmony.

Darshana (Darśana) Worldview or vision.

Dhāraṇā Control of the senses.

Dharma The way of truth in action; right-doing.

Dharmas Ultimate constituents of existence according to Sarvastivada.

Dhyāna Concentrated awareness.

Duḥkha (P: Dukkha) Unwholesomeness of life directed by selfish grasping and hatred because of ignorance; suffering.

Dvaita Dualistic metaphysics, especially Madhva's school of Vedanta.

Guṇa The ultimate mass-energy constituents of things; according to Samkhya, the constituitive threads of *prakriti,* namely *sattva, rajas,* and *tamas.*

Guru Spiritual teacher.

Hsiao Filial love.

I-Ching (Book of Changes) Ancient text explaining the process of change according to the movements of *yin* and *yang.*

Indra Principal Vedic deity.

Jāti Literally, "birth"; one's class as determined by birth.

Jen What makes a person human; human-heartedness.

Jina In Jainism, one who has conquered ignorance and the passions.

Jīva Life-principle or soul; living thing.

Jñāna Knowledge.

Kālī Dark goddess who overcomes death and destruction.

Kāma Enjoyment, especially sensual enjoyment. One of the four aims of life.

Karma Action, especially person-making actions.

Kevalin A liberated person.

Kōan A meditative question to break down dualistic thinking in Zen.

Krishna (Kṛṣṇa) Hindu deity symbolizing the way of loving devotion.

Kshatriya (Kṣatrīya) Ruling and military class responsible for security.

Kung-an The question-answer practice (called *kōan* in Japanese Zen) for going beyond dualistic thinking in Ch'an.

Li (1) The principle that makes something what it is; (2) ritual; (3) what is proper.

Liṅga The symbol of Śiva.

Mādhyamaka Middle Way philosophy.

Mahābhārata Great epic of India.

Mahāyāna Form of Buddhism emphasizing the *Bodhisattva* ideal of compassion.

Māyā Creative power of reality.

Mīmāṁsā Indian philosophical system concerned with action, ritual, and hermeneutics.

Moksha (Mokṣa) Liberation from bondage.

Nāstika Traditions (Jaina, Buddhist, and Carvaka) that reject the authority of the Vedas.

Naya Standpoint or perspective from which things are known.

Neti, Neti Literally, "not this, not this." The negative way of reaching *Brahman*.

Nirvāṇa (P: Nibbana) The peace that is attained by eliminating suffering.

Niyama Yogic techniques of spiritual purification.

Nyāya Indian philosophical tradition of logic and epistemology.

Pāramitā The perfections characterizing the way of the *Bodhisattva*.

Prajāpati The Vedic god of creation.

Prajñapāramitā The wisdom that reaches reality as it truly is; a group of texts that explain this wisdom.

Prakriti (Prakṛti) In Samkhya, the ground of material and mental existence.

Prāṇa The life-force.

Prānāyama Yogic techniques for regulating the life-energy.

Pratītyasamutpāda (P: Paṭicca Samuppāda) The Buddha's insight that interdependent arising is the nature of existence.

Pudgala (1) Jain word for material existence. (2) Buddhist term for substratum of personal existence.

Purusha (Puruṣa) Literally "person." In Vedas, the proto-person that became this existence. In Samkhya, the self as pure subject.

Purushartha (Puruṣārtha) *Dharma, artha, kama,* and *moksha* as fundamental aims of life.

Rajas The *guna* of *prakriti* responsible for cosmic energy and action.

Rāmāyana Indian epic poem that tells the story of the god Rama.

Rig Veda (Ṛg Veda) Hymns of knowledge used in Vedic rituals.

Rinzai Japanese Zen tradition that emphasizes *kōan* practice.

Rita (Ṛta) The normative structure of reality according to Vedic thought.

Samādhi Final absorption into the true self.

Sāṁkhya Dualistic Indian philosophical tradition that takes reality to be of the nature of either *prakriti* or *purusha*.

Saṁsāra The cycle of death, life, and re-death.

Sannyāsin One who has renounced worldly life in favor of spiritual seeking.

Sarvāstivāda Buddhist tradition that emphasizes the *dharmas* as ultimate constituents of the processes of existence.

Sat-Chit-Ānanda The absolute being, awareness, and bliss that characterizes Brahman.

Satkāryvāda Theory of causality that claims effects preexist in their causes.

Satori In Zen, the awakening to true existence.

Sattva In Samkhya, the constituent of *prakriti* making possible mental activity.

Satya Truth.

Shakyamuni (Śakyamuni) Title of the Buddha. Literally "Sage of the Sakya [clan]."

Shintō Japanese religious tradition that emphasizes the way of the Kami (spiritual powers of nature and humanity) in restoring the natural purity and order of things.

Shiva Natarāj The god Shiva as Lord of the Dance.

Shiva (Śiva) Hindu god.

Shōbōgenzō Dōgen's main work, the "Treasury-eye of the True Teaching."

Shu Reciprocity.

Shudra (Śūdra) Serving class.

Sōtō Japanese Zen tradition that emphasizes sitting meditation.

Śramana A seeker of truth.

Śūnyatā Emptiness of independent and permanent being.

Sūtra A brief verbal formula encapsulating an important idea.

Svabhāva Having independent existence.

Syāt Conditionality of knowledge because of limited perspective.

T'ai-chi The Great Ultimate, source of *yin* and *yang*.

Tamas The *guna* responsible for inertia and dullness.

Tao The nameless source and way of existence.

Taoism Chinese philosophical tradition of Lao Tzu and Chuang Tzu.

Tapas The transforming heat-energy of austerity.

Tathāgata Title of the Buddha. Literally. "Thus-gone," meaning gone to enlightenment.

Tat Tvam Asi "You are That," that is, the identity of innermost Self and *Brahman.*

Te The functioning of *Tao.*

Theravāda The Buddhist tradition practiced in Sri Lanka, Cambodia, Thailand, and Burma.

Tirthaṇkara In Jainism, a "Ford-maker," who has shown the way across the river of suffering.

Upanishad (Upaniṣad) Texts that form the concluding portion of the Veda.

Vāc Speech; the Vedic goddess of speech.

Vaisheshika (Vaiśeṣika) Realistic and pluralistic Indian philosophical tradition.

Vaishya (Vaiśya) The producing class.

Varṇa System of social classification ideally based on qualification and social function.

Veda The knowledge that transforms and saves; sacred texts containing such knowledge.

Vedanā Sensation or feeling.

Vedānta Indian philosophical tradition based on the Upanishads.

Vishishtadvaita (Viśiṣṭādvaita) Nondualistic Vedanta tradition that admits differences, usually associated with Ramanuja.

Vishnu (Viṣṇu) Hindu god.

Wu-wei Doing nothing except what proceeds freely and spontaneously from one's own nature.

Yama Lord of the dead.

Yang Positive principle of cosmic energy.

Yi Righteousness.

Yin Negative principle of cosmic energy.

Yoga Discipline of mind and body.

Yogācāra Buddhist tradition championed by Asanga and Vasubandhu emphasizing the practice of overcoming ignorance.

Zazen Zen discipline for attaining enlightenment.

Zen Form of Buddhism developed and practiced in China, Korea, and Japan that emphasizes the establishment of mindfulness.

Pronunciation Guide

The following guidelines will help the reader correctly pronounce the Sanskrit, Pāli, Chinese, and Japanese terms encountered in this book.

SANSKRIT AND PĀLI TERMS

Because Pāli consonants and vowels are pronounced like Sanskrit, the reader may achieve correct pronunciation of both Pāli and Sanskrit terms by observing the following guidelines. Pāli equivalents of Sanskrit words are given in parentheses in the glossary.

Because Sanskrit has more letters than the Roman alphabet, it is necessary to combine diacritical marks with Roman letters to represent the sounds contained in Sanskrit. The following examples show how to pronounce the Sanskrit vowels and consonants that differ from usual English equivalents.

a as u in but
$\bar{a}$ as a in f$a$ther
i as i in tin
$\bar{i}$ as i in mach$i$ne
u as u in f$u$ll
$\bar{u}$ as u in r$u$le
$\d{r}$ as ri in river

e as *ay* in s*ay*

ai as *ai* in *ai*sle

o as *o* in g*o*

au as *ow* in c*ow*

$\dot{m}$ nasalizes and lengthens the preceding vowel, like the *o* in French *bon*

$\d{h}$, which sometimes replaces *s* or *r* at the end of a word, has the effect of lengthening the preceding vowel.

Most consonants can be pronounced as in English; exceptions are

c as *ch* in *ch*urch

g as *g* in *g*o

$\d{s}$ and *ś* as in *sh* in *sh*ape

Aspirated consonants—*th, ph, bh, kh, gh, ch, jh, dh* — are pronounced like the *th* in an*th*ill, the *ph* in she*ph*erd, the *bh* in ab*h*or, and so on.

Theoretically each syllable, which consists of one or more consonants and the accompanying vowel, receives equal emphasis. In practice, however, the main accent is usually placed on the next-to-last syllable if it contains a long vowel ($\bar{a}, \bar{\imath}, \bar{u}$), otherwise on the third-to-last syllable.

In the body of the text, a simplified form of transliteration has been used. The following chart shows how the standard transliteration has been simplified.

Standard Form	Simplified Form
c, ch	ch
m, ṁ	m
n, ṇ, ñ	n
ṛ	ri
ś, ṣ	sh
t, ṭ	t
th, ṭh	th
a, ā	a
i, ī	i
u, ū	u

In the glossary, Sanskrit and Pāli words are transliterated in the standard way, with proper diacritical marks to show how they should be pronounced.

CHINESE TERMS

There are two systems for romanizing Chinese, Wade-Giles, and Pinyin. Pinyin, the more recent system, standard in the People's Republic, follows English phonetic rules of pronunciation for the most part. The older, Wade-Giles system, which is used because most of the available English translations of Chinese texts have used it, is not always phonetic. The following table shows how to convert to the Pinyin equivalents, enabling the reader to pronounce them according to the phonetic rules given at the end of the table.

Cha	*zha*	chüan	*juan*
chai	*zhai*	ch'üan	*quan*
chan	*zhan*	chüeh	*jue*
chang	*zhang*	ch'üeh	*que*
chao	*zhao*	chün	*jun*
che	*zhe*	ch'ün	*qun*
chei	*zhei*	erh	*er*
chen	*zhen*	ho	*he*
cheng	*zheng*	hsi	*xi*
chi	*ji*	hsia	*xia*
ch'i	*qi*	hsiang	*xiang*
chia	*jia*	hsiao	*xiao*
ch'ia	*qia*	hsieh	*xie*
chiang	*jiang*	hsien	*xian*
ch'iang	*qiang*	hsin	*xin*
chiao	*jiao*	hsing	*xing*
ch'iao	*qiao*	hsiu	*xiu*
chieh	*jie*	hsiung	*xiong*
ch'ieh	*qie*	hsü	*xu*
chien	*jian*	hsüan	*xuan*
ch'ien	*qian*	hsüeh	*xue*
chih	*zhi*	hsün	*xun*
ch'ih	*chi*	i	*yi*
chin	*jin*	jan	*ran*
ch'in	*qin*	jang	*rang*
ching	*jing*	jao	*rao*
ch'ing	*qing*	je	*re*
chiu	*jiu*	jen	*ren*
ch'iu	*qiu*	jeng	*reng*
chiung	*jiong*	jih	*ri*
cho	*zhuo*	jo	*ruo*
ch'o	*chuo*	jou	*rou*
chou	*zhou*	ju	*ru*
chu	*zhu*	juan	*ruan*
chua	*zhua*	jui	*rui*
chuai	*zhuai*	jun	*run*
chuan	*zhuan*	jung	*rong*
chuang	*zhuang*	ka	*ga*
chui	*zhui*	kai	*gai*
chun	*zhun*	kan	*gan*
chung	*zhong*	kang	*gang*
ch'ung	*chong*	kao	*gao*
chü	*ju*	ke,ko	*ge*
ch'ü	*qu*	kei	*gei*

ken	*gen*	po	*bo*
keng	*geng*	pou	*bou*
ko,ke	*ge*	pu	bu
k'o	*ke*	shih	*shi*
kou	*gou*	so	suo
ku	*gu*	ssŭ, szˇu	*si*
kua	*gua*	sung	*song*
kuai	*guai*	szŭ,ssŭ	*si*
kuan	*guan*	ta	*da*
kuang	*guang*	tai	*dai*
kuei	*gui*	tan	*dan*
k'uei	*kui*	tang	*dang*
kun	*gun*	tao	*dao*
kung	*gong*	te	*de*
k'ung	*kong*	tei	*dei*
kuo	*guo*	teng	*deng*
lieh	*lie*	ti	*di*
lien	*lian*	tu	*du*
lo	*luo*	tuan	*duan*
lün	*lun*	tui	*dui*
lung	*long*	tun	*dun*
lüan	*luan*	tung	*dong*
lüeh	*lue*	t'ung	*tong*
mieh	*mie*	tzŭ	*zi*
mien	*mian*	tsŭ	*ci*
nieh	*nie*	tiao	*diao*
nien	*nian*	tieh	*die*
nung	*nong*	t'ieh	*tie*
nü	*nu*	tien	*dian*
nüeh	*nue*	t'ien	*tian*
o	*e*	ting	*ding*
pa	*ba*	tiu	*diu*
pai	*bai* ·	to	*duo*
pan	*ban*	t'o	*tuo*
pang	*bang*	tou	*dou*
pao	*bao*	tsa	*za*
pei	*bei*	ts'a	*ca*
pen	*ben*	tsai	*zai*
peng	*beng*	ts'ai	*cai*
pi	*bi*	tsan	*zan*
piao	*biao*	ts'an	*can*
pieh	*bie*	tsang	*zang*
p'ieh	*pie*	ts'ang	*cang*
pien	*bian*	tsao	*zao*
p'ien	*pian*	ts'ao	*cao*
pin	*bin*	tse	*ze*
ping	*bing*	ts'e	*ce*`

tsei	*zei*	ts'ui	*cui*
tsen	*zen*	tsun	*zun*
ts'en	*cen*	ts'un	*cun*
tseng	*zeng*	tsung	*zong*
ts'eng	*ceng*	ts'ung	*cong*
tso	*zuo*	yeh	*ye*
ts'o	*cuo*	yen	*yan*
tsou	*zou*	yu	*you*
ts'ou	*cou*	yung	*yong*
tsu	*zu*	yü	*yu*
ts'u	*cu*	yüan	*yuan*
tsuan	*zuan*	yüeh	*yue*
ts'uan	*cuan*	yün	*yun*
tsui	*zui*		

Pronunciation Guide for the Pinyin Chinese Romanization System

Vowels:

1. "ao" is pronounced "ow." For example, hao = "how."
2. "ou" is pronounced "oe." For example dou = "doe" (as in female deer).
3. "a" is pronounced "ah." For example, hang = "hong" (rhymes with the English word "song").
4. "o" is pronounced similar to the English sound "oo" in the word "book." For example, song = "soong."
5. "ui" is pronounced "uay." For example, hui = "huay."
6. "e" is pronounced "uh." For example, neng = "nung" (rhymes with the English word "hung").
7. There is variation in pronunciation for words ending in "i." When "i" follows compound consonants such as "sh," it is prounoued as though followed by an "r." Thus shi = "sure," zhi = "zher," and chi = "cher." However, when "i" follow a single consonant such as "l," "q," or "n," no "r" sound is added. Thus li = "lee," qi = "chee," and ni = "nee."

Consonants:

1. "x" is pronounced similar to the English letter "s." For example, xuan = "swan," xi = "see," xin = "sin."
2. "q" is pronounced "ch." For example, qi = "chee," qian = "chian."
3. "zh" is pronounced like the English letter "j." For example, zhi = "jer," zhang = "jong," zhen = "Jen."
4. "c" is pronounced similar to the English letter "ts." For example, cui = "tsway."

JAPANESE TERMS

Japanese consonants are usually pronounced according to English phonetic rules. Japanese vowels are pronounced as follows:

a as in f*a*ther
e as in m*e*t
i as in mach*i*ne
o as in *o*h
u as in r*u*le

An exception occurs when a vowel is long, as, for example, the $\bar{o}$ in Dōgen, in which case it is pronounced twice as long as the usual vowel.

Index

Abhidharma, 143, 183–86
  Sarvastivada, 185–86
  Theravada, 184–85
Abhinivesha (fear of death), 61
Action, knowledge and, 318–20
Activities of the body, mindfulness
  of, 177
Adi Granth (Guru Granth Sahib),
  117
Advaita, 123, 220
  qualified, 81, 88–90
  of Shankara, 81, 82–88
Age of Great Unity, 326
Agni (Vedic diety), 16, 95
Ahamkara ("I-maker"), 58
Ahimsa (nonhurting), 39–40, 62,
  123, 124–25
Ahmad, Shaikh, 120
Ajatasatru, King, 29
Akbar, 118–19
Alaya vijnana (store
  consciousness), 219, 221,
  222
Al-Ghazali, 109–11
Al-Hallaj, 114
Alienation, 338
Analects (Lun Yu), 259
Animals, in wheel of becoming,
  173
Aparigraha (nongrasping), 40–41,
  62
Apparent change, theory of, 86
Aquinas, Thomas, 111
Aranyaka, 5
Ardhanaraishvara, 104
Arhant, 141
Arhat ("noble one"), 197–98
Arjuna, 45
Artha, 47, 48, 49
Artha Shastra, 5
Asanas (postures), 63
Asanga, 144, 218, 223, 226–29
Asatkaryavada (nonexistence of
  the effect), 83–84
Asceticism, Sufi, 112–13, 114–15
Ashoka, King, 137
Ashrama (life-stages), 51–52
Asmita (ego-force), 61
Asrar-I Khudi (Secrets of the Self)
  (Iqbal), 129–30
Asteya (nonstealing), 40, 62
Atharva Veda, 4–5
Atman, 10, 21–22, 24–25
Attachment (raga), 61
Aurangzeb, 119–20
Aurobindo, Sri, 7, 123, 125–27
Autobiography (Gandhi), 124
Avalokita, 199, 200
Averroes (Ibn Rushd), 111
Aversion (dvesha), 61
Avicenna (Ibn Sina), 110, 111–13
Avidya (ignorance), 168–72
  of a garden hose, 168–70

of interdependent arising,
  170–72

Badr-ud-Din, 113
Becoming, wheel of. See Wheel of
  becoming
Becoming forces, 172
Bergson, Henri, 326, 327
Bhagavad Gita, 5, 44–46, 94, 97
Bhakti (loving devotion), 98–99
Bhaskara, 6–7
Bhisma, 51
Billah, Khwaja Baqi, 120
Birth, in wheel of becoming, 172
Bodhidharma, 233, 234–35
Bodhisattva, 141
Bodily positions, mindfulness of,
  177
Bodily processes (rupa), 157
Body, mindfulness of activities of,
  177
Body awareness, 176–77
Body-mind, in wheel of becoming,
  171
Bondage
  in Jainism, 30–34
  yoga and, 61
Book of Changes (I-Ching), 259,
  328
Book of Chuang Tzu, 235, 294
Book of History (Shu Ching), 259
Book of Mencius (Meng Tzu), 259
Book of Poetry (Shi Ching), 259
Book of Rites (Li Chi), 259
Brahmacarya (sexual purity), 40
Brahman, 10
  functions of, 131
  matter vs., 91
  quest for, 20–21, 24–25
  Ramanuja on, 89–90
  relations between world and, 81
  unchanging reality of, 82
Brahmana, 5
Brahmana varna, 50
Breathing, mindfulness of, 176–77
Brihadaranyaka Upanishad, 24, 81
Buddha, the ("Enlightened
  One"), 96, 137, 141, 148–64
  India in time of, 138–39
  life of, 148–55
    enlightenment quest, 151–53
    the four signs, 149–51
    optimism of, 154–55
    self of, 209
  teachings of, 155–64
    Four Noble Truths, 155–60
    Noble Eightfold Path, 155,
      160–64
    on suffering, 155–60
Buddha-nature, 243
Buddhi (intelligence), 58
Buddhist philosophies, 135–250
  absolutist interpretations of, 205

central teaching of, 137–38
challenge to Neo-Confucianism,
  304–5
Chinese, 145, 263–64
  Ch'an school, 264
  Hua-yen tradition, 263
  Pure Land school, 264
  T'ien-t'ai tradition, 263
chronology of events and
  thinkers, 136
in India, 138–39
interdependent arising (pratitya
  samutpada), 153, 157,
  167–80, 183
  conditioned existence
    principle, 167–68
  implications of, 174–75
  mindfulness, 175–80
  wheel of becoming, 168–74
in Korea and Japan, 145–46. See
  also Zen Buddhism
Madhyamaka (Middle Way)
  tradition, 142, 143–44,
  203–16
  Chinese adaptation of, 263–64
  defined, 203–4
  emptiness, 211–16
  Nagarjuna philosophy,
    143–44, 203, 204–11
  overview of, 203–4
Mahayana, 139–42, 218
  foundational texts of, 194
  spread of, 140
  as nastika (unorthodox system),
    6
Perfection of Wisdom
  (prajnaparamita), 193–201
  defined, 194–95
  Diamond Sutra
    (Vajracchedika), 193–94,
    196–98
  Heart Sutra, 193–94, 198–201
  reading in, 194–96
  texts of, 193–94
Sarvastivada tradition, 142, 143,
  182–90
  Abhidharma, 183–86
  Arguments against substance,
    186–90
  teachings of, 182–83
Theravada-Mahayana split,
  139–42
Tibetan, 144, 203
in the West, 146
Yogacara School, 142–45, 218–19
  arguments against realism,
    224–26
  Chinese adaptation of, 263–64
  consciousness, 220–24
  existence in, 219–20
  knowledge of reality, 226–29
  overview of, 218–19
Zen, 146, 203, 231–50

foundations of, 233–35
koans, 239, 241–42
overview of, 231–33
stages of, 244–50
Taoist influences on, 235–36
teachings of, 243–44
Zazen, 238–41

Cakrayana, Ushasta, 25
Candrakirti, 213
Carvaka, as *nastika* (unorthodox system), 6
Castes (*jatis*), 49–51, 116
Causality
  arguments against permanence and, 188–89
  Indian theory of, 55–57
  Shankara on, 83
Ceremonial activities, as embodiments of *li*, 273
Chaitanya, 119
Ch'an Buddhism, 243–44
Chandogya Upanishad, 23, 25, 81, 132
Chang Tsai, 314
Chang Tung-sun, 326–28
Ch'an tradition, 145
Ch'eng brothers, 314
Cheng Chung-ying, 339
Ch'eng Hao, 265, 309–13
Ch'eng I, 309–13
Cheng-ming (rectification of names), 276
Ch'eng Yi, 265
Chiang Ch'ing, 331
Chih liang-chih (innate knowledge of the good), 318
Ch'i (material force), 310, 315
Chinese philosophies, 257–343
  basic characteristics of, 265–67
  Buddhism, 145, 263–64
    Ch'an school, 264
    Hua-yen tradition, 263
    Pure Land school, 264
    T'ien-t'ai tradition, 263
  Chang Tung-sun, 326–28
  chronology of, 256
  Confucianism, 258–59, 270–84
    Confucius, 257, 258, 259, 270–71
    filial piety (*hsiao*) in, 274–75
    Hsun Tzu, 259, 280–81, 283–84, 314
    humanity (*jen*) in, 259, 265, 271–73, 311–13, 316–17, 321, 339
    Mencius, 259, 280–83
    propriety (*li*) in, 273–74
    rectification of names in (*cheng-ming*), 276
    righteousness (*yi*) in, 275–76
    as state religion, 325
    virtue in, 276–81
  early medieval developments, 262–63
  Fung Yu-lan, 331–34
  Hsiung Shih-li, 328–31
  K'ang Yu-wei, 325–26
  legalism, 262

Mao Tse-tung, 333–34
Mohism, 260
Neo-Confucianism, 264, 265, 304–21
  Buddhist challenge to, 304–5
  Ch'eng Hao, 265, 309–13
  Ch'eng I, 309–13
  Chou Tun-i, 307–9, 315
  Chu Hsi, 265, 313–17
  Han Yu, 264, 305–6, 314
  jen and, 311–13, 316–17
  Li Ao, 306
  Ou-yang Hsiu, 307
  principle and material force in, 309–11
  Tai Chen, 320–21
  Wang Yang-Ming, 265, 317–20
  post-Mao thought, 337–40
  pre-Confucian China, 257–58
  School of Names, 260–61
  Taoism, 259–60, 287–301
    Chuang Tzu, 260, 287, 293–301
    influence on Zen Buddhism, 235–36
    Lao Tzu, 235, 257, 259–60, 266, 287–90, 317
    Tao, 235, 265, 290–93
    Yin and *yang* 261–63, 291, 308, 316
Chinghis Khan, 106
Ching period, 265
Chinul, 145
Chogyechong school, 145
Chou dynasty, 258
Chou Tun-i, 307–9, 315
Chuang Tzu, 260, 287, 293–301
  argument from perspectives, 298–99
  argument from skepticism, 299–301
  on complementariness of opposites, 296–98
  on relativity of distinctions, 294–96
Chu Hsi, 265, 313–17
Chung Yung (*Doctrine of the Mean*), 259
Closing, concept of, 329
Cognitive framework, universal, 300–301
Comparison, knowledge through, 72–73
Complementariness of opposites, 296–98
Concentration, 239
  dharana, 64
  stages of, 164
Conditioned existence, principle of, 167–68
Conduct, in Noble Eightfold Path, 160, 161
Confucianism, 258–59, 270–84
  filial piety (*hsiao*) in, 274–75
  Hsun Tzu, 259, 280–81, 283–84, 314
  humanity (*jen*) in, 259, 265, 271–73
    Chinese modernization and, 339

Neo-Confucianism and, 311–13, 316–17
  Mencius, 259, 280–83
  propriety (*li*) in, 273–74
  rectification of names in (*cheng-ming*), 276
  righteousness (*yi*) in, 275–76
  as state religion, 325
  virtue in, 276–81
    as element of learning, 277–78
    familial relationships and, 278–79
    human nature and, 279–81
Confucius, 257, 258, 259, 270–71
Conquerors (*jinas*), 28, 29, 38–39
Consciousness, 171, 185, 220–24
  defiled, 221
  discursive, 221
  fundamental, 221–22
  intentional, 221
  kinds of, 221–23
  nature and function of, 218, 220
  processes of, 157, 219
  as source, 223–24
  store, 219, 221, 222
Constituents, ultimate, 186
Construction-deconstruction-reconstruction technique, 195–96
Contact, in wheel of becoming, 171
Continuity, Sarvastivada on, 186
Correlative terms, pairs of, 297
Cosmic Person, Hymn to, 17
Craving, in wheel of becoming, 172
Craving (*trishna*), 158–60

Dadu, 117–18
Darshana (faith), 8, 38–39
Death
  Buddhist view of, 138
  fear of, 61
Deconstruction, 195–96
Defiled consciousness, 221
Deities
  Vedic, 16–17
  in wheel of becoming, 173
Demons, in wheel of becoming, 173
Deng Xiaoping, 337
Dengyo Daishi (Saicho), 146, 231
Desire, control of, 8
Destructive *karmas*, 33
Development of the Philosophy of Change (Hsiung), 330
Dewey, John, 326, 327
Dhammapada, 158, 163–64
Dharana (concentration), 64
Dharma (moral order), 11, 47–48, 49, 123, 139, 183
Dharma Shastras, 5, 44
Dhyana, 64
Diamond Sutra (*Vajracchedika*), 193–94, 196–98
Digha Nikaya, 29
Din-i Ilahi, 119
Discursive consciousness, 221

Discursive thought
kinds of, 227–28
knowledge free of, 228–29
Distinction, relativity of, 294–96
Doctrine of the Mean (*Chung Yung*), 259
Dogen, 146, 232, 236, 237, 239
Dream objects, 84–85
Dualism (*Dvaita*), 81, 90–92, 220
Duhka (impermanence), 142
Duhkha (suffering), 155–56, 158
Dvesha (aversion), 61

Education, Confucian view of, 277–78, 280
Effect(s)
nonexistence of the, 83–84
preexistence of, 55–57
Ego-force (*asmita*), 61
Eisai, 232
Empirical School, 265
Emptiness, 144, 145, 188–201, 211–16
conception of, 193
practicing, 214–16
understanding, 211–14
Enlightened One. *See* Buddha, the ("Enlightened One")
Enlightenment
arising of, 222
Buddha's quest for, 151–53
living, 240–41
nirvana, 142, 159–60, 211
Epic period of Indian philosophy, 5
Error, perceptual, 86–88
Essentialist view of existence, 186–87
Establishment of Mindfulness, 176, 177, 178, 179
Evil
Chinese thought on, 282–83
origins of, 314
Existence
conditioned, 167–68
essentialist view of, 186–87
"many-sidedness" (*anekanta*) of, 36–37
oneness of, 113
Vedas on origins of, 17–19
in Yogacara, 219–20
Experience, Zen's view of, 236–38

Faith
Buddhist, 142
darshana, 8, 38–39
as pillar of Islam, 107
Fallacies, inferential, 72
Familial virtues, 267
Family, respect for, 275
Fariduddin, Shaikh, 112
Fasting, as pillar of Islam, 108
Fear of death (*abhinivesha*), 61
Feeling(s)
mindfulness of, 177–78
in wheel of becoming, 171
Filial piety (*hsiao*), 274–75
Five agencies, theory of, 261, 262–63, 308

Five Classics, 259
Five pillars of Islam, 107–8
Ford-makers (*Tirthankaras*), 28, 29, 38
Four Books, 259
Four Noble Truths, 155–60
Four signs, the, 149–51
Fu, Charles, 339
Full awareness, 238
Function-substance unity, 330
Fundamental Verses on the Middle Way, 205
Fung Yu-lan, 331–34

Gandhi, Mohandas K., 7, 41–42, 123, 124–25
Gao Ertai, 338
Gaudapada, 6–7
Ghosts, in wheel of becoming, 174
Good, origins of, 314
Goodness, Chinese thought on, 281–84
Grasping, in wheel of becoming, 172
Great commentaries period of Indian philosophy, 6–7
Great Harmony, 335
Great Learning, The (*Ta Hsueh*), 259, 266, 276–77, 319
Great Ultimate, 307–8, 315–16
Great Whole, 332–33
Gunas, 45, 46, 82
Guru Granth Sahib (*Adi Granth*), 117

Han Fei Tzu, 262
Han Yu, 264, 305–6, 314
Haribhadra, 30–31, 41
Heart Sutra, 193–94, 198–201
Hell, in wheel of becoming, 173
Hemacandra, 41
Hinduism, 114–18
History of Chinese Philosophy (Fung Yu-lan), 331, 334
Honen, 146, 231
Hosso school, 231
Hsiao (filial piety), 274–75
Hsiung Shih-li, 328–31
Hsun Tzu, 259, 280–81, 283–84, 314
Hui-nan Tzu, 262–63
Hui-neng, 240
Hui Shih, 260
Hu Jiwei, 337
Humanism, 271
science and, 339
Humanity (*jen*), 259, 265, 271–73
Chinese modernization and, 339
morality and, 321
Neo-Confucianism and, 311–13, 316–17
Human perfection, Chinese thought on, 265–67
Humans, in wheel of becoming, 173–74
Hundred Days' Reform of 1898, 325
Hung-jen, 240

Ibn Arabi, 113

Ibn Rushd (Averroes), 111
Ibn Sina (Avicenna), 110, 111–13
I-Ching (*Book of Changes*), 259, 328
Ideal life, Lao Tzu on, 288
Identity
arguments against, 189
Sarvastivada on, 186
Ignorance, 168–72
of a garden hose, 168–70
of interdependent arising, 170–72
as primary affliction, 218
Illness, suffering of, 150
"I-maker" (*ahamkara*), 58
Impermanence (*duhka*), 142
Indian philosophies, 1–134
Aurobindo, 7, 123, 125–27
Buddhism, 138–39
chronology of, 2
dominant features of, 7–11
Gandhi, 7, 41–42, 123, 124–25
historical overview, 3–7
Iqbal, 123, 127–30
Islam, 106–20
basic teachings of, 107–8
defined, 107
Muslim-Hindu interactions, 114–18
politics and, 118–20
Sufism, 109–14
Sunni, 109
Jainism, 28–42
bondage in, 30–34
historical context, 29–30
impact of, 41–42
liberation in, 34–36
as *nastika* (unorthodox system), 6
primary virtues in, 39–41
"three jewels" of, 36–39
on knowledge, 67–76
through comparison, 72–73
through inference, 70–72
objects of, 73–76
perceptual, 68–70
problem of, 67–68
through testimony, 73
Mimamsa, 6, 78–80
Radhakrishnan, 7, 123, 130–32
Samkhya, 6, 54–60, 82–83
causality, 55–57
dualistic theory of reality, 54–55
evolution of the world, 57–60
society and the individual in, 44–52
Bhagavad Gita, 5, 44–46, 94, 97
human aims, 46–51
life-stages, 51–52
theistic developments in, 94–104
Kali, 95, 99–101
Shiva, 94–95, 101–4
Vishnu, 95–99
Upanishads, 5, 19–26
Atman quest, 10, 21–22, 24–25
Brahman quest, 20–21, 24–25
key questions of, 20
Prajapati teaches Indra, 23–24
tat tvam asi, 25–26

356

Vedanta, 6, 81–92
  Madhva's dualism, 81, 90–92
  Ramanuja's qualified
    nondualism, 81, 88–90
  Shankara's nondualism, 81,
    82–88
Vedas, 14–26
  dieties, 16–17
  Indus culture and, 14–15
  on origins of existence, 17–19
  rita, 10, 17, 124
  yoga, 6, 15, 60–65
    forces of bondage and, 61
    purpose of, 60
    as self-discipline, 46
    techniques of, 62–65
Indra, 23–24, 95
Indrabhuti, 29–30
Indra (Vedic diety), 16, 23–24
Indus culture, 14–15
Inference
  knowledge through, 70–72
  as Vaisheshika knowledge
    category, 75
Innate knowledge of the good
  (*chih liang-chih*), 318
Inquiry into Confucianism, An
  (Hsiung), 330
Insight (*samyak darshana*), 35, 38
Intelligence, goodness through,
  283–84
Intelligence (*buddhi*), 58
Intentional consciousness, 221
Interdependent arising (*pratitya*
    samutpada), 153, 157,
    167–80, 183
  conditioned existence principle,
    167–68
  implications of, 174–75
  mindfulness, 175–80, 184–85
    body awareness, 176–77
    establishment of, 176, 179–80
    of feelings, 177–78
    of mind, 178
    of objects of mind, 178–79
    practice of, 179–80
  wheel of becoming, 168–74
    aspects of ignorance, 168–70
    hub of, 172–73
    ignorance of, 170–72
    realms of existence, 173–74
    release from, 174
Introduction to Modern New
    Confucianism, An (Zheng
    Jiadong), 339
Iqbal, Mohammed, 123, 127–30
Isha Upanishad, 124
Islam, 106–20
  basic teachings of, 107–8
    five pillars, 107–8
    spiritual realization, 108
  defined, 107
  Muslim-Hindu interactions,
    114–18
    Dadu, 117–18
    Guru Nanak, 116–17
    Kabir, 116
  politics and, 118–20
  Sūfism, 109–14

Al-Ghazali, 109–11
Ibn Sina's metaphysics of
  divine love, 111–13
Sufi path, 113–14
Sunni, 109
Iwasaki, Yaeko, 242

Jahan, Shah, 119
Jainism, 28–42
  bondage in, 30–34
  historical context, 29–30
  impact of, 41–42
  liberation in, 34–36
  as *nastika* (unorthodox system), 6
  primary virtues in, 39–41
  "three jewels" of, 36–39
Japan, Buddhism in. *See* Zen
  Buddhism
Jatis (castes), 49–51, 116
Jen (humanity), 259, 265, 271–73
  Chinese modernization and, 339
  morality and, 321
  Neo-Confucianism and, 311–13,
    316–17
Jinas (Conquerors), 28, 29, 38–39
Jinnah, 127
Jiva (soul), 31
Jizya (military support tax), 120
Jodo (Pure Land) School, 146, 231

Kabir, 116
Kalama, Arada, 152
Kali, 95, 99–101
Kalkin, 96
Kama, 47, 48–49
K'ang Yu-wei, 325–26
Kant, Immanuel, 327
Karma, 11, 33–34
Karmic bondage, 32–33
Karmic matter, 32
Kashyapa, Maha, 233
Katha Upanishad, 20
Kegon school, 231
Kena Upanishad, 22
Khudi (self-affirmation), 128
Kingdom of God Is Within You,
  The (Tolstoy), 124
Knowability, Sarvastivada on, 186
Knowledge, 6, 67–76, 82–83, 187
  action and, 318–20
  arguments against permanence
    and, 188
  arguments against unity and,
    189–90
  Buddhist views of, 143
  through comparison, 72–73
  false, 79
  through inference, 70–72
  limitations of, 37
  of love, 26
  means of, 68–73
  objects of, 73–76
  perceptual, 68–70
  practice as criterion of, 295
  problem of, 67–68
  purpose of, 288
  of reality, 226–29
    free from discursive thought,
      228–29

free of personal defilements,
  228
ordinary, 226–27
scientific, 226–27
self-knowledge, 278
through testimony, 73
of universal entity, 190
Knowledge and Culture (Chang),
  327
Koans, 239, 241–42
Kobo Daishi (Kukai), 146, 231
Korea, Buddhism in, 145
Krishna, 44–45, 55, 58, 94–99
Kshatriya varna, 50
Kukai (Kobo Daishi), 146, 231
Kumarajiva, 145
Kung-sun Lung, 260
Kurma, 96

Lao Tzu, 235, 257, 259–60, 266,
  287–90, 317
Legalism, 262
Letting go, 176, 236
Lewis, C.S., 327
Li, 309, 310
Li Ao, 306
Liberation
  Indian philosophy on, 10
  in Jainism, 34–36
Li Chi (*Book of Rites*), 259
Life, Upanishads on, 5
Life Divine, The (Aurobindo), 125
Life-stages (*ashrama*), 51–52
Linga, 101–2, 103
Li (propriety), 273–74
Living enlightenment, 240–41
Li Zehou, 338, 339
Lord of the Dance (*Nataraja*),
  102–3
Lotus Sutra, 231
Love
  Ibn Sina's metaphysics of
    divine, 111–13
  knowledge of, 26
Loving devotion (*bhakti*), 98–99
Lu Chiu-yuan, 265
Lu Hsiang-shan, 318

Madhva, 6–7, 81, 90–92
Madhyamaka (Middle Way)
  tradition, 142, 143–44,
  203–16
  Chinese adaptation of, 263–64
  defined, 203–4
  emptiness, 211–16
    practicing, 214–16
    understanding, 211–14
  Nagarjuna philosophy, 203,
    204–11
    the Buddha in, 209–10
    causal conditions in, 207–8
    causality in, 205–7
    method of, 205
    motion in, 208
    nirvana in, 211
    Noble Fourfold Truth in,
      210–11
  overview of, 203–4
Mahabharata, 5, 44, 48

Mahat, 58
Mahavira, 29–30
Mahayana Buddhism, 139–42, 218
  foundational texts of, 194
  spread of, 140
Maitreyanatha, 144
Mallisena, 41
Mandukya Upanishad, 24
Manu Shastra, 5
Many-sidedness *(anekanta)* of
  existence, 36–37
Mao Tse-tung, 333–34
Marshall, Sir John, 15
Marxism-Leninism, 333–34
Mass-energy *(pudgala),* 31
Material force *(ch'i),* 310, 315
Matsya, 96
Matter
  Brahman vs., 91
  in Indian philosophies, 46
Mecca, pilgrimmage to, 108
Meditation, 64, 176, 265
Mencius, 259, 280–83
Meng Tzu (Book of Mencius), 259
Mental activity, 185
Mental discipline, in Noble
  Eightfold Path, 160, 161
Mental processes *(nama),* 157
Middle Path, 160
Middle Way. *See* Madhyamaka
  (Middle Way) tradition
Mimamsa, 6, 78–80
Mind, states of, 178
Mindfulness, 175–80, 184–85
  body awareness, 176–77
  establishment of, 176, 179–80
  of feelings, 177–78
  of mind, 178
  of objects of mind, 178–79
  practice of, 179–80
Modernization, post-Mao thinking
  and, 338–40
Modern period of Indian
  philosophy, 7
Mohenjo Daro, 14–15
Mohism, 260
Moksha, 36, 47, 49, 51
Morality
  human nature and, 321
  Indian philosophy on, 10
Moral justice, universal, 10
Moral order *(dharma),* 11, 47–48,
  49, 123, 139, 183
Moral rules, function of, 289–90
Motion, as Vaisheshika knowledge
  category, 75
Motion, kinds of, 75
Mo Tzu, 260
Mou Zongsan, 339
Muhammad, 107
Mukoan, 242
Mumonkoan, 233
Mundaka Upanishad, 20, 81
Muslim renaissance, 127
Muslims, 106. *See also* Islam
  Hindu interactions with,
    114–18
  Dadu, 117–18
  Guru Nanak, 116–17

Kabir, 116
saints, 115–18

Nagarjuna philosophy, 143–44,
  203, 204–11
  the Buddha in, 209–10
  causal conditions in, 207–8
  causality in, 205–7
  method of, 205
  motion in, 208
  nirvana in, 211
  Noble Fourfold Truth in, 210–11
Namadeva, 115
Nama (mental processes), 157
Nanak, Guru, 116–17
Naqshbandi movement, 120
Narasimha, 96
Nataraja (Lord of the Dance),
  102–3
Naturalism, 271
Negation
  Brahman view of, 20–21
  uses of, 297
Neo-Confucianism, 264, 265,
  304–21
  Buddhist challenge to, 304–5
  Ch'eng Hao, 265, 309–13
  Ch'eng I, 309–13
  Chou Tun-i, 307–9, 315
  Chu Hsi, 265, 313–17
  Han Yu, 264, 305–6, 314
  jen and, 311–13, 316–17
  Li Ao, 306
  Ou-yang Hsiu, 307
  principle and material force in,
    309–11
  Tai Chen, 320–21
  Wang Yang-Ming, 265, 317–20
Neti, neti, 94
*New Doctrine of Consciousness-
  Only, The,* 328
New History of Chinese Philosophy
  (Fung Yu-lan), 334
*New Rational Philosophy, The
  (Hsin li-hsueh)* (Fung Yu-
  lan), 332
Nichiren school, 146, 231
Nihilism, 212
Nikayas, 139
Nimbarka, 6–7
Nirvana (enlightenment), 142,
  159–60, 211
Niyama, 62
Noble Eightfold Path, 140, 141,
  155, 160–64
Noble Fourfold Truth, 137–38, 140,
  210–11
Nonattachment, Indian
  philosophy on, 11
Nondualism, 123
  qualified, 81, 88–90
  of Shankara, 81, 82–88
Nonexistence
  of the effect *(asatkaryavada),*
    83–84
  as Vaisheshika knowledge
    category, 75–76
Nongrasping *(aparigraha),* 40–41,
  62

Nonhurting *(ahimsa),* 39–40, 62,
  123, 124–25
Nonsense of Nonsense, The (Ibn
  Rushd), 111
Nonsense of Philosophers, The
  (Al-Ghazali), 111
Nonstealing *(asteya),* 40, 62
Nothingness, attainment of, 152
Nyaya, 6, 83, 187
  perceptual error in, 86
Nyaya-Vaisheshika theory of
  knowledge, 6, 67–76, 82–83
  the knower and, 76
  means of knowledge, 68–73
  objects of knowledge, 73–76
  problem of knowledge, 67–68

Old age, suffering of, 149
Oneness of existence, Sufi theory
  of, 113
"On Practice" (Mao), 334
Opposites, complementariness of,
  296–98
Ordinary knowledge, 226–27
Origin beliefs in Indian
  philosophy, 17–19
Origins, Hymn of, 17
Outcastes, 51
Ou-yang Hsiu, 307

Panchatantra, 48
Paramitas, path of, 141–42
Paraushrama, 96
Parjapati, 23–24
Parsva, 29
Particularity, as Vaisheshika
  knowledge category, 75
Parvati, 104
Patanjali, 60, 113
Perception
  determinate and indeterminate,
    69
  illusory, 86
  verification of, 69–70
Perceptual error, 86–88
Perceptual knowledge, 68–70
Perceptual processes, 157
Perfection of Wisdom
  (prajnaparamita), 143,
  193–201
  defined, 194–95
  Diamond Sutra (Vajracchedika),
    193–94, 196–98
  Heart Sutra, 193–94, 198–201
  reading in, 194–96
  texts of, 193–94
Periods, classification by, 4
Permanence, arguments against,
  187–89
Perpetual transformation, 329
Personal defilements, knowledge
  free of, 228
Perspective(s)
  argument from, 298–99
  transcendental, 301
  unlimited, 298–99
Philosophical systems period of
  Indian philosophy, 6
Philosophy of Humanity (Jin), 339

Philosophy of Life (Fung Yu-lan), 332
Philosophy-science distinction, 332
Physical processes, 157
Pilgrimmage to Mecca, 108
Plato, 327
Poets, Hindu devotional, 115
Politics, Islam and, 118–20
Pomnang tradition, 145
Postures (*asanas*), 63
Practical character of Indian philosophy, 7–8
Prajapati, 23–24
Prajnaparamita (Perfection of Wisdom), 143, 193–201
  defined, 194–95
  Diamond Sutra (*Vajracchedika*), 193–94, 196–98
  Heart Sutra, 193–94, 198–201
  reading in, 194–96
  texts of, 193–94
Prakriti, 54, 57–60, 82
Prana, 63
Pratitya samutpada. See Interdependent arising (*pratitya samutpada*)
Prayer, as pillar of Islam, 107
Predication, conditional, 37–38
Processes, 184
  Buddha's view of, 157
  centrality of, 131–32
Propriety (*li*), 273–74
Pudgala (mass-energy), 31
Pure Land Buddhism, 146, 231
"Pure mind," 243
Purification in Jainism, 34–36
Purusha, 54–55, 58–60
Purushartha, 47

Qasim, General, 106
Qualified nondualism (*vishistadvaita*), 81, 88–90
Quality, as Vaisheshika knowledge category, 74
Quality of life, Indian criteria for, 9
Qur'an, 107

Radhakrishnan, Sarvepalli, 7, 123, 130–32
Raga (attachment), 61
Rajas, 45, 46, 58, 82
Rama, 95, 96
Ramakrishna, 7
Ramananda, 116
Ramanuja, 6–7, 81, 88–90
Ramaputra, Udraka, 152
Ramayana, 5, 44
Realism, Yogacara arguments against, 224–26
Reality. *See also* Knowledge
  Buddhist views of, 142
  independent, 138
  knowledge of, 226–29
    free from discursive thought, 228–29
    free of personal defilements, 228

  ordinary, 226–27
  scientific, 226–27
Mimamsa on, 78–80
Sarvastivada on, 185
Shankara on, 82
Vedanta on, 81–92
Reason, role of, 110–11
Reconstruction, 195–96
Reconstruction of Religious Thought, The (Iqbal), 127
Rectification of names (*cheng-ming*), 276
Religion
  Indian philosophy and, 9
  Iqbal's reinterpretation of, 128–29
Renunciation, 150–51
Revival of Religious Sciences, 110–11
Right action, in Noble Eightfold Path, 160, 162–63
Right concentration, in Noble Eightfold Path, 160, 163–64
Right effort, in Noble Eightfold Path, 160, 163
Righteousness (*yi*), 275–76
Right intention, in Noble Eightfold Path, 160, 162
Right livelihood, in Noble Eightfold Path, 160, 163
Right mindfulness, in Noble Eightfold Path, 160, 163
Rightness, goodness vs., 281
Right speech, in Noble Eightfold Path, 160, 162
Right view, in Noble Eightfold Path, 160, 161–62
Rig Veda, 3, 4–5, 15–19, 124
Rinzai form of Zen Buddhism, 232
Rita, 10, 17, 124
Roy, Ram Mohun, 7
Rudra, 103
Rupa (bodily processes), 157
Ruskin, John, 124
Russell, Bertrand, 326, 327

Saicho (Dengyo Daishi), 146, 231
Saints, Muslim, 115–18
Samadhi, 64–65
Sama Veda, 4–5
Samkhya, 6, 54–60, 82–83
  on causality, 55–57
  dualistic theory of reality, 54–55
  on evolution of the world, 57–60
Samyak darshana (insight), 35, 38
Samyutta Nikaya, 167–68
Sanskrit language, 15
Sarvastivada, 142, 143, 182–90
  Abhidharma, 185–86
  arguments against substance, 186–90
  features of, 187
  identity and, 189
  permanence and, 187–89
  unity and, 189–90
  universality and, 190
  teachings of, 182–83

Satkaryavada, 55–56, 83–84
Satori (awakening of enlightenment), 239
Sattva, 45, 46, 58, 82
Satyagraha (truthfastness), 124
Satya (truth), 40, 123
Sautrantika, 143, 182
Sayings (*Lun-yu*) (Confucius), 272
School of Mind, 265
School of Names, 260–61
School of Principle, 265, 318
Science
  humanism and, 339
  modern, 111
Science-philosophy distinction, 332
Scientific knowledge, 226–27
Secondary *karmas*, 33
Secrets of the Self, The (Iqbal), 127
Self, the
  Buddhist views of, 142, 209
  forgetting, 215
  Indian philosophies on, 9, 21
  interrelatedness of society, culture, and, 337–38
  Mimamsa on, 78–80
  Samkhya and, 54–60
  unchanging, 138
  Vedanta on, 81–92
  yoga and, 60–65
Self-affirmation (*khudi*), 128
Self-discipline, 8
Self-knowledge, 8, 278
Self-transformation, 265
Sensation, processes of, 157
Senses, in wheel of becoming, 171
Sexual activity, 62
Sexual purity (*brahmacarya*), 40
Shabda (testimony), 79–80
Shakti, 104
Shakyamuni, 233
Shang dynasty, 257
Shankara, 6–7, 81, 82–88
  theory of perceptual error of, 87–88
Shari'ah (Muslim Holy Law), 108
Sharif of Ahmadnagar, Shah, 115
Sharing, as pillar of Islam, 108
Shastra of Yajnavalkya, 5
Shen-hsiu, 240
Shi Ching (*Book of Poetry*), 259
Shingon school, 146, 231
Shinran, 231
Shinto tradition, 231
Shiva, 94–95, 101–4
  as Lord of the Dance, 102–3
  as symbol of the unmanifest, 103–4
Shivaji, 115
Shobogenzo ("Treasury-Eye of the True Teaching"), 232
Shu Ching (*Book of History*), 259
Shudra varna, 49
Shunyata. See Emptiness
Shvetaketu, 25
Siddhartha Gautama. *See* Buddha, the ("Enlightened One")
Sikh religion, 115, 116–17
Sino-Japanese War, 325

Sita, 95
Skepticism, argument from, 299–301
Social organization, Aurobindo's theory of, 125–27
Social reform, Confucian view of, 271
Son tradition, 145
Soto Zen, 232
Soul ($jiva$), 31
Spirit, evolution of, 126
Spirit of Chinese Philosophy, The (Fung Yu-lan), 331, 333
Spring and Autumn Annals (Ch'un Ch'iu), 259
Stages of Bodhisattva Practice, The (Asanga), 226
Stages of yoga practice (Yogacarabhumi), 144
Store consciousness (alaya vijnana), 219, 221, 222
Substance
  arguments against, 186–90
  features of, 187
  identity and, 189
  permanence and, 187–89
  unity and, 189–90
  universality and, 190
  conception of, 186–87
  as Vaisheshika knowledge category, 73–74
Substance-function unity, 330
Suffering
  Buddhist view of, 138, 155–60
  duhkha, 155–56, 158
  Indian approach to problem of, 7–8
  Noble Truths of, 155–60
  in wheel of becoming, 172
Sufism, 109–14
  Al-Ghazali, 109–11
  Ibn Sina's metaphysics of divine love, 111–13
  Suvi path, 113–14
Sui dynasty, 145
Sung period, 264–65
Sunni Islam, 109
Sunyata (emptiness), 142
Supernaturalism, 271
Sutras, 6
Svabhava, 183, 185
Svatahpramanyavada, 79
Synthesis of Yoga (Aurobindo), 125

Tagore, 7
Ta Hsueh (The Great Learning), 259, 266, 276–77, 319
Tai Chen, 320–21
Taittiriya Upanishad, 21
Taj Mahal, 119
Tamas, 45, 46, 58, 82
T'ang dynasty, 145
Taoism, 259–60, 287–301
  Chuang Tzu, 260, 287, 293–301
  argument from perspectives, 298–99
  argument from skepticism, 299–301

on complementariness of opposites, 296–98
on relativity of distinctions, 294–96
influence on Zen Buddhism, 235–36
Lao Tzu, 235, 257, 259–60, 266, 287–90, 317
Tao (inner Way), 235, 265, 290–93
Tao Te Ching, 287, 289
Tao (the Way), 288
Taqi, Shaikh, 116
Tat tvam asi, 25–26
Tattvartha Sutra, 40
Tendai tradition, 231
Tenda (T'ien-t'ai) school, 146
Testimony
  knowledge through, 73
  shabda, 79–80
Theism in Indian philosophies, 94–104
  Kali, 95, 99–101
  Shiva, 94–95, 101–4
  Vishnu, 95–99
Theravada Abhidharma, 184–85
Theravada tradition, 139–42
Thirty Verses (Trimsika Karika), 145, 222, 224
"Three jewels" of Jainism, 36–39
Tiananmen Square incident, 339
Tibetan Buddhism, 144, 203
Tirthankaras (Ford-makers), 28, 29, 38
Tolerance, Indian philosophy on, 10
Tolstoy, Leo, 124
Transcendental perspective, 301
Transformation, perpetual, 329
"Treasury-Eye of the True Teaching" (Shobogenzo), 232
Treasury of Metaphysics, A (Vasubandhu), 144
Treatise on the Way and Its Power, The (Tao Te Ching), 287
Trimsika Karika (Thirty Verses), 145, 222, 224
Trishna (craving), 158–60
True Pure Land School, 231
Truth
  in Indian philosophy, 8–9
  post-Mao thinking on, 337–38
Truthfastness (satyagraha), 124
Truth (satya), 40, 123
Tukaram, 115
Tung Chung-shu, 262–63
Turiya, 24
Tu Wei-ming, 339
Twenty Verses, 220
Twenty Verses with Commentary (Vimsatika Karika), 144–45
Two nations, theory of, 127
Two truths, theory of, 210–11

Uddalaka, 25
Unity, arguments against, 189–90
Universal essences, as Vaisheshika knowledge category, 75

Universality, arguments against, 190
Universe, origin of, 261–62
Unto This Last (Ruskin), 124
Upanishads, 5, 19–26
  Atman quest, 21–22, 24–25
  Brahman quest, 20–21, 24–25
  key questions of, 20
  Prajapati teaches Indra, 23–24
  tat tvam asi, 25–26

Vac (Vedic diety), 16
Vaibhasika, 143, 182
Vairocana, Buddha, 231
Vaisheshika. See Nyaya-Vaisheshika theory of knowledge
Vaishya varna, 49, 50
Vajracchedika (Diamond Sutra), 193–94, 196–98
Vallabha, 7
Vamana, 96
Varna, 49–51
Varuna (Vedic diety), 17
Vasubandhu, 144, 218, 220–24
Vatsyayana, 49
Vedanta, 6, 81–92
  Madhva's dualism, 81, 90–92
  Ramanuja's qualified nondualism, 81, 88–90
  Shankara's nondualism, 81, 82–88
Vedas, 14–26
  dieties, 16–17
  Indus culture and, 14–15
  on origins of existence, 17–19
  rita, 17
Vedic period, 4–5
Via negative, 94
Vice, 185
Virocana, 23
Virtue(s), 185
  as basis of government, 276–77, 279–80
  in Confucianism, 276–81
  as element of learning, 277–78
  familial relationships and, 278–79
  human nature and, 279–81
  familial, 267
  Neo-Confucian, 305–6
  personal embodiment of, 276
Vishistadvaita (qualified nondualism), 81, 88–90
Vishnu, 95–99
  forms of, 95–97
  Krishna, 44–45, 55, 58, 94–99
Vision
  awakening, 38
  in Indian philosophy, 8
Vivekananda, 7
Volition, 170–71
Volitional processes, 157

Wang Ruoshui, 338, 339
Wang Yang-Ming, 265, 317–20
West, Buddhism in the, 146
Wheel of becoming, 168–74

aspects of ignorance, 168–70
hub of, 172–73
ignorance of, 170–72
realms of existence, 173–74
release from, 174
Whitehead, Alfred North, 326
Wing-tsit Chan, 318, 327
Wisdom, in Noble Eightfold Path, 160, 161
Wonhyo, 145
Wu-ti, Emperor, 234
Wu-wei (nonaction), 290, 291

Xiao Jeifu, 339

Yajnavalkya, 5, 20, 25
Yajur Veda, 4–5
Yamuna, 6–7
Yen Tzu, 312
Yin and *yang*, 261–63, 291, 308, 316
Yi (righteousness), 275–76

Yoga, 6, 15, 60–65
forces of bondage and, 61
purpose of, 60
as self-discipline, 46
techniques of, 62–65
Yogacara School, 142–45, 218–19
arguments against realism, 224–26
Chinese adaptation of, 263–64
consciousness, 220–24
kinds of, 221–23
nature and function of, 218, 220
as source, 223–24
store, 219, 221, 222
existence in, 219–20
knowledge of reality, 226–29
free from discursive thought, 228–29
free of personal defilements, 228

ordinary, 226–27
scientific, 226–27
overview of, 218–19
Yoga Sutra, 60
Yu Tzu, 274–75

Zazen (seated meditation), 232, 238–41
aims of, 239–41
Zen Buddhism, 146, 203, 231–50
foundations of, 233–35
koans, 239, 241–42
overview of, 231–33
stages of, 244–50
Taoist influences on, 235–36
teachings of, 243–44
Zazen, 232, 238–41
Zhang Dainian, 339
Zhaozhou, 236–37, 242
Zheng Jiadong, 339